Heirs of the Vikings

YORK MEDIEVAL PRESS

York Medieval Press is published by the University of York's Centre for Medieval Studies in association with Boydell & Brewer Limited. Our objective is the promotion of innovative scholarship and fresh criticism on medieval culture. We have a special commitment to interdisciplinary study, in line with the Centre's belief that the future of Medieval Studies lies in those areas in which its major constituent disciplines at once inform and challenge each other.

All enquiries of an editorial kind, including suggestions for monographs and essay collections, should be addressed to: The Academic Editor, York Medieval Press, Department of History, University of York, Heslington, York, YO10 5DD (E-mail: pete.biller@york.ac.uk)

Details of other York Medieval Press volumes are available from Boydell & Brewer Ltd.

Heirs of the Vikings

History and Identity in Normandy and England, c.950–c.1015

Katherine Cross

THE UNIVERSITY *of York*

YORK MEDIEVAL PRESS

First published 2018
Paperback edition 2021

A York Medieval Press publication
in association with The Boydell Press
an imprint of Boydell & Brewer Ltd
PO Box 9, Woodbridge, Suffolk IP12 3DF, UK
and of Boydell & Brewer Inc.
668 Mt Hope Avenue, Rochester, NY 14620–2731, USA
website: www.boydellandbrewer.com
and with the
Centre for Medieval Studies, University of York

ISBN 978 1 903153 79 6 hardback
ISBN 978 1 903153 97 0 paperback

A CIP catalogue record for this book is available
from the British Library

The publisher has no responsibility for the continued existence or accuracy
of URLs for external or third-party internet websites referred to in this book,
and does not guarantee that any content on such websites is,
or will remain, accurate or appropriate

To my parents

Contents

Illustrations

Plate

Maps

Acknowledgements

I am most grateful to the following people and organisations for their assistance and support – given in varied but essential forms – in the research for and preparation of this book. My thanks to Antonio Sennis, Haki Antonsson, Sarah Foot, Susan Irvine, Lesley Abrams, Heather O'Donoghue, Sophie Page, David d'Avray, Caroline Palmer, Peter Biller, the readers for Boydell and Brewer, Jaś Elsner and the Empires of Faith team, colleagues at the British Museum, the Arts and Humanities Research Council, University College London, Wolfson College, Oxford, the Leverhulme Trust; and to my parents, all my family, Steve Morgan and Lyra Morgan.

This book is produced with the generous assistance of the Leverhulme Trust, Wolfson College and the Lorne Thyssen Research Fund for Ancient World Topics

Abbreviations

AASS	*Acta Sanctorum quotquot tot orbe coluntur* (Antwerp and Brussels, 1643–1940)
Abbo	Abbo of Fleury, *Life of St Edmund*, in *Three Lives of English Saints*, ed. M. Winterbottom (Toronto, 1972), pp. 65–87
Æthelweard	*Chronicon Æthelweardi: The Chronicle of Æthelweard*, ed. A. Campbell (London, 1962)
ANS	*Anglo-Norman Studies*
ASC	Anglo-Saxon Chronicle. Quotations are taken from the various volumes of *The Anglo-Saxon Chronicle: A Collaborative Edition*, ed. D. Dumville and S. Keynes (Cambridge, 1983-). Translations are given from *The Anglo-Saxon Chronicles*, trans. M. Swanton (London, 1996; rev. edn 2000).
ASC A	*Volume 3. MS A*, ed. J. M. Bately (1986)
ASC B	*Volume 4. MS B*, ed. S. Taylor (1983)
ASC C	*Volume 5. MS C, A semi-diplomatic edition with introduction and indices*, ed. K. O'Brien O'Keeffe (2001)
ASC D	*Volume 6. MS D*, ed. G. P. Cubbin (1996)
ASC E	*Volume 7. MS E*, ed. S. Irvine (2004)
ASE	*Anglo-Saxon England*
BHL	*Bibliotheca Hagiographica Latina*
BSAN	*Bulletin de la Société des Antiquaires de Normandie*
Christiansen	*Dudo of St Quentin: History of the Normans*, trans. E. Christiansen (Woodbridge, 1998)
EETS	Early English Text Society
EHD	*English Historical Documents*, ed. by David C. Douglas, 10 vols (London, 1953–1977; 2nd edn London, 1979-), I: *c.500–1042*, ed. D. Whitelock (1979)
EHR	*English Historical Review*
EME	*Early Medieval Europe*
es	extra series
ns	new series
os	original series
ss	supplementary series
F	*Recueil des Actes des Ducs de Normandie (911-1066)*, ed. M. Fauroux, Mémoires de la Société des Antiquaires de Normandie, 36 (Caen, 1961)
HSC	*Historia de Sancto Cuthberto*, ed. T. Johnson South (Cambridge, 2002)
HSJ	*Haskins Society Journal*

Lair   Dudo of Saint-Quentin, *De Moribus et Actis Primorum Normanniae Ducum: Auctore Dudone Sancti Quinini Decano*, ed. J. Lair (Caen, 1865)
MGH   *Monumenta Germaniae Historica*
S   *The Electronic Sawyer: Online Catalogue of Anglo-Saxon Charters* <http://www.esawyer.org.uk/> [accessed 19/05/2013]
TRHS   *Transactions of the Royal Historical Society*
VPSN   *The Anglo-Saxon Chronicle: A Collaborative Edition, Volume 17. The Annals of St Neots with Vita Prima Sancti Neoti*, ed. D. Dumville and M. Lapidge (1985)

Note on Terminology

The term 'Viking' has developed an ethnic usage in modern historiography, which stems from contemporary sources that refer to Scandinavian raiders as, for example, *'ferox gens'*. This idea of raiders as an 'ethnicity' in themselves is a development I wish to investigate. Therefore, in order not to confuse separate issues, I retain a more specific use of the word 'viking', to mean raiders and armies intent on gaining tribute, slaves and plunder. As such, it is spelt with a lower-case 'v'. In this usage, it is closer to the Old Norse word from which it stems, *víkingr*, and the Old English word used by contemporaries, *wicing*, which was used to translate the Latin *pirata*. In using 'Viking Age' I follow the bulk of the historiography in referring to the period when Scandinavian vikings were active, roughly c.750–1100. See Christine Fell, 'Modern English "Viking"', *Leeds Studies in English* 18 (1987), 111–23; Christine Fell, 'Old English *Wicing*', *Proceedings of the British Academy* 72 (1986), 295–316.

'Normans' presents a similar problem: for ease of understanding, I have used this term to apply to viking leaders and Scandinavian immigrants in the land granted to Rollo and his companions after 911. I have referred to Rollo and his successors as 'dukes' for similar reasons, although this title was not used until later. These issues are discussed further in Chapter Five.

Names are given according to the context in which they appear: thus we meet Hinguar in medieval texts, but Ívarr when referring to the historical figure. In some cases I have used the form common in modern English usage, such as Cnut.

Map 1. England, c. 1000

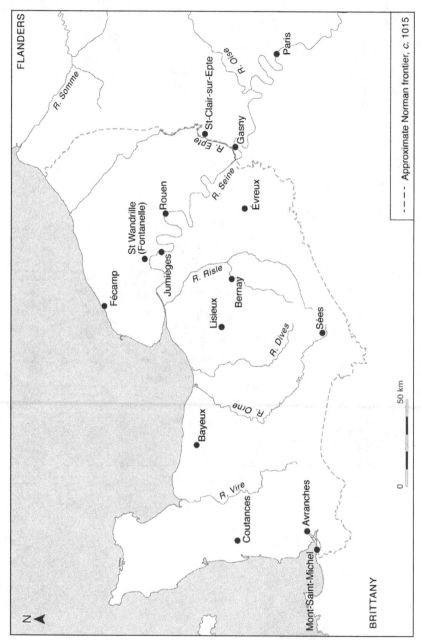

Map 2. Normandy, c. 1015

FLANDERS

R. Somme

St-Clair-sur-Epte

Gasny

R. Epte

R. Oise

Paris

R. Seine

Évreux

Rouen

St Wandrille
(Fontanelle)

Jumièges

Fécamp

R. Risle

Bernay

Lisieux

R. Dives

Sées

R. Orme

Bayeux

R. Vire

Coutances

Avranches

Mont-Saint-Michel

BRITTANY

N

0   50 km

- - - - Approximate Norman frontier, c. 1015

Introduction: The Problem of Viking Identity

After Edward the Confessor's death in 1066, three men claimed the English throne: William of Normandy, Harold Godwineson and Harald Hardrada (Haraldr Sigurðarson). Teachers and historians alike identify these claimants as Norman, English and Norwegian respectively.[1] But Viking Age identities were not this simple. The conflicts of 1066 were one focused moment in a long history of shifting ethnic relations, which were perceived differently by various participants.

William presented himself as a Norman, *Normannus*. But, had he been asked, Harold Godwineson would probably have identified William as *Francus* rather than *Normannus*, reserving that label for Harald Hardrada.[2] For the inhabitants of England, *Normannus* retained its original meaning of a man from the north. Harald Hardrada, for his part, would have recognized himself in that term, but for him it now took on a new distinction: in his praise-poetry, as *Nóregs dróttinn* (the lord of Norway), he was king of the *Norðmeðr* – literally, the Northmen, but in this context distinguishing the Norwegians from the Danes.[3] The differing terminologies, and especially the overlapping and sometimes contradictory meanings of 'Northman' as an ethnonym, arose during the Viking Age. They reveal a wider issue: divergent, and highly political, perceptions of the value of viking heritage.

For, had the claimants in 1066 been asked who among them was of viking blood, the distinctions would have become even more blurred. Harald Hardrada is the obvious candidate. Scholars have called Harald 'one of the last of the Vikings': prior to becoming king of Norway, he was a Varangian mercenary and raider in Russia and Byzantium.[4] Historians have surmised that Harald Hardrada attacked England near York because it had been the centre of a tenth-century viking kingdom, and he probably expected the

---

[1] R. A. Brown, *The Normans and the Norman Conquest* (Woodbridge, 1969; 2nd edn 1985), pp. 1–5, 118.

[2] S. Harris, *Race and Ethnicity in Anglo-Saxon Literature* (New York, 2003), p. 136; H. Thomas, *The English and the Normans: Ethnic Hostility, Assimilation and Identity, 1066–c.1220* (Oxford, 2003), pp. 32–4. See e.g. ASC C 1066, which uses 'Normenn' for Norwegians; ASC D 1051–52 uses 'frenciscum' and 'frencisra manna' for Normans.

[3] Þjóðólfr Arnórsson, *Stanzas about Haraldr Sigurðarson's leiðangr*, ed. D. Whaley, in *Poetry from the Kings' Sagas 2: From c.1035 to 1300*, ed. K. E. Gade, 2 vols. (Turnhout, 2009), I, 154, 157. 'Norðmenn' is also used in Steinn Herdísarson, *Nizarvísur*, ed. K. E. Gade, in *Poetry from the Kings' Sagas 2*, ed. Gade, I, 363.

[4] B. Crawford, 'The Vikings', in *From the Vikings to the Normans, 800–1100*, ed. W. Davies (Oxford, 2003), pp. 41–71 (p. 69); F. Stenton, *Anglo-Saxon England* (Oxford, 1943, 1971; repr. 2001), pp. 427–8.

people there to be more receptive to his rule.[5] But William the Conqueror also called himself *Normannus* because of his viking ancestors. William traced his descent and ducal authority from his great-great-great-grandfather, Rollo the viking; the people he ruled over were still called *Normanni* because of their viking origins.[6] Even Harold Godwineson, renowned as the last 'native' Anglo-Saxon king of England, was half Danish:[7] his mother was from Denmark and closely linked to the family of Swein Forkbeard and Cnut the Great, the viking kings. But it was by promoting his status as a leading Englishman that he became king.[8] Each claimant to the English throne shaped his identity by either emphasizing or downplaying his Scandinavian heritage. For each man, Scandinavian – specifically viking – identity aligned him with a different group of supporters. A claim to viking identity was a potent, but precarious, force in England in the eleventh century. Many people who lived in England believed their ancestors to be Scandinavian vikings – but many considered vikings to be their nation's enemies.

Viking identity was used politically in northern Europe throughout the Viking Age. During the ninth, tenth and eleventh centuries, the actions of vikings – sea-borne Scandinavian raiders – profoundly altered the political, social and cultural landscape of the medieval world. Through viking activity and Scandinavian settlement, the histories of the British Isles, the Frankish Empire and the Scandinavian countries of Denmark and Norway became interlinked. These connected histories created the situation in 1066. However, interpretations of the viking past developed differently in the various regions. Thus the meaning of Scandinavian heritage and its relevance to identity appeared differently to the inhabitants of England and those of Normandy. William the Conqueror and his men proudly claimed viking roots. Harold Godwineson preferred to emphasize the English side of his identity, while Harald Hardrada believed the inhabitants of northern England to be sympathetic to the viking past, in preference to southern rule. Why and how did viking identity come to mean such different things in England and Normandy?

In order to answer this question, we need to look at identities in England and Normandy comparatively. The two regions were affected by similar

---

[5] L. Musset, *Les invasions: le second assaut contre l'Europe chrétienne, VIIe–XIe siècles* (Paris, 1965; 2nd edn 1971), pp. 138–9; M. K. Lawson, *The Battle of Hastings 1066* (Stroud, 2002), p. 37.

[6] See the statements of William's chaplain and biographer: *The Gesta Guillelmi of William of Poitiers*, ed. R. H. C. Davis and M. Chibnall (Oxford, 1998), pp. 72–3, 116–19.

[7] I. Walker, *Harold: the Last Anglo-Saxon King* (Stroud, 1997); Lawson, *Battle of Hastings*, p. 13.

[8] *The Life of King Edward*, ed. F. Barlow (Oxford, 1962; 2nd edn 1992), pp. 48–9, written by a supporter of the Godwinesons, calls Harold 'a true friend of his race and country' ('amicus[que] gentis suę et patrię').

events in the First Viking Age: a period of raids followed by conquest and settlement. However, because different historians have studied the two regions separately, and utilized different source material in each case, the experiences of their inhabitants have often appeared dissimilar. The particular processes which led to the divergent histories of England and Normandy in the tenth century cannot be identified without comparison. This book distinguishes some of the different forces bearing on identity in England and Normandy. These forces transformed viking identity to such a degree that the Norman Conquest of England is regularly presented – by historians as it was by contemporaries – as a clash between two ethnically distinct peoples:[9] that is, between two innately different groups, the members of each united by shared heritage, homeland and descent. However, as the complex attachments to the viking past suggest, the unity and distinctiveness of such groups prove to be an imagined order imposed on a more messy social reality.

Viking Age identities

The politicization of viking identity, and varied perceptions of Scandinavian ethnicity, arose from the processes of settlement and assimilation in different regions. During the Viking Age, Scandinavians migrated to regions across the northern world. In Iceland and Greenland, they established new settlements in largely uninhabited regions, but everywhere else, migrants interacted with existing populations. These interactions took many forms: in Ireland, vikings established towns of their own, such as Dublin; in northern Francia, viking armies took over long-standing cities and fortifications. In some regions of England, there is evidence of widespread rural settlement, by women as well as men; whereas, in Russia, it seems that a small incoming elite established dynastic control. Scandinavian settlers and natives formed new alliances and intermarried in most of their settlements (the temporary militaristic control in Brittany may possibly be an exception). But their presence also led to the adoption of new ethnonyms (in the case of the Normans and the Rus') and labels of distinction (such as the 'light' and 'dark' foreigners in Ireland). Wherever they encountered existing populations, vikings and Scandinavian settlers fundamentally altered the experience and expression of ethnic relations.

This book examines two regions of Scandinavian settlement: England, and the area of northern Francia that became Normandy. From the perspective of Scandinavian settlers, the establishments of communities in England and Francia were similar processes. At first, viking bands created winter bases for extended raids. By the last quarter of the ninth century, they were intent on

---

[9] E.g. Thomas, *English and the Normans*.

settlement and conquest. Vikings seized control in Brittany and Normandy, and in northern and eastern England. The Bretons soon expelled the vikings, but the new rulers of Normandy led by Rollo made an agreement with the French king Charles the Simple, just as Guthrum, the new king of East Anglia, made an agreement with Alfred in England. In Normandy at least, vikings seem to have brought their households with them: evidence for the presence of Scandinavian women in England suggests a similar process.[10] Several waves of immigration arrived in both regions. Indeed, many of the vikings who settled in the Cotentin area of Normandy seem to have come via the British Isles. The processes of Scandinavian settlement in both regions involved significant political and demographic change.

Such changes almost always result in reconfigurations of ethnic relations. The significant level of migration that must have taken place in both areas – whether we take the minimal or maximal view in each case – meant an influx of new inhabitants, displaying different cultural, religious, linguistic and social traits, and importing new ways of life. In addition, immigrants seem in several cases to have maintained links with their homelands, at least for a time. Processes of integration, such as intermarriage and religious conversion, may have reduced divisions created by these cultural and social differences but, equally, may have created new categories.[11] Moreover, ethnic distinctions between incomers and existing inhabitants could be emphasized when aligned with other forms of social stratification. If, as has been claimed (both for Viking Age settlers and participants in all migrations), the majority of primary settlers were adult males,[12] then the lower social status of women and children would inevitably have fed into perceptions of ethnic relations; similarly, in a conquest situation, the elite position of incomers would have reinforced their separation from their subordinates. Finally, changes in political systems and dynasties frequently encourage new ways of under-standing past migrations and conquests, and the relationship of inhabitants to their rulers, as a means of justifying the new situations.

Normandy's early development resembles the establishment of Scandinavian rulers in England. Although historians dispute the numbers of settlers, both migrations may be characterized as elite takeovers. Existing inhabitants remained and found methods of accommodation. The archbishop

---

[10] J. Kershaw, *Viking Identities: Scandinavian Jewellery in England* (Oxford, 2013), pp. 245–7.

[11] A parallel may be drawn with anthropological studies of modern America, such as that of N. Glazer and D. Moynihan, *Beyond the Melting-pot* (Cambridge, MA, 1963), which have revealed, rather than integration, the persistence of ethnic self-awareness and networks among urban migrants: T. H. Eriksen, *Ethnicity and Nationalism* (London, 1993; 2nd edn 2002), p. 9.

[12] Although this presumption is increasingly subject to revision: S. McLeod, *The Beginning of Scandinavian Settlement in England: The Viking 'Great Army' and Early Settlers, c. 865–900* (Turnhout, 2014), pp. 79–101, esp. pp. 100–1.

of Rouen negotiated with Rollo to spare the city in the late ninth century.[13] Likewise, the archbishop of York and the community of St Cuthbert played essential roles in the creation of new societies in Northumbria. Neighbouring authorities also began to interact with viking settlers through the church. Letters between Archbishop Hervey of Rheims, Pope John X and Archbishop Wito of Rouen testify to the concern of the Christian authorities to integrate the viking princes into their world.[14] Pope Formosus, in the 890s, had raised similar concerns with the English bishops.[15] For those experiencing it, therefore, the processes of settlement by Scandinavians in Normandy, Northumbria, East Anglia and the Five Boroughs (the towns in the English midlands ruled by Scandinavian *jarls* and *holds*) were comparable in many ways.[16] The tenth-century inhabitants of England and Normandy accepted vikings, who had terrorized them in attacks, as neighbours and rulers. This comparison highlights their divergent strategies for doing so.

Reassessments of ethnicity in the Viking Age were not simply a result of demographic change. The activities of the Northmen, and the necessities of accommodation, profoundly challenged western Christians' world-views and prompted them to reconsider their own roles.

Viking attacks presented a new and real threat from a largely unknown Scandinavian world. Alcuin of York, writing in the wake of the 793 attack on Lindisfarne, expressed the trauma that the viking raids inflicted not only on the monks of St Cuthbert, but on the world-views of the Northumbrians

---

[13] Dudo states that this took place in 876 (*Dudo of St Quentin, History of the Normans,* trans. E. Christiansen (Woodbridge, 1998; hereafter Christiansen), p. 35; Dudo of Saint-Quentin, *De Moribus et Actis Primorum Normanniae Ducum: Auctore Dudone Sancti Quinini Decano*, ed. J. Lair (Caen, 1865; hereafter Lair), pp. 151–3); J. Le Maho, 'Les Normands de la Seine à la Fin du IXe Siècle', in *Les fondations scandinaves en Occident et les débuts du duché de Normandie: Colloque de Cerisy-la-Salle (25–29 septembre 2002)*, ed. P. Bauduin (Caen, 2005), pp. 161–79 (pp. 176–9), and 'Les premières installations normandes dans la basse vallée de la Seine (fin du IXe siècle)', in *La progression des Vikings, des raids à la colonisation*, ed. A.-M. F. Héricher (Rouen, 2003), pp. 153–69 (pp. 165–7), suggests that this agreement must have been made later, around 898.

[14] 'Epistolae Ioannis Papae IX', in *Sacrosancta Concilia ad Regiam editionem exacta...,* ed. P. Labbé and G. Cossart, 16 vols. (Paris, 1671–72), IX, cols 483–94. The Pope concerned was in fact John X: E. Searle, 'Frankish Rivalries and Norse Warriors', *ANS* 8 (1986), 198–213 (p. 204, n. 26). See further forthcoming work by Lesley Abrams.

[15] *Cartularium Saxonicum*, ed. W. de Gray Birch, 3 vols. (London, 1885–99), no. 573 (II, p. 214); trans. in *English Historical Documents, I: c.500–1042*, ed. D. Whitelock (London, 1955; 2nd edn 1979), pp. 890–2. The second part of this letter is a post-Conquest forgery supporting the claims of Canterbury to primacy over York, but the first half appears to be genuine.

[16] *Jarls* and the lower-ranking *holds* were Scandinavian terms for hereditary landowners.

to whom he addressed his letter and the Frankish court from which he wrote:

> We and our fathers have now lived in this fair land for nearly three hundred and fifty years, and never before has such an atrocity been seen in Britain as we have now suffered at the hands of a pagan people. Such a voyage was not thought possible.[17]

As Alcuin's words show, the attack came from an unexpected direction – the remote lands of the north, for so long envisaged as the true periphery of the world. When Alcuin lamented that 'such a voyage was not thought possible' – or, in Dorothy Whitelock's more poetic translation, 'it was not thought that such an inroad from the sea could be made' – he expressed his disbelief that the north could impinge on civilized Christian lands.[18] Early medieval geographers, as the heirs of classical traditions, painted the British Isles at the edge of the world map, with only vague and occasional references to a place further north called Thule.[19] The explosion of viking raids across the North Sea transformed these peripheral northern lands from far-away fantasy to the real habitation of dangerous, pagan peoples.

This new and forceful awareness prompted the inhabitants of England and Francia to reorient themselves, accommodating lands and peoples to the north within their perspectives. Those living in Anglo-Saxon kingdoms now drew further towards the centre of the world. No longer did they inhabit the last islands on earth; as the map expanded, so they gained a more centralized place.[20] One strategy for dealing with the threat was to try to domesticate the north. The translator of the *Old English Orosius*, working at the court of King Alfred, inserted the testimony of the northern travellers Ohthere and Wulfstan

---

[17] Alcuin of York to King Ethelred, 793: *Alcuin of York*, trans. S. Allott (York, 1974), no. 12, p. 18; *Alcuini sive Albini Epistolae, MGH, Epistolae*, IV (Berlin, 1895), ed. E. Dümmler, no. 16, p. 42: 'Ecce trecentis et quinquaginta ferme annis, quod nos nostrique patres huius pulcherrime patrie incole fuimus, et numquam talis terror prius apparuit in Brittannia, veluti modo a pagana gente perpessi sumus, nec eiusmodi navigium fieri posse putabatur.'

[18] *EHD*, ed. Whitelock, p. 842; P. Sawyer, 'Scandinavians and the English in the Viking Age', H. M. Chadwick Memorial Lecture 5, 1994 (Cambridge, Department of ASNaC, 1995), p. 3, argued that there are no special connotations to the sea in this sentence, but that Alcuin simply spoke of a 'loss' or 'ruin'. However, this argument is based on his reading of the word 'naufragium', which appears in Haddan and Stubbs's edition (*Councils and Ecclesiastical Documents relating to Great Britain and Ireland*, ed. A. W. Haddan and W. Stubbs, 3 vols. (Oxford, 1869–73), III, 493), but should in fact be 'navigium' as in Dümmler's edition.

[19] F. L. Michelet, *Creation, Migration, and Conquest: Imaginary Geography and Sense of Space in Old English Literature* (Oxford, 2006), pp. 124–31; N. Howe, 'An Angle on this Earth: Sense of Place in Anglo-Saxon England', *Bulletin of the John Rylands University Library of Manchester* 82 (2000), 3–27 (pp. 4–6, 10, 12).

[20] Michelet, *Creation, Migration, and Conquest*, p. 141.

into his geographical description.[21] Ohthere reported on lands far north of the viking homelands, occupied by the *Finnas* and *Beormas* and *Cwenas*, thereby presenting Denmark and Norway as well-known and explored in comparison. Moreover, these accounts further centralized Alfred's court: not only was it now firmly fixed as an integral part of Christendom, far from the edges of the world, but it attracted men from all directions, from the exotic north as well as the familiar south-east.[22] Knowledge of the northerners, elsewhere depicted as barbarous and strange, established a significant place in the world for the Anglo-Saxons.

In their early contacts with Danes, the Franks similarly attempted to domesticate the north. Frankish interest in Denmark had increased following Charlemagne's conquest of neighbouring Saxony, after which Frankish annals began to depict Danes as a threat, but also as allies of the Frankish rulers. The image of Christendom expanding in all directions suited the annalists who recorded early Frankish contacts with Danes, including missionary attempts.[23] Such an image placed Francia at the centre of a Christian Empire which was gradually drawing the pagan peripheries within its civilizing borders. However, the onset of increasingly severe raids soon challenged this narrative. As at Alfred's court, the threat of viking raids from these unknown regions stimulated geographical curiosity: the first sentence of *De situ orbis*, an anonymous treatise of the late ninth century, identifies ignorance of the vikings' sea journeys as a reason for compiling knowledge of the world.[24] However, knowledge of the north could rarely be found in geographical authorities, and this limited intelligence could not prevent invasion.

Thus viking activity not only forced western European Christians to redraw their conceptual maps of the world, but also raised questions about Christianity's role and future within that world. Unfruitful missionary attempts to Scandinavia and repeated attacks on Christian churches challenged the idea of a triumphant, expanding Christendom. In another letter, Alcuin wondered 'What assurance can the churches of Britain have, if Saint Cuthbert

---

[21] *Two Voyagers at the Court of King Alfred: The Ventures of Ohthere and Wulfstan together with the Description of Northern Europe from the Old English Orosius*, ed. N. Lund, trans. C. Fell (York, 1984). See further I. Valtonen, *The North in the Old English Orosius: A Geographical Narrative in Context* (Helsinki, 2008).

[22] Michelet, *Creation, Migration, and Conquest*, pp. 26, 138.

[23] See further I. Wood, 'Missionaries and the Christian Frontier', in *The Transformation of Frontiers From Late Antiquity to the Carolingians*, ed. W. Pohl, I. Wood and H. Reimitz, The Transformation of the Roman World 10 (Leiden, 2001), pp. 209–18.

[24] *Anonymi Leidensis De Situ Orbis Libri Duo*, ed. R. Quadri (Padua, 1974), p. 3; Michelet, *Creation, Migration, and Conquest*, p. 27; S. Lamb, 'Knowledge about the Scandinavian North in Ninth-Century England and Francia', *Quaestio Insularis* 8 (2007), 82–93.

and so great a company of saints do not defend their own?'[25] A century later, Abbo of St-Germain attempted, in his poem on the siege of Paris in 885–86, to answer his own question about the fate of Francia:

> O France, tell me, I pray you, what became of your strength and might,
> With which you once could overcome and subdue kingdoms that were
>   Often far stronger than you? Your weakness has come from three
>   sins...[26]

Thus Christians sought explanations for the success of pagans and their own inability to resist them, despite having God and the saints on their side; these explanations often invoked the sins of the entire national or geographical community, Britain or Francia. Moreover, Christian religious rhetoric and concepts provided them with a means of strongly distinguishing themselves from their new enemies. So Alcuin wrote to the monks of Wearmouth-Jarrow, invoking a scriptural text that was redeployed frequently throughout the Viking Age by Christian writers seeking to create distance between themselves and their assailants:[27]

> You live near the sea from which this danger first came. In us is fulfilled what once the prophet foretold: 'From the North evil breaks forth, and a terrible glory will come from the Lord' (Jer. 1.14, Job 37.22). See, the pirate raids have penetrated the north of our island.[28]

---

[25] Alcuin of York to Bishop Higbald, 793: *Alcuin of York*, trans. Allott, no. 20, p. 36; *Alcuini Epistolae*, ed. Dümmler, no. 20, p. 57: 'Quae est fiducia aeclesiis Brittanniae, si sanctus Cudberhtus cum tanto sanctorum numero suam non defendit?'

[26] Abbo of St-Germain, *Viking Attacks on Paris: the Bella Parisiacae urbis of Abbo of Saint-Germain-des-Prés*, ed. and trans. N. Dass (Paris, 2007), pp. 96–7: 'Francia, cur latitas vires, narra, peto, priscas, / Te maiora triumphasti quibus atque iugasti / Regna tibi? Propter vitium triplexque piaclum...' On Abbo's depiction of vikings, see N. Dass, 'Temporary Otherness and Homiletic History in the Late Carolingian Age: A Reading of the *Bella Parisiacae urbis* of Abbo of Saint-Germain-des-Prés', in *Difference and Identity in Francia and Medieval France*, ed. M. Cohen and J. Firnhaber-Baker (Farnham, 2010), pp. 99–113.

[27] Also found in *Miracula Sancti Benedicti: Les Miracles de Saint Benoit*, ed. E. de Certain (Paris, 1858), Bk. 2, ch. 1 (p. 95); in addition, Bk. 1, ch. 33 (p. 74) quotes Jeremiah 25. 8–11: 'ecce ego mittam et assumam universas cognationes aquilonis'; Abbo of Fleury, *Life of St Edmund*, in *Three Lives of English Saints*, ed. M. Winterbottom (Toronto, 1972), pp. 65–87, ch. 5 (p. 72). Byrhtferth of Ramsey, *Vita Oswaldi*, in *Byrhtferth of Ramsey: the Lives of St Oswald and St Ecgwine*, ed. M. Lapidge (Oxford, 2009), v. 5 (p. 158) also quotes Jeremiah 25. 8–9, apparently copying from the *Miracula Sancti Benedicti*. See further S. Coupland, 'The Rod of God's Wrath or the People of God's Wrath?', *Journal of Ecclesiastical History* 42 (1991), 535–54 (p. 537).

[28] Alcuin of York to Wearmouth and Jarrow: *Alcuin of York*, trans. Allott, no. 16, p. 40; *Alcuini Epistolae*, ed. Dümmler, no. 19, p. 55: 'Vos maritima habitatis, unde pestis primo ingruit. In nobis impletum est, quod olim per prophetam praedictum est: "Ab aquilone inardescunt mala et a Domino formidolosa laudatio veniet". Ecce fugax latro boreales insulae nostrae partes pervasit.'

Yet here Alcuin warned that the pagan north itself was beginning to impinge on England. He cautioned the monks that they lived next to the sea, which was the source of trouble, and linked the quotation from Jeremiah not to Scandinavia, but to the viking presence in the north of Britain. His words were prescient for, in both England and Francia, raiders soon turned into settlers. Indeed, Normandy was so-called because this region of Scandinavian settlement gained the name *Normannia* among the Franks – the same term used for the original homelands of the vikings.[29] The importance of distinction, and in some cases the desirability of elision, between the two places named *Normannia* became a central theme in formulations of Norman identity. Scandinavian settlement meant the establishment of new lands of Northmen; the north and its people now existed within the borders of regions formerly considered part of Christendom. What had previously been a conceptual division between distant pagan barbarians and civilized Christian kingdoms now became a real issue encountered in local societies.

The presence of vikings in western Europe therefore invoked a variety of images, stereotypes and ideas in Anglo-Saxon and Frankish culture. In many ways, vikings appeared as completely 'Other', the pagan or barbarian foils to Christians' self-images. With the escalation of conflict during the Viking Age, demonization of Scandinavian enemies served an immediate explanatory and patriotic purpose. However, Scandinavia and Norse culture also chimed with familiar aspects of local cultures and related to concepts of the past. The 'Germanic' heritage of Anglo-Saxon and Frankish culture, both in its explicit historical expression and in isolated features of pagan survival, 'heroic' values or vernacular language, found many points of similarity with the newcomers. They were not as alien as the rhetoric of Otherness implied. Thus, in some senses, vikings appeared as equivalent to 'ancestors' or long-lost relatives of the inhabitants of north-west Europe. Indeed, Janet Nelson suggested comparing evidence from England and the Continent in order to investigate the paradox by which images of the viking 'Other' developed in the Viking Age, but individual Danes still took part in political life and behaved as integral members of these societies: this book answers that suggestion.[30] The tension between vikings as ancestors and vikings as Other continued throughout the Viking Age and the period explored in this book, developing

---

[29] L. Musset, 'Un aspect de l'esprit medieval: la "cacogéographie" des Normands et de la Normandie', in L. Musset, *Nordica et Normannica: recueil d'études sur la Scandinavie ancienne et médiévale, les expéditions des Vikings et la fondation de la Normandie* (Paris, 1997), pp. 233–42 (first published in *Revue du Moyen Âge latin*, II (1946), 129–38), p. 236.

[30] J. Nelson, 'England and the Continent in the Ninth Century: II, the Vikings and Others', *TRHS* 6th s., 13 (2003), 1–28 (p. 13). See also E. Roesdahl, 'What May We Expect? On the Problem of Vikings and Archeology in Normandy', in *La progression des Vikings, des raids à la colonisation*, ed. A.-M. F. Héricher (Rouen, 2003), pp. 207–13 (p. 210).

in new ways. Norman histories, for instance, constantly negotiated their subjects' position between claiming viking heritage and distinguishing them from barbarian Northmen. The dual function of vikings as both ancestors and Other made them especially 'good to think with' for English, Norman and Frankish writers: that is, their narratives about vikings were often really narratives about themselves, a means of self-definition and an arena to work out the contradictory appearance of similarities and differences in their own social worlds.[31] This was especially the case for those exploring the limits of ethnic boundaries, which assert the significance of difference but are only necessitated, as a means of distinction, by some degree of similarity.[32] As the following chapters show, political actors in England and Normandy used these dual identifications in order to buttress their own authorities and negotiate identities.

England and Normandy in comparison

Among the areas of Scandinavian settlement, the regions that became England and Normandy provide the most intriguing cases for comparison in terms of viking identities. Apparent differences between Viking Age developments in the two regions in many cases derive from the different research agendas that have been pursued. Chris Wickham and David Bates have both drawn attention to the 'national' historiographies that, on the whole, continue to deal independently with their own regions.[33] Historians of viking England have paid little attention to leaders and rulers, instead asking questions primarily about the nature and scale of settlement.[34] The evidence of place-names, the statements of law codes and the identification of Scandinavian elements in Domesday Book encouraged conclusions about long-term change rather

---

[31] The phrase comes originally from C. Lévi-Strauss, *Totemism*, trans. R. Needham (London, 1964 [1962]), p. 89. Cf. the discussion of Jews in late medieval Europe in D. C. Klepper, *The Insight of Unbelievers: Nicholas of Lyra and Christian Reading of Jewish Text in the Later Middle Ages* (Philadelphia, 2007), p. 61.

[32] S. Malešević, *The Sociology of Ethnicity* (London, 2004), p. 3.

[33] C. Wickham, *Problems in Doing Comparative History* (Southampton, 2005), pp. 2–7, 18; D. Bates, 'Britain and France in the Year 1000', *Franco-British Studies* 28 (1999), 5–22 (p. 5, n. 1; p. 19).

[34] D. Hadley and J. Richards, 'Introduction: Interdisciplinary Approaches to the Scandinavian Settlement', in *Cultures in Contact: Scandinavian Settlement in England in the Ninth and Tenth Centuries*, ed. D. Hadley and J. Richards (Turnhout, 2000), pp. 3–15 (p. 5). For a long time, the only exception was Alfred Smyth's research into the ruling dynasty of Dublin and York (A. Smyth, *Scandinavian Kings in the British Isles 850–880* (Oxford, 1977)), but his reliance on later literary sources was criticized; C. Downham has more recently investigated this dynasty through contemporary evidence: *Viking Kings of Britain and Ireland: the Dynasty of Ívarr to AD 1014* (Edinburgh, 2007).

than the fast-moving transfer of political power. The different polities which viking armies and rulers established in England – the kingdom of York, the Five Boroughs, Guthrum's kingdom of East Anglia – are often treated as one.[35] In contrast, historians of Scandinavian settlement in Francia have focused on political history, so that the names of Rollo and his successors remain central to any account of Normandy's origins. More recently, there have been some successful attempts at integrating the Frankish experience with other areas assaulted by vikings and settled by Scandinavians.[36] This book continues along that route. Comparison with the areas settled by Scandinavians in England will highlight those characteristics attributable specifically to processes of conquest, settlement and cultural interaction.

In fact, broadly speaking, England and Normandy experienced similar histories of raiding and settlement: violent attacks and military campaigns increased in intensity during the ninth century, culminating in territorial conquests by viking armies. In each area of the Anglo-Saxon and Frankish kingdoms where vikings settled, a Scandinavian minority established political control over existing inhabitants. Thus in both England and Normandy immigrants and natives co-existed. Yet the two regions show contrasting pictures of subsequent acculturation and the meanings of viking identity – at least, when viewed through the lens of existing scholarship.

Interpretations of early Normandy have separated broadly along 'Scandinavian' and 'Frankish' lines.[37] After the Second World War, French historians began to abandon long-held views of the Scandinavian character of Normandy in favour of institutional, cultural and social continuity with the Carolingian past.[38] According to these researchers, viking settlers in Normandy rejected Scandinavian culture and rapidly assimilated into the Frankish world. There remain few archaeological traces that are demonstrably Scandinavian.[39] It is claimed that the Old Norse language rapidly died

---

[35] As pointed out by L. Abrams, 'Edward the Elder's Danelaw', in *Edward the Elder, 899–924*, ed. N. Higham and D. Hill (London, 2001), pp. 128–43 (p. 133).

[36] E.g. *Les fondations scandinaves en Occident*, ed. Bauduin.

[37] M. de Boüard, 'De la Neustrie Carolingienne à la Normandie féodale: Continuité ou discontinuité?', *Bulletin of the Institute of Historical Research* 28 (1955), 1–14.

[38] P. Bauduin, *La Première Normandie (Xe –XIe siècles): Sur les frontières de la Haute Normandie: Identité et construction d'une principauté* (Caen, 2004), pp. 25–7; see also the Preface by R. Le Jan, pp. 9–10. H. Prentout, *Essai sur les origines et la fondation du duché de Normandie* (Paris, 1911), presents the case for Scandinavian impact. The most influential post-war interpretations were made by Musset (in particular *Les invasions* and the studies collected in *Nordica et Normannica*, among hundreds of articles on these subjects) and A. d'Haenens, *Les Invasions Normandes, Une Catastrophe?* (Paris, 1970).

[39] L. Mazet-Harhoff, 'The Incursion of the Vikings into the Natural and Cultural Landscape of Upper Normandy', in *Viking Trade and Settlement in Continental Western Europe*, ed. I. S. Klæsøe (Copenhagen, 2010), pp. 81–122 (pp. 82–4) gives an overview of the Scandinavian finds relating to Normandy, but also suggests that

11

out. The centres of population, diocesan and county structures remained the same as they had been in Carolingian times – there was simply a change of personnel at the elite levels.[40] The 'Frankish' school of thought still currently dominates, although more recent research has nuanced the certainty of these conclusions and cast more light on the process of settlement.[41] Moreover, the findings of these studies do not link directly to the scale of migration: Bates argued for a significant number, though still a minority, of Scandinavian settlers in Normandy, attributing the lack of Scandinavian characteristics to the processes of assimilation.[42]

Nevertheless, a few voices maintain that Scandinavian elements persisted. Notably, Eleanor Searle proposed that Scandinavian kinship structures underlay the foundation and expansion of Normandy.[43] However, others pointed out that Frankish society may have been built upon similar patterns of kinship.[44] Lesley Abrams has recently taken another angle on the Scandinavian impact, with particular focus on language. She has emphasized that Norse-speaking immigrants had diverse experiences across Normandy, which were obscured by later sources created after the triumph of Rollo's family.[45] This family's assimilation and political dominance may therefore have created the anomalous situation in Normandy. No one would deny that the vikings' seizure of power in Normandy must have had considerable contemporary repercussions, but it has proved difficult to identify a specifically Scandinavian impact. Cultural contact exerted pressure in one direction

the scarcity of finds results from a lack of excavation. L. Abrams, 'Early Normandy', *ANS* 35 (2013), 45–64 (pp. 48–51) discusses further reasons for the low survival of evidence displaying 'Scandinavian' characteristics.

[40] L. Musset, 'Gouvernés et Gouvernants dans le Monde Scandinave et dans le Monde Normand', *Recueils de la Société Jean Bodin* 23 (1968), 439–68; *idem*, 'Les Domaines de l'Époque Franque et les Destinées du Régime Domanial du IXe au XIe Siècle', *BSAN* 49 (1946), 7–97; *idem*, 'Monachisme d'Époque Franque et Monachisme d'Époque Ducale en Normandie: Le Problème de la Continuité', in *Aspects du Monachisme en Normandie (IVe–XVIIIe siècles)*, ed. L. Musset (Paris, 1982), pp. 55–74; J. Yver, 'Les Premières Institutions du duché de Normandie', in *I Normanni e loro espansione in Europa nell' alto medioevo* (Spoleto, 1969), pp. 299–366; more recently, F. Lifshitz, 'La Normandie carolingienne: essai sur la continuité, avec utilisation de sources négligées', *Annales de Normandie* 48 (1998), 505–24.

[41] See especially the studies in *La Normandie vers l'an mil: études et documents*, ed. F. de Beaurepaire and J.-P. Chaline (Rouen, 2000).

[42] D. Bates, *Normandy Before 1066* (London, 1982), pp. 15–24; Abrams, 'Early Normandy', p. 48. Roesdahl, 'What May We Expect?', pp. 208–9, asks why the situation in Normandy should be so different from other areas, and suggests possible cultural dynamics that might have been causes.

[43] E. Searle, *Predatory Kinship and the Creation of Norman Power, 840–1066* (Berkeley and Los Angeles, 1988); Searle, 'Frankish Rivalries'.

[44] M. Gelting, 'Predatory Kinship Revisited', *ANS* 15 (2003), 107–20 (p. 107); see the review by D. Bates in *Speculum* 65 (1990), 1045–7.

[45] Abrams, 'Early Normandy'.

only: from the absence of Norse cultural markers it would appear that, by the end of the tenth century, the immigrant vikings had assimilated to Frankish culture.

The Scandinavian influence on England, though no less controversial, is generally considered to be more significant. For most of the twentieth century, the question of scale has focused the debate.[46] In support of mass migration from Scandinavia, scholars attributed distinctive features of northern and eastern England to the viking period. Later references to the 'Danelaw' were supplemented with investigations into the Scandinavian origins of legal, administrative and social institutions and terminology. Frank Stenton presented this view at length, drawing especially on linguistic evidence in support of two waves of migration. Philologists pointed to the predominance of Scandinavian elements in place-names (and personal names) as evidence of dense Scandinavian settlement and linguistic influence. Place-names derived from Old Norse elements map convincingly onto the regions where written sources state that viking armies settled – the north and east of England.

In contradiction to this view of mass migration, in his *Age of the Vikings* of 1962, Peter Sawyer argued for minimal levels of Scandinavian settlement. Sawyer dismissed the reliability of contemporary written sources, claiming that they greatly exaggerated the size of viking armies; he asserted, furthermore, that the settlers were all members of these armies, and rejected the idea of an unrecorded secondary migration.[47] Opinions divided according to the nature of the evidence each scholar privileged, but it was clear that both arguments required refinement. For example, Sawyer significantly rethought his position in the light of advances in place-name studies: he credits the work of Gillian Fellows-Jensen in convincing him that there continued to be new Scandinavian settlements in the tenth and eleventh centuries.[48] Moreover, local studies indicated that not only the density but the patterns of settlement varied in different regions.[49] However, the question of Scandinavian impact

---

[46] D. Hadley, *The Vikings in England: Settlement, Society and Culture* (Manchester, 2006), pp. 3–6; Hadley and Richards, 'Introduction', p. 4; S. Trafford, 'Ethnicity, Migration Theory and the Historiography of the Scandinavian Settlement in England', in *Cultures in Contact*, ed. Hadley and Richards, pp. 17–39 (pp. 18–21) gives a useful overview of the debate.

[47] P. Sawyer, *The Age of the Vikings* (London. 1962; 2nd edn 1971). Sawyer's work was matched by similar re-interpretations of the viking period in Francia by Lucien Musset and Albert d'Haenens: see A. d'Haenens, 'Les Invasions Normandes dans l'Empire Franc au IXe Siècle', in *I Normanni e loro espansione*, pp. 233–98 (esp. pp. 240–1).

[48] Sawyer, *Age of the Vikings*, pp. vi, 148–76.

[49] E.g. L. Abrams, 'Scandinavian Place-Names and Settlement-History: Flegg, Norfolk and East Anglia in the Viking Age', in *Vikings and Norse in the North Atlantic: Proceedings of the Fourteenth Viking Congress*, ed. A. Mortensen and S. Arge (Torshavn, 2005), pp. 307–22.

remained bound up with the issue of the scale of settlement.[50] Scholars on all sides of the debate presented Scandinavian linguistic, cultural, administrative or legal influence (or lack thereof) as evidence of mass (or minimal) migration.

In the last twenty years, researchers have moved away from the issue of scale to examine processes of settlement and acculturation. In doing so, they have recognized the importance of interdisciplinary and collaborative projects. Dawn Hadley and Julian Richards' edited volume *Cultures in Contact* drew together researchers in many different disciplines to suggest new avenues of research and to produce a more complex view of accommodation and integration in the British Isles. New archaeological evidence added further material for this approach. The Coppergate excavations at York between 1979 and 1981 revealed 40,000 objects, which sparked a re-interpretation of the 'viking capital' of York. Since its inception in 1997, the Portable Antiquities Scheme has recorded small finds from around the country, increasing the artefactual evidence of Scandinavians in England exponentially.[51] Research into these discoveries has produced sophisticated analyses of the Scandinavian contribution to material culture.

In response to their findings, researchers have coined the term 'Anglo-Scandinavian' to refer to the culture and society of Danish-settled areas of England in the Viking Age. Different types of evidence reveal a complex process of acculturation between migrants and natives, which resulted in the creation of new forms of societal organization and display. For instance, stone sculpture from northern England bears resemblance to contemporary Scandinavian styles and in some cases illustrates scenes from Norse mythology, but includes elements from an Anglo-Saxon background – including the very tradition of such stone-carving.[52] Stonework artists in England developed new types of monument, such as the hogback, out of this fusion.[53] Similarly, women's brooches made in East Anglia and near Lincoln followed Scandinavian fashions, but used Anglo-Saxon forms and fittings. Moreover, there are a number of 'Scandinavian' brooch types and styles found only in England.[54] Research into these aspects of material culture and social organization implies that the interaction of Danish settlers and

---

[50] Cf. B. Ward-Perkins, 'Why Did the Anglo-Saxons Not Become More British?', *EHR* 115 (2000), 513–33; Trafford, 'Ethnicity, Migration Theory', suggests why this issue has been discussed more profitably for the Anglo-Saxon settlement.

[51] Kershaw, *Viking Identities*, p. 2.

[52] D. Stocker, 'Monuments and Merchants: Irregularities in the Distribution of Stone Sculpture in Lincolnshire and Yorkshire in the Tenth Century', in *Cultures in Contact*, ed. Hadley and Richards, pp. 180–212; P. Sidebottom, 'Viking Age Stone Monuments and Social Identity in Derbyshire', *ibid*, pp. 213–35.

[53] R. Bailey, *Viking Age Sculpture in Northern England* (London, 1980), pp. 85–100.

[54] J. Kershaw, 'Culture and Gender in the Danelaw: Scandinavian and Anglo-Scandinavian Brooches', *Viking and Medieval Scandinavia* 5 (2009), 295–325; Kershaw, *Viking Identities*, pp. 222, 229–36.

Anglo-Saxon inhabitants created a new culture of fusion, in contrast to the one-sided assimilation of vikings in Normandy.

In the definition of 'Anglo-Scandinavian' society, several scholars have introduced the concept of identity.[55] They have interpreted these cultural products as deliberate assertions of ethnic identity, which demonstrated their users' links to Scandinavia, and also connection to their immediate local regions. In their introduction to *Cultures in Contact*, Hadley and Richards state that 'an important aim of this volume is to open up new interdisciplinary dialogue', before listing the types of evidence used: 'documentary, archaeological, artefactual, and linguistic evidence'.[56] Note that this list does not include literary material. Indeed, medieval written sources contain no equivalent to the new term 'Anglo-Scandinavian'. Sawyer's comments on the written sources, despite the criticism they received, have taught researchers of the viking impact a general wariness in the use of literary texts. But this discrepancy between the 'identity' expressed in material culture and in texts at least needs elucidating. Moreover, these studies rarely entangle their research with discussions of the contemporaneous development of a unified English identity, which, in contrast, classify texts as their primary sources of evidence.[57] The relationship between a developing English identity and the posited 'Anglo-Scandinavian' identity deserves consideration. Literary sources therefore provide an opportunity to investigate ethnic relations across England.

The absence of literary studies from the agenda constitutes the major difference between approaches to identity in England and Normandy. In contrast to the focus on Scandinavian material culture in England, it was literary sources that sparked modern interest in Norman identity. Successive eleventh- and twelfth-century historians produced texts devoted to the Norman people as a distinct group. Dudo of St-Quentin, William of Jumièges, William of Poitiers, Robert of Torigni and Orderic Vitalis, as well as a number of anonymous monks, detailed the exploits of the Norman *gens* and attributed their achievements to their distinctive Norman character. These histories led modern scholars to an appreciation of the constructed nature of Norman identity. In 1976, R. H. C. Davis referred to the enigma of 'The Normans and

---

[55] L. Abrams, 'Diaspora and Identity in the Viking Age', *EME* 20 (2012), 17–38; Kershaw, *Viking Identities*; M. Innes, 'Danelaw Identities: Ethnicity, Regionalism and Political Allegiance', in *Cultures in Contact*, ed. Hadley and Richards, pp. 65–88; D. Hadley, 'Viking and Native: Rethinking Identity in the Danelaw', *EME* 11 (2002), 45–70.

[56] Hadley and Richards, 'Introduction', p. 3.

[57] Harris, *Race and Ethnicity in Anglo-Saxon Literature*; S. Foot, 'The Making of *Angelcynn*: English Identity before the Norman Conquest', *TRHS* 6th s. 6 (1996), 25–49; S. Reynolds, 'What Do We Mean by "Anglo-Saxon" and Anglo-Saxons"?', *Journal of British Studies* 24 (1985), 395–415 (repr. in S. Reynolds, *Ideas and Solidarities of the Medieval Laity* (Aldershot, 1995), no. III); P. Wormald, '*Engla Lond*: The Making of an Allegiance', *Journal of Historical Sociology* 7 (1994), 1–24.

their Myth': from the eleventh century to the present, historians viewed the Normans as a distinct and united people, but what that meant and who it included was never constant.[58] Davis thus recognized Norman identity as a creation of the inhabitants of Normandy. It was an extreme example of the general truth that 'What no nation can be without is an image or myth with which it can identify itself... it is usually flexible and capable of being gradually transformed.'[59] Subsequent researchers investigated in detail how historical texts created this identity.[60]

Historians of the medieval period increasingly came to recognize that *all* identities are constructed by those who use them, and *all* identities continue to mutate over time. In this respect, Normandy was not unique, though many clung to the suggestion that it was an extreme example.[61] Rather, in the texts of Norman identity we are able to view the process more clearly than in most cases. This base of literary sources makes Norman identity a useful comparison with Scandinavian identity in England.

Norman historians created a strong narrative of the origins and characteristics of the Norman people. They attributed the Normans' success as conquerors in England, Sicily and the Levant to their *Normanitas*, which flourished among not just the dukes but the entire people. The earliest of these histories, which subsequent historians followed, was Dudo of St-Quentin's *De moribus et actis primorum Normanniae ducum*. Dudo devoted much time and emphasis to the viking past, describing how Rollo the viking leader became the first of the Norman dukes. Moreover, the collective name he used – *Normanni* – was the same word that their neighbours used for viking raiders throughout the ninth and tenth centuries. This word came from the Old Norse for 'North men', a fact which demonstrates the deliberate identification of the inhabitants of Normandy with vikings. Again, however, the development of Norman identity has been viewed in isolation from the identities of the Normans' neighbours, the Franks. The effect of the Normans on Frankish identity has been assumed to be minimal, because Norse culture seems to have had little influence in France. Yet the Normans did not forget their viking roots. While Scandinavian culture may have declined, there remained a specifically 'viking' element in the texts of Norman identity.

These differing pictures of assimilation and identity in England and Normandy present a clear problem. Settlers in Normandy rapidly assimilated

---

[58] R. H. C. Davis, *The Normans and Their Myth* (London, 1976), pp. 12–14.

[59] Davis, *Normans and Their Myth*, p. 49.

[60] N. Webber, *The Evolution of Norman Identity, 911–1154* (Woodbridge, 2005); E. Albu, *The Normans in Their Histories: Propaganda, Myth, and Subversion* (Woodbridge, 2001); C. Potts, '*Atque unum ex diversis gentibus populum effecit*: Historical Tradition and the Norman Identity', *ANS* 17 (1995), 139–52; G. A. Loud, 'The *Gens Normannorum* – Myth or Reality?', *ANS* 4 (1982), 104–16.

[61] Searle, *Predatory Kinship*, p. 2; M. Chibnall, *The Normans* (Oxford, 2000), p. 3.

to Frankish society, whereas settlers in England developed their own 'Anglo-Scandinavian' culture, which was full of Norse forms and elements. Yet contemporaries spoke of 'Normans' as a people, but no comparable term existed in England. The texts of Norman identity described how they, as a people, had come from Scandinavia and terrorized Francia in years of viking raids. In tenth-century England, on the other hand, no one produced texts identifying with vikings, not even in the Anglo-Scandinavian milieu of north-east England. Culture and identity appear to have been disconnected.

So, this book poses the problem: how did identities in England and Normandy develop as a result of Scandinavian settlement? Identification with vikings and Scandinavian origins cannot be mapped onto the persistence of Norse culture. Nor was there a simple connection between the creation of a new ethnicity (such as Norman identity) and the creation of a new culture (such as the Anglo-Scandinavian culture discerned in northern England). Given that the creation of identities was not the result of a general expression of cultural distinctions, we should ask who manipulated identities in England and Normandy. The dominant political authorities present a striking difference. The Norman dukes originated as a viking dynasty, whereas the West Saxon kings took dominance over all England by conquering regions from viking rulers. Were the identities of ordinary people determined by the holders of political power?

Ethnicity and identity in medieval studies

The central problem, then, is that of ethnicity. The settlement of Scandinavian migrants in England and in Normandy meant that, in the tenth and eleventh centuries, a significant proportion of both populations had viking ancestors. Texts from both societies suggest that innate personal qualities and contemporary societal organisation derived from such descent. Yet they do not wholly agree on the nature of those qualities or the effect on society: as this book explores, the meaning attributed to Scandinavian ancestry, and the circumstances in which it was acknowledged, emphasised or denied, manifested in varied ways. Moreover, in scholarship and in popular discourse, the impact of the vikings on the ethnic make-up of the British population – and, to some extent, inhabitants of Normandy – constitutes a major source of interest.[62]

---

[62] As well as those works already cited, see for example C. Downham, 'Viking Ethnicities: A Historiographic Overview', *History Compass* 10 (2012), 1–12; P. Dottelonde, 'Normandie: la chasse aux ancêtres vikings', *L'Histoire* 49 (1982), 99–102; F. Guillet, 'Le Nord Mythique de la Normandie: des Normands aux Vikings de la fin du XVIIIe siècle jusqu'à la Grande Guerre', *Revue de Nord* 360-1 (2005), 459–71. On genetic testing, see J. Kershaw and E. C. Røyrvik, 'The "People of the British Isles" Project and Viking Settlement in England', *Antiquity* 90 (2016), 1670–80; E. C.

While vikings have also played a role in visions of national and regional identity, emphasis consistently falls on the basic components of ethnicity – descent, a distinct origin and a shared past.

Researchers in viking studies, as Hadley has demonstrated, have generally relied on outmoded or under-theorized paradigms of ethnicity.[63] Although recent interdisciplinary research has raised interest in issues of identity, research in different disciplines is often conducted against the background of contrasting theoretical frameworks. For instance, projects analysing DNA samples either of medieval burials or current populations have been used as evidence of migration and ancestry.[64] Results from these kinds of studies may be helpful in mapping the movements of particular genetic characteristics. Yet they tell us nothing about perceived, and therefore socially real, identities.[65] Recognition of the complex connections between genetic relations, culture and ethnic identities, and the multifarious possible approaches, has stimulated increasing interest in these areas. This has extended to dealing with conflict and ethnicity among vikings, although this has so far been ultimately a project of categorization.[66]

Modern concepts of ethnicity have exerted a slower impact on viking studies because the field has fallen between two discussions of ethnicity in the medieval period. The first, the debate over the 'ethnogenesis' of barbarian peoples in the fourth and fifth centuries, problematized the relationships between identity, solidarity, organization and status. Although there has been fierce disagreement about the role and origin of ethnic traditions in group formation, the discussion as a whole emphasized the fluid, subjective nature of identities.[67]

Hirschman and D. Panther-Yates, 'Peering Inward for Ethnic Identity: Consumer Interpretation of DNA Test Results', *Identity* 8 (2008), 47–66; following a similar model to the People of the British Isles Project, researchers from the Universities of Leicester and Caen are currently investigating genetic heritage in the Cotentin.

[63] Hadley, 'Viking and Native', especially p. 70.

[64] E.g. G. Bowden, P. Balaresque, T. King and others, 'Excavating Past Population Structures by Surname-Based Sampling: the Genetic Legacy of the Vikings in Northwest England', *Molecular Biology and Evolution* 25.2 (2008), 301–09.

[65] Hadley, 'Viking and Native', p. 69.

[66] C. Downham, '"Hiberno-Norwegians" and "Anglo-Danes": Anachronistic Ethnicities in Viking Age England', *Mediaeval Scandinavia* 19 (2009), 139–69, for discussion.

[67] H. Wolfram, '*Origo et religio*. Ethnic traditions and literature in early medieval texts', *EME* 3 (1994), 19–38; *Strategies of Distinction: the Construction of Ethnic Communities, 300–800*, ed. W. Pohl and H. Reimitz (Leiden, 1998). These historians draw on ideas from R. Wenskus, *Stammesbildung und Verfassung. Das Werden der frühmittelalterlichen Gentes* (Cologne, 1961). In dispute, see A. Gillett, 'Ethnogenesis: A Contested Model of Early Medieval Europe', *History Compass* 4 (2006), 241–60 (pp. 247–52); P. Heather, 'Disappearing and Reappearing Tribes', in *Strategies of Distinction*, ed. Pohl and Reimitz, pp. 95–111.

The second important discussion of medieval ethnicity relates to the later Middle Ages and the concept of frontier.[68] Explorations of specific situations have emphasized how political, ethnic, cultural and economic boundaries rarely correspond, and provided many examples of cultural exchange (and other kinds of interaction such as economic networks) across ethnic boundaries.[69] A frontier society can be imagined as a 'middle ground' where cultural exchange could take place and accommodations to differences evolved through necessity.[70] The insights from frontier societies may be deepened with reference to English and Norman societies, both of which can be seen as frontiers between Christian Europe and the pagan Scandinavian world.

Scholars involved in both discussions recognize ethnic identity as a 'situational construct'.[71] The same individual is able to present himself or herself as a member of various groups, depending on context. In particular, ethnic identity arises *for* something, in the pursuit of a political purpose or material benefit. Ethnicity is in this way relative: the group identities of others are recognized in a way that relates to the identity of the perceiver, and vice versa. The views of the outsider and the insider are different, but dependent, facets of identity. Frequently, individuals may manipulate their behaviour based on externally recognized characterizations of ethnicity. The anthropologist Frederik Barth's work refuted the idea that ethnic groups with distinctive cultures emerged in isolation, proposing rather that ethnicity is constructed only in relation to others – through contact.[72] Studying a single ethnic group is therefore of limited usefulness, as this approach disregards both the purpose and the negotiation of ethnicity.

However, contributions to both 'ethnogenesis' and frontier debates have been built on the basic assumption that ethnic groups are real and active entities. Yet this assumption has been challenged within the social sciences in recent years. Rogers Brubaker has pointed out that ethnic groups are not bounded or internally homogeneous, and their members do not share the same interests and actions.[73] Ethnic groups are constituted by members

---

[68] *Frontiers in Question: Eurasian Borderlands, 700–1700*, ed. D. Power and N. Standen (Basingstoke, 1999); *Medieval Frontier Societies*, ed. R. Bartlett and A. MacKay (Oxford, 1989); R. Bartlett, *The Making of Europe* (London, 1993), esp. pp. 197–242.

[69] R. Burns, *Muslims, Christians and Jews in the Crusader Kingdom of Valencia: Societies in Symbiosis* (Cambridge, 1983); T. Glick, *Islamic and Christian Spain in the Early Middle Ages* (Boston, 2005), pp. 165–93.

[70] D. Power and N. Standen, 'Introduction', in *Frontiers in Question*, pp. 1–31 (pp. 10–11, 22–25).

[71] P. Geary, 'Ethnic Identity as a Situational Construct in the Early Middle Ages', *Mitteilungen der Anthropologischen Gesellschaft in Wien* 113 (1983), 15–26.

[72] *Ethnic Groups and Boundaries: The Social Organization of Culture Difference*, ed. F. Barth (London, 1969).

[73] R. Brubaker, *Ethnicity Without Groups* (Cambridge, MA, 2004), pp. 7–27.

believing they exist: they do not function as organizations and communities in themselves. Therefore, it is necessary to separate the discourse of group identity from actual social and political organization. This approach is essential if we are to understand *why* people believe in ethnic groups. As Brubaker has emphasized:

> ...we cannot rely on common sense here. Ethnic common sense – the tendency to partition the social world into putatively deeply constituted, quasi-natural intrinsic kinds – is a key part of what we want to explain, not what we want to explain things *with*; it belongs to our empirical data, not to our analytical toolkit.[74]

In other words, the focus of this investigation is not real social groups: it is the belief in group membership, and the effect that belief had on action. Our sources' statements about ethnicity constitute the data examined in the five main chapters. They are not factual reports of ethnic groups but participants in the discourse of identity.

Thus studies which trace the development of a particular identity – the 'emergence' of the English or the Normans, for example – risk confusing their own analytical concepts with the categories of the societies they investigate.[75] Instead of taking this approach, in this book I analyse the changing significance of viking and Scandinavian identities during the tenth and eleventh centuries, in order to investigate the forces which transform historical events and processes into focuses of ethnicity. The investigation goes beyond the statements of texts about identity, for the sources themselves had a role to play in manipulating ethnicity.

For this reason, we cannot simply adopt the medieval concept of *'gens'*, most often translated as 'people' or 'race', which early medieval writers used in a variety of contexts. Around 900, Regino of Prüm stated that 'the various nations of peoples differ in their descent, customs, language and law'.[76] Notably, the physical appearance of different peoples, now of central importance to everyday concepts of ethnicity, was not often invoked as a mark of distinction.[77] The learned construction of this term owed a lot to the story

---

[74] Brubaker, *Ethnicity Without Groups*, p. 9.

[75] Cf. A. Wimmer, *Ethnic Boundary Making: Institutions, Power, Networks* (Oxford, 2013), p. 206.

[76] *Reginonis Abbatis Prumiensis Chronicon*, ed. F. Kurze, *MGH*, SS rer. Germ. 50 (Hanover, 1890), p. xx: 'diversae nationes populorum inter se discrepant genere moribus lingua legibus'. On Regino, see *History and Politics in Late Carolingian and Ottonian Europe: the Chronicle of Regino of Prüm and Adalbert of Magdeburg*, ed. S. Maclean (Manchester, 2009).

[77] R. Bartlett, 'Medieval and Modern Concepts of Race and Ethnicity', *Journal of Medieval and Early Modern Studies* 31 (2001), 39–56 (p. 53); S. Reynolds, *Kingdoms and Communities in Western Europe, 900–1300* (Oxford, 1984), p. 302; Thomas, *English and the Normans*, p. 348.

of the tower of Babel, rather than contemporary experience. Consequently, as Patrick Geary has pointed out, the distinctions drawn in practice bore little relation to formally articulated criteria.[78] Explanations of *gentes* merely constituted one discursive strategy among many used in the negotiation of ethnicity.

The structure of the book

This book focuses on the years *c.* 950–*c.* 1015, in which period the political authorities of England and Normandy were comparable. Although their populations were mixtures of long-term inhabitants and immigrants, both societies were unified under single leaderships – at least in theory. Moreover, in this period, writers showed significant interest in the viking past, which arose from its perceived relevance to their contemporary situations.

The study begins around 950 AD. In the 940s, the viking societies of Normandy and York both went through political crises. Louis IV and Hugh the Great invaded Normandy and exiled the infant Norman leader Richard I; the West Saxon King Eadred violently asserted his dominance over the Northumbrians who had chosen the Norse King Eric. These crises had opposite outcomes for the viking rulers. Richard I established himself as the sole ruler of the principality of Normandy, although it remained within the French kingdom. On the other hand, 954 marked the expulsion of the last viking king of York. From that point forwards the English king ruled all of the former Anglo-Saxon kingdoms, including Danish-settled areas. Therefore, we compare England with Normandy: each region was ruled by one dynasty, and contained populations descended from a mixture of Scandinavian settlers and pre-viking 'natives'.

The comparison ends in *c.* 1015. By this point, ethnic relations were very different in the two regions. In Normandy, Dudo of St-Quentin composed his *De moribus et actis primorum Normanniae ducum*, and thereby established the history of the Normans' origins which would dominate future historiography. In England, the kingdom formed in the tenth century remained united, but the West Saxon dynasty of kings was threatened. In 1016, England was conquered by Cnut, and a new chapter of English–Danish relations began. Therefore, the comparison concludes before Cnut's conquest and the divergent fates of England and Normandy.

The period under consideration began almost 100 years after the initial Scandinavian settlements. Identities were flexible and open to reformulation; they could be manipulated according to political advantage. The difference between 'vikings', 'English' and 'Franks' was asserted at a societal level.

---

[78] Geary, 'Ethnic Identity as a Situational Construct', pp. 19–24.

Individuals, many of whom had mixed heritage, found themselves able to associate with different groups more freely.

Comparisons between England and Normandy have often been suggested but rarely attempted in any depth.[79] There are numerous aspects on which the two regions of Scandinavian settlement could be compared in terms of political, social or cultural history. In this book, I focus on the second half of the tenth century and the early eleventh century, and the entirety of the two regions. It is thus not a study of two 'viking' polities as such, but an investigation into the processes of assimilation and identification in two similar historical contexts. The comparison pursued here explores the variety of ways in which Scandinavian and viking heritage was employed as a means of negotiating ethnic relations. Or, to put it another way, what did it mean to claim or assign viking identity in these two societies?

Interpretations of the viking and Scandinavian past appear in written sources of various genres from the period *c.* 950–*c.* 1015: genealogy, history (in both dynastic and chronicle form), hagiography (saints' lives, miracles and translations), charters and law codes. In most of these cases, the nature, quantity and survival of evidence from England and Normandy is broadly similar, although their narratives of viking activity and its effects often diverge considerably.

This investigation concentrates its analysis on the literary aspects of written sources in order to focus discussion on perceived identities. Research into material and linguistic evidence has illuminated complex processes of cultural interaction in regions of Scandinavian settlement. However, since socially relevant identities are subjective, dependent on perceptions and not directly correlated to culture, this evidence is difficult to interpret in terms of intergroup dynamics. Written evidence expresses opinions and provides insight into mentalities, and can therefore increase our understanding of how identities were perceived and activated. Through its focus on literary sources, this study will complement work on cultural interaction and offer some possibilities of interpretation.

This form of comparison is intended to highlight differences and similarities in two comparable societies, in order to explain historical divergence. Chris Wickham has proposed a useful method in approaching such historical comparison. He employs Carlo Ginzburg's concept of '*spie*', or 'clues', as a

---

[79] L. Musset, 'Pour l'étude comparative de deux fondations politiques des Vikings: le royaume d'York et le duché de Rouen', in *idem, Nordica et Normannica*, pp. 157–72; F. Stenton, 'The Scandinavian Colonies in England and Normandy', *TRHS* 4th s. 37 (1945), 1–12. In addition, some scholars have successfully used material from one region to shed light on the other: G. Fellows-Jensen, 'Les noms de lieux d'origine scandinave et la colonisation viking en Normandie: Examen critique de la question', *Proxima Thulé* 1 (1994), 63–103.

means of focusing on comparable elements that illuminate reasons for difference.[80] In this book, I apply a similar approach to a problem which hinges on people's beliefs – why did viking identity develop differently in England and Normandy? The *spie* employed, therefore, should be clues to the creation and manipulation of those beliefs: in what contexts was the viking past invoked in an identitarian sense? When we have answered this question, then we can ask *who* used it in this way and for what purposes. Our *spie* should thus illuminate different manifestations of ethnic narratives, so that we can isolate when the viking past was or was not used. Different contexts – particularly forms of historical writing and representations of the past – which were important to identity in these societies now become *spie* through which we examine the uses of viking and Scandinavian identity in England and Normandy.

Chapter 1 discusses genealogical identity in Normandy and England. The concern for identity inherited from ancestors was displayed through the production of genealogies, usually tied to the heritage of ruling houses. Chapter 2 continues this discussion to explore the connected phenomenon of origin myths. Investigating these sources shows the perceived relationships of Scandinavian migrants and their host peoples in the distant and more recent past.

While genealogies and origin myths frequently invoked a distant Scandinavian heritage, historical narratives also considered the recent past of viking invasions and wars between Frankish, English and Scandinavian armies. Rewritings and reinterpretations of these events can be related directly to contemporary concerns about ethnic identity and heritage in the societies for which they were produced. Chapters 3 and 4 compare the historical narratives produced in England and Normandy, which predominantly appeared in hagiographical form. Many similarities emerge in how monastic writers and ruling elites presented the viking past in saints' *vitae* and *miracula*, although the actual historical content of the narratives promoted either side of the Channel differed markedly.

Finally, Chapter 5 examines how histories of viking activity and Scandinavian settlement related to regional and territorial identities within England and Normandy. To what extent did contemporaries perceive areas most affected by these histories to be socially, politically and culturally distinct, and in what circumstances did they attribute such distinction to the viking past? In this chapter, I compare the evidence of land charters from England and Normandy, in order to investigate the use of ethnonyms and terminology for inhabitants of different regions, as well as the ways in which historical justifications underpinned claims to territorial authority. In the case of England, however, it also proves necessary to consider a selection of legal

---

[80] Wickham, *Problems in Doing Comparative History*, pp. 12–15. For the original idea, see C. Ginzburg, 'Morelli, Freud and Sherlock Holmes: Clues and Scientific Method', *History Workshop* 9 (1980), 5–36.

texts from the early eleventh century, written by Archbishop Wulfstan II of York, which impose an ethnic explanation for a regional divide.

In each chapter, the sources used exemplify how identities were constructed, manipulated and disseminated throughout society. As Walter Pohl has argued, a text cannot be treated 'as evidence for the natural existence of ethnic communities'. It may be a reflection of contemporary perceptions of group identities, and at the same time 'part of strategies to give shape to these communities'.[81] Medieval writers may not have thought of their actions in those terms, perhaps, but they participated in the assertion of ethnic narratives for political gain. The viking past and present offered compelling material for these ethnic narratives. Modern historians of Scandinavian settlement frequently invoke Maitland's famous caution, 'we must be careful how we use our Dane';[82] we should keep in mind that these medieval writers were just as careful.

Placing England and Normandy in comparative perspective raises new questions about ethnicity in each region. In particular, this book frequently highlights the similarity between the actions of the English kings in manipulating ethnic relations and those of the Norman dukes. This pairing of secular rulers is partly a result of the extant written material, but the survival of this evidence results from the comparability of their actions. English kings and Norman dukes followed similar strategies in the presentation and establishment of their authority. In addition, they both concerned themselves with their subjects' identities as a means of ensuring loyalty. Much of this comparison, therefore, juxtaposes the actions of a 'native' dynasty with an 'immigrant', Scandinavian dynasty. Their parallel achievements demonstrate that successful rule was not 'ethnic'. More importantly, the comparison allows us to investigate the extent to which a medieval ruler actively determined his subjects' ethnicity.

This issue is particularly significant in the next two chapters, which compare constructions of genealogical identity in England and Normandy. In both regions, genealogy was the preserve of rulers, but gained relevance and meaning for a much wider range of people. Anglo-Saxon and Norman genealogies incorporated the distant, mythical Scandinavian past into the family histories of their ruling houses, thereby showing how the Northmen – though still imbued with pagan, alien associations – had become part of their peoples' stories.

---

[81] W. Pohl, 'Telling the Difference: Signs of Ethnic Identity', in *Strategies of Distinction*, ed. Pohl and Reimitz, pp. 17–69 (p. 21).

[82] F. Maitland, *Domesday Book and Beyond: Three Essays in the Early History of England* (Cambridge, 1897; repr. 1987), p. 139.

1

Genealogy: Building a Viking Age Dynasty

DE REGUM FRANCORUM

Primus rex Francorum Chloio.
Chloio genuit Glodobode.
Ghlodobedus genuit Mereveo.
Mereveus genuit Hilbricco.
Hildebricus genuit Genniodo.
Genniodus genuit Hilderico.
Childericus genuit Chlodoveo.
Chlodoveus genuit Theodorico,
    Chlomiro, Hildeberto, Hlodario.
Chlodharius genuit Chariberto,
    Ghundrammo, Chilberico, Sigiberto.
Sigibertus genuit Hildeberto.
Hildebertus genuit Theodoberto et Theoderico.
Et ante Hilbericus genuit Hlodhario.
Hlodharius genuit Dagabertum.[1]

CANTWARA

Aeðelberht Uihtreding
Uihtred Ecgberhting
Ecgberht Erconberhting
Erconberht Eadbalding
Eadbald Eðilberhting
Eðilberht Iurmenricing
Iu:menric Oes[...]
Oese Ocging
Ocga Hengesting
Hengest Uitting
Uitta Uihtgilsing
Uihtgils Uegdaeging
Uegdaeg Uodning
Uoden Frealafing[2]

At first glance, early medieval genealogies such as these present information on origins and ancestry, and therefore seem to provide the basis for an understanding of ethnicity. However, examination of these texts rapidly reveals that their claims are by no means accurate, that they were constantly reworked, and that they are highly selective in content.[3] It is doubtful whether Merovech and Hengest – let alone Woden – were real historical figures; certainly, they accrued a body of fantastic legend attached to their names. Meanwhile, the selection in these two texts completely bypasses all the women who must have played essential roles in the descent of these kings. The genealogies' applicability, moreover, was malleable: the first claimed to represent all the Frankish kings, its neatness hiding multiple kingdoms and dynastic complexity; the second is entitled merely the Kings of Kent, but Hengest came to be seen as the forefather of all Anglo-Saxons.

---

[1] *Catalogi Regum Francorum Praetermissi*, ed. B. Krusch, *MGH*, SS rer. Merov., 7 (Hanover, 1920), pp. 850–5 (p. 851).

[2] D. Dumville, 'The Anglian Collection of Royal Genealogies and Regnal Lists', *ASE* 5 (1976), 23–50 (p. 31).

[3] L. Genicot, *Les Genealogies*, Typologie des Sources du Moyen Âge Occidental, 15 (Turnhout, 1975).

We must, therefore, investigate the context, reception and adaptation of the genealogical formulations in order to understand how descent and ethnicity interacted.

This chapter investigates the impact of the Viking Age on genealogy produced in England and Francia. Anglo-Saxon and Frankish genealogies produced before the mid-tenth century were restricted to royal lines. Concepts of ethnicity in these texts were therefore entangled with issues of royal legitimacy. Early medieval genealogies emerge as complex texts which, far from being simple records of biological descent, were ultimately ideological statements.[4] As such, they are indeed invaluable evidence for identity, not biological but social: they represent the subjective perception and political impact of constantly evolving ethnic relations.

We may therefore expect the events of the Viking Age, in which Scandinavians became a political force and significant demographic within England and Francia, to be reflected in genealogical texts. As we shall see, this was indeed the case, but Scandinavian influence manifested very differently in the two regions. The West Saxon royal genealogy expanded to include Scandinavian ancestors, but that of the Frankish kings did not. It was instead an entirely new aristocratic genealogy of the Normans that asserted viking identity in Francia. This chapter explores how and why these divergent situations arose, analysing the relationship between power structures and genealogical texts.

A complication arises in this comparison, since the formal characteristics of genealogies from England and Francia differed considerably and thus conveyed varied types of information. The earliest Anglo-Saxon royal genealogies were written in the vernacular, and often possess rhythm and alliteration that may derive from oral poetic origins. Frankish royal genealogies, on the other hand, were always in Latin, and contain references that suggest familiarity with Latin literature. Moreover, they seem to have been inspired by biblical genealogies, being written in the form 'x genuit y'. In this they differ again from Anglo-Saxon royal genealogies, which are retrograde, starting with an individual and working backwards. These distinctions suggest different origins for the two traditions, oral in the case of the Anglo-Saxon texts and literate in Francia. Nevertheless, by the mid-ninth century, these were all literary texts, for which we can on occasion determine manuscript transmission and associated alterations.[5] They frequently appear

---

[4] D. Dumville, 'Kingship, Genealogies and Regnal Lists', in *Early Medieval Kingship*, ed. P. Sawyer and I. Wood (Leeds, 1977), pp. 72–104.

[5] The fullest studies of the relationships between the manuscripts are given in K. Sisam, 'Anglo-Saxon Royal Genealogies', *PBA* 39 (1953), 287–348; Dumville, 'Anglian Collection'; D. Dumville, 'The West Saxon Genealogical List: Manuscripts and Texts', *Anglia* 104 (1986), 1–32; see also Dumville, 'Kingship, Genealogies and Regnal Lists', p. 90.

in similar manuscript contexts: as prefaces for law codes, in historical collections and in encyclopaedic compendia. In these contexts they were mined for information (certainly by medieval historians, as we shall see) or, more widely, they made a visual impression of authority, likely on a secular as well as a clerical audience.[6]

Of perhaps greater significance than origin is the differing logic of the two formats. The first Anglo-Saxon genealogies were pedigrees, beginning with a single individual and counting the generations in reverse: they thus demonstrated the legitimacy of an individual ruler. The Frankish model, conversely, began at the remote end and presented the line of direct descent, sometimes with agnatic lines included: its claims were thus greater, displaying the entire legitimate royal family, and by implication excluding all others. These formats were not inflexible throughout the Viking Age, but they do suggest different perspectives on genealogy and its social role.

The different Frankish and Anglo-Saxon traditions of genealogy have also resulted in a divergence in modern approaches. Scholars of the Anglo-Saxon royal genealogies have applied insights from anthropological studies, which show that genealogies in oral societies reflect contemporary, rather than past, ethnic groupings and political alliances. Accordingly, genealogies change to suit new political and social realities.[7] New links between genealogies are forged to represent new contemporary relationships, while more remote generations which have lost their relevance are discarded. David Dumville, in an important discussion of early medieval genealogies from the British Isles, has shown how a common ancestor was used to establish political relationships between dynasties: a case in point is the 'Anglian collection' of Anglo-Saxon royal genealogies, which – presented as a group – established the common descent from Woden of the kings of Bernicia, Deira, Mercia, Lindsey, East Anglia and Kent.[8] Likewise, Susan Reynolds has pointed out that in medieval society the idea of common descent, and associated narratives, were 'more often the result than the cause of social and political solidarity'.[9] That is, the production of genealogies reflected current societal realities, and belief in common ancestors arose within groups *after* they perceived their common identity.

---

[6] Dumville, 'Kingship, Genealogies and Regnal Lists', p. 75; J. Stodnick, '"Old Names of Kings or Shadows": Reading Documentary Lists', in *Conversion and Colonization in Anglo-Saxon England*, ed. C. E. Karkov and N. Howe (Tempe, 2006), pp. 109–31 (p. 131).

[7] L. Bohannan, 'A Genealogical Charter', *African Journal of the International African Institute* 22 (1952), 301–15; *Literacy in Traditional Societies*, ed. J. Goody (Cambridge, 1968); J. La Fontaine, 'Descent in New Guinea: an Africanist View', in *The Character of Kinship*, ed. J. Goody (Cambridge, 1973), pp. 35–51.

[8] Dumville, 'Kingship, Genealogies and Regnal Lists', esp. p. 82; Dumville, 'The Anglian Collection'.

[9] Reynolds, 'What Do We Mean by "Anglo-Saxon" and "Anglo-Saxons"?', p. 405.

These insights have not been applied to Frankish genealogies, presumably because of their scholarly and Latin presentation, which does not suggest an oral origin. Yet, in the period we are discussing, adaptations to both Anglo-Saxon and Frankish genealogies were made primarily by scribes working in partially literate societies. The process of moulding genealogies to contemporary situations may occur more rapidly in an oral tradition, but it may usefully be applied to the medieval world.[10] Considering how manuscripts were copied and texts adapted, there was ample opportunity for superfluous elements to be omitted or changed. We may therefore pursue a similar approach with both English and Frankish traditions, in which we analyse these 'textes vivants' as referring primarily to contemporary social and political relationships.[11]

Royal genealogy

At the time of viking settlement in England and Normandy, Anglo-Saxon and Frankish genealogies were restricted to the lines of kings. Although they were often produced by clerics, they may be seen as productions of the court, or ecclesiastical institutions associated with the ruling family. Courtly origins are suggested, firstly, by the propagandist nature of the content. The Carolingians used genealogy to assert their legitimacy as replacements for the Merovingian kings, by reworking Merovingian royal genealogies to show the rise of the Carolingian mayors of the palace[12] and by including both Merovingian and saintly ancestors in their own line.[13] Notably, the Carolingian genealogists presented royal blood as transmitted through a Merovingian princess,

---

[10] D. Thornton, 'Orality, Literacy and Genealogy in Early Medieval Ireland and Wales', in *Literacy in Medieval Celtic Societies*, ed. H. Pryce (Cambridge, 1998), pp. 83–98 (pp. 85–9).

[11] Genicot, *Les Genealogies*, p. 27.

[12] See for example the Merovingian genealogies in Paris, Bibliothèque Nationale lat. 4628A, printed in *Catalogi Regum Francorum Praetermissi*, ed. Krusch, pp. 853–5. H. Reimitz, 'Anleitung zur Interpretation: Schrift und Genealogie in der Karolingerzeit', in *Vom Nutzen des Schreibens: Soziales Gedächtnis, Herrschaft und Besitz*, ed. W. Pohl and P. Herold, Forschungen zur Geschichte des Mittelalters 5 (Vienna, 2002), pp. 167–81 (pp. 178–9).

[13] The earliest genealogy of the Carolingian family themselves, which all subsequent texts follow to some extent, derived from Paul the Deacon's 784 *History of the Bishops of Metz* (*Pauli Warnefridi Liber de Episcopis Mettensibus*, ed. G. Pertz, MGH, SS, 2 (Hanover, 1829), 260–8): see R. McKitterick, *History and Memory in the Carolingian World* (Cambridge, 2004), pp. 67, 124–5. The genealogical list is printed in *Genealogiae Karolum*, ed. G. Waitz, MGH, SS, 13 (Hanover, 1881), pp. 245–6. See further Reimitz, 'Anleitung zur Interpretation', p. 170; O. G. Oexle, 'Die Karolinger und die Stadt des heiligen Arnulf', *Frühmittelalterliche Studien* 1 (1967), 250–364 (pp. 252–79) proposes that the genealogy also promoted the interests of the See of Metz.

Blithild; another woman, Begga, the daughter of Pippin I, also carried the Pippinid family identity and forged the link with St Arnulf's line.[14] Thus, in a Frankish context, marriage was used as a key method for adding ancestral links to the upper reaches of the royal genealogy, a method that was not available in the exclusively masculine Anglo-Saxon genealogical tradition. However, West Saxon genealogies also transmitted ideological messages from royal centres. The manuscript contexts of genealogical texts often suggest that they were court productions. For example, a genealogy known as the West Saxon Genealogical Regnal List circulated with historical texts associated with the court of Alfred – the Anglo-Saxon Chronicle and the Old English version of Bede's *Historia ecclesiastica*. Sarah Foot has emphasized the importance of these texts in the development of an 'English' identity under Alfred.[15]

In Francia, a boom in royal genealogical production began under Charlemagne, from the 780s onwards; for the West Saxons, a similar process took place around a century later, under Alfred. It seems unlikely that Carolingian actions influenced the West Saxons in this respect: the similarities in their genealogical productions probably stem more generally from similar methods of dynastic promotion, coupled with an emphasis on learning. These two cases indicate that early medieval genealogies reflect changes in political relationships partly because they were used as ideological tools by the dynasties they represented.

Increases in production under the Carolingians and West Saxons included the expansion of genealogical information, but more generally a proliferation of texts presenting that information in a variety of formats and frameworks. The genealogies produced for the sons of Louis the Pious, and later for King Lothair (954–86), appear in different lists, poems and sketched family trees.[16] Likewise, in contrast to the genealogies of other Anglo-Saxon kingdoms, the forms in which West Saxon genealogies were presented were very varied, and frequently updated. Several versions were often presented in a single manuscript. The scribe of Cotton Tiberius B v, an eleventh-century

---

[14] I. Wood, 'Genealogy Defined by Women: the Case of the Pippinids', in *Gender in the Early Medieval World: East and West, 300–900*, ed. L. Brubaker and J. M. H. Smith (Cambridge, 2004), pp. 234–56 (esp. pp. 236–42).

[15] Foot, 'The Making of *Angelcynn*', pp. 32, 35–41; G. Molyneaux, 'The *Old English Bede*: English Ideology or Christian Instruction?', *EHR* 124 (2009), 1289–1323, has an alternative view of the Old English Bede, but he suggests (p. 1305) that the traditional association with Alfred was what suggested the inclusion of the West Saxon Genealogical Regnal List in CUL, Kk.3.18 (2004) – earlier manuscripts of the Old English Bede do not include this genealogical text.

[16] *Regum Francorum Genealogiae*, ed. G. Pertz, MGH, SS, 2 (Hanover, 1829), pp. 308–14; *Genealogiae Karolum*, 242–8; *Carmen de Exordio Gentis Francorum* ed. E. Dümmler, *MGH*, Poetae latini aevi Karolini, 2 (Berlin, 1884), pp. 141–5; Reimitz, 'Anleitung zur Interpretation', pp. 176–7; C. Klapisch-Zuber, *L'Ombre des Ancêtres: Essai sur l'imaginaire médiévale de la parenté* (Paris, 2000), pp. 112–17 describes the earliest family tree sketches; see also her *L'Arbre des Familles* (Paris, 2003).

encyclopaedic compilation, included three genealogical texts relating to the West Saxon kings, and in the early twelfth-century *Textus Roffensis* we find four West Saxon genealogies. The multiplication of lists relating to the West Saxon kings demonstrates the growth in the dynasty's importance and the recognition of them as kings of the entire English people. The latest, unique list in the *Textus Roffensis* begins: 'Ðis ys angel cynnes cyne cynn Þe her ge mearcod is', thus explicitly denoting the West Saxons as kings of the nation of the English.[17] The existence of varied texts presenting similar information suggests that the ideological statements of genealogical relationships were deployed in specific contexts and for specific purposes.

With this in mind, it is noteworthy that two new genealogical texts presenting similar information were produced during the reign of King Alfred: the West Saxon Genealogical Regnal List, which appears in seven manuscripts, usually as a preface to the Chronicle, laws and historical texts, and the pedigree of Alfred's father Æthelwulf, which appears in the Anglo-Saxon Chronicle *s.a.* 855.[18] Both genealogies present the pedigree of Alfred and his father, Æthelwulf, but the second text extends further back in time, counting the generations ultimately back to Adam and Christ. The West Saxon Genealogical Regnal List was perhaps the most accessible genealogical text of the Anglo-Saxon period, but the pedigree of Æthelwulf was also very influential. The pedigree's influence derived primarily from its status as the fullest expression of the genealogy of the West Saxon kings.

The pedigree of Æthelwulf

The importance of Æthelwulf's pedigree is demonstrated by its role within the Anglo-Saxon Chronicle. After this 855 annal, the Chronicle – which, throughout earlier entries, is full of information on kings' pedigrees – ceases to present royal ancestors beyond immediate parents. The Chronicle produced in the reign of Alfred had established his right to rule in the pedigree of his father. As it was updated in succeeding years, the direct succession of the descendants of Æthelwulf meant that genealogy did not need to be called upon any further to establish legitimacy. Moreover, because of the vikings' destruction of the royal lines of neighbouring kingdoms, the Chronicle now concerned itself solely with the royal house of the West Saxons.

The 855 pedigree has a sense of being the final word on the subject of genealogy. It contains more generations than any other genealogical text dating from the Anglo-Saxon period. This extensive lineage was probably a source of status in itself: in oral societies, it has been observed that royal pedigrees tend to be longer than those of their subjects.[19] The pedigree was extended in two ways. Firstly, Æthelwulf's pedigree contradicted

---

[17] Rochester Cathedral Library MS A.3.5 (*Textus Roffensis*), I, fol. 101r.
[18] Dumville, 'The West Saxon Genealogical List: manuscripts and texts'.
[19] Thornton, 'Orality, Literacy and Genealogy', p. 89.

earlier genealogical notes relating to the West Saxons in the Chronicle, as it contained several further generations in between Æthelwulf and Cerdic – in this, it agreed with the West Saxon Genealogical Regnal List. Secondly, the pedigree was lengthened at the remote end, in what appears to have been a novel development: the Chronicle is certainly the earliest text in which we find these remote generations recorded.[20] Previous texts run back to Woden, or to Geat. This new section of the West Saxon pedigree went all the way back to Adam, and thus God ('et pater noster id est Christus'). Such an origin was unprecedented in all the Chronicle's genealogical entries, and the lengthened pedigree established Æthelwulf's right to rule on a number of levels. The genealogy given for Æthelwulf in 855 related many more generations further back into the remote past than any previous genealogy, including the West Saxon Genealogical Regnal List. In comparison, the genealogies of earlier kings now appear somewhat petty. The distant generations also included new key ancestors who provided additional qualities for the ruling family.

The pedigree, as given in manuscript B of the Chronicle, runs as follows:

Se Aþelwulf wæs Ecgbrihting, Ecgbriht Ealhmunding, Ealhmund Eafing, Eafa Eopping, Eoppa Ingilding, Ingild wæs Ines broþor Westsexna cinges, ˥ he heold þæt rice .xxxvii. wintra ˥ eft ferde to Sancte Petre ˥ þær his feorh gesealde; ˥ hie wæran Kenredes suna, Cenred wæs Ceolwalding, Ceolwald Cuþing, Cuþa Cuðwining, Cuþwine Ceawlining, Ceawlin Cynricing, Cynric Creoding, Creoda Cerdicing, Cerdic wæs Elesing, Elesa Esling, Esla Gewising, Gewis Wigging, Wig Freawining, Freawine Freoþogaring, Freoþogar Branding, Brand Bældæging, Bældæg Wodening, Woden Frealafing, Frealaf Fining, Finn Godwulfing, Godulf Geating, Geata Tætwaing, Tætwa Beawing, Beaw Sceldweaing, Scyldwa Heremoding, Heremod Itermoning, Itermon Haðraing, Haðra Hwalaing, Hwala Bedwiging, Bedwig Sceafing; <i>d est filius Noe, se wæs geboren on þære earce Noes; Lamech, Matusalem, Enoc, Iared, Malalehel, Camon, Enos, Seth, Adam primus homo; et pater noster, id est Christus.[21]

The pedigree includes important ancestors known from earlier genealogies: Ine, the great king who, it is commented, died in Rome; Cerdic, the first West Saxon to arrive in Britain; Gewis, from whom the West Saxons were originally called Gewisse, according to Bede; Woden and Geat, euhemerized gods. Beyond Geat, the names are new additions to the genealogy, and we may surmise that they also held particular significance. These new ancestors

[20] Sisam, 'Anglo-Saxon Royal Genealogies', pp. 315–16: several names have dropped out of the Parker manuscript here, apparently through scribal error, while others are added; manuscripts B and C are closer to the original of the 'common stock'.

[21] *The Anglo-Saxon Chronicle: A Collaborative Edition, Volume 4. MS B*, ed. S. Taylor (1983), *s.a.* 856 (pp. 32–3). This text appears under the year 855 in manuscripts ADE, and 856 in C (no year is given in B).

related to the identity of the West Saxons, but also to the status of the genealogy itself.

The claim to descent from Adam cannot have reflected particularly on the ethnic identities of the English people. Everyone, including semi-human species such as giants, was considered to be descended from Adam. Descent from Adam was not intended to demonstrate ethnic or royal identity, but gave a Christian interpretation to the entire genealogy, despite its incorporation of pagan gods such as Woden and Geat. The addition of the biblical generations from Adam to Noah made a clear statement of Christian belief; the inclusion of figures previously revered as gods then became an assertion of these individuals' historical, mortal natures.

At the same time as incorporating biblical ancestors, the pedigree of Æthelwulf added several further generations apparently drawn from Germanic or Scandinavian legend. The figure who joined the two traditions was Sceaf, who bore a Germanic name, but was said to have been a son of Noah born in the Ark. This statement poses a problem. Medieval genealogists knew that Noah had three sons, Shem, Ham and Japheth, from whom were descended the peoples of Asia, Africa and Europe respectively.[22] Did the addition of Sceaf therefore make his descendants a fourth race of Germanic kings, distinct from all the other peoples of the world?[23] Or did these two authorities remain unreconciled? The inclusion of Noah Christianized the pagan names in the genealogy, but at the same time the linking figure of the ark-born son contradicted the Bible.

Subsequent adapters of the pedigree struggled with these issues. Alfred's biographer Asser preferred 'Seth' to 'Sceaf', although he also included Seth son of Adam several generations back. Kenneth Sisam suggested that this may be a scribal mistake related to Japheth, the son of Noah from whom the Europeans were believed to be descended.[24] Byrhtferth of Ramsey, in his *Historia regum* of c.1000, has 'Sem', a different son of Noah.[25] Given that Asser was Byrhtferth's source, this may have been Asser's original reading, too. A later list of the West Saxon genealogy, found only in the *Textus Roffensis*, solves the problem differently, by simply including both figures: this section runs 'Đa wæs noe. Þa wæs sem. Đa wæs scyf. Se wæs in tham arken geboran.'[26]

---

[22] Bartlett, 'Medieval and Modern Concepts of Race and Ethnicity'; see T. D. Hill, 'The Myth of the Ark-Born Son of Noe and the West-Saxon Royal Genealogical Tables', *Harvard Theological Review* 80 (1987), 379–83, for possible sources for the idea of a fourth son.

[23] Hill, 'Myth of the Ark-Born Son', makes this suggestion; C. Davis, 'An Ethnic Dating of *Beowulf*', *ASE* 35 (2006), 111–29 (p. 120), extends it to all Germanic peoples.

[24] Sisam, 'Anglo-Saxon Royal Genealogies', p. 316; See e.g. *The Historia Brittonum: 3. The 'Vatican' Recension*, ed. D. Dumville (Cambridge, 1985), p. 71.

[25] *Symeonis monachi opera omnia*, ed. T. Arnold, RS 75, 2 vols. (London, 1882–85), II, 69.

[26] *Textus Roffensis*, I, f.101r. For a detailed discussion of these issues, see D. Anlezark, 'Sceaf, Japheth and the Origins of the Anglo-Saxons', *ASE* 31 (2002), 13–46, but it

This solution adequately reconciled the traditions, but Sceaf no longer distinguished his descendants from the other peoples of the world. That previous genealogists did not come to a similar solution perhaps indicates the importance of this function.[27]

Sceaf was the most distant of a series of Germanic names bridging the divide between Geat and Noah. The sources of these names are unknown, but some of them are to be found in other contexts. Sceaf's name appears also in the Old English poems *Widsith* and *Beowulf*. Amid the catalogue of Germanic rulers, peoples and heroes recounted in *Widsith*, Sceaf is described as the ruler of the Langobards, whereas in *Beowulf* 'Scyld Sceafing' – a name which probably implies a father, Sceaf – is the first king of the Danes. In including Sceaf and the associated list of Germanic names, the genealogist's primary intention, like that of the *Widsith*-poet, may have been to evoke a wide Germanic epic past rather than a single national tradition.

On the other hand, several of the names held particular Danish associations. Heremod appears twice in *Beowulf* as a former Danish leader.[28] Moreover, *Beowulf*, having introduced the Danish line with Scyld Sceafing, continues to his son Beow, a succession which appears to match Scyldwa and his son Beaw in the genealogy.[29] However, the 855 pedigree differs from *Beowulf* in that Scyldwa is separated from Sceaf by six generations. These intervening generations, which supply several names without analogues elsewhere in early medieval literature, prevent any easy line of transmission being drawn between *Beowulf* and the West Saxon pedigree.[30] 'Sceafing' in *Beowulf* could, of course, mean a more distant descendant of Sceaf, or something else entirely.[31] Nevertheless, Ealdorman Æthelweard, in his

is worth noting that the text referred to here is a West Saxon genealogy and not an Anglian one as he assumes.

[27] D. Cronan, '*Beowulf* and the Containment of Scyld in the West Saxon Royal Genealogy', in *The Dating of Beowulf: A Reassessment*, ed. L. Neidorf (Cambridge, 2014), pp. 112–37 (pp. 126–7).

[28] *Beowulf: An Edition*, ed. B. Mitchell and F. Robinson (Oxford, 1998), p. 78, ll. 901–15; pp. 104–5, ll. 1709–22.

[29] Beow, confusingly, appears in the manuscript as Beowulf the Dane (not the hero of the poem). *Beowulf*, ed. Mitchell and Robinson, pp. 47, 49; ll. 18–19, 53.

[30] A. C. Murray, '*Beowulf*, the Danish Invasions, and Royal Genealogy', in *The Dating of Beowulf*, ed. C. Chase (Toronto, 1981), pp. 101–11, hints that the West Saxon pedigree was used as a source by the *Beowulf*-poet; Cronan, '*Beowulf* and the Containment of Scyld', rebuts this claim: although some of his arguments, such as his dependence on his own formulation of 'genealogical convention', are difficult to accept, we should note in particular the comments on the archaic, non-West Saxon forms of the names in the genealogy (pp. 121–3).

[31] William of Malmesbury, *Gesta Regum Anglorum*, ed. R. A. B. Mynors, R. M. Thomson and M. Winterbottom, 2 vols. (Oxford, 1998), I, pp. 176–7 stated that Sceaf arrived 'sleeping with a sheaf of wheat laid by his head, and hence was called Sheaf' ('posito ad caput frumenti manipulo dormiens, ideoque Sceaf nuncupatus').

Chronicon of the 980s, omitted the generations between Sceaf and Scyld from King Æthelwulf's pedigree, perhaps because he knew of the relationship alluded to in *Beowulf*.[32]

It seems very likely that the Chronicle compiler believed Scyldwa to have been an ancestor of the Danish kings. The unglossed name in the genealogy is the earliest secure reference, but all other early uses of 'Scyld' and 'Scyldings' refer to Danes. *Beowulf*, which may well pre-date Æthelwulf's pedigree, not only introduces 'Scyld Scefing' at the outset, but continues to describe the Danish kings as 'Scyldings' throughout. Significantly, the tenth-century *Historia de Sancto Cuthberto* uses the term *Scaldingi* for the Danes who came to England in the ninth century (apparently referring to the whole Great Army).[33] To an English audience, such a term would have appeared as a patronymic, and thus suggested an ancestor named Scyld. Therefore it seems that the genealogist of the West Saxon kings wanted to credit them with ancestors who not only established their English royalty (Woden and Geat), but also their Danish royal origins (Scyld).[34]

These analogues in English texts do not establish conclusively that Danes in England also held such a belief. There has been some disagreement over the precise relationship of Scyld in the West Saxon genealogies and Skjöldr in later Old Norse genealogical material. Certainly, we cannot use the Old Norse material as evidence for belief in late ninth-century England. Old Norse genealogies containing Skjöldr all date from much later and some were influenced by the Anglo-Saxon lists.[35] Yet some Icelandic genealogies actually contain two figures named Scyld/ Skjöldr – one apparently derived from the Anglo-Saxon pedigree, but another that might represent an older tradition.[36] References in Old Norse sources to the Skjǫldung dynasty help us little, since they all date from the twelfth century onwards.

However, Roberta Frank's evidence from skaldic poetry indicates that the Old Norse equivalent term, *skjöldungr*, was used politically in relation to three Scandinavian kings in the first half of the eleventh century: Cnut the Great, Óláfr Haraldsson and Magnus the Good.[37] She links the use of the term to these kings' viking activities in England and claims to the English throne.

---

[32] Sisam, 'Anglo-Saxon Royal Genealogies', pp. 317–18.

[33] *Historia de Sancto Cuthberto*, ed. T. Johnson South (Cambridge, 2002; hereafter HSC), pp. 48, 50. See p. 139 below for the dating of this text.

[34] Murray, 'Beowulf, the Danish Invasions, and Royal Genealogy'.

[35] Faulkes, 'Earliest Icelandic Genealogies', pp. 115–19. The poem *Ynglingatál* may have originally been composed earlier than the twelfth- and thirteenth-century contexts it is found in but, given the general approach to genealogy taken here, we cannot expect it to represent the ninth-century genealogy accurately at such a late date.

[36] A. M. Bruce, *Scyld and Scef: Expanding the Analogues* (London, 2002), p. 56.

[37] R. Frank, 'Skaldic Verse and the Date of Beowulf', in *The Dating of Beowulf*, ed. Chase, pp. 123–39 (pp. 126–7).

The association with Cnut is particularly clear. The skald Óttarr svarti, in a composition of around 1027, referred to Cnut as 'Strong Skjǫldungr' in his reference to the battle of Ashingdon.[38] A few years earlier, another skald, Þórðr Kolbeinsson, related Cnut's arrival in England in 1014:

And the Skjǫldungr, Knútr, who pounded the keel-paths [SEA], again ran his longships ashore onto the shallows of the land-spit.[39]

Although there was not a clear dynastic content to the word in these verses, Frank has suggested that Cnut's skalds used this title to demonstrate his continuity with earlier generations of viking conquerors in England.

Combined with the evidence of the *Historia de Sancto Cuthberto*, this would appear to relate more specifically to the dynasty of Ívarr and Halfdanr. Indeed, Sigvatr Þórðarson's *Knútsdrápa*, also composed for Cnut around 1027, in two mirroring verses matches that king's victories in England to Ívarr's conquest of York in 867:

And Ívarr, who resided at York, had Ælla's back cut with an eagle.

And Knútr soon defeated or drove out the sons of Æthelred, and indeed, each one. [40]

These verses – composed by Icelandic skalds for a Danish king of England – suggest that Scandinavian use of the term 'Skjǫldungr' referred to the actions of vikings in England, and perhaps specifically to the dynasty of Ívarr. The references in the *Historia de Sancto Cuthberto* and in Cnut's praise poetry both imply widespread knowledge of the term, which suggests that it may have been in use in the later ninth century, too. Although later traditions may diverge, at the time of this genealogy's composition it seems that the West Saxon kings looked back to ancestors who established their royalty in a way that was convincing not only to the English peoples but also to the Danes in the northern kingdom.

Although they did not have a written genealogy of the northern kings, as they did for other Anglo-Saxon dynasties, in this pedigree Alfred and his

---

[38] Óttarr svarti, *Knútsdrápa*, ed. M. Townend, in *Poetry from the Kings' Sagas 1: From Mythical Times to c.1035*, ed. D. Whaley, 2 vols. (Turnhout, 2012), II, 779: 'Skjǫldungr, vannt und skildi | skœru verk, inn sterki'.

[39] Þórðr Kolbeinsson, *Eiríksdrápa*, ed. J. Carroll, in *Poetry from the Kings' Sagas 1*, ed. Whaley, I, 507: 'Enn at eyrar grunni | endr Skjǫldungr of renndi, | sás kjǫlslóðir kníði, | Knútr langskipum útan'. On the dates of these verses, see M. Townend, 'Contextualizing the "Knútsdrápur": Skaldic Praise-Poetry at the Court of Cnut', *ASE* 30 (2001), 145–79 (p. 162).

[40] Sigvatr Þórðarson, *Knútsdrápa*, ed. M. Townend, in *Poetry from the Kings' Sagas 1*, ed. Whaley, II, 651–52: 'Ok Ellu bak, | at, lét, hinns sat, | Ívarr ara, | Jórvík, skorit'; 'Ok senn sonu | sló, hvern ok þó, | Aðalráðs eða | út flæmði Knútr'. The date is given by Townend, 'Contextualizing the "Knútsdrápur"', p. 162.

successors were demonstrating their relationship to these Danish rulers. The inclusion of Scyld during the ninth century suggests that, although Alfred's kingdom had never been united with the regions ruled by Danes, members of the West Saxon court saw the English and Danish kingdoms as a single political community. Davis has suggested that this genealogy was composed on the occasion of Guthrum's baptism under Alfred's sponsorship. However, the term 'Scylding', if it was dynastically linked, related to Ívarr and Halfdanr: the connections of the East Anglian King Guthrum either to the term or to that dynasty are unclear. While various texts refer to family relationships between Ívarr, Halfdanr and Ubba, none includes Guthrum within this kin group. Historical traditions such as those explored in Chapter 4 emphasized Alfred's encounter with Guthrum of East Anglia, but the genealogies suggest his interest in Ívarr and York.

Further evidence that Alfred promoted this extended genealogy of his dynasty emerges from Asser's *Life of Alfred*. This text, written during the king's lifetime, applied the Chronicle pedigree to Alfred and recounted the generations back to Adam. Asser began with the genealogy, so that it acted almost as a preface to the biography, introducing Alfred by his royal blood. Notably, Asser's comment on the euhemerized divine ancestor Geat reveals the contemporary view that this was a figure 'whom the pagans worshipped for a long time as a god', for which he (erroneously) cited Sedulius in support.[41] He thus transferred Bede's gloss on Woden to the more recently added ancestor, Geat – and omitted Christ himself from the distant end of the genealogy. In addition, Asser elaborated on the ancestry of Osburh, Alfred's mother, indicating that she was of Gothic or Jutish descent. Asser stated that Osburh could trace her lineage back to Stuf and Wihtgar, the first Jutes to arrive in Britain, but who, he claimed, were even then Cerdic and Cynric's relatives and subordinates.[42] These statements and general emphasis placed King Alfred within a broad tradition of Germanic kingship, which included Angles, Saxons, Jutes, Goths and Danes: a royalty that was acceptable to all in his kingdom and neighbouring polities.

The lengthened pedigree including Sceaf and Scyld also influenced later compilers, who continued to employ its material in other contexts throughout the Anglo-Saxon period. Genealogical lists in Cotton Tiberius B v and the *Textus Roffensis* appear to be abstracted from the Chronicle entry of 855.

---

[41] *Asser's Life of King Alfred*, ed. W. Stevenson (Oxford, 1904, repr. 1959), p. 3: '...quem Getam iamdudum pagani pro deo venerabantur. Cuius Sedulius poeta mentionem facit in Paschali metrico carmine...'; *Alfred the Great*, ed. S. Keynes and M. Lapidge (London, 1983), pp. 67, 229.

[42] *Asser's Life of King Alfred*, ed. Stevenson, p. 4: 'Mater quoque eiusdem Osburh nominabatur... quae erat filia Oslac, famosi pincernae Æthelwulfi regis. Qui Oslac Gothus erat natione; ortus enim de Gothis et Iutis, de semine scilicet Stuf et Wihtgar, duorum fratrum et etiam comitum... accepta potestate Uuectae insulae ab avunculo suo Cerdic rege et Cynric filio suo, consobrino eorum...'

Dennis Cronan has recently argued that 'this genealogical claim [to Danish ancestry] was probably stillborn' in the Alfredian period, and thus had little propaganda value.[43] However, these later genealogical lists demonstrate that, because it showcased the longest list of West Saxon ancestors, Æthelwulf's pedigree from the Chronicle became the most authoritative and influential source of information on the royal genealogy. The West Saxon Genealogical Regnal List, despite existing in a greater number of copies and, as a distinct and prominent text, being more easily accessible, was not drawn upon in the same way. However, Cronan's discussion highlights the fact that the claim to Scylding descent was strategically deployed and exerted influence purely in the field of genealogy. Much as the inclusion of Woden in earlier royal genealogies had not implied the continuation of pagan belief, so the presence of Sceaf and Scyld in the English royal genealogy did not confer Danish identity in any broader sense.

Æthelweard's West Saxon genealogy

The pedigree was developed further by Ealdorman Æthelweard, in his *Chronicon* written in the 980s. In writing his Latin *Chronicon*, Æthelweard drew primarily on the Anglo-Saxon Chronicle. Because of his use of this one clear source, and his convoluted 'hermeneutic' Latin, Æthelweard's creativity has often been overlooked.[44] Recently, however, studies by Mechthild Gretsch, Wojtek Jezierski and Scott Ashley have emphasized Æthelweard's role as author, and the *Chronicon* as a creative work with its own independent value.[45] Seeing Æthelweard, to use Ashley's words, 'less as a slave to his sources and more as a conscious manipulator of them', allows us to appreciate the secular, aristocratic view of history and genealogy presented in his pages.[46]

The differences in Æthelweard's version of the West Saxon genealogy may therefore provide evidence of a deliberate adaptation, reflecting a developing conception of English ethnicity. Æthelweard wrote in a changed political context, a hundred years after the pedigree was first composed. We may confidently identify Æthelweard with the ealdorman of that name, apparently responsible for the south-western provinces, who witnessed

---

[43] Cronan, '*Beowulf* and the Containment of Scyld', pp. 133–6.

[44] M. Winterbottom, 'The Style of Æthelweard', *Medium Ævum* 36 (1967), 109–18; M. Lapidge, 'The Hermeneutic Style in Tenth-Century Anglo-Latin Literature', *ASE* 4 (1975), 67–111; L. Whitbread, 'Æthelweard and the Anglo-Saxon Chronicle', *EHR* 74 (1959), 577–89.

[45] M. Gretsch, 'Historiography and Literary Patronage in Late Anglo-Saxon England: The Evidence of Æthelweard's *Chronicon*', *ASE* 41 (2012), 205–48; S. Ashley, 'The Lay Intellectual in Anglo-Saxon England: Ealdorman Æthelweard and the Politics of History', in *Lay Intellectuals in the Carolingian World*, ed. P. Wormald and J. L. Nelson (Cambridge, 2007), pp. 218–45; W. Jezierski, 'Æthelweardus Redivivus', *EME* 13 (2005), 159–78.

[46] Ashley, 'Lay Intellectual', p. 219.

royal charters between 973 and 998.[47] He also appears in the Anglo-Saxon Chronicle under the year 994, as a negotiator for Æthelred with the viking Óláfr Tryggvason; Æthelweard's name is also recorded in the resulting treaty, known as II Æthelred. In writing his *Chronicon*, Æthelweard began his history from Creation, before focusing on Britain and the arrival of the English. The narrative ends in 973, but the contents page includes two further chapters, on Edward the Martyr 'et de nece ipsius' and Æthelred 'et de actibus eius'.[48] No trace of these sections remains – they were probably never completed – but the chapter-list indicates that Æthelweard wrote during the reign of Æthelred. Since he referred to Arnulf of Flanders as if he were still alive, we may deduce that the prologue at least was written before 988, when Arnulf died.[49]

Æthelweard made two significant changes to the West Saxon genealogy. Firstly, he omitted the biblical section of the pedigree beyond Sceaf to Adam. It has been suggested that Æthelweard was using an earlier version, as (because of this) his pedigree of Æthelwulf is considerably shorter than that found in the Chronicle.[50] However, we do not have any evidence of any such version, and it is more likely that he simply chose not to include the genealogy further than Sceaf. Genealogy was one of Æthelweard's central interests as he composed his *Chronicon*, which took the form of a letter to his Saxon relative Matilda about their common family. He had investigated various lines of research, and would certainly have been aware that Æthelwulf's genealogy existed back to Adam.[51] Æthelweard was more than a translator, especially when it came to genealogy, and he was clearly engaging with his original text here. His omission of the biblical sections probably related to his focus on the history of the West Saxon royal family – of which he was a member. Adding ancestors back to Adam would have universalized his narrative, rather than presenting a specifically English history.

Instead of completing the pedigree back to Adam, Æthelweard made a second significant adaptation: he elaborated the story of Sceaf, explicitly tying him to his Scandinavian origins. He significantly shortened the section between Sceaf and Geat, thus placing more emphasis on 'Danish' ancestors than other Germanic names. Æthelweard related that

> This Sceaf arrived with one light ship in the island of the ocean which is called Skaney, with arms all round him. He was a very young boy, and unknown to the people of that land, but he was received by them, and they

---

[47] *Chronicon Æthelweardi: The Chronicle of Æthelweard*, ed. A. Campbell (London, 1962; hereafter Æthelweard), p. xv. A charter of 997 (S891) called him 'Occidentalium prouinciarum dux'.

[48] E. Barker, 'The Cottonian Fragments of Æthelweard's Chronicle', *Historical Research* 24 (1951), 46–62 (p. 53).

[49] Æthelweard, p. xiii, n. 2.

[50] Anlezark, 'Sceaf, Japheth and the Origins of the Anglo-Saxons', pp. 19–20.

[51] Ashley, 'Lay Intellectual', p. 233.

guarded him with diligent attention as one who belonged to them, and elected him king. From his family King Æthelwulf derived his descent.[52]

Perhaps Sceaf's identification with the 'ark-born son' of Noah is related to this tale of his arrival in a boat. We do not find this exact narrative independently elsewhere but, despite a dislocation by a generation, it clearly derives from the same origins as *Beowulf*'s king Scyld Sceafing, whose unknown family 'had adventured him over seas, alone, a small child'.[53] Although Æthelweard associated these origins with Sceaf, he did give him a son named Scyld. In *Beowulf*, Scyld Sceafing and his son Beowulf were immediately identified as Danish; Æthelweard, in his genealogy, emphasized these Scandinavian origins by mentioning the island of Skaney. The single manuscript witness to *Beowulf* dates from around the year 1000, and thus indicates English interest in the Danish heroic past at this time. Æthelweard's expansion of the genealogy also testifies to such an interest.

Æthelweard sought to connect his own family history to that of the Danes whom he encountered in England. What began as an expression of political relationship between Alfred and the new Danish elite of the ninth century was still – or once again – relevant in the late tenth century. It is tempting to attribute Æthelweard's interest in Danish heritage to his personal involvement in negotiating with viking leaders in the 990s. However, it seems that he wrote his *Chronicon* in the early 980s: in fact, he specifically stated that no viking raids had troubled England since the Battle of *Brunanburh* in 937.[54] It is therefore more likely that, in his pedigree of Æthelwulf, Æthelweard responded to everyday contexts in which he saw English and Danish interaction. The genealogy presented a reasonable explanation for the interconnected social relationships between Anglo-Saxons and Danes within England.

Æthelweard had a relatively positive view of the Danes, notwithstanding some of the later content of his *Chronicon*. He obviously knew people who spoke Old Norse and was particularly interested in Scandinavian

---

[52] Æthelweard, p. 33: 'Ipse Scef cum uno dromone aduectus est in insula oceani que dicitur Scani, armis circundatus, eratque ualde recens puer, et ab incolis illius terrae ignotus. Attamen ab eis suscipitur, et ut familiarem diligenti animo eum custodierunt, et post in regem eligunt; de cuius prosapia ordinem trahit Aðulf rex'.

[53] *Beowulf*, trans. M. Alexander (Harmondsworth, 1973), p. 52; *Beowulf*, ed. Mitchell and Robinson, p. 49, ll. 45–46: 'Þe hine æt frumsceafte forð onsendon | ænne ofer yðe umborwesende'. Murray, 'Beowulf, the Danish Invasions, and Royal Genealogy', p. 108, presents an explanation for the different attribution of the same description, to Scyld in *Beowulf* and Sceaf in Æthelweard's *Chronicon*. He suggests that the two authors interpreted the annotation to a common genealogical source as applying to different individuals because it was attached to 'Scyld Sceafing' (equally, the annotation could have derived from the poem and been used by Æthelweard).

[54] Æthelweard, p. 54; Ashley, 'Lay Intellectual', p. 221.

religion, although disapproving.[55] Others were more hostile, and this may be reflected in their reluctance to include Sceaf as the connecting link between the Germanic and biblical sections of the genealogy. We can perhaps associate Æthelweard's version of the genealogy with his position as a powerful layman who interacted with Danes in political life. Much as Byrhtferth and Asser, both well-educated clerics, attempted to reconcile the genealogy with the biblical history with which they were familiar, so Æthelweard appears to have rejected the textual evidence against his knowledge that Scyld was the son of Sceaf. All the genealogies, however, include Scyld – the one ancestor who seems to have meant something to the Danish population as well.[56] Æthelweard's adaptation indicates, as does the *Beowulf* manuscript of c.1000, that the subjects of the English kings continued to perceive Sceaf and Scyld as distant but distinctively Danish royal ancestors throughout the Viking Age.

In incorporating this Danish element into their royal genealogy, the West Saxon kings of England diverged from their Frankish counterparts. Although the West Saxon approach resembled Carolingian genealogical production in many ways, no members of the Frankish royal family developed any Scandinavian aspect into their heritage.

The differences in format, language and origin may have made Anglo-Saxon royal genealogy more open to Scandinavian influence than was Frankish royal genealogy. It is worth considering whether the West Saxon incorporation of 'Danish' ancestors was more feasible because the Anglo-Saxon genealogical tradition was closer to the genealogical traditions which vikings brought with them. Since Old Norse and Old English seem to have been mutually intelligible, a genealogist might have found it relatively simple to amalgamate vernacular texts in these two languages, whereas the process would not have suggested itself so readily to someone dealing with Latin and Old Norse.[57] Because of the significance and proliferation of genealogies in later Old Norse literature, it has frequently been assumed that such genealogies as existed later derived from Viking Age oral traditions.[58] Certainly, if Old Norse genealogies did exist in this period, they must have been orally

---

[55] For Æthelweard's knowledge of some Old Norse see pp. 70–1 and other examples in the text such as Ealdorman Æthelwulf's body taken 'in loco qui *Northuuorthige* nuncupatur, iuxta autem Danaam linguam Deoraby' (Æthelweard, p. 37); M. Townend, *Language and History in Viking Age England: Linguistic Relations Between Speakers of Old Norse and Old English*, Studies in the Early Middle Ages 6 (Turnhout, 2002), pp. 110–28.

[56] With the exception of Æthelwulf's pedigree in the Parker Chronicle, where some names have dropped out apparently through scribal error: Sisam, 'Anglo-Saxon Royal Genealogies', pp. 315–16.

[57] On mutual intelligibility: Townend, *Language and History in Viking Age England*, esp. pp. 181–5.

[58] See the useful discussion in J. Quinn, 'From Orality to Literacy in Medieval Iceland',

kept, since writing in Scandinavian society was restricted to brief runic inscriptions. However, we know very little about such traditions, and lack convincing evidence that they originated this early. Given the highly context-dependent approach to genealogy pursued here, later Old Norse genealogical texts cannot be used as evidence for the traditions of Viking Age people.

Moreover, Old Norse genealogies may well have actually been influenced by Anglo-Saxon traditions, rather than developing in parallel. The earliest Scandinavian manuscripts containing genealogical lists included Old Norse versions of the Anglo-Saxon royal genealogies alongside the Scandinavian royal families – which suggests that the latter were produced in a certain format in imitation of the Anglo-Saxon lists.[59] For these reasons, we should be cautious about attributing too much importance to the possible similarities between the Anglo-Saxon and hypothetical Scandinavian traditions. Language may have eased assimilation, but this in itself became a focus of identitarian discourse.

Frankish royal genealogy

Within Viking Age Frankish texts, the only hint of an idea of Scandinavian ancestry may be found in Ermold the Black's poem for Louis the Pious, in which he narrates the baptism of Louis's godson, the Danish King Harald Klak, in 826.[60] After describing the fierce character and beautiful appearance of the Danes, Ermold claimed that, from this people, 'it is said, the line of the Franks descended'. The common Scandinavian heritage of the Franks and other Germanic peoples was a newly fashionable idea among Carolingian scholars, but this was generally restricted to the relationship between their languages.[61] Ermold developed the implications further by indicating that, because he was 'moved to pity for his ancestral stock', Louis the Pious sought to convert the Danes to Christianity.[62] Ermold then had Louis dictate a long sermon to the missionary bishop, Ebo of Rheims, in which he recapped the key events of Christian belief and history. In the opening of this account, Ermold described Adam as both 'the first man' ('hominem primum') and 'our

---

in *Old Icelandic Literature and Society*, ed. M. Clunies Ross (Cambridge, 2000), pp. 30–60 (pp. 46–50).

[59] A. Faulkes, 'The Earliest Icelandic Genealogies and Regnal Lists', *Saga-Book* 29 (2005), 115–19.

[60] On Ermold, see T. X. Noble, *Charlemagne and Louis the Pious: Lives by Einhard, Notker, Ermoldus, Thegan, and the Astronomer* (University Park, 2009), pp. 119–25.

[61] R. Frank, 'Germanic Legend in Old English Literature', in *The Cambridge Companion to Old English Literature*, ed. M. Godden and M. Lapidge (Cambridge, 1991; 2nd edn 2013), pp. 82–100 (pp. 87–9); M. Coumert, *Origines des Peuples: Les récits de Haut Moyen Âge occidental (550–850)* (Paris, 2007), pp. 363–7, 373–8.

[62] *Carmina in honorem Hludovici*, ed. E. Dümmler, *MGH*, Poetae Latini aevi Carolini, 2 (Berlin, 1884), 5–79 (p. 59): 'Unde genus Francis adfore fama refert. | Victus amore dei generisque misertus aviti...'.

parent' ('nostrum parentem').[63] Thus, the same image that we encountered in the West Saxon pedigree – of two related peoples, in this case Danes and Franks, descended equally from Adam – appeared within Ermold's text.

However, this connection was never incorporated into a specifically genealogical text and we find no mention of it thereafter. Ermold invoked it for another purpose: to explain Louis's missionary impulse to the Danes. Frankish royal genealogies written for the sons of Louis the Pious, and throughout the ninth and tenth centuries, seem overwhelmingly preoccupied with more immediate dynastic instabilities. For the Carolingians, the viking settlers in the Seine valley and in Brittany – although threatening in other ways – did not constitute the most pressing concerns to their own royal legitimacy. Competition between adult male heirs, the divisions of kingdoms, claims to the imperial title and the challenge posed by the rise in aristocratic power and the resulting potential usurpers (particularly the Robertians) all provided more immediate threats. From the beginning of the tenth century, various Carolingian kings emphasized their royal bloodline more strongly. The kings' charters referred to their ancestors more often, and Louis IV's epitaph laid great weight on his royal blood.[64] Accordingly, the later Carolingian genealogical texts stress recent generations of the royal patriline above all else, firmly denying the existence of cadet branches. Hincmar of Rheims selectively employed genealogical information to present Charles the Bald as the rightful successor to the kingdom of Lotharingia in 869.[65] Likewise, in the tenth century a new Carolingian genealogy down to Lothair IV ensured that there were no rogue claimants to the throne by demonstrating how all segmentary lines ran out: they end in a bishop or virgin saint, or a childless death, or only illegitimate children. The compiler traced descent from each of the sons of Louis the Pious in detail (though only through the male lines) until, in each case, he could say that 'finem fecit illi successioni' or 'illa successio deperiit'.[66] His detailed explanation presented a case for the descendants of Charles the Bald as the only surviving legitimate Carolingians. In this period of instability, genealogists seem to have been more concerned to impose limits on the Carolingian dynasty – and thus those with a claim to rule – than to present bonds of relationship with other powerful families.

The usurping dynasty of the Robertians, become the Capetians, did not produce genealogy to justify their new position, however. It appears that such texts were no longer an effective instrument of royal identity. Frankish scholars continued to copy Carolingian genealogies, but did not join the Capetians to them by ties of blood (despite their ancestral links to the Carolingians).

[63] *Carmina in honorem Hludovici*, ed. Dümmler, p. 60.
[64] A. Lewis, *Royal Succession in Capetian France: Studies on Familial Order and the State* (Cambridge, MA, 1981), p. 5.
[65] Annals of St Bertin, *s.a.* 869; Reimitz, 'Anleitung zur Interpretation', pp. 171–2.
[66] *Genealogiae Karolum*, p. 247.

Contemporaries perceived 987 to mark the end of the Carolingian dynasty, and continued to consider Hugh Capet as a usurper.[67] King lists did include the Capetians, but their lineage was not glorified in the way of earlier kings, and genealogical links were not made with their predecessors.[68] One of the reasons for this was that the Capetian links to the Carolingians were not unique. From the mid-tenth century onwards, local aristocracies had begun to emphasize their own links to the Carolingian family.[69] Carolingian blood had become a mark of nobility, not a guarantee of royalty. In this context, Frankish noble families began to produce genealogies of their own lineages.

Aristocratic genealogy

While Frankish royal genealogy lost it significance in the later tenth century, Frankish aristocracies began to promote their own dynastic identities. Counts and dukes had grown in prominence during the late Carolingian period, to the point that Hugh Capet rose from being duke of the Franks to becoming king in 987. As royal authority weakened and the royal principality shrank to an area around the Île de France, the higher aristocracy increasingly wielded effective local power.[70] The cultivation of aristocratic lineages seems to have developed partly in an endeavour to tie aristocratic power to geographically defined patrimonies and familial inheritance. Georges Duby and Karl Schmid posited that, from around the year 1000, a change took place in how aristocratic families organized themselves: the large kin group bound by horizontal ties was reorganized into the patrilinear *Geschlecht*.[71] Of course, this model has limitations; as Constance Brittain Bouchard has pointed out, the definition of family included much more than the practice of inheritance.[72] However, the model of *Geschlecht* describes a developing trend in aristocratic self-presentation, often based primarily on genealogical constructions.

---

[67] Lewis, *Royal Succession*, p. 17.

[68] Lewis, *Royal Succession*, pp. 106–9; Dumville, 'Kingship, Genealogies and Regnal Lists', pp. 96–102 on king-lists.

[69] Lewis, *Royal Succession*, p. 34.

[70] J. Dunbabin, *France in the Making, 843–1180* (Oxford, 2nd edn 2000), p. 162.

[71] T. Bisson, 'Nobility and Family in Medieval France: A Review Essay', *French Historical Studies* 16 (1990), 597–613; see especially K. Schmid, 'Zur Problematik von Familie, Sippe und Geschlecht, Haus und Dynastie beim mittelalterlichen Adel. Vorfragen zum Thema: "Adel und Herrschaft im Mittelalter"', *Zeitschrift für die Geschichte des Oberrheins* 105 (1957), 1–62. Lewis, *Royal Succession*, pp. 3–4; R. H. Bloch, *Etymologies and Genealogies: A Literary Anthropology of the French Middle Ages* (Chicago, 1983), pp. 66–70.

[72] C. B. Bouchard, *Those of My Blood: Constructing Noble Families in Medieval Francia* (Philadelphia, 2001).

Indeed, aristocratic families began to commission and produce specifically genealogical texts in the tenth and eleventh centuries. This phenomenon emerged first in northern France. Georges Duby records that, by 1109, genealogies had been produced for the counts of Flanders, Vendôme, Anjou and Boulogne: several versions in some cases. During the twelfth century, the practice spread throughout the kingdom of France.[73] The very earliest texts promoting dynastic identities were produced for the counts of Flanders (Witger's *Genealogia Arnulfi Comitis* of *c.* 960) and their neighbours, the dukes of Normandy (Dudo of St-Quentin's *De moribus et actis primorum Normanniae ducum*, composed around 1000). For reason of their idiosyncrasies and debt to other genres, both have at times been dismissed from surveys of genealogies.[74] Since these were the first productions of this kind, their authors had no genre or convention to follow; royal genealogies provided the only available model. Moreover, these two dynastic texts reveal the available ideas about lineage identity developing among Frankish elites. And it was through one of these texts, Dudo's *De moribus*, that the Norman dukes proudly laid claim to Scandinavian heritage.

Dudo of Saint-Quentin's genealogy of the Norman dukes

Dudo of Saint-Quentin's *De moribus et actis primorum Normanniae ducum* is a narrative history that was commissioned by the Norman Duke Richard I and his son Richard II. Written between 994 and *c.* 1015, the *De moribus* was the first historical text of sizable length to have been produced in Normandy after the viking conquest of 911.[75] It is a complex and idiosyncratic text, but essential to understanding the origins of Normandy.[76] Although Henri Prentout's

---

[73] G. Duby, 'Remarques sur la littérature généalogique en France aux XIe et XIIe siècles', in G. Duby, *Hommes et Structures de moyen âge* (Paris, 1973), pp. 287ff. (pp. 289–90).

[74] L. Genicot, 'Princes Territoriaux et Sang Carolingien: La Genealogia Comitum Buloniensium', in *idem, Études sur les Principautés Lotharingiennes* (Louvain, 1975), pp. 217–306 (p. 220): Witger's text 's'apparente plus à une pièce liturgique qu'à une genealogie'; Duby, 'Remarques sur la littérature généalogique', p. 288, dismissed Dudo's text because of its extended historical form. On the relationships between genealogies and dynastic histories, see L. Shopkow, 'Dynastic History', in *Historiography in the Middle Ages*, ed. D. M. Deliyannis (Leiden, 2003), pp. 217–48 (pp. 218–22).

[75] Recent evidence and arguments have demonstrated the likelihood that Dudo wrote the majority of his text in the earlier part of this period: F. Lifshitz, *Viking Normandy: Dudo of St Quentin's Gesta Normannorum* <http://www.the-orb.net/orb_done/dudo/dudintro.html> [accessed 10/02/2013]; M. Arnoux, 'Before the *Gesta Normannorum* and beyond Dudo: Some evidence on early Norman historiography', *ANS* 22 (2000), 29–48 (p. 41). Traditionally, the *De moribus* has been dated after 1015, since Dudo appears in a charter of this date (F18) without the title of *decanus* ascribed to him in the *De moribus*. The date 911 is, of course, the generally accepted date of the 'Treaty of St-Clair-sur-Epte', by which Charles the Simple granted land to Rollo and his companions.

[76] Dudo of Saint-Quentin, *De Moribus et Actis Primorum Normanniae Ducum: Auctore Dudone Sancti Quinini Decano*, ed. J. Lair (Caen, 1865; hereafter Lair); *Dudo of St*

lengthy study of 1916[77] demonstrated the historical inaccuracy of much of the *De moribus*, more recently the interest of historians and literary scholars in Dudo's work has revived. Several studies have revealed how this rich text gives us insight into early Norman mentalities and the province's place within Frankish and Scandinavian cultures.[78] In particular, the *De moribus* provides valuable and rewarding evidence for the Norman ducal family's self-perception, and the image they wanted to present to their neighbours.

Lineage is central to the *De moribus*, giving the work its structure and narrative drive. The *De moribus* opens with the Scandinavian origins of the Normans, proceeding to dedicate a book to each successive viking or Norman leader. Throughout, Dudo's focus was firmly centred on Richard I, his original patron, to whose life and acts half the work is dedicated. The earlier sections of the history provide a genealogy of Duke Richard and explain how he came to achieve his power and greatness. His life is prefigured from the prefaces onwards, and the Norman achievement hinted at by Dudo in prophetic passages addressed to Rollo and William, Richard's father and grandfather, reaches its culmination in the life of Duke Richard.

Dudo's text presented the Norman lineage down to Duke Richard I as a patrilinear succession, in which the family identity as well as ducal authority passed from father to son. Although many of the Norman dukes had several children, Dudo presented single, outstanding sons as the clear inheritors of the title. Other siblings he omitted or passed over with only a casual mention. Thus Dudo mentioned only one son of William Longsword – Richard I – and he did not even name Richard's mother.[79] The structure of the work followed the patriline without hesitation, and ignored other family members. Dudo streamlined the Norman ducal family just as the Frankish aristocracy did, in

---

Quentin, *History of the Normans*, trans. E. Christiansen (Woodbridge, 1998; hereafter Christiansen).

[77] H. Prentout, *Étude Critique sur Dudon de Saint-Quentin et son Histoire des Premiers Ducs Normands* (Caen, 1916).

[78] See especially *Dudone di San Quintino*, ed. P. Gatti and A. Degl'Innocenti (Trento, 1995); L. Shopkow, 'The Carolingian World of Dudo of Saint-Quentin', *Journal of Medieval History* 15 (1989), 19–37; F. Lifshitz, 'Translating "Feudal" Vocabulary: Dudo of Saint Quentin', *HSJ* 9 (2001), 39–56; E. Searle, 'Fact and Pattern in Heroic History: Dudo of Saint-Quentin', *Viator* 15 (1984) 119–37; B. Pohl, *Dudo of St Quentin's Historia Normannorum: History, Tradition and Memory* (York, 2015).

[79] One of the introductory poems to the work is addressed to Richard II's uncle, Count Rodulf, who was not William Longsword's son, but was also the son of this unnamed woman, usually called Sprota. Richard I's children are recorded: although he had none by his first wife, Emma, he had two sons (Geoffrey and William, named) and two daughters (unnamed) 'ex concubinis' (Lair, p. 289; Christiansen, p. 63); Dudo wrote that after Richard's marriage to Gunnor, 'in the course of time he begot five male and three female children on her' (Christiansen, p. 164; Lair, p. 290: 'ex ea processu temporis quinque masculinae prolis pignora, femineaeque genuit tria'). Some of their names have been added in two of the manuscripts but were not originally by Dudo.

an effort to maintain regional authority and to prevent the division of their possessions.

The Norman commission of this text celebrating their family line strongly resembled the action of their neighbours and rivals, the counts of Flanders. In perhaps 959–60, a monk named Witger had produced a genealogy for the counts of Flanders – the first of its kind.[80] Witger emphasized the qualities and Christian virtues of the counts, especially the current Count Arnulf and his son Baldwin III. The implication is clear, and occasionally made more explicit, that these qualities passed through the family line: they are described as innate ('indolis'), often physical ('vultu decorum') and following the example of the father ('exemplo patris'). In connection with these qualities, the genealogy's central theme is the transfer of the comital title from father to son. The descent of the counts of Flanders appeared to be a straightforward transmission in a single vertical line, from Baldwin I to Baldwin II, to Arnulf, to Baldwin III. Witger referred to a brother, Adelulf, but swiftly followed this reference with an account of his premature death, thereby closing off an alternative line of descent.[81] Drawing inspiration from the Carolingian line, Witger presented the transmission of the comital title as largely comparable to that of royal authority. In this respect, Witger's presentation of the Flanders genealogy, although embedded in a liturgical format and arising from a particular historical moment, prefigured the model of descent which eleventh- and twelfth-century aristocracies claimed for themselves.[82]

A similar genealogical model was the structuring principle of Dudo's text. Each book focused on one Norman leader as its subject, but it is more than serial biography. The family connections between Rollo, William and Richard were emphasized, foreshadowed, and provided strong links between the sections of the work.

The first book of the history is dedicated to Hasting, a viking leader contemporary with Rollo but with no family relationship. Yet this brief section occupied an important place within the formation of the lineage identity. Dudo used the deeds of Hasting to display the nature of the Danes (or Dacians, as he called them), firmly establishing the background from which the Normans came. He set up the viking activities of Hasting as a foil to the viking Rollo, to whom he dedicated the second book. Dudo showed that Hasting behaved in every way opposite to Rollo, both in terms of his

---

[80] *Genealogiae Comitum Flandriae*, ed. L. C. Bethmann, *MGH, SS*, 9 (Hanover, 1851), pp. 302–4. On the context and date of composition, see E. Friese, 'Die "Genealogia Arnulfi comitis" des Priesters Witger', *Frühmittelalterliche Studien* 23 (1989), 203–43.

[81] An eleventh-century note found on the back of a charter highlights how far this patrilinear 'bloodline' differed from the real experience of family. Arnulf and Adelulf are described as uterine brothers, and the note explains the reciprocal adoptive relationship between their families: *Genealogiae Comitum Flandriae*, p. 304.

[82] See further Friese, 'Die "Genealogia Arnulfi comitis" des Priesters Witger', esp. pp. 237–40.

disregard for the holy places of Francia and his willingness to submit to the king for money. Rollo's virtues were thus emphasized in comparison: when he finally converted, this act seemed all the more honourable in contrast to Hasting's earlier false baptism. The Dacians stated that Hasting, who came from the 'same nation' as Rollo, 'was marked out by a good omen, and he made a good beginning; but he was fated to die a bad death in the end'.[83] Hasting's origins contributed to Norman identity and demonstrated the Normans' viking background, and this explains his place in the *De moribus*: a kind of originary ancestor.[84]

Rollo, as the founder of the Norman dynasty, occupies a much more significant section. Throughout the second book, Dudo inserted metrical passages which provide prophecy about Rollo's offspring achieving greatness, as well as the viking leader himself. He predicted that, with the commingling of Francia and the Dacians, 'then will she [Francia] breed and give birth, and pregnant, bring forth | Kings and archbishops, dukes also and counts, nobles of high rank... And they will rejoice in new and continuing progeny.'[85] Such a claim so early in the narrative provides a firm indication of where it leads. Given that peace and greatness will be achieved by the flourishing of Rollo's lineage (as well as his conversion), it is appropriate that we follow this lineage throughout the history. The fate of Normandy itself – the land Rollo demanded as 'a perpetual possession for the progeny of his progeny' – is inextricably linked to the lineage.[86] The book dedicated to Rollo grounds the origins of that lineage in the viking past.

The interests of the dynasty were safeguarded as the narrative continued into the book concerning William Longsword. With this aim, Dudo frequently employed metrical passages to prophesy and exhort his characters. William's desire to become a monk, though laudable as it showed his Christian fervour, presented a danger to the all-important patriline. While we know that William became the father of Richard, as did Dudo, at the critical moment he interjected: 'Cease keeping the vows! For you and for us there is need for | Your seed; for to you is a brilliant duke to be born.'[87] Later in the book, Dudo exhorted William again, to abandon fear for his chastity and to father

---

[83] Christiansen, pp. 36–7; Lair, pp. 154: 'ista gente', 'bono omine auspicatus est, bonoque initio coepit; sed malum finem exitumque sortitus est'.

[84] See further F. Amory, 'The Viking Hasting in Franco-Scandinavian Legend', in *Saints, Scholars and Heroes: Studies in Medieval Culture in Honour of Charles W. Jones*, ed. M. King and W. Stevens, 2 vols. (Collegeville, 1979), II, 265–86.

[85] Christiansen, p. 28; Lair, p. 144: 'Gignet producens, expurget, proferet ingens | Reges, pontificesque, duces, comites, proceresque... Atque novo quorum, gaudebunt, perpete foete'.

[86] Christiansen, p. 47; Lair, p. 167: 'in sempiternum per progenies progenierum possessionem'.

[87] Christiansen, p. 58; Lair, p. 180: 'Desine vota; necesse tibi nobisque fueris | Semine; namque tuo nascetur dux luculentus'.

children, just as his counts implored. William's desire for chastity would not be affected, he reasoned, because he indulged in sexual activity for a higher reason: 'for the sake of preserving the succession by hereditary right'.[88] The propagation of the patriline thus became a virtue in itself.

Dudo used this virtue and the value inherited from a strong lineage to justify the position of duke of the Normans. For this reason, the final, longest book, concerning Richard I, continued to stress the language of kinship. The theme of genealogy continued throughout Richard's life, as Dudo reflected back on his ancestors. Richard was introduced as the legitimate heir to Normandy precisely because he had 'sprung from the most celebrated seed of a brilliant and most noble stock'.[89] Indeed, much of the book concerns Richard's childhood, and as an individual personality he is largely absent from these sections. Rather, the qualities inherited from his ancestors were emphasized: Dudo interspersed these early chapters with metrical sections praising Richard's parents and grandparents. Richard was above all 'famed for his ancestry'.[90] It was also kinship that acted as a motivation for those who helped Richard. Count Bernard of Senlis explicitly alluded to his affection for his 'best-beloved nephew' as the reason for providing help, while king Harald of Dacia acted 'on account of his love for his relation Richard'.[91] Dudo showed the wider kin group protecting the interests of the ducal patriline. This patrilinear model strongly resembles that constructed by Witger for the counts of Flanders, and later those of other Frankish nobles.

But Dudo's construction of the Norman genealogy differed from those of the dukes' neighbours in one particularly significant respect: the lack of a royal connection. Both Dudo and Witger used genealogy to establish the origins of their patrons' families and the sources of their authority, but Witger's strategy was to present the counts of Flanders as an offshoot of the Carolingian royal house. Indeed, his text began with a copy of the Carolingian genealogy, from which he drew the line of the counts.[92] Witger's genealogical presentation seems to have been part of a more general emphasis on Carolingian heritage among the counts of Flanders, which is most clearly indicated by the name of the count at the time, Arnulf – the same as the Carolingians' saintly forebear.

The royal ancestor of the counts, Judith, is highlighted in Witger's Carolingian genealogy and cross-referenced to the next page, where the

---

[88] Christiansen, p. 63; Lair, p. 185: 'geniali jure conservandae successionis'.

[89] Christiansen, p. 94; Lair, p. 218: 'insignissimo luculentae et nobilissimae prosapiae semine exortus'.

[90] Christiansen, p. 105; Lair, p. 230: 'insignis prosapiae'.

[91] Christiansen, p. 111; Lair, p. 235: 'ille nepos meus dilectissimus'. Christiansen, p. 114; Lair, p. 239: 'ob amorem Ricardi, sui propinqui'. Dudo presents Harald as a king, but he may in reality have been a viking ruler of Bayeux. See Christiansen, p. 200, n. 248 on Bernard's identity.

[92] See Friese, 'Die "Genealogia Arnulfi comitis" des Priesters Witger', pp. 215–17 on the manuscript context and order of the text.

'*Sancta Prosapia*' of the counts of Flanders begins from her. In emphasising this female linkage, Witger imitated the strategy found in the Carolingian genealogy, in which royalty was established as stemming from the daughter of a Merovingian king. This connection through Blithild occurs in the first line of Witger's royal genealogy, mirrored by Judith's marriage to Baldwin in the first line of his comital genealogy. Moreover, because the text begins with Count Baldwin's marriage to Judith, the counts' nobility and title appeared to arise from their Carolingian heritage. Witger's text thus produced a legitimating lineage of power for the counts of Flanders, but one that depended on the royal line.[93]

Aristocratic genealogies written in the eleventh century similarly emphasized their families' links to the Carolingians. They reflect the prestige associated with Carolingian ancestry at this time, and the general belief that the aristocracy descended from royal origins. Adalbero of Laon (Dudo's own bishop and patron) wrote in a work addressed to King Robert in the 1010s that 'The pedigrees of nobles descend from the blood of kings.'[94] The late-eleventh-century genealogy of the counts of Boulogne, which Genicot has studied in detail, began from Priam – named as the Trojan ancestor of the Frankish kings – and recounted the genealogies of the Frankish kings down to Louis V and the end of the Carolingian dynasty.[95] The genealogy of the counts of Boulogne followed, stemming from Louis's uncle Charles, Duke of Lower Lorraine. This genealogy, which related also to the counts of Namur, became quite widespread. Other examples followed suit: Carolingian heritage was thus one of the markers of Frankish nobility in the late tenth and eleventh centuries. As in each case the line descended from the Carolingian family, so the principality appeared to pass from royalty to prince like an appanage. Some manuscripts of the genealogy of the counts of Namur and Boulogne contain, in addition, reference to their contemporary Capetian kings. These genealogies were statements of aristocratic power, but not a power independent of royalty.

Dudo, unlike Witger and the genealogists of other noble houses, studiously avoided making too much of the Norman dynasty's royal connections. In fact, by referring to two royal marriages, he explicitly rejected the importance of such connections. Most significantly, Dudo claimed that Rollo married Gisla, supposedly the daughter of Charles the Simple, which would have provided a parallel to Judith's role in the Flanders genealogy. Gisla may even have been Dudo's own creation, but he portrayed her in a negative light.[96] He told a

---

[93] There were additional reasons for Witger to emphasize particular Carolingian ancestors here – such as establishing a connection with Compiègne: Friese, 'Die "Genealogia Arnulfi comitis" des Priesters Witger', pp. 218–19, 237.

[94] Adalbéron de Laon, *Poème au Roi Robert*, ed. C. Carozzi (Paris, 1979), p. 2: 'Stemmata nobilium descendunt sanguine regum'.

[95] Genicot, 'Princes Territoriaux et Sang Carolingien'.

[96] J. Nelson, 'Normandy's Early History since *Normandy Before 1066*', in *Normandy and*

story in which Gisla received two male visitors from Charles without telling Rollo:

> And when Gisla had seen her father's knights she sent them off to a house where they would not be seen by her husband Robert [i.e. Rollo]; and she gave them all sorts of good things, and made them stay much too long.[97]

The visit became a source of shame for Rollo, whose counts goaded him for his effeminacy ('they said that Robert had never known her as a lawful husband') until he had the two Frankish knights executed.[98] Because of this, the incident ultimately disrupted the relationship between the Norman leader and the Frankish king. Dudo did not dwell on this consequence, however. He immediately moved on to the important point that William Longsword, Rollo's successor as Norman ruler, was not Gisla's son, and therefore the Carolingian family had made no contribution to the Norman lineage.[99]

In his final book, Dudo showed the Norman dynasty achieving a new strength and independence from the Franks. Richard I's first wife, Hugh the Great's daughter Emma, was not the one to provide him with an heir. Indeed, Dudo's comments on Emma might be read as somewhat barbed: she was known to be 'fit for the mingling of wedded procreation, and for the proper embrace of a pleasurable bedding, and not at all reluctant to submit to the force of masculine insemination' – but she never had a child.[100] Instead, it was a 'heavenly girl... of Dacian lineage' who produced the 'true heir to the dear line'.[101] Thus the culmination of the genealogical progress was not the individual duke, but the independence of the Norman lineage on both sides. Dudo had the Norman nobles specify that God led them to this point 'so that an heir to this land might be born to a Dacian father and mother'.[102] Gunnor, Richard's second wife and Richard II's mother, was still alive at the time of writing and probably one of Dudo's patrons. But this was more than personal

---

Its Neighbours, 900–1250: Essays for David Bates, ed. D. Crouch and K. Thompson (Turnhout, 2011), pp. 3–15 (pp. 9–12), summarizes the reasons for scepticism about this marriage.

[97] Christiansen, p. 53; Lair, p. 173: 'Gisla autem, quum vidisset milites patris sui, quadam domo, ne viderentur a Rotberto suo conjuge, seposuit; cunctaque bona illis largiens, nimis diu morari fecit.'

[98] Christiansen, p. 53; Lair, p. 173: 'Dicebant igitur Rotbertum eam non cognovisse maritali lege'.

[99] He was the son of Poppa, Rollo's first wife according to Dudo (daughter of the chief Berengar, probably of Rennes): Christiansen pp. 38–9, 54; Lair, pp. 157, 174.

[100] Christiansen, p. 138; Lair, p. 264: 'apta genialis connubii commistioni, congruentique delectabilis concubitus amplexioni, masculini seminis viribus minime differt succumbere'.

[101] Christiansen, p. 139; Lair, pp. 264–5: 'coelestis virgo... stirpe Dacigena'; 'Nascetur haeres germinis almi'.

[102] Christiansen, p. 164; Lair, p. 289: 'ut patre matreque Dacigena haeres hujus terrae nascatur'.

praise. After all, Dudo did not shy away from naming the children of Richard I's concubines.[103] In other Frankish genealogies, women were used to link families together. Dudo, on the other hand, presented Richard I's second wife, Gunnor, as the ideal bride and mother because she was *not* a member of another lineage: through her, the Norman dukes could continue with purely Norman blood.

In practice, of course, the Norman dukes used marriage in much the same way as other nobles. Eleanor Searle has suggested that the marriage of Richard I to Gunnor was used to unite two previously distinct groups of Scandinavians in Normandy.[104] Moreover, later generations of Normans did involve themselves in marriages with the houses of Flanders and the Breton counts: notably, William the Conqueror was married to Matilda of Flanders, whose mother Adela's first husband was William's uncle, Duke Richard III. In his presentation of the marriage to Gunnor, however, Dudo was making a claim for the independence of Norman power and the distinctiveness of Norman ethnicity. Dudo's rejection of Carolingian or Capetian blood, and celebration of a pure Dacian heir, separated the Normans from their neighbours.

Dudo's *De moribus*, when viewed as a text structured by genealogy, reveals the lineage which the Norman dukes wished to display to their Frankish neighbours. Like other powerful nobilities, they copied the tools of royal power, such as the cultivation of lineage identity, to secure their families' positions. However, instead of demonstrating how their territory and title descended from royal power, the Norman dukes claimed independence.

They did so by embracing, rather than rejecting, their viking origins. The establishment of their family's authority over Normandy was generally associated with a grant from Charles the Simple in 911, but the importance of this concession could be diminished by the assertion that they had conquered it themselves. Moreover, their viking origins lingered in the minds of their Frankish neighbours: Richer of Rheims referred to the Normans as 'pirates' throughout his tenth-century history.[105] While used by others as an insult, viking roots were transformed by Dudo and the Norman dukes into a source of independent identity. This strategy was so powerful that, from the end of the eleventh century, other Frankish magnates also created narratives of conquering heroic ancestors, independent from royalty.[106] Some of these legendary ancestors were even vikings, like Siegfried the Dane, ancestor of the counts of Guines. The chronicler Lambert of Ardres (writing between 1198

---

[103] Christiansen, p. 163; Lair, p. 289.

[104] Searle, 'Fact and Pattern', pp. 133–7.

[105] Richer of St-Rémi, *Histories*, ed. J. Lake, 2 vols. (Cambridge, MA, 2011).

[106] J. Dunbabin, 'Discovering a Past for the French Aristocracy', in *The Perception of the Past in Twelfth-Century Europe*, ed. P. Magdalino (London, 1992), pp. 1–14 (pp. 5–7); Bouchard, *Those of My Blood*, p. 29.

and 1206) made Siegfried at once the rightful heir of the counts of Guines and a Danish viking, whom he described as 'second in status after the king' of Denmark ('a rege secundus') – just like Rollo's father in the *De moribus* (discussed further in Chapter 2).[107] Dudo's genealogical strategy provided a powerful model for the shaping of a lineage.

Aristocratic genealogy in Anglo-Saxon England

The comparison between English and Frankish genealogical texts highlights the complete lack of aristocratic genealogy produced in Viking-Age England. Although genealogical production flourished, it remained restricted to the royal patriline until after the Norman Conquest. We must ask, therefore, why did no English equivalent of Dudo compose such a genealogical text for any of the Anglo-Scandinavian rulers?

In England (unlike in Ireland) there was no learned group whose responsibility it was to maintain genealogies.[108] To some extent, this role was played by clerics, who were the compilers and scribes of the manuscripts, and whose religious institutions maintained them. However, the most accomplished tenth-century English genealogist, Æthelweard, was a layman, so clerical involvement was far from an official or exclusive role. Moreover, genealogical information had a much greater significance than merely explaining the origins of the king. Distant ancestors like Cerdic may have been seen as the ancestors not only of the kings, but of the entire West Saxon aristocracy, or even the past of the entire ethnic group.[109]

Yet, in England, production of genealogical texts aided the strength of the ruling dynasty to the exclusion of others. The pedigree of Æthelwulf was composed in its final form in the reign of Alfred, as an assertion of the permanent establishment of the dynasty. Alfred's brothers, father and grandfather had all been kings before him. By the tenth century it was increasingly unlikely that anyone outside the direct descent from Æthelwulf would become king. In such circumstances, written claims to rule were unlikely to be necessary – indeed, would appear subversive. While genealogical production was linked to royal power it would have been impolitic to produce new aristocratic patrilines back to the founding ancestor. Frankish aristocratic genealogies were dynastic claims to localized power – something that West Saxon kings in their new English kingdom sought to forestall.

---

[107] Below, pp. 68–9; *Lamberti Ardensis historia comitum Ghisnensium*, ed. J. Heller, *MGH*, SS, 24 (Hanover, 1879), pp. 566–8; Lambert of Ardres, *The History of the Counts of Guines and Lords of Ardres*, trans. L. Shopkow (Philadelphia, 2001), pp. 58–61 (p. 3 for the date of composition).

[108] J. E. Caerwyn Williams, *The Court Poet in Medieval Ireland*, Sir John Rhys Memorial Lecture 1971 (London, 1971); Thornton, 'Orality, Literacy and Genealogy', p. 83.

[109] Davis, 'Cultural Assimilation', pp. 32–3.

The West Saxon kings appear to have prevented the formation of strong aristocratic lineages. Many ealdormen, like Ealdorman Æthelweard, seem to have originated from branches of the West Saxon royal house, but they did not establish separate lineages. Cyril Hart has demonstrated this for the family of Ealdorman Æthelstan 'Half King', who in the mid-tenth century 'at the height of his power governed in virtual autonomy a province the size of Normandy', in the shape of the ealdormanry of East Anglia.[110] Although his son, Æthelwold, succeeded him as ealdorman, the family had little influence by the reign of Æthelred. As the title of ealdorman remained a royal appointment, rather than a hereditary office, English kings could dilute the influence of any family or individual whose local support grew too great.[111] English kings in the later tenth century may have been particularly concerned about local rulers of Northumbria. Edgar and Æthelred appointed men from eastern England to the ealdormanry of Northumbria, and arranged for the archbishopric of York to be held in plurality with a southern see; Whitelock suggested that they were chosen as suitable because of their experience in areas of Danish settlement, but also to avoid candidates with too much personal support locally.[112]

The West Saxons' monopoly on genealogy, coupled with their tight control on emergent aristocratic families, prevented the production of specifically aristocratic genealogies like those from Flanders and Normandy. The boundaries of acceptable aristocratic interest in genealogy are revealed by Ealdorman Æthelweard's Latin *Chronicon* of the late tenth century. Æthelweard was a powerful ealdorman, as was his son Æthelmær after him, and he was also a member of a cadet branch of the royal family. He was, therefore, a prominent aristocrat who may have attempted to convert his honours and property into the inheritance of his lineage. Moreover, Æthelweard's *Chronicon* was explicitly concerned with his family history. In the prologue, Æthelweard addressed his work to his Saxon relative Matilda, whom he also addressed directly later in the narrative.[113] He defined the scope of his work as a clear explanation of the English side of 'our common family and also about the migration of our nation'.[114]

---

[110] C. Hart, 'Athelstan "Half King" and his Family', in C. Hart, *The Danelaw* (London, 1992), pp. 569–604 (p. 569).

[111] P. Stafford, *Unification and Conquest: A Political and Social History of England in the Tenth and Eleventh Centuries* (London, 1989), pp. 156–9 (the house of Bamburgh provides an exception in the far north); C. Insley, 'The Family of Wulfric Spott: an Anglo-Saxon Mercian Marcher Dynasty?', in *The English and their Legacy, 900–1200: Essays in Honour of Ann Williams*, ed. D. Roffe (Woodbridge, 2012), pp. 115–28.

[112] D. Whitelock, 'The Dealings of the Kings of England with Northumbria in the Tenth and Eleventh Centuries', in *The Anglo-Saxons: Studies in Some Aspects of Their History and Culture, Presented to Bruce Dickins*, ed. P. Clemoes (London, 1960), pp. 70–88 (pp. 73–6, 78–9).

[113] Æthelweard, pp. 1–2, 39.

[114] Æthelweard, p. 1: 'communis prosapiae, generis quoque et migratione'.

Æthelweard had a significant interest in his own family history, and a considerable amount of information appears to have been available to him. Not only did he display familiarity and pride when relating his family tree, but he expected Matilda, to whom he was writing, to be able to fill in the gaps. Æthelweard lamented his ignorance over the fate of one of the two sisters that King Æthelstan had sent to Otto I for marriage, and told Matilda that 'it is your task to bring information to our ears, for you have not only the family connection but the capacity, since distance does not hinder you'.[115] Thus links of kinship were acknowledged and maintained across time as well as space. They were simply not written down so frequently when they were not being used to justify royal power. Ashley has argued that 'the hegemonic cultural presence of the Alfredian royal lineage' prevented aristocracy from emphasizing the identities of their own lineages.[116] Certainly, Æthelweard identified himself closely with the royal family in this text – and, in fact, gave no distinct information about his own branch of the family. In this respect it is significant that Æthelweard did not recount his closest relatives, his father and grandfather. Thus Æthelweard left his family connection vague, and did not identify himself as royal. He used the genealogy of the royal family to represent his own, but did not claim to be 'throne-worthy' himself.

As discussed above, Æthelweard's information came from a culture that preserved genealogies in interacting oral and literary forms. Æthelweard's relationship to the royal family of the West Saxon dynasty meant that much of his information was available in genealogical king lists and in the Anglo-Saxon Chronicle, which he used extensively in writing his own *Chronicon*.[117] He claimed that he had learned of his relationship with Matilda from his parents, proceeding to explain their family links in detail. His prologue includes an intricate account of the intermarriages of the Saxon and West Saxon royal families. His detailed knowledge extended in several directions, tracing the descendants of various individuals, rather than simply their own relationship. Æthelweard was exceptional in that he included several branches of the family, including those of his female relatives – a rare mention of women in Anglo-Saxon genealogical tradition. It was, after all, through Eadgyth (Æthelstan's sister who married Otto) that he was related to Matilda herself. From his explanation we can see that women were the ones who connected the family with others further afield; the women Æthelweard refers to in his prologue were all sent abroad to marry. However, there is no suggestion in his discussion that Matilda was any less English in deriving that origin from a female ancestor.

---

[115] Æthelweard, p. 2: 'uestrum hoc opus est innotescere auribus nostris, quae non solum affinitate sed et potestate uideris obpleta, nulla intercapedine prohibente'.

[116] Ashley, 'Lay Intellectual', p. 237.

[117] E. Barker, 'The Anglo-Saxon Chronicle Used by Aethelweard', *Bulletin of the Institute of History Research* 40 (1967), 75–91.

In this respect, Æthelweard's *Chronicon* contrasted with other Anglo-Saxon texts listing patrilinear genealogical information and also expanded considerably on any possible written source material. Both the extent of his knowledge and the way he presented it demonstrate that Æthelweard was, as he claimed, using the genealogical memory cultivated by his family. Moreover, his view of the preceding generations structured the way he thought about the past and constituted an organizing principle for his work.[118] Æthelweard's interest in genealogy does not seem to have been born out of a desire to aggrandize himself or his authority.[119] His history, based around a genealogical framework and impetus, sought to establish an identity for himself and for his cousin Matilda's English side of the family. The ease with which he connected his ancestors to a chronological history associated with the West Saxon kingdom reveals that members of the English aristocracy, at least, had a perception of their own descent that was closely connected to that of the royal family. However, aristocratic expressions of that descent were also curtailed by the dominance of the West Saxon kings.

Anglo-Scandinavian dynasties

West Saxon kings were assisted in this policy by the dynastic discontinuity of Anglo-Scandinavian rulers in northern and eastern England. We know very little about most of these rulers: many are bare names in chronicles or are only known to us by examples of their coinage. Hadley has described the resulting picture as 'a bewildering catalogue of rulers'.[120] Three Scandinavian 'kings' seem to have ruled East Anglia before its conquest by Edward the Elder but, apart from Guthrum, we know little of them. Scandinavian rulers dominated the kingdom of York for a much longer period but, in any circumstances, dynastic continuity would have been difficult to achieve against the disruption of periods of direct West Saxon rule. In addition, the number of kings of York in the period 876–954 not only makes a chronology difficult to construct but testifies to significant disputes over the kingdom, which resulted in a frequent turnover of rulers. The clearest attempt to construct a chronology has been made by Clare Downham, who has argued that York and Dublin were both ruled by the dynasty of Ívarr throughout this period.[121] Ívarr may be identified with the Hinguar of the *Passio Eadmundi*

---

[118] E. van Houts, 'Women and the Writing of History in the Early Middle Ages: the Case of Abbess Matilda of Essen and Aethelweard', *EME* 1 (1992), 53–68 (p. 68); Jezierski, 'Æthelweard redivivus', pp. 176–7.

[119] P. Wormald, 'Æthelweard (d. 998?)', *Oxford Dictionary of National Biography* (Oxford, 2004) <http://www.oxforddnb.com/view/article/8918> [accessed 24 July 2013]. Ashley, 'Lay Intellectual', pp. 224–5, for Æthelweard's power deriving from his links with the royal family.

[120] D. Hadley, '"Hamlet and the Princes of Denmark": Lordship in the Danelaw, c.860–954', in *Cultures in Contact*, ed. Hadley and Richards, pp. 107–32 (p. 107).

[121] Downham, *Viking Kings*.

with reasonable confidence – the viking who killed King Edmund of East Anglia.[122] Many of Downham's identifications, though plausible, remain unproven, as they are generally based on the coincidence of names between the Anglo-Saxon Chronicle or coinage and the Irish annals. Her thesis represents a possible example of a Scandinavian dynasty asserting control over York for some eighty years. However, the behaviour of the descendants of Ívarr as described by Downham suggests that this was a disparate kin-group of competing individuals. Indeed, she claims that 'dynastic infighting' was the major weakness of the kingdom of York, resulting in its permanent conquest by West Saxon kings.[123]

Of more relevance for a discussion of identity is the lack of clear evidence for the cultivation of Ívarr's lineage in England. Downham has identified the kings of York as various descendants of Ívarr, who were apparently related as cousins. The relationship to one renowned ancestor would bear comparison with Anglo-Saxon identities, but contemporary references to descent from Ívarr were minimal, and are found only in Irish sources.[124] If we accept that references to Scyldings also related to Ívarr, as discussed above, then this would suggest some form of royal dynastic consciousness. The Scandinavian kings of York do not seem to have patronized any form of written document and so we are unlikely to find comparable evidence to that of the West Saxon kings and Norman dukes. As Townend highlighted in relation to the lack of surviving York praise-poetry, dynastic promotion pursued primarily in oral form is unlikely to have left traces precisely because, once the dynasty had lost influence in York, no one who cared was left to maintain the tradition.[125] It may be that a dynastic identity was fostered through stone sculpture or coinage.[126] Downham presents the evidence of coinage as the sole example that kings promoted their lineage in York. However, the images she has associated with their dynasty – Thor's hammer and a sword – may more readily be taken as symbols of kingship more generally.[127] The apparent lack of lasting dynastic promotion among the Scandinavian kings of England meant that later West Saxon kings were not troubled by members of rival royal lineages, nor local loyalty to them, once the last king of York had been expelled in 954.

---

[122] Smyth, *Scandinavian Kings in the British Isles*, p. 202. See Chapter Three. For a clear summary of the evidence for the career and identity of Ívarr, see McLeod, *Beginning of Scandinavian Settlement*, pp. 113–15, 118–19.

[123] Downham, *Viking Kings*, p. 135.

[124] See B. Hudson's review in *Speculum* 84 (2009), 703–5, and B. Hudson, *Viking Pirates and Christian Princes: Dynasty, Religion, and Empire in the North Atlantic* (Oxford, 2005), pp. 19–20.

[125] M. Townend, 'Whatever Happened to York Viking Poetry? Memory, Tradition and the Transmission of Skaldic Verse', *Saga-Book* 27 (2003), 48–90 (p. 80).

[126] Sidebottom, 'Viking Age Stone Monuments and Social Identity', pp. 232–3.

[127] Downham, *Viking Kings*, pp. 119–20.

Conclusion

This discussion of Viking-Age genealogy in England and Francia brings us to two comparative points.

Firstly, different patterns of genealogical production both derived from and contributed to the different power structures in England and Francia. In the mid-ninth century, genealogy was restricted to royal patrilines on both sides of the Channel. However, the increasing scope and centralization of West Saxon royal power in England led to this single dynasty's complete dominance in terms of lineage identity: the kings of the new English kingdom seem to have prevented aristocratic families from consolidating power, title or land in a single line. In effect, royal power prohibited aristocratic genealogy. In Francia, on the other hand, the weakening of royal power in the tenth century led to the opposite situation. With the decline of the Carolingian dynasty, aristocratic lineages flourished, concentrating power, land and titles as hereditary attributes. Concomitantly, genealogical production was adopted by these lineages. It was because of these opposing situations that the Scandinavian presence in England and Francia manifested itself differently in genealogies. English kings, holding a monopoly on genealogy, appropriated Scandinavian ancestors for their own line – perhaps in order to undermine the emergence of a rival dynasty. In Francia, however, it was an aristocratic lineage – Rollo's Norman rulers, one among many families developing a semi-independent regional power base – that asserted Scandinavian ancestry. In both England and Francia, therefore, genealogists responded to the presence of Scandinavian settlers in the shaping of dynastic identity. In both cases also, Danish or viking identity was used as a source of power.

These observations have implications for the application of anthropological understandings of genealogy to the early medieval context. Although most often employed in the discussion of literacy and orality, the anthropological concept of a 'genealogical charter' has also illuminated the relationship between identity and dynastic power. David Dumville's discussion, in particular, has highlighted how genealogies reflect and validate the power structure of a given society, and therefore that they must be flexible.[128] Our comparison here reveals that this is a two-way process, in that genealogies were also used as a tool in consolidating that power, precisely because of their relevance to identity. Dumville emphasized that genealogies, if they are to reflect contemporary political and social relationships, require an 'area of ambiguity' that allows reconfiguration and manipulation in changing circumstances. Yet genealogies need to be flexible enough to accommodate not only changes in the ruling dynasty or

---

[128] Dumville, 'Kingship, Genealogies and Regnal Lists', pp. 85–9.

newly subordinate under-kings, but also changes in the structure of power itself. The West Saxons rose to dominance over all the former Anglo-Saxon kingdoms; Frankish noble families rose at the expense of the West Frankish king. These developments were not merely changes in personnel, but changes to the very nature of the relationships that constituted the power structure.

For this reason, therefore, early medieval genealogists were engaged in a creative process. Genealogies did not follow the same conventions across the early Middle Ages, and we cannot make rules for *how* they express power. Anglo-Saxon royal genealogies reflected political relationships through distant common ancestors, but power relations in Frankish royal and noble genealogies were more often expressed through emphasis on particular marriages between dynasties. These differing strategies depended on culturally and historically specific perceptions of how families worked and the role of genealogies themselves. In the tenth and eleventh centuries, developing family structures meant that the significance of genealogies also changed. Moreover, genealogies may have presented one message when presented as a corpus (such as the Anglian collection or Witger's combined Carolingian and Flanders genealogy), but single, widely disseminated texts relating to one family gave a very different message.

This need for historical specificity in comparing genealogies brings us to the second comparative point. The means by which Scandinavian ancestry was asserted in the West Saxon genealogy, on the one hand, and the Norman genealogy, on the other, differed significantly. We deduce that the West Saxons claimed Danish royal ancestors from the names that were added to their genealogy, and these names' uses in other contexts: in the genealogical texts themselves there is no glossing or explanation that these were specifically 'Danish'. In fact, the addition of these names, and the use of 'Scyldings' in a range of Old English, Latin and Old Norse texts, suggests a shared cultural understanding between English and Scandinavian audiences. The West Saxon kings incorporated heroic figures that were known to be Danish, from their own traditions and perhaps from Scandinavian traditions – from this fact, I suggest that their prime interest in those figures was their Danish heritage. If the suggestion is accepted, then this constitutes a cultural signifier of identity. It was not until the late tenth century that a genealogy, produced by the ealdorman Æthelweard, explicitly connected these figures to Scandinavia.

Dudo's history of the Norman dukes, on the other hand, explicitly and repeatedly asserted their Scandinavian heritage as such. Yet his structure of ancestral descent, as well as the names and details he gives, follows Latin texts and Frankish tradition, rather than Old Norse legend. It is, of course, difficult to trace Dudo's sources, and to assess the contribution of oral tradition to his narrative. It is noteworthy that the figures he mentions do not appear in Old Norse skaldic poetry or sagas, although Rollo's establishment of Normandy is referred to in *Heimskringla*.[129] This absence could be due to Normandy's lack of communication with Scandinavian courts from the early eleventh century onwards, and thus the obliteration of these narratives from the Old Norse tradition, but the most likely suggestion seems to be that these stories were relatively newly created, perhaps by Dudo himself.[130] Thus, the genealogical line that was explicitly 'viking' drew primarily on Frankish, rather than Scandinavian tradition.

This distinction is intriguing. On the one hand, a claim to Danish identity used Danish cultural signifiers, and on the other, a claim to viking identity used explicit statement drawing primarily on Frankish culture. The immediate explanation is that audience dictated presentation. It would be pointless to present Scyld and Sceaf to a Frankish audience if they had never heard of them; since the Franks perceived vikings through their history of plunder and paganism, these were the details necessary to assert a viking identity *in this context*. In England, however, the West Saxons perhaps aimed to present a more specific message, against a particular dynasty – claiming royalty through Scyld and Sceaf, rather than Danishness in particular, in order that a Danish audience would accept them. In this case the names Scyld and Sceaf, and associated legend, were used as a point of communication and similarity between English and Dane. In a Frankish context, conversely, no specifically Scandinavian tradition was necessary to claim viking ancestry.

These contrasts applied not only to the rulers whose genealogies incorporated Scandinavian ancestors, but to the entire peoples they represented. Indeed, the distant generations of a genealogy appear to have related both to the people and to the ruling dynasty, leading back to the people's myth of origins. The next chapter explores the importance of Scandinavia and the Viking Age in the formulation of English and Norman myths of ethnic origins.

---

[129] Snorri Sturluson, *Heimskringla*, ed. B. Aðalbjarnarson, Íslenzk Fornrit 26–7, 2 vols. (Reykjavik, 1941), I, 124–5; trans. A. Finlay and A. Faulkes (London, 2011), p. 72. As here, the earliest Old Norse reference to Rollo also calls him 'Ganger-Hrolf', and is found in the twelfth-century *The Book of Settlements: Landnámabók*, trans. H. Pálsson and P. Edwards (Winnipeg, 1972), pp. 119–20. Because of this reference, Rollo has been identified with the protagonist of Göngu-Hrólfs Saga, but this later composition bears no relation to the early Norman duchy: J. Hartmann, *The Göngu-Hrólfssaga: A Study in Old Norse Philology* (New York, 1912), pp. 53–5.

[130] For an overview of Normandy's Old Norse connections, see L. Abrams, 'England, Normandy and Scandinavia', in *A Companion to the Anglo-Norman World*, ed. C. Harper-Bill and E. van Houts (Woodbridge, 2003), pp. 43–62.

2

Origin Myths: A People for a Dynasty

The genealogies examined in the previous chapter counted generations back to 'founder ancestors' of a dynasty or of an entire *gens*. Thus the Merovingian dynasty took their name from Merovech, while the West Saxons located their origins in the figure of Cerdic, the first of their people to arrive in Britain.[1] Placed within genealogical lists, these names held meaning only because they were attached to a deeper store of historical narrative: origin myths, which recounted the actions of the founder ancestors. In the person of the founder ancestor, the boundaries between dynasty and people often seemed to dissolve. Like genealogies, these origin myths (usually called *origines gentium* by modern historians) echoed and referred to contemporary ethnic relations. An origin myth for a people that no longer existed would cease to be recounted, since the motive for recounting the narrative was to explain the existence of contemporary groups. Individuals within such histories were representative of group identities currently important in the perceptions of writers and audience.

Origin myths have been used to discuss the actual pasts of Germanic peoples during the 'Age of Migrations' but, given their fluid nature and the chronological distance at which they were usually written, they are extremely unreliable as evidence of the events they describe.[2] The designation of 'myth' is perhaps a little misleading, since it implies a separate genre from other forms of history. In fact, we know of these *origines gentium* from their places in conventional histories such as Bede's *Historia ecclesiastica* and Jordanes's *Getica*, in which they are not treated differently from other historical events.[3] Moreover, as we shall see in this chapter, writers continued to create such tales as ethnic relations developed. They are united more by function than

---

[1] Merovech's name appears in Merovingian genealogies: an earlier origin story appears to have been that Merovech's father was a sea monster, a Quinotaur: I. Wood, 'Defining the Franks: Frankish Origins in Early Medieval Historiography', in *Concepts of National Identity in the Middle Ages*, ed. S. Forde, L. Johnson and A. Murray (Leeds, 1995), pp. 47–57 (p. 49).

[2] Wolfram, '*Origo et religio*'; W. Goffart, 'Does the Distant Past Impinge on the Invasion Age Germans?', in *On Barbarian Identity: Critical Approaches to Ethnicity in the Early Middle Ages*, ed. A. Gillett (Turnhout, 2002), pp. 21–37.

[3] W. Goffart, *The Narrators of Barbarian History (A.D. 550–800)* (Notre Dame, 2005); J. Martínez Pizarro, 'Ethnic and National History ca. 500–1000', in *Historiography in the Middle Ages*, ed. Deliyannis, pp. 43–87 (p. 43); R. Hachmann, *Die Goten und Skandinavien* (Berlin, 1970), pp. 15–35.

literary genre.[4] However, early medieval origin myths tended to employ a common vocabulary and increasingly referred to their earlier precursors.[5] Susan Reynolds has emphasized that Scandinavian ancestry was as much a part of this vocabulary as descent from Troy or Noah's Ark.[6] Scholars have treated accounts of Scandinavian origins as somehow more historical than other myths, but such origins were similarly a literary creation, and eventually became a topos, employed by early medieval writers in much the same way.[7] These traditions then influenced perceptions of the Scandinavian origins of raiders and migrants in the Viking Age.

Since origin myths were closely linked to genealogies, they often appear in combination with them within historical writing. Hence, in this chapter, we continue to discuss two of the same key texts: Dudo's *De moribus et actis primorum Normanniae ducum* and Æthelweard's *Chronicon*. Written within twenty years of each other, they present origin myths for the Normans and English respectively. Both Dudo and Æthelweard located these peoples' origins in Scandinavia. However, we see a similar divide as in the construction of their genealogies. In narrating Scandinavian origins, Æthelweard developed an existing origin myth through his knowledge of Danish language and culture. Dudo's vision of the Normans' Scandinavian background, on the other hand, drew primarily on Frankish conceptions of the north and Frankish conventions surrounding origin myths.

Manuscripts containing genealogical lists also highlighted the importance of founder-ancestors to ethnic origins. A number of short texts associated with genealogies described the origins and relationships of ethnic groups in similar genealogical terms. For example, a text known as the Frankish Table of Nations appears immediately before the Merovingian genealogy in two manuscripts, listing the descent from three brothers of various Germanic peoples.[8] More comprehensive items explained how the various peoples of the world got their names, usually from a founder-ancestor or king. Several such items are collected together in Lambert of St Omer's Liber Floridus (*c*.1120). One of these, entitled 'The Names Given to Peoples, from kings and kingdoms or from the situation of kingdoms', follows a simple pattern: 'Frigia

---

[4] L. Boje Mortensen, 'Stylistic Choice in a Reborn Genre: The National Histories of Widukind of Corvey and Dudo of St Quentin', in *Dudone di San Quintino*, ed. P. Gatti and A. Degl'Innocenti (Trento, 1995), pp. 77–102 (p. 81).

[5] Pizarro, 'Ethnic and National History', pp. 71, 79–81.

[6] S. Reynolds, 'Medieval *Origines Gentium* and the Community of the Realm', *History* 68 (1983), 375–90 (pp. 378–9).

[7] W. Goffart, *Barbarian Tides: The Migration Age and the Later Roman Empire* (Philadelphia, 2006), pp. 56–72 on Jordanes's creation of the idea; Coumert, *Origines des Peuples*, pp. 177–96 and pp. 367–8 on its later employment in histories of the Lombards and Franks.

[8] St Gall Stiftsbibliothek 732 and Paris Bibliothèque Nationale lat.4628A.

a Friga. Dardani a Dardano. Danai a Danao… Saxones a saxo'.[9] Such connections show the widespread assumption of the equivalence of royal and ethnic
identity. Æthelweard, likewise, included several such examples in his explanation of how the name of the Kentish royal dynasty, the 'Escingas', derived
from a king named Esc: 'as the Romans [got their name] from Romulus,
the Cecropids from Cecrops, and the Tuscans from Tuscus'.[10] Although
elsewhere we find an eponymous founder-ancestor for the Franks ('Francio'
in Fredegar's *Chronicle*), in this particular list in the Liber Floridus their name
is given a different kind of source: 'Franci a ferocitate'.[11] The character of the
Frankish people beyond their royal family often figures in accounts of their
origins – a symptom of the importance of the aristocracy as well as the king.

Such discrepancies in accounts of Frankish origins were widespread,
but rarely problematic to compilers and readers. As early as the 820s or
830s, Frechulf of Lisieux's World Chronicle recorded two different origin
myths.[12] One account reports that the Franks came originally from the
isle of Scandza. In this account, Frechulf clearly followed Jordanes's *Getica*,
applying the topos of Scandinavian origins to the Franks for perhaps the first
time.[13] Many national histories of the early Middle Ages did the same: by
repeating originary elements, these conventional origin stories positioned
ethnic groups within a political community.[14] Frechulf's other origin myth
was the well-known tale of the Franks' Trojan origins, and the election of
Francio as their first king. The earliest appearances of this myth are in the *Liber
Historiae Francorum* (which relates their descent from Priam and Antenor) and
Fredegar's *Chronicle* where, in light of the differences in their accounts, they
appear to be independent of each other. Gregory of Tours did not mention
the myth: it seems to have been a learned creation of the seventh century, and
was referred to increasingly often after this period.[15] Like all origin myths,

---

[9] *Lamberti S. Audomari Canonici Liber Floridus*, ed. A. Derolez (Ghent, 1968), pp. 99–100
(fol. 49): 'Nomina a regnis et regibus vel a situ regnorum gentibus imposita'.

[10] Æthelweard, p. 18: 'ut a Romulo Romani, et Cecrope Cecropidae, et a Tusco Tusci.'
He was apparently drawing on Isidore's *Etymologies*: Gretsch, 'Historiography and
Literary Patronage', p. 235.

[11] R. Gerberding, *The Rise of the Carolingians and the Liber Historiae Francorum* (Oxford,
1987), p. 12, gives various etymologies for the name of the Franks.

[12] *Frechulfi Lexoviensis Episcopi Opera Omnia*, ed. M. I. Allen, Corpus Christianorum
Continuatio Mediaevalis CLXIX–CLXIXA, 2 vols. (Turnhout, 2002), II, 147–8 (I, 2,
26).

[13] Coumert, *Origines des Peuples*, pp. 367–8; S. Ghosh, 'The Barbarian Past in Early
Medieval Historical Narrative' (unpublished doctoral thesis, University of Toronto,
2009), pp. 229–35.

[14] Reynolds, 'Medieval *Origines Gentium*', pp. 378–9.

[15] Gerberding, *Rise of the Carolingians*, p. 20; Wood, 'Defining the Franks', pp. 51, 53;
M. Innes, 'Teutons or Trojans? The Carolingians and the Germanic Past', in *The Uses
of the Past in the Early Middle Ages*, ed. Y. Hen and M. Innes (Cambridge, 2000), pp.
227–49 (p. 248).

the inception of the Trojan story probably arose as a way to negotiate ethnic relationships. In this case, it is likely that the Franks' relationship to Aeneas, the founder of Rome, demonstrated their contemporary relationship with the Gallo-Roman inhabitants of Francia.[16] It also established the Franks' relationship with the Roman Church.

English origin myths also mediated contemporary relationships. Hengest and Horsa, the ancestors of the Kentish royal family, continued throughout the period to enjoy prestige and importance as the first Anglo-Saxons to arrive in Britain. As a single English kingdom formed, they ceased to be linked directly to Kent but instead represented the English as a whole. For example, the recension of the *Historia Brittonum* made for King Edmund by an English adapter in 944 omitted most of the Anglo-Saxon genealogies found in the earlier versions. The compiler included only the lineage of Hengest and Horsa.[17] Immediately afterwards, he measured the passage of time between their arrival and the beginning of Edmund's reign, thus linking the earliest invaders directly with the current king. The *Historia Brittonum* as a whole related to the conflicts and contacts between the Anglo-Saxons and the Britons; despite being thoroughly reworked by an Anglo-Saxon editor, the text continued to be preoccupied with these relationships. Thus the genealogy it included was the one which related to the most significant historical event in these relations, the arrival of the Anglo-Saxons. As such, it defined the *Saxones* as one people, now headed by King Edmund. Because the origin myth of the Anglo-Saxons was at root a narrative of conflict with the Britons, the primary ethnic boundaries it constructed were those between English and British. It was not until the tenth century that an English writer, Ealdorman Æthelweard, connected the origin myth to the Danes, as discussed later in this chapter.

Other than Hengest and Horsa, by the later ninth and tenth centuries, genealogical texts generally focused on West Saxon founder ancestors. Thus the West Saxon Genealogical Regnal List began with the arrival of Cerdic in Britain, and established the legitimacy of virtually all subsequent kings with the phrase 'his family goes back to Cerdic' ('þæs cynn gæð to Cerdice'). The West Saxons had originally been called the Gewissae, which Asser explained as a name derived from Cerdic's ancestor, Gewis. However, we encounter few references to Gewis in Anglo-Saxon texts, and no recorded deeds are

---

[16] Innes, 'Teutons or Trojans?', p. 248, where he also suggests the alternative view that it may have arisen earlier as part of an alliance between Franks and Roman leaders. Ghosh, 'Barbarian Past', pp. 97–101 makes a convincing argument that the Trojan origin myth both connected the Franks to and distinguished them from their Roman neighbours: his argument provides a parallel to the case I make in this chapter for the origins of the Normans alongside the Franks.

[17] *Historia Brittonum*, ed. Dumville, p. 83; pp. 4–6 for dating and origins of this recension.

associated with him. Other Anglo-Saxon royal lines also recorded eponymous ancestors: the East Anglian dynasty of Wuffings, for example, originally traced their ancestry back to a pre-migration figure, Wuffa, while the Mercian kings, the Iclingas, were said to be descended from Icel. Yet similarly, the genealogies are the only records the Anglo-Saxons made about these figures and their history before the migration to Britain. Once the migration itself was distant in time, it could be perceived as a rite of passage, and so when the Anglo-Saxons came to write down their own histories, they equated their group origins with their ancestors' arrival in Britain. Within this world-view, migration made a people.

Scandinavian origins

Migration was a central element of origin myths composed in England and Normandy, and the Viking Age brought new interest in migration from Scandinavia in particular. Both Dudo and Æthelweard described the Scandinavian origins of the migrating dynasties – and peoples – that they discussed. Their sources of information, however, were significantly different. Dudo, the only writer in early Normandy to treat Scandinavia in any detail, turned to the common vocabulary of Scandinavian origin myths that he would have encountered in Latin histories and treatises. Doing so not only made him appear learned, but placed the Norman dukes within an existing system of references. Unlike the genealogies of their neighbouring aristocracies, Dudo's history of the Norman dukes represented a distinct ethnic group. This was only possible because the Norman dukes came from parallel, rather than identical, origins to the Frankish kings.

In describing the Normans' ethnic background, Dudo fitted them into a familiar narrative of ethnogenesis. His discussion of the origins of the Danes was derived from literary works. From the very beginning of the history, Dudo drew on standard works of history and geography: his first line of prose was derived from Paulus Orosius, Jordanes and Isidore.[18] Dudo presented the Danes – and thus the Normans – as a *gens* comparable to the Franks, Goths and Lombards, thereby boosting their claim to greatness; in particular, by including similarities and connections with the Franks, he cemented the Norman place in the contemporary political sphere.

Dudo introduced the Dacians, the ancestors of the Normans, as one group among many Germanic peoples:

...there dwell savage and barbarous peoples, which are said to have sprung forth in various different ways from the island of Scanza, hemmed in on both sides by the Ocean, like a swarm of bees from a hive, or like a

[18] Christiansen, p. 182, n. 60.

sword from a scabbard; as barbarians will. For there lies the region of the great multitudes of Alania, the exceedingly fertile site of Dacia, and the far-extended reaches of Getia... And wild peoples, warlike and 'foreboding Mars' inhabit this extensive corner; that is, the Getae (also called Goths), the Sarmatians, and the Amacsobii, the Tragoditae, and the Alans, and many other people who dwell in and cultivate the Maeotid Marshes.[19]

Dudo's geography was confused, but it allowed him to draw the connections he needed. The ideas of Germany as 'germinating' many nations, and of many peoples emerging from Scanza like bees from a hive, both taken from Jordanes, were common concepts in other national histories.[20] This first chapter linked the Dacians to a number of Germanic peoples, notably the Alans, a combination also made by Abbo of Fleury in the *Passio Sancti Eadmundi*.[21] Dudo explicitly compared the customs of the Dacians to those of the Getae, 'who are also called Goths', the barbarians considered responsible for the fall of Rome. This identification of Geats and Goths was also common, and the comparison may be considered shorthand for a Germanic barbarian background.

In casting the Dacians as barbarians, Dudo was not being derogatory, but aligning them with Frankish origins. A number of hints in these early passages associated them with the origin myth of the Franks. The Germanic peoples were located in the 'Maeotid Marshes', or Sea of Azov, just where the *Liber Historiae Francorum* indicated the Franks escaped after their flight from Troy.[22] Moreover, Dudo picked up on this Trojan origin – the very beginning of the Frankish story in the *Liber Historiae Francorum* – and applied it also to the Danes:

And so the *Daci* call themselves *Danai*, or Danes, and boast that they are descended from Antenor; who, when in former times the lands of Troy were laid waste, slipped away through the middle of the Greeks and penetrated the confines of Illyria with his own men.[23]

---

[19] Christiansen, p. 15, Lair, p. 129: '...commorantur ferae gentes et barbarae, quae ex Canza insula, Oceano hinc inde circumsepta, velut examen apum ex canistro, seu gladius e vagina, diversitate multimoda dicuntur prosiluisse... Est namque ibi tractus quam plurimis Alaniae, situsque nimium copiosus Daciae, atque meatus multum profusus Getiae... Quos protense anfractus amplitudinis furentes incolunt populi, praemonente Marte bellicosi scilicet Getae, qui et Gothi, Sarmatae et Amacsobii, Tragoditae et Alani, quamplurimaeque gentes, Meotidibus paludibus excolendo commorantes.'

[20] Reynolds, 'Medieval *Origines Gentium*', pp. 378–9.

[21] Abbo of Fleury, *Life of St Edmund*, p. 73. See further Chapter Three.

[22] Christiansen, p. 15; Lair, p. 129; *Liber Historiae Francorum*, ed. B. Krusch, MGH, SS rer. Merov., 2 (Hanover, 1888), 215–328 (pp. 241–3).

[23] Christiansen, p. 16; Lair, p. 130: 'Igitur Daci nuncupantur a suis Danai, vel Dani, glorianturque se ex Antenore progenitos; qui, quondam Trojae finibus depopulatis, mediis elapsus Achivis, Illyricos fines penetravit cum suis.'

It has been noted that this passage lacks coherence, given that *'Danai'* refers to Greeks and Antenor was a Trojan.[24] But Dudo's aim was achieved. By indulging in a little word-play, he was able to make the Danes share a common ancestor with the Franks: Antenor. Like Ermold the Black, nearly two centuries earlier, Dudo sought to define the relationship between the Normans and the Franks through an ethnic connection. It should be noted that Dudo presented Antenor as the ancestor of all the Danes, rather than elucidating a genealogical connection between Frankish and Danish kings. This ethnographical introduction prepared the ground for the emergence of the Normans within Francia.

Thus as Dudo produced his history, he drew on the vocabulary of *origines gentium*. He presented the Normans as the leaders of a people comparable to the Franks by using recognizable details and patterns from myths of ethnogenesis. Whereas the West Saxon genealogist responsible for the pedigree of Æthelwulf had created a similar effect by incorporating names that invoked Germanic epic, Dudo drew on classical and early medieval Latin literature. The cultural sphere chosen was different, but the method was largely similar. Both created a certain feeling of antiquity and an aura of authenticity, though in each case the specific details may have lacked accuracy.

However, the Normans' relationships with the Franks could be problematic. To counter this, Dudo also stressed the Normans' distinctiveness from the Franks: they were a different branch of the same family. The more recent migration and the specifically viking heritage of the Normans asserted this distinctiveness. The Normans would never be merely Franks, because their viking ancestors made their difference inherent. Their viking origins were dramatized through the person of Hasting, and continued to be important throughout the *De moribus*. Dudo even contrasted their viking heritage favourably with Frankish connections. In one episode, the loyalties of William Longsword, the son of a Frankish mother, were called into question by a magnate named Riulf. Riulf claimed that William was too much of a Frank, for he 'was begotten on the noblest stock of the Frankish race, has procured Frankish friends for himself... he wants to give the land which we own to his own kinsmen to be possessed by their heirs'.[25] William needed to demonstrate his worth like a viking, to prove himself a man of the north and not a Frank. He found men 'who made their act of association, fealty and support in the manner of the Danes', rejecting Frankish conventions, and descended upon his enemies 'as the wolves attack sheep'.[26]

---

[24] Christiansen, p. 183, n. 75.

[25] Christiansen, p. 64; Lair, p. 187: 'nobilissimo Franciscae stirpis semine genitus, Francigenas amicos acquirit sibi... Terram autem quam possidemus parentibus suis in haeredem suorum possessionem dabit.'

[26] Christiansen, p. 67; Lair, p. 190: 'qui... judiciumque foederis fideique, et adjutorium, more Dacorum, facientes'; 'ut agnos lupi'.

Although Normandy still maintained some links with Norway and Denmark, it is unlikely that this text was intended for or accessed by a northern audience (although Saxo Grammaticus knew it later).[27] The Scandinavian and especially viking origins of the Normans expressed their relationships with their neighbours: Franks, Bretons and English. In order to align the Normans with both Franks and Danes, Dudo's text contained a number of passages which functioned as origin myths for the Norman people. The detailed description of their background in Dacia and Scanza linked them to other Germanic tribes, particularly the Franks. Dudo then provided reasons for viking activity at this specific time – a combination of overpopulation, Scandinavian custom and increased royal power. Dudo invoked commonplaces about the Germanic peoples' 'wanton lasciviousness', which led to overpopulation: 'and so, by mingling together in illicit couplings they generate innumerable children'. As a result, there was not enough land in Dacia to go around, and young men were expelled by lot to conquer new lands for themselves, according to 'a very old custom' enforced by the king.[28] These factors he described in 'ethnic' terms: it was the character, culture and social organization of the Danes which drove their young men abroad.

Dudo dedicated a considerable part of the first two books of the *De moribus* to the more recent political conditions of the viking homelands. Having located Danish origins in the connected regions of Dacia in the east and Scanza in the north, the action moves between these two locations. Even excusing Dudo's erroneous geography, it is highly unlikely that the events he described as taking place in the viking homelands had any basis in reality;[29] rather, he used the Scandinavian background to create a parallel situation to that of the Normans and the Franks. Dudo introduced the Norman dynasty first of all by describing the situation of Rollo's father in Dacia:

> Never had he bowed the nape of his neck to any king, nor had he done service or entrusted his own hands into the hands of any man by way of commendation. As owner of almost the whole of the kingdom of Dacia, he won for himself lands adjacent to Dacia and Alania and subjected their peoples to his might and power in several battles.[30]

---

[27] K. Friis-Jensen, 'Dudo of St-Quentin and Saxo Grammaticus', in *Dudone Di San Quintino*, ed. Gatti and Degl'Innocenti, pp. 11–28; Saxo Grammaticus, *Gesta Danorum: The History of the Danes*, ed. K. Friis-Jensen, trans. P. Fisher, 2 vols. (Oxford, 2015), I, 20–1.

[28] Christiansen, p. 15; Lair, p. 129: 'petulanti nimium luxu exardescentes... illinc soboles innumeras obscena illiciti connubii commixtione patrando generant'; 'veterrimo ritu'.

[29] Although this cannot be completely dismissed: the emphasis on growing royal power as a cause of the Viking Age is echoed in later Scandinavian histories. For a full discussion of such issues, and Dudo's sources, see Prentout, *Étude Critique*, pp. 33–46, 114–60.

[30] Christiansen, p. 26; Lair, p. 141: 'qui nunquam colla suae cervicis cuipiam regi

This 'all-powerful leader' ('dux praepotentissimus') was distinct from the Dacian king, who threatened the young Dacian men with expulsion and the seizure of their 'lands and land-grants' ('fundis... atque beneficiis').[31] His power over the wide lands he ruled was effective, and won by his own force; it was also hereditary, passing on to his sons Rollo and Gurim. This structure of power or 'monarchia', independent of and sometimes in opposition to the king, prefigured the future state of the dukes of Normandy beside France.[32] Thus, Dudo used the Scandinavian past to comment on the new Frankish–Norman boundary.

Dudo was the only contemporary writer to deal with the Scandinavian past of the vikings or Normans in any detail. Frankish writers possessed little interest and considerable ignorance about the viking homelands of Denmark and Norway. The anonymous author of one ninth-century geographical tract, known as the *De situ orbis* of the Anonymous Leidensis, claimed that he was moved to write because of the viking raids, and his brothers' ignorance of the Scandinavian north. However, he sought information from written author-ities, such as Aethicus Ister's *Cosmographia*, rather than travellers from these regions.[33] Within Normandy, most writers came originally from other regions of Francia, and employed the Frankish vision of Scandinavia in the service of Norman distinction. Their audience and context were Frankish rather than Norse – they did not need to engage with the realities of Scandinavian life. In hagiographical texts, references to Norman origins generally began with the viking arrival in Francia, rather than in the Scandinavian homelands. Their brief references to Scandinavia used ideas from western geographies concerning the north. The tenth-century *Vita Romani*, composed in Rouen, described the Danes as 'a nation from the extreme ends of the sea and the unknown islands', a concept mirrored exactly in the eleventh-century *Translatio Severi*, which stated that they came 'from the most remote northern islands of the sea'.[34] Beyond these geographical introductions, Norman and Frankish writers displayed little curiosity or imagination when it came

---

subegit nec cujuslibet manibus, gratia servitii, manus suas commendando commisit. Qui Daciae regnum pene universum possidens, affines Daciae et Alaniae terras sibi vindicavit, populosque sibi praeliis quamplurimis vi et potestate subjugavit.'

[31] Christiansen, p. 26; Lair p. 142.

[32] Lair, p. 143; Ademar of Chabannes, *Chronicon*, ed. G. Waitz, *MGH*, *SS*, 4 (Hanover, 1891; repr. 1968), 106–48 (p. 127): 'omnisque eorum Normannorum, qui iuxta Frantiam inhabitaverant...'.

[33] *Anonymi Leidensis De Situ Orbis Libri Duo*, ed. Quadri; Lamb, 'Knowledge about the Scandinavian North'.

[34] *Vita Romani*, in F. Lifshitz, *The Norman Conquest of Pious Neustria: Historiographic Discourse and Saintly Relics, 684–1090* (Toronto, 1995), p. 250: 'gentem... ab extremis finibus maris et ignotis insulis'; trans. in F. Lifshitz, 'The dossier of Romanus of Rouen: The political uses of hagiographical texts' (unpublished doctoral thesis, Columbia University, 1988), p. 257; *Translatio Severi*, in *Texte français et latin des vies des Saints du diocèse de Coutances et Avranches avec des notions préliminaires et l'histoire*

to the Scandinavian homelands. This gave Dudo free rein to mould the Scandinavian past – including transposing it to a different location – to suit his broader narrative.

English views of Scandinavia, though rare, were characterized by the curiosity and imagination that Frankish views lacked. The Alfredian writer of the *Old English Orosius*, taking a very different approach from the Anonymous Leidensis, elaborated on Scandinavian geography by adding informed eyewitness accounts from northern travellers Ohthere and Wulfstan.[35] Ealdorman Æthelweard demonstrated both curiosity and imagination in his *Chronicon*: firstly, in his adaptations to the West Saxon genealogy, as discussed in the previous chapter, and then as he continued his claims to Danish ancestry in his version of the English origin myth. Like other versions, this late tenth-century adaptation of the Chronicle account of the *adventus saxonum* concentrated on Hengest as 'the first earl of the English people and their leader out of Germany'.[36] But Æthelweard elaborated some new aspects relating to English origins, developing an explicit and informed connection with Denmark.

Æthelweard seems to have adapted his genealogical information for its accuracy in relation to Scandinavian genealogy, or at least language. The names in Æthelweard's genealogy of Hengest and Horsa differ from those given by Bede: he amalgamated Bede's 'Wehta' and 'Witta', and inserted 'Withar', which corresponds to the Old Norse divine name *Viðarr*.[37] Similarly, in his pedigree of Æthelwulf, 'Bældæg' became 'Balder', or the Old Norse *Baldr*. Indeed, in the thirteenth century the Icelander Snorri Sturluson made the same change in the *Prose Edda*, identifying this figure in the genealogy as 'Beldegg, [whom] we call Baldr'.[38] Æthelweard's linguistic knowledge is also displayed in his sections on ninth- and tenth-century viking wars, in which he improved on the Anglo-Saxon Chronicle's forms of Old Norse personal and place names.[39] However, the inclusion of Withar (for *Viðarr*) and Balder suggests Æthelweard's familiarity with Scandinavian religion as well. The

---

des Reliques de chaque Saint, ed. E. A. Pigeon, 2 vols. (Avranches, 1892–98), II, 56–77 (p. 56): 'a remotis septentrionalibus maris insulis'.

[35] *The Old English Orosius*, ed. J. Bately, EETS, ss, 6 (London, 1980), pp. 13–18. Valtonen, *The North in the* Old English Orosius, pp. 256–7, 472.

[36] Æthelweard, p. 18: 'primus consul et dux de Germania... gentis Anglorum'; see Jezierski, 'Æthelweard redivivus', pp. 166–7 for Æthelweard's use of the origin myth to construct one English people.

[37] Æthelweard, pp. xx, 9, 18. Townend, *Language and History in Viking Age England*, pp. 121–7 demonstrates that Æthelweard used Scandinavian sources for these details.

[38] Æthelweard, pp. xxxvi, 33; Snorri Sturluson, *Edda: Prologue and Gylfaginning*, ed. A. Faulkes (London, 2nd edn 2005), p. 5: 'Beldegg, er vér kǫllum Baldr'; Snorri Sturluson, *The Prose Edda*, trans. J. Byock (London, 2005), p. 7.

[39] Townend, *Language and History in Viking Age England*, pp. 110–21.

equation of the Anglo-Saxon ancestors with Norse gods must have been suggested to him by their close relationship to Woden.

Indeed, Æthelweard was explicit about the nature of Woden, whose name he also improved to reflect Norse pronunciation.[40] Listing this name (*Vuothen*) in the genealogy of Hengest and Horsa, he did not speak of an ancient error, but referred to the beliefs of his Scandinavian contemporaries, stating that 'the heathen northern peoples are overwhelmed in so great a seduction that they worship [him] as a god to the present day, that is to say the Danes, Norwegians and also the Svebi'.[41] While the presence of Woden may have been a 'convention' for Bede, Æthelweard clearly connected the name with the Oðinn worshipped by Danish neighbours in England.[42] In his addition of these details, Æthelweard displayed his knowledge of contemporary Danish language and religion; it is noteworthy that he found the ancestral past of the English the most suitable place for its application.

Æthelweard's elaboration of the genealogies was matched by his elucidation of details in the Anglo-Saxon origin myth.[43] Again, he related the details of the Anglo-Saxons' distant past to contemporary Danes. Æthelweard added nothing to Bede's explanation of the land of Old Saxony, even though he was writing to a Saxon relative, Matilda. Rather, he preferred to focus on 'Anglia uetus', the original home of the Angles, which he located among the Danes. As in his versions of the genealogies, Æthelweard displayed his familiarity with the language of the Danes by including Danish place-names; he explained that 'Anglia uetus' 'has as its capital the town known in the Saxon language as Schleswig, but by the Danes as Hedeby'.[44] This familiarity appears to have come through contact with the Danes; the other example of such an association being drawn with the lands around Hedeby is in the reported account of Ohthere the Dane's travels in the *Old English Orosius*.[45] Æthelweard, however, alluded to what 'the common people say', rather than copying from Ohthere.[46] In this passage, Æthelweard not only displayed a

---

[40] Townend, *Language and History in Viking Age England*, p. 122.

[41] Æthelweard, p. 9: 'In tanta etenim seductione oppressi aquilonales increduli ut deum colunt usque in hodiernam diem, viz. Dani, Northmanni quoque, et Sueui.'

[42] Dumville, 'Kingship, Genealogies and Regnal Lists', p. 79, described Bede's use of Woden as merely a 'convention'. On Æthelweard's interest in Woden, see A. Meaney, 'Æthelweard, Ælfric, the Norse Gods and Northumbria', *Journal of Religious History* 6 (1970), 105–32 (pp. 105–8).

[43] For further adaptations made by Æthelweard to the Anglo-Saxon origin myth, see Gretsch, 'Historiography and Literary Patronage', pp. 218–29.

[44] Æthelweard, p. 9: 'Porro Anglia uetus... habens oppidum capitale, quod sermone Saxonico Slesuuic nuncupatur, secundum uero Danos, Haithaby'. Townend, *Language and History in Viking Age England*, p. 119.

[45] *Old English Orosius*, ed. Bately, p. 16: 'on þæm landum eardodon Engle, ær hi hider on land coman'. Although they appear to be Ohthere's own words, it seems most likely that this was an addition from the English scribe/recorder.

[46] Æthelweard, pp. 7, 9: 'quae nunc uulgo...nuncupatur'.

familiarity with the area that had not been present in any previous account of Anglo-Saxon origins, but actually changed Bede's narrative in a small but significant way. Bede had claimed that the old land of the Angles had been deserted from the migration up to the present day, thus depicting a wholesale migration of an entire people. Æthelweard, on the other hand, omitted this passage and displayed its falsity by relating the contemporary names for its capital – which was, of course, a busy emporium during the Viking Age. In doing so, he revealed that the land of 'Anglia uetus' was not deserted by the migration, but remained a site of continued activity. This raised the suggestion that those currently living in 'Anglia uetus' were related to the pre-migration Angles.

Æthelweard used both terms *Angli* and *Saxones* for his pre-migration ancestors so that, in a connected passage, he made this area the domain also of the Saxons.[47] The Britons are said to have asked the Saxons for help because 'they had heard that in those days the nation of the Saxons was active in piracy in the whole coastal stretch from the river Rhine to Donia, which is now called Denmark by the common people...'.[48] Again, the link with the homeland of the Danes was reinforced. The similarity went even further than this: the behaviour of the Anglo-Saxons in this distant past was essentially the same as that of the vikings: they were 'active in piracy' ('esse piratico in opere') in those times, a phrase we might equally associate with Danish vikings (and indeed *piraticus* was a common description).[49]

In an earlier period, before the Viking Age, the Anglo-Saxon origin myth had stimulated a feeling of relationship with the continental Saxons. This manifested itself in missions to the still-pagan Saxons, notably the mission of Boniface. In one of his letters of 738, Boniface appealed to the Anglo-Saxons to pray for the conversion of the continental Saxons. They should be concerned, he stated, because they derived from the same origin as the Saxons: 'Have pity on them, because their repeated cry is: "We are of one and the same blood and bone".'[50] Just as Ermold the Black had claimed that Louis the Pious was moved to convert the Danes because of their relationship to the Franks, so

---

[47] Ashley, 'Lay Intellectual', pp. 231–2, argues that Æthelweard used 'Angli' to denote the converted 'Saxon' people, which would suggest the importance of conversion in the ethnogenesis of the English. Gretsch, 'Historiography and Literary Patronage', p. 237 suggests that Æthelweard's preference for 'Angli' avoided confusion with the continental Saxons.

[48] Æthelweard, p. 7: 'Nam illis diebus agilem audierunt esse piratico in opere gentem Saxonum in tota maritima a Rheno fluuio usque in Doniam urbem, quae nunc uulgo Danmarc nuncupatur...'

[49] E.g. Æthelweard, pp. 45, 50.

[50] *The Anglo-Saxon Missionaries in Germany...*, trans. C. H. Talbot (London, 1954), p. 96; *Die Briefe des heiligen Bonifatius und Lullus*, ed. M. Tangl, MGH, Epp. sel., 1 (Berlin, 1916), p. 75: 'Miseremini illorum, quia et ipsi solent dicere: "De uno sanguine et de uno osse sumus"'.

Boniface saw common ancestry as a stimulus to conversion.[51] But by the later tenth century, this relationship was no longer being emphasized in the same way. Æthelweard's *Chronicon* is one place where we might expect to find it retained, given his Saxon recipient, but he barely alludes to their common origin in this respect.[52] He may have been aware of the varied Saxon narratives of origins which, in the ninth and tenth centuries, gave different accounts of their relationship to the English.[53] As the belief in a special mission to their Saxon cousins was no longer relevant, a similar belief in the need to evangelize the Danes may have arisen. We have little comparable written evidence for English mission to Scandinavia in the tenth and eleventh centuries, although it is apparent that it did happen.[54] The perceived relationship with the Danes may be one explanation for this missionary activity.

Æthelweard's claim to Danish origins may also have related to a more general interest in the Danish heroic past among English elites in the late tenth century. We have already encountered *Beowulf*, the only extant manuscript of which was copied around the year 1000. There are other hints that tales of Danish heroes were fashionable at the time. Most intriguing is a fragment of a frieze from the Old Minster, Winchester, which appears to show a scene from the story of Sigmund, now known from the saga of the Volsungs (see Plate 1). The stone relief carving seems to show parts of two scenes. On the left stands a man in mail armour and with a straight sword. On the right is a bound man, lying on his back with a wolf pressing down upon him. The wolf's head is directly in his face, and the wolf's tongue is clearly depicted entering the man's mouth. This scene bears striking resemblance to an episode in which Sigmund, bound in stocks, freed himself by biting the tongue from a wolf which was mauling him. Martin Biddle suggested that the fragment originally formed part of a longer frieze narrative, perhaps recounting the saga to

---

[51] See above, pp. 41–2.

[52] On connections between England and Ottonian Saxony in the tenth century, see K. Leyser, 'The Ottonians and Wessex', in K. Leyser, *Communications and Power in Medieval Europe: The Carolingian and Ottonian Centuries*, ed. T. Reuter (London and Rio Grande, 1994), pp. 73–104. However, the arguments I put forward here stand in contrast to Leyser's view of Æthelweard's *Chronicon*, which he described as an expression of 'community' between Anglo-Saxons and Old Saxons (p. 84). Yet, as explored above, Æthelweard specified that he presented the English side of Matilda's family in distinction from her Saxon ancestors and he rewrote the origin myth to omit Saxon ancestry.

[53] I. Wood, 'Beyond Satraps and Ostriches: Political and Social Structures of the Saxons in the Early Carolingian Period', in *The Continental Saxons from the Migration Period to the Tenth Century: An Ethnographic Perspective*, ed. D. Green and F. Siegmund (Woodbridge, 2003), pp. 271–90 (pp. 280–4); on Æthelweard's knowledge of Widukind of Corvey's *Deeds of the Saxons*, see van Houts, 'Women and the Writing of History', p. 65.

[54] L. Abrams, 'The Anglo-Saxons and the Christianization of Scandinavia', *ASE* 24 (1995), 213–49, esp. p. 216.

Plate 1. Fragment of stone frieze from Winchester Old Minster: Winchester Cathedral CG WS 98. Photo © Dr John Crook (www.john-crook.com) / Winchester Excavations Committee.

a greater extent. The dates within which the sculpture can be placed are *c*. 980 to 1093.[55] Biddle suggested that the reign of Cnut is the most likely context for the frieze's commission, given its Danish subject matter.[56] However, the rebuilding of the Old Minster, especially the work on the east end in 980–94, where the frieze was situated, is most likely on archaeological grounds. Such an early dating for this sculpture would reinforce the impression Æthelweard gives of an emphasis on the shared cultural heritage of English and Danes, cultivated in the West Saxons' heartland. Moreover, the saga of the Volsungs, including one representation of this same episode, appears less ambiguously on tenth-century stone sculpture from Scandinavian settlement areas in northern England.[57] The evidence of stone sculpture may thus suggest that the popularity of Danish heroic narrative in Wessex derived from communication with Scandinavian settlers and their descendants.

Æthelweard's *Chronicon* reflects a tenth-century view of the Anglo-Saxons' and the Danes' shared origins. As discussed in the previous chapter, this connection was created in genealogies produced for Alfred, who made a treaty with Guthrum and faced other Danish rulers in the North and Midlands, in order to reflect desired political relationships. Æthelweard elaborated the connection, which he applied to himself as well as the royal house, when it became politically relevant once again. He would certainly have identified some, if not all, of the viking attackers of the late tenth century as Danes. But Æthelweard may also have identified a Danish element in the existing population of England, particularly in the regions of Northumbria and East Anglia. His generalization of the Danish connection in the origin myth, which applied to the whole people, suggests that the Danish and Anglo-Saxon populations within England had come to be perceived as different branches of the same ethnic group. However, the viewpoint was more nuanced than this. The Danes of Æthelweard's time were equated not with contemporary English people, but with the Anglo-Saxons of the distant, pre-migration past. They behaved as pirates, and they had not undergone the civilising process of Christianity. In this way, the view of the Danes we find in Æthelweard's *Chronicon* is similar to that of evolutionary anthropology viewing supposedly 'primitive' peoples as 'contemporary ancestors'.[58] This attitude has been

---

[55] The style, which has been described as 'Romanesque', would suggest later; however, the archaeological context constitutes a more objective means of dating.

[56] M. Biddle, 'Excavations at Winchester, 1965', *Antiquaries Journal* 46 (1966), 308–32 (pp. 329–32); M. Biddle, 'Narrative Frieze', in *The Golden Age of Anglo-Saxon Art, 966–1066*, ed. J. Backhouse, D. H. Turner and L. Webster (London, 1984), pp. 133–5. L. Kopár, *Gods and Settlers: The Iconography of Norse Mythology in Anglo-Scandinavian Sculpture* (Turnhout, 2012), pp. 47–51 is highly sceptical of a pre-Conquest dating for this sculpture: she surveys alternative readings.

[57] Kopár, *Gods and Settlers*, pp. 23–56 (pp. 44–5 for the possible Sigmund and the wolf scene).

[58] A view which was frequently accompanied by a missionary impulse similar to

frequently overlooked because it is often retained in modern historians' discussions of 'pre-Christian' society.

The essential distinguishing factors in Æthelweard's presentation of English and Danes were twofold: settlement in Britain, and conversion to Christianity. Migration had begun the Anglo-Saxon process of ethnogenesis, but it was conversion to Christianity that had cohered them as one people, and characterized the key distinction that Æthelweard observed between contemporary English and Danes. Æthelweard repeatedly emphasized this distinction by referring to viking forces as *pagani* and *barbari* throughout his *Chronicon*.[59] He referred quite explicitly to Scandinavian paganism in his description of Woden, and actually equated such belief with named 'northern peoples' (*aquilonales*). In this respect it is noteworthy that Æthelweard, when reporting Guthrum's death, referred to him as 'Borealium rex Anglorum', which Campbell translates as 'king of the Scandinavian English'.[60] In Æthelweard's eyes, Guthrum and his men seem to have gained membership of the English people, albeit as a distinct group. The details which follow suggest why Æthelweard labelled Guthrum in this way, distinct from the other *pagani* and *barbari*. Firstly, Æthelweard's perception related to Guthrum's rule over part of England, East Anglia, whereby he became a migrant rather than a pirate. Secondly and even more importantly, Guthrum had converted to Christianity. Æthelweard reiterated the details of Guthrum's baptism: he had gained an English name (Æthelstan) from his English godparent (Alfred). At the same time as taking on these new ethnic signifiers, it seems, Æthelweard considered that Guthrum had taken on a new English identity. However, he gave no hint that this process operated among any other Scandinavians in England.

In Normandy, Dudo also emphasized the pagan religion and gods of the vikings and used conversion as a means of ethnic transition. He described graphically how they blessed their voyages by 'making [human] sacrifices in honour of their god Thor'.[61] While Scandinavian and viking heritage separated the Normans from the Franks, and at the same time made them distant relatives, a pagan identity would not allow them to integrate within a Frankish political community as equals. The Normans were now Christians, too, and their conversion formed the second part of Dudo's narrative of ethnogenesis.

---

that of Boniface and Ermold: e.g. C. Young, *Contemporary Ancestors: A Beginner's Anthropology for District Officers in Africa* (London, 1940).

[59] When referring specifically to vikings, Æthelweard used *Dani* 14 times, *barbari* 32 times and *pagani* 17 times.

[60] Æthelweard, p. 47.

[61] Christiansen, pp. 15–16; Lair, pp. 129–30: 'sacrificabant olim venerantes Thur, Deum suum'.

Viking myths

In order to separate the Normans from their pagan Danish ancestors, Dudo included a further origin myth in the form of a vision received by Rollo during his viking years. The vision bears the weight of an origin myth throughout Dudo's history, and this was the passage which later historians seized upon to fulfil this function in their own works. Rollo's prophetic dream vividly presented his destiny:

> ...and one night, while sleep was gently creeping over his drowsy limbs from the jaws of Lethe, he seemed to behold himself placed on a mountain, far higher than the highest, in a Frankish dwelling. And on the summit of this mountain he saw a spring of sweet-smelling water flowing, and himself washing in it, and by it made whole from the contagion of leprosy and the itch, with which he was infected; and finally, while he was still staying on top of that mountain, he saw about the base of it many thousands of birds of different kinds and various colours, but with red left wings, extending in such numbers and so far and so wide that he could not catch sight of where they ended, however hard he looked. And they went one after the other in harmonious incoming flights and sought the spring on the mountain, and washed themselves, swimming together as they do when rain is coming; and when they had all been anointed by this miraculous dipping, they all ate together in a suitable place, without being separated into genera or species, and without any disagreement or dispute, as if they were friends sharing food. And they carried off twigs and worked rapidly to build nests; and furthermore, they willingly yielded to his command, in the vision.[62]

Dudo immediately followed the dream with an explanation of its meaning. Only a Christian prisoner (who was 'tinged with a divinely inspired foreknowledge') was able to interpret it.[63] Dudo seems to have been inspired by the interpretation of dreams by Joseph in the Bible, and also the vision of

---

[62] Christiansen, pp. 29–30; Lair, p. 146: '...quadam nocte, soporifera lethei malis quiete per membra leniter serpente, videre videbatur praecellentissimis quodam praecelsiore Franciscae habitationis monte se positum: ejusque montis in cacumine fontem liquidum et odoriferum, seque in eo ablui et ab eo expiari contagione leprae et prurigine contaminatum; denique illius montis cacumine adhuc superstes, circa basim illius hinc inde et altrinsecus, multa millia avium diversorum generum, varii coloris, sinistras alas quin etiam rubicundas habentium, quarum diffusae longe lateque multitudinis inexhaustam extremitatem perspicaci et angustato obtutu non poterat comprehendere; caeterum congruenti incessu atque volatu eas sibi alternis vicibus invicem cedentes, fontem montis petere, easque se convenienti natatione sicuti solent tempore futurae pluviae abluere, omnibusque mira infusione delibutis, congrua eas statione sine discretione generum et specierum, sine ullo contentionis jurgio, mutuo vicissim pastu quasi amicabiliter comedere; easque deportatis ramusculis festinanti labore nidificare: quin etiam suae visionis imperio voluntarie succumbere'.

[63] Christiansen, p. 30; Lair, p. 146: 'praesagioque divinae inspirationis aspersus'.

Constantine.[64] The latter was particularly relevant as a prophecy of imperial power and military victory. Constantine's vision of being cleansed from leprosy was employed in the Donation of Constantine to symbolize the emperor's baptism, and so it symbolized Rollo's baptism in the *De moribus*.[65]

The symbols in the dream were explained by the Christian prisoner. Much of the dream concerned the achievements of Rollo and his successors in building a new Church from the pagans they would convert, and in restoring 'devastated cities'.[66] These aspects drove Rollo to strive for such goals throughout the book. But the other aspect of his greatness, that 'men of different kingdoms will kneel down to serve you', is of particular relevance to the formation of the Norman people.[67] For this is what was signified by the birds who ate together 'without being separated into genera or species'. The Normans, the dream prophesied, were a people made up of many others. Their unifying feature was allegiance to one leader, to Rollo and afterwards his descendants. From this dream onwards, therefore, the definition and fate of the Norman people was aligned to the fate of this one dynasty.

There is no recorded tradition of Rollo's dream before Dudo's text was written. Although this could be because of the sparse historical record coming from tenth-century Normandy, it has the mark of being Dudo's creation. The symbols and their explanations were derived from literary models. Moreover, the dream is typical of the *De moribus*. In the previous chapter, Dudo used a dream to instruct Rollo to go to England.[68] This dream was also interpreted by a Christian as a prophecy of baptism. Although he generally used it in metrical passages, prophecy was a standard technique for Dudo in the *De moribus*.

Throughout the work, Dudo referred back to the dream to explain the trajectory of the Norman story. It was first used as a motivation for Rollo, keeping him on track towards his true purpose. When Rollo and his band seemed to be deviating from the future for which readers knew he should be aiming, Dudo reassured them that 'he still remembered the vision that

---

[64] V. Jordan, 'The Role of Kingship in Tenth-Century Normandy: Hagiography of Dudo of Saint Quentin', *HSJ* 3 (1991), 53–62 (p. 54).

[65] Christiansen, p. 188, n. 134. *Constitutum Constantini*, ed. H. Fuhrmann, *MGH*, Fontes iuris, 10 (Hanover, 1968), 69–74; trans. in *Carolingian Civilization: A Reader*, ed. P. Dutton (Peterborough, Ont., 1993), pp. 13–19. The link with the Donation of Constantine is discussed in B. Pohl, 'Translatio imperii Constantini ad Normannos: Constantine the Great as a possible model for the depiction of Rollo in Dudo of St. Quentin's *Historia Normannorum*', *Millennium: Yearbook on the Culture and History of the First Millennium* 9 (2012), 297–339 (pp. 320–6), and Pohl, *Dudo's* Historia Normannorum, pp. 212–13. See P. Dutton, *The Politics of Dreaming in the Carolingian Empire* (Lincoln and London, 1994), p. 37.

[66] Christiansen, p. 30; Lair, p. 146: 'vastatarum urbium [moenia]'.

[67] Christiansen, p. 30; Lair, p. 147: 'tibi homines diversorum regnorum serviendo accubitati obedient'.

[68] Christiansen, pp. 28–9; Lair, pp. 144–5.

had told him to set out for Francia'.[69] It continued to be a signpost, as Dudo connected Rouen with 'the mount of the church, where you saw yourself joyful'.[70] And he even made Rollo's men, all fully aware of the dream, become participants in its unravelling, knowingly placing in their mouths the suggestion that 'perhaps the interpretation of your vision directs us to this very country'.[71]

The importance of the dream is demonstrated by its reappearance at the end of the work, which firmly established it as the root of dynastic and Christian power in Normandy. When chronicling Duke Richard I's admirable qualities and actions towards the Church, Dudo reminded his readers of the journey that brought them here. Once again, the prophetic dream was presented as a motivation. Richard saw that he should build an even greater church at Fécamp, 'for this is the hill on which my grandfather saw himself standing, through the salutary mystery of the holy vision'.[72] Moreover, Richard's knowledge of the vision implied that it had passed into oral family legend by this time. It was soon to be known much more widely.

For, although it is long, complex and full of unusual words and turns of phrase, the *De moribus* seems to have been popular. The work itself still exists, in various forms, in fourteen manuscripts, with a further known manuscript no longer extant.[73] Leah Shopkow has speculated that it was aimed at a Frankish audience, but Lars Boje Mortensen's suggestion that the *De moribus* was intended as a school text seems most convincing. Dudo even referred to the recipients of his book as 'Norman academies' and 'Frankish high-schools'.[74] We may thus imagine the work's first audience as broadly clerical, within and beyond the Norman borders. However, as Mortensen points out, clergy may well have provided access to a lay elite: it is clear that the ducal court – and perhaps their neighbouring nobles – constituted an important audience for Dudo's *De moribus*, particularly given Benjamin Pohl's suggestion that early copies were illuminated with narrative scenes.[75] Moreover, Dudo's history served as a base-text for future Norman historians

---

[69] Christiansen, p. 32; Lair, p. 148: 'memor semper visionis monentis ad Franciam proficisci'.

[70] Christiansen, p. 35; Lair, p. 153: 'En mons ecclesiae, quo te gaudere videbas'.

[71] Christiansen, p. 36; Lair, p. 153: 'Forsan interpretatio tuae visionis vertetur in finibus istis'.

[72] Christiansen, p. 165; Lair, p. 290: 'Hic namque mons est in quo meus avus se stantem... salutifero divinae visionis oraculo conspexit.'

[73] The manuscripts are described in Pohl, *Dudo's* Historia Normannorum, pp. 18–33, and discussed in detail pp. 34–108. This work supersedes G. Huisman, 'Notes on the Manuscript Tradition of Dudo of St Quentin's Gesta Normannorum', *ANS* 6 (1983), 122–35.

[74] Shopkow, 'Carolingian World'; Mortensen, 'Stylistic Choice in a Reborn Genre', pp. 100–1; Christiansen, p. 7; Lair p. 120: 'Northmannica... gymnasia'; 'scholis... Franciscis'.

[75] Pohl, *Dudo's* Historia Normannorum, pp. 166, 193–5.

including William of Jumièges, Orderic Vitalis and Robert of Torigni. William omitted the narrative of Rollo's dream, but referred to it in passing in a way that suggested it would be familiar to his readers; Robert reinstated the passage into his history.[76] Other historians also showed awareness of the episode. The mid-eleventh-century *Inventio et Miracula Sancti Vulfranni* reflects a strikingly similar idea of Rollo uniting diverse peoples into the Normans, although it does not refer directly to the vision.[77] The *Annals of St Neots*, composed in post-Norman Conquest England, retells the story of Rollo's dream in a new form, in which the birds are recast as bees.[78] These two texts raise the possibility that the narrative circulated beyond the written histories that survive: the significant divergences imply a knowledge of the episode, but rule out direct copying. They suggest, therefore, that the origin myth of Rollo's dream passed rapidly into oral circulation, just as Dudo's text implied.

However, the contexts of written transmission were significant to the enshrinement of the episode as an origin myth. A short history composed at the abbey of Fécamp before 1001, and discussed in greater detail in the next chapter, includes a passage of the *De moribus* referring to Rollo's vision.[79] This passage in the Fécamp Chronicle is valuable evidence for the early composition of the *De moribus*, and reveals the importance of the narrative's association with Fécamp abbey. Rollo's vision functioned not only as the origin myth of the Norman people, but also as an important episode in the history of the abbey, and thus benefited from an additional impetus to its promotion. The ducal relationship with the Norman Church, and with this abbey in particular, played a central role within the narrative and in its propagation.

No writer used England's viking past or the conversion of viking rulers in England in a comparable way; it seems that the dynastic patronage of the Norman dukes was an essential and distinctive factor in shaping Norman identity in this direction. In particular, it was the Normans' partnership with the Church, and commission of a cleric to write a Latin text, that ensured the

---

[76] *The Gesta Normannorum Ducum of William of Jumièges, Orderic Vitalis and Robert of Torigni*, ed. E. van Houts, 2 vols. (Oxford, 1992) includes six later adaptations, including that of Robert of Torigni, who added in passages of Dudo's text which William of Jumièges had omitted; William's comment is on p. 6: 'Sane genealogiam Rollonis... necnon somnium eius... ab hystorica serie desecui'; Robert's insertion of Dudo's account of the dream may be found at pp. 40–3.

[77] *Inventio et Miracula Sancti Vulfranni*, ed. J. Laporte, in *Mélanges. Documents publiés et annotés par Dom. J. Laporte et al.* 14th s. (Rouen, 1938), 1–87 (p. 27).

[78] *The Anglo-Saxon Chronicle: A Collaborative Edition: Volume 17. The Annals of St Neots with Vita Prima Sancti Neoti*, ed. D. Dumville and M. Lapidge (Cambridge, 1985), pp. 73–5.

[79] Arnoux, 'Before the *Gesta Normannorum*'; the text is edited at pp. 43–6.

long-term survival of this narrative. However, the Norman origin myth may also have circulated orally, particularly the story of Rollo's dream. It is worth considering, therefore, whether any now lost narratives were composed in England, particularly in areas ruled by Danes. Considering the complete absence of written evidence from ninth- and tenth-century Danish England, and the much more tenuous relationships of Anglo-Scandinavian rulers with ecclesiastical institutions, such narratives would have been composed and transmitted orally, within secular (or even pagan) milieux. Matthew Townend has argued for the composition of (now lost) skaldic poetry at Anglo-Scandinavian courts, which suggests one possible context.[80] Alternatively, existing inhabitants of these regions may have devised narratives to explain the presence of new rulers. Either way, we do not have contemporary textual evidence comparable to Dudo's *De moribus*.

Historical and literary texts composed after the Norman Conquest provide hints of alternative origin myths giving the Danes a more prestigious role.[81] Gaimar's *Estoire des Engleis*, an Anglo-Norman vernacular history, appears to record one such myth. Of course, this text, written in 1136–37, dates from much later than those we have been examining, but it may well have drawn on regional traditions from the East Midlands.[82] Although much of Gaimar's narrative was derived from written sources such as the Anglo-Saxon Chronicle and the *Life of Dunstan*, and indeed Geoffrey of Monmouth's *Historia regum Britanniae*, there are many elements that do not originate in a prior written source. The *Estoire des Engleis* gave the Danes a pre-history in northern and eastern England, including the story of Haveloc, who became king of both Denmark and parts of England. Gaimar situated his version of this narrative, which is found elsewhere in parallel but independent sources, in Arthurian Britain.[83] As such, it is a witness to local Lincolnshire legends that provided a pseudo-historical explanation for the regional presence of Danes in positions of power.

Gaimar justified the viking raids on England by presenting the Danes as holding a prior claim. Adapting the Anglo-Saxon Chronicle's account of the first viking raid on Portland, he stated:

> They [the Danes] then returned home and enlisted their allies with the intention of coming to Britain to seize the island from the English, for they

---

[80] Townend, 'Whatever Happened to York Viking Poetry?'.

[81] On the range of (later) medieval narratives relating to Danish rights to rule in England, see E. C. Parker, 'Anglo-Scandinavian Literature and the Post-Conquest Period' (unpublished D.Phil. thesis, University of Oxford, 2013), pp. 160–71.

[82] E. Parker, '*Havelok* and the Danes in England: History, Legend, and Romance', *The Review of English Studies* ns 67 (2016), 428–47 (pp. 430, 446).

[83] S. Kleinman, 'The Legend of Havelok the Dane and the Historiography of East Anglia', *Studies in Philology* 100 (2003), 245–77; the different versions are summarized in *Havelok*, ed. G. V. Smithers (Oxford, 1987), pp. xvi–xxxiv.

had reached the decision, between them, and claimed that this country was part of their heritage, and that many of their ancestors had established an inheritance claim before any English had even arrived or before anyone from Saxony came to live there. King Danr, who was born in Denmark, had ruled over the kingdom, as had Adelbricht and Haveloc, and they named others who had done so. It was on this basis that they claimed it to be true that Britain was their rightful inheritance.[84]

The reference to a King Danr is particularly suggestive, since this figure is only known from Danish sources.[85] Gaimar therefore seems to have used a combination of English historical texts, local oral tradition, and possibly Danish information (perhaps mediated through English informants) to create his own narrative of Danish priority. Later in the work, Gaimar used these narrative elements to argue against the importance of Cerdic. He reported that Cnut negotiated with Edmund Ironside by subverting the well-established West Saxon origin myth:

> Our Danish ancestors, I'll have you know, have been ruling here for a very long time. Almost a thousand years before king Cerdic came to the throne, Danr was king. Cerdic was your ancestor, and king Danr was mine. A Dane held the land in chief from God. It was Mordred who granted Cerdic his fief; he never held in chief, and your family is descended from him...[86]

This passage provided a very different view of Danish origins in England, located even further in the distant past. The precise extent to which Gaimar drew upon oral narratives and otherwise unrecorded traditions from the North-East is unknown, but the very existence of his alternative origin myth reminds us that written Anglo-Saxon accounts, although they presumed to represent all subjects, always emanated from political and ecclesiastical centres. Indeed, even this apparently oral narrative seems to have served the interests of King Cnut, although it is not clear whether these narratives were created or appropriated during his reign, or whether they were connected

---

[84] Geffrei Gaimar, *Estoire des Engleis*, ed. I. Short (Oxford, 2009), pp. 114–15, ll. 2071–86: 'Puis realerent en lur païs / si asemblerent lur amis; / en Bretaigne voldrent venir, / as Engleis la voldrent tolir / car entr'els eurent esgardé / e dit ke ço est lur herité / e mulz homes de lur linage / urent le regne en heritage / ainceis kë Engleis i entrast / ne home de Sessoigne i habitast: / li reis Danes tint le regnez, / ki de Denemarch[e] fu nez, / si fist Ailbrith e Haveloc, / e plus en nomerent ovoc, / purquai il distrent pur verité / Bretaigne ert lur dreit herite'.

[85] A. Bell, 'Gaimar's Early "Danish" Kings', *PMLA* 65 (1950), 601–40 (p. 630).

[86] Gaimar, *Estoire des Engleis*, ed. Short, pp. 234–7, ll. 4315–24: 'e bien sachez loi[n] gtenement / l'urent Daneis nostre parent / prés de mil anz l'out Dane aince[i]s / ke unc i entrast Certiz li reis. / Certiz, ço fu vostre ancïen, / e li reis Danes fu le mien. / Daneis le tint en chef de Deu, / Modret donat Certiz son feu: / il ne tint unkes chevalment, / de lui vindrent vostre parent'.

to Cnut at a later date.[87] While Cnut's skalds in the early eleventh century invoked the viking past of Ívarr as his precursor, the justification here is situated in a more distant past than the Viking Age. Gaimar's references to early Danish kings in England served the purpose of a legal claim to priority over the well-known Anglo-Saxon origin myth. The importance of descent from an original founding king remains unquestioned in Gaimar's text. Instead of the Viking Age, as employed by Dudo in Normandy, here an ancient claim and migration was still the basis of ethnic inheritance. The West Saxons may not have been completely successful in imposing the superiority of their dynasty over all, but the assumptions which underlay that claim, especially the centrality of royal ancestral descent, were accepted as a powerful source of identity and difference.

Conclusion

In their presentation of origin myths, Dudo and Æthelweard continued in the manner in which they had presented genealogies. Dudo drew primarily on those conventions which he encountered in his Frankish cathedral library, both in terms of topoi associated with origin myths and in his presentation of Scandinavia. Æthelweard, on the other hand, seems to have derived his information on Denmark, Old Norse language and religion from his Scandinavian contemporaries. Moreover, while Dudo's history stands basically alone in Francia and even in Normandy as evidence for interest in Scandinavia, Æthelweard's reimagining of Anglo-Saxon origins seems to have reflected a wider fashion for the Danish heroic past among Anglo-Saxon elites.

Both presented narratives of Scandinavian origins, but using different signs and stores of knowledge. The distinction between ethnic groups needed to be signified in a way that everyone involved could understand. In creating a genealogy and origin myth, a Viking Age scholar drew upon those traditions that had relevance for his or her audience, rather than completing a checklist of cultural attributes. Here the distinction between ethnic boundary and cultural content delineated by the anthropologist Frederik Barth is useful. Barth's approach reoriented the focus of intergroup relations on the 'ethnic *boundary* that defines the group, not the cultural stuff that it encloses'.[88] The 'cultural stuff' used by Æthelweard did derive from Old Norse language and culture, because he presented Scandinavian origins as a point of connection between English and Dane, in a context where such signifiers would have been recognized. Dudo, conversely, used the 'cultural stuff' of learned Latin geography and cosmography to make a similar claim to Scandinavian

---

[87] *Havelok*, ed. Smithers, p. lvii.

[88] F. Barth, 'Introduction', in *Ethnic Groups and Boundaries: The Social Organization of Culture Difference*, ed. F. Barth (London, 1969; reissued 1998), pp. 9–38 (p. 15).

ethnicity, because his audience was familiar with that material. Dudo's employment of Scandinavian ethnicity served to distinguish the ethnic boundary between Normans and Franks, rather than creating a connection as Æthelweard had done.

Both Dudo and Æthelweard therefore required a further element to create ethnic boundaries between Scandinavians in general, and the specific peoples they described. Christianity served this essential function in both Æthelweard's and Dudo's myths of origins. In both cases, it was conversion to Christianity that distinguished the people (English or Normans respectively) from the Danes. These narratives demonstrate the intertwined understanding of ethnicity and religion in this period. Origin myths were two-stage processes, involving both migration and conversion in order that a new people would emerge. Moreover, in the Norman myth of origins in particular, Christian obedience was equated with allegiance to the ruler.

Our vision of these origin myths and their significance is complicated by the possibility of co-existing and interacting oral narratives. Yet, in general, it is apparent that for an origin myth to successfully shape perceptions of ethnic relations it needed elite backing. Only the patronage of the wealthy and powerful could provide the resources required for the production and control of these ethnic narratives, generally through their canonisation in written texts and dissemination through ecclesiastical networks. Formalisation in verse by a court skald would have provided an alternative, but little evidence of such activities from these contexts now remains.

The role of elites in cultivating origin myths and genealogy thus derived in large part from their dominance of cultural production in general. Moreover, their influence – as patrons and sponsors even more than as creators – is visible in the roles given to English kings and Norman dukes within these ethnic narratives. The founders of Anglo-Saxon dynasties, such as Hengest and Horsa, or Cerdic and Cynric, were kings who stood for the people as a whole. Similarly, in Dudo's account of Rollo's dream, it was primarily allegiance to the viking leader and his dynasty that actually constituted Norman identity. The role of elites, and rulers in particular, in identity formation is a thread that will continue to be relevant throughout the following chapters.

Moreover, in the texts examined so far, there is a clear distinction between Norman engagement with the recent viking past and the preference of Anglo-Saxon writers for locating Scandinavian heritage far back in remote generations and distant origins. Nevertheless, writers did address the English experience of the First Viking Age in historical writing. The next chapter compares how writers in England and Normandy presented the recent past of viking invasion and Scandinavian settlement. In both regions, this past was interpreted primarily by monastic or clerical writers at institutions patronized by English and Norman rulers: thus we shall continue to explore the key issues of Christian identity and the role of ruling families.

3

Hagiography I: Ruin and Restoration

This chapter and the next explore how inhabitants of England and Normandy in the tenth and early eleventh centuries perceived the recent viking past. During this period, historians and hagiographers looked back on the viking raids and wars which afflicted Francia and England in the ninth century, and the subsequent Scandinavian conquest and settlement of certain regions. Writers imposed their own interpretations on the earlier conflicts and, as these chapters will demonstrate, dominant narratives emerged in England and Normandy respectively. This chapter investigates the creation and dissemination of these dominant narratives, exemplified in England by two texts describing the martyrdom of St Edmund, and in Normandy by the Fécamp Chronicle, which was closely linked to Dudo's *De moribus*. The English vision of the viking past presented a conflict between Christian Anglo-Saxons and pagan vikings, with solely temporary effects. In Normandy, on the other hand, Christianity was seen to transform viking conquerors and unite them with local people. Investigation of earlier evidence for the cults of St Edmund in England and St Romanus in Normandy, however, suggests that the establishment of these narratives replaced alternative visions of the viking past. Rather than being witnesses to dramatically different events, the dominant narratives responded to contemporary ethnic relations in England and Normandy around the year 1000.

Furthermore, despite the different narratives that emerged either side of the Channel, these texts reflect remarkably similar contexts of literary production. Firstly, it is noteworthy that, in both regions, interpretations of the viking past predominantly emerged in hagiographical texts (the Fécamp Chronicle, as explained below, is in part a compilation of hagiographies). Framing the events described within this genre had the effect of attributing moral and supernatural significance to interactions between vikings and others. The explanation for this, however, most properly resides in the fact that, leaving aside the 'official' histories of the Anglo-Saxon Chronicle and Dudo's *De moribus*, hagiography was the primary means of literary and historical composition in the tenth and early eleventh centuries in both England and Normandy.[1] This brings us to a second point, which is that these texts were composed in or for monastic institutions, often recently reformed, founded

---

[1] A. Gransden, *Historical Writing in England c. 550 to c. 1307* (London, 1974), pp. 67–9, 78–87.

or refounded. Many were participants in the wider tenth-century movement for monastic reform; at its broadest, this movement can be seen to include the re-establishment of ecclesiastical institutions after the disruptions of the Viking Age, even if these houses were not always conformed to monastic discipline. As a result, these communities were particularly interested in their institutions' histories, partly as a means of justifying reform and partly as a focus for constructing their own communal identities. Such interests led to the increased production in hagiography, and the perceived relevance of the viking past within such narratives.

While the similarities of these contexts in England and Normandy explain the comparability of the texts explored in this chapter and the next, the roles played by vikings in their narratives differed considerably. Hagiography provided a powerful framework and a persuasive instrument for shaping ethnic relations, but it was flexible to the requirements of different perspectives and interests, which varied with changing political and social contexts.

England: St Edmund

The recent past of viking invasion remained a potent memory in tenth-century England. However, it was not until the last quarter of the century that new histories of the period were produced.[2] The Anglo-Saxon Chronicle continued to record contemporary events, but much more sparsely and unevenly, particularly from the middle of the century. The ninth-century Chronicle's terse record of events remained the standard narrative of viking history, and formed the basis of many later accounts, such as Æthelweard's *Chronicon*.[3] These accounts elaborated the Chronicle's bare details with new interpretations of the viking conflicts and their effects.

The ninth-century annals in the Anglo-Saxon Chronicle focused overwhelmingly on conflict with the viking armies. Even though the chroniclers were working in the midst of viking attack, they described the actions of their enemies in terms of facts, not invective. As Alice Jorgensen has shown, a formula emerged in the Chronicle for the description of conflict with the vikings, so that in each case the same information was replicated: how many ships arrived, where the battle was fought, who was killed, and

---

[2] On the background to this textual production, and the creation of a common past, see S. Foot, 'Remembering, Forgetting and Inventing: Attitudes to the Past in England at the End of the First Viking Age', *TRHS* 6th s. 9 (1999), 185–200.

[3] Many of the surviving manuscripts of the Chronicle were made during the tenth or early eleventh century: MS A was updated throughout the tenth century; MS B probably copied 977–79; MS G copied between 1001 and 1013. See introductions in *The Anglo-Saxon Chronicles*, trans. by M. Swanton (London, 1996; rev. ed. 2000), and the various volumes of *The Anglo-Saxon Chronicle: A Collaborative Edition*, ed. D. Dumville and S. Keynes (Cambridge, 1983–).

who 'controlled the battlefield' ('wælstowe geweald').[4] Sometimes, the ninth-century chroniclers sought to downplay the threat posed by the vikings, in contrast to their later successors. The section of the Chronicle covering the years 892/93 to 896, which was originally written as one text,[5] minimized the effects of the viking armies on the English people:

> The raiding-army, by the grace of God, had not altogether utterly crushed the English race; but they were a great deal more crushed in those three years with pestilence among cattle and men, most of all by the fact that many of the best of the king's thegns there were in the land passed away in those three years.[6]

Other contemporary texts from England, including those into which the voice and opinions of the author intrude further, were similarly understated. Asser, writing his biography of Alfred at the end of the ninth century, was more interested in the development of Alfred's character than military details. In fact, he apologized for his tendency to 'veer off course' ('circumferamur') when he paused in his main narrative to insert Chronicle passages.[7] Those who had experienced the conflicts of the ninth and early tenth centuries did not demonize their enemies, nor did they wish viking destruction to appear catastrophic for the English. Both of these trends developed with chronological distance from the events.

The main outlet for addressing the viking past in the tenth century, and the only place where we find original composition, was in hagiography. There was a considerable amount of hagiographical composition in the late tenth century, including the Lives of Oswald, Ecgwine, Swithun, Dunstan, Æthelwold, and Wulfstan, and the Passion of Æthelberht and Æthelred, not to mention the work of Ælfric. Yet there is very little reference to the Danes in any of these texts. England's viking past featured in the hagiographies of three saints, whose legends are examined in this and the following chapter. Often still using the Chronicle as a basis of historical evidence, hagiographers elaborated episodes of viking aggression and English response. These texts

---

[4] A. Cowen, 'Writing Fire and the Sword: The Perception and Representation of Violence in Viking Age England' (unpublished doctoral thesis, York University, 2004), p. 48; e.g. ASC E 837, 999.

[5] J. Bately, 'The Compilation of the Anglo-Saxon Chronicle Once More', *Leeds Studies in English* 16 (1985), 7–26 (pp. 12–18); C. Clark, 'The Narrative Mode of the Anglo-Saxon Chronicle before the Conquest', in *Words, Names and History: Selected Writings of Cecily Clark*, ed. P. Jackson (Cambridge, 1995), pp. 3–19 (8–10).

[6] ASC A 896: 'Næfde se here, Godes þonces, Angelcyn ealles forswiðe gebrocod, ac hie wæron micle swiþor gebrocede on þæm þrim gearum mid ceapes cwilde 7 monna, ealles swiþost mid þæm þæt manige þara selestena cynges þena þe þær on londe wæron forðferdon on þæm þrim gearum'.

[7] *Asser's Life of Alfred*, p. 19; *Alfred the Great*, ed. Keynes and Lapidge, p. 74.

produced a new and influential vision of the ninth-century conflicts, which transformed the events they described into ethnic conflicts.

Vikings played central roles in the pre-Conquest narratives of these three saints, which were all written in the mid- to late tenth century. They appeared as the killers of St Edmund of East Anglia, first in Abbo of Fleury's *Passio Sancti Eadmundi* and then in Ælfric's English version, The Life of St Edmund; the Cuthbertine community presented them as major actors in a number of St Cuthbert's posthumous miracles in the *Historia de Sancto Cuthberto*; and, finally, they featured in the anonymous *Vita Prima Sancti Neoti* and the (also anonymous) Old English Life of Saint Neot, which similarly involved posthumous interaction of the saint with the vikings. The cults of the latter two saints are investigated in the next chapter; here we shall concentrate on the most well-known and influential texts, those relating to St Edmund of East Anglia, who was killed by vikings in 869.

There were saints other than Edmund killed by vikings, but this death in itself did not guarantee holy status in England or in Francia. Vikings killed Bishop Baltfrid of Bayeux (858) and Bishop Lista of Coutances (890), among others, but they never became the recipients of hagiographical narratives or martyr-cults.[8] John Blair's handlist of Anglo-Saxon saints adds four more martyrs of the vikings to the list, but only two of these, Beocca and Edor of Chertsey, who may have been the recipients of a local cult, were killed in the ninth century.[9] The others, Ælfheah and Eadnoth, were victims of the raids of the early eleventh century.[10] The saintly qualifications of both were called into doubt later in the century, when the characterization of vikings as the natural enemy of Christianity was less accepted.[11] Lanfranc, doubting that the archbishop's refusal to pay a ransom really qualified him as martyr, had

---

[8] P. Bouet, 'Les Translations de Reliques en Normandie (IXe–XIIe siècles), in *Les Saints dans la Normandie médiévale. Colloque de Cerisy-la-Salle (26–29 septembre 1996)*, ed. P. Bouet and F. Neveux (Caen, 2000) pp. 97–108 (p. 108); D. Planavergne, 'Les Normands avant la Normandie: Les invasions scandinaves en Neustrie au IXe siècle dans l'hagiographie franque', in *Les fondations scandinaves en Occident*, ed. Bauduin, pp. 37–52 (pp. 50–1).

[9] J. Blair, 'A Handlist of Anglo-Saxon Saints', in *Local Saints and Local Churches in the Early Medieval West*, ed. A. Thacker and R. Sharpe (Oxford, 2002), pp. 495–565; J. Blair, 'The Chertsey Resting-Place List and the Enshrinement of Frithuwold', in *The Origins of Anglo-Saxon Kingdoms*, ed. S. Bassett (Leicester, 1989), pp. 231–6, cites a thirteenth-century Chertsey cartulary that he believes may indicate a continuing cult, revived by the invention of the relics by Æthelwold (963–84) – a similar period to the hagiographies examined here.

[10] Eadnoth (killed at Assandun, 1016): Blair, 'A Handlist of Anglo-Saxon Saints', pp. 528–9; Ælfheah (killed by his captors at Greenwich): ASC E 1011–1012.

[11] C. Fell, 'Edward King and Martyr and the Anglo-Saxon Hagiographic Tradition', in *Ethelred the Unready: Papers from the Millenary Conference*, ed. D. Hill (Oxford, 1978), pp. 1–13 (p. 8); *The Life of St Anselm by Eadmer*, ed. R. Southern (London, 1962), pp. 49–54.

to be convinced of Ælfheah's holiness. According to Anselm's biographer, Eadmer, he even stressed that it was 'the words of the English' which labelled the vikings as 'the pagan enemies of God'. Anselm managed to convince him, however, by explaining that by standing up to his 'pagan persecutors' and trying to convert them, Ælfheah acted as a witness of Christ.[12] Lanfranc then commissioned a Life of Ælfheah, which further justified his claim to martyrdom on more conventional grounds.[13] Of all the victims of the vikings, only Edmund was the recipient of pre-Conquest hagiography. As a result, his *Passio* and *Life* strongly influenced contemporary and subsequent views of the viking past.

As the earliest detailed description of vikings murdering an Anglo-Saxon saint, Abbo of Fleury's *Passio Sancti Eadmundi* exerted significant influence on later historians and hagiographers. Abbo's narrative may have contributed something to the Chronicle's account of Ælfheah's death, but its greatest impact came after the Conquest. Excerpts from Abbo's descriptions of the origins of vikings, the havoc they wreaked, and the nature of their crimes appear in several post-Conquest texts, including the *Liber Eliensis* and Hugh Candidus's Peterborough Chronicle.[14] Although borrowed by those writing history in the twelfth century, the authority of the *Passio* stemmed not only from its relative antiquity, but actually from its hagiographical nature. As the accepted account of a powerful and popular saint's martyrdom, the basic facts of its narrative had become unassailable.

Abbo's *Passio Sancti Eadmundi* placed the historical figures of King Edmund, the viking Hinguar and their followers within a hagiographical narrative framework for the first time. The text was composed at the request of the monks of Ramsey, where Abbo was a visiting teacher between 985 and 987.[15] The abbey was founded as a Benedictine house in 966 and, after Abbo's time there, it became a centre of historical production.[16] Gransden has suggested that Abbo wrote the *Passio* as a model hagiographical text

---

[12] *Life of St Anselm*, p. 51: 'ut verbis utar Anglorum'; 'inimici Dei pagani'; p. 52: 'paganis persecutoribus'.

[13] *Vita Elphegi* (BHL 2518–19), ed. D. van Papenbroeck, *AASS*, Apr. XIX (Antwerp, 1675), pp. 631–41.

[14] J. Barrow, 'Danish Ferocity and Abandoned Monasteries: The Twelfth-century View', in *The Long Twelfth-Century View of the Anglo-Saxon Past*, ed. M. Brett and D. A. Woodman (Aldershot, 2015), pp. 77–93 (pp. 83, 89, 93); *Liber Eliensis*, ed. E. O Blake (London, 1962), pp. 52–3; *The Chronicle of Hugh Candidus, a Monk of Peterborough*, ed. W. T. Mellows (London, 1949), pp. 22–4.

[15] M. Mostert, *The Political Theology of Abbo of Fleury* (Hilversum, 1987), pp. 40–5; R. Pinner, *The Cult of St Edmund in Medieval East Anglia* (Woodbridge, 2015), pp. 34–5.

[16] *Byrhtferth of Ramsey*, ed. Lapidge, p. xviii (see n. 13 for his refutation of the commonly used date 969). Abbo's pupil Byrhtferth produced a considerable number of historical works: pp. xxx–xliv.

for the monks of Ramsey.[17] As claimed in its preface, Abbo's text was the earliest testimony of Edmund's martyrdom, although it was composed over a century after Edmund's death in 869. There is evidence of local veneration in East Anglia soon after his death, and the cult centre was established at Bury St Edmunds.[18] Nevertheless, it was the monks of Ramsey who eventually commissioned his *Passio*. Abbo's preface, addressed to Dunstan, archbishop of Canterbury, makes it clear that the text was intended for a much wider audience than the people of East Anglia. If so, the intention was successful, as Edmund became widely venerated throughout England and the Continent.[19]

The *Passio Sancti Eadmundi*'s dedicatory letter explains that Abbo had been called upon to write the work when at Ramsey. He wrote that he had learned of the story from Dunstan, who in turn had heard it many years earlier, when Edmund's armour-bearer, an eyewitness, had recounted it in his old age to King Æthelstan. Abbo then described the arrival of the Anglo-Saxons in Britain (ch.1), and the landscape of East Anglia (ch.2), before focusing on King Edmund, whom he described as a Saxon (ch.3). Here, highlighting a theme he would return to throughout the text, Abbo presented Edmund as the perfect Christian ruler (ch.4).[20] Next, he introduced the Danes and their leader, Hinguar, and stated that they were sent by the devil to try the holy Edmund. Abbo took the opportunity to describe the evil characteristics and habits of the Danes, which were demonstrated through their activities in Britain (chs.5–6). The main scene of the martyrdom then begins. Abbo described how Hinguar sent his messenger to Edmund with the proposal that he should pay tribute and submit to him as a sub-king (ch.7). Edmund, after consulting with his bishop, sent back a messenger rejecting the offer (chs.8–9). At Hinguar's arrival, Edmund threw away his weapons, and was seized, before being tortured and shot with arrows. Perceiving that Edmund would not give up his faith, Hinguar ordered that he be executed (ch.10). The Danes departed, taking the king's head and throwing it into the forest to prevent an honourable burial (ch.11).

After the Danes had left, the few remaining Christians returned from hiding and sought to rejoin the head to the body. Edmund's head was miraculously enabled to talk, calling 'Here, here, here!' to draw them to it. The searchers found the head guarded by a wolf, whose hunger was held in

---

[17] A. Gransden, 'Abbo of Fleury's *Passio Sancti Eadmundi*', *Revue Benedictine* 105 (1995), 20–78 (p. 40).

[18] S. Ridyard, *The Royal Saints of Anglo-Saxon England* (Cambridge, 1988), pp. 211–33; A. Gransden, 'The Legends and Traditions Concerning the Origins of the Abbey of Bury St Edmunds', *EHR* 100 (1985), 1–24.

[19] A. Bale, 'Introduction: St Edmund's Medieval Lives', in *St Edmund, King and Martyr: Changing Images of a Medieval Saint*, ed. A. Bale (York, 2009), pp. 1–25 (p. 11).

[20] Mostert, *Political Theology*, explores Abbo's views in detail.

check by God (ch.12). After this, Abbo narrated Edmund's burial, followed by accounts of miracles demonstrating the sanctity of his body, most notably its incorruption (chs.13–17).[21]

The *Passio Eadmundi* placed viking invaders in the roles of villains characteristic of hagiography. In order to establish a saint's holiness, hagiographers made explicit and implicit parallels with established saints. The passions of the Roman martyrs, which delineated a struggle between Christians and pagans, were well known in tenth-century England and Francia, and the conventions of these narratives were employed to establish the sanctity of more recent holy men and women.[22] Accordingly, in order to present Edmund as a holy martyr, Abbo presented the saint in a similar situation and as endowed with similar characteristics to the Roman martyrs, while his enemies were made to resemble the persecutors of the early Christians. In the *Passio*, vikings are presented as persecutors, judges, executioners and tyrants, in descriptions that owed more to the trials of the early Roman martyrs than warfare in Anglo-Saxon England. For example, in the *gesta martyrum* the judge played an essential role in eliciting the confession of faith from the Christian.[23] In the *Passio Eadmundi*, the exchange of messengers and the ensuing torture deviated slightly from the conventional format, but functioned in the same way. Abbo recalled the *gesta martyrum* through the language of Roman law.[24] In the next section, Edmund was explicitly compared to Christ, while the 'tyrannus' Hinguar was called 'Pilatum praesidem'.[25] By transforming vikings into such hagiographic villains, Abbo's *Passio Sancti Eadmundi* opposed the pagan Scandinavians to the Christian English. Abbo depicted Edmund, the former king of East Anglia, as a martyr for the Christian faith. Edmund's qualities of Christian kingship were highlighted by the tyranny and impiety of his adversaries. To achieve this contrast, Abbo presented the war in which Edmund died as a religious conflict, and his enemies as demonic villains.

This characterization of Edmund's viking enemies was attributed to their ethnicity. Abbo's introduction established that the evil actions of Hinguar and his companions could be seen as representative of Danes more generally. He introduced Edmund's persecutors with a detailed explanation of what it meant to be a Dane:

---

[21] Abbo of Fleury, *Life of St Edmund* (hereafter Abbo).

[22] A. Thacker, 'In Search of Saints: the English Church and the Cult of Roman Apostles and Martyrs in the Seventh and Eighth Centuries', in *Early Medieval Rome and the Christian West. Essays in Honour of Donald A. Bullough*, ed. J. Smith (Leiden, 2000), pp. 247–77; C. Rauer, 'The Sources of the *Old English Martyrology*', *ASE* 32 (2003), 89–109.

[23] L. Grig, *Making Martyrs in Late Antiquity* (London, 2004), pp. 59–78 (esp. p. 69).

[24] E.g. Abbo, p. 77: 'forensibus causis intersunt'.

[25] Abbo, p. 78.

These, it is certain, are so cruel by their natural ferocity that they are unable to be softened by the ills of men: indeed, since people among them feed on human flesh...[26]

He thus presented evil as an intrinsic attribute of the vikings, although his description verged on denying them human status at all. This evil emerged from the Danes as natural and unchangeable, demonstrated and reinforced by wicked behaviour such as cannibalism.[27] Abbo stated that they came from a distant, foreign land in the north, which in itself was an explanation for their difference:

> ...since they came steeled with the cold of their own wickedness from that corner of the earth where he [Lucifer] placed his seat who, through elevation, desired to be equal to the Most High.[28]

This link with the devil was maintained throughout the *Passio*. Hinguar, Edmund's persecutor, in particular, and the Danes in general, were repeatedly referred to as the 'limbs' or 'ministers' of the devil.[29] Abbo only just stopped short of characterizing them as demons themselves. Instead, he emphasized the physical link with Satan, which made them innately predisposed to act maliciously. When Edmund addressed Hinguar with the words 'son of the devil, well do you imitate your father', the audience were reminded of inheritance through both nature and nurture. Abbo's words reinforced the moral implications of ancestry.[30]

The Danes' demonic inheritance resulted in paganism. Abbo made this, too, a function of their ethnic make-up, not a choice or an error. The

---

[26] Abbo, p. 72: 'quas certum est adeo crudeles esse naturali ferocitate ut nesciant malis hominum mitescere, quando-quidem quidam ex eis populi uescuntur humanis carnibus...'.

[27] Abbo refers to the Danes as *Antropofagi*, who were normally situated in the East, but Abbo's connection of Danes with Scythians might imply that this detail is ultimately derived from Pliny or Herodotus: the positioning of dog-headed cannibals in Scandinavia can be seen on the Hereford Mappa Mundi and in the ninth-century correspondence between Rimbert, missionary to the north, and Ratramnus of Corbie: see R. Bartlett, *The Natural and the Supernatural in the Middle Ages* (Cambridge, 2008), pp. 97–100. In medieval Europe, cannibalism was used to suggest the semi-human status of minority groups: B. Bildhauer, 'Blood, Jews and Monsters in Medieval Culture', in *The Monstrous Middle Ages*, ed. B. Bildhauer and R. Mills (Toronto, 2003), pp. 75–83; J. J. Cohen, *Hybridity, Identity and Monstrosity in Medieval Britain: On Difficult Middles* (New York and Basingstoke, 2006), pp. 139–73.

[28] Abbo, p. 71: 'Nec mirum, cum uenerint indurati frigore suae malitiae ab illo terrae uertice quo sedem suam posuit qui per elationem Altissimo similis esse concupiuit.' The significance of the far north in the Anglo-Saxon world is explored in Valtonen, *The North in the Old English Orosius*.

[29] Abbo, p. 71: 'unus ex suis membris' (in contrast, Edmund is 'membrum Christi', p. 78); p. 76: 'cuius sectator praecipuus'; p. 79: 'Dani, ministri diaboli'.

[30] Abbo, p. 76: 'Bene, filius diaboli patrem tuum imitaris'.

Northmen, he wrote, 'follow the Antichrist more than all other peoples' and, in consequence, were driven to behave as viking raiders against Christians: 'and most greatly the Danes, who, too close neighbours with the western regions, engage in piracy around them with frequent raids'.[31] Abbo went so far as to claim that the Danes sought to convert Christians to devil-worship: however, there is very little evidence that Danes did encourage others to take up their religion.[32] Later in the text, he approved the Christians' speculation that the Danes' actions sprang from their religious hatred of Christianity, 'that the worshippers of a foreign sect had hidden the head of the martyr out of malice to our faith'.[33] His statements served to emphasize the religious nature of the war between Christians and vikings.

The viking persecutors in the *Passio Eadmundi* were constructed in this extreme way in order to highlight the opposite qualities of their English victims. The primary purposes of the text, as a hagiography, were to convince of Edmund's sanctity, imbue him with the qualities of martyr and promote his cult more widely. Abbo also moulded Edmund as his ideal of Christian kingship.[34] Perhaps because it was intended as a model text, the vikings in the *Passio* were placed in several of the standard roles for hagiographical persecutors: they were in turns tyrants, judges and executioners. In contrast to each of these roles, Edmund was made to display the correct exercise of God-given power.

In pursuit of these goals, Abbo made Edmund a representative of the English people. This was conveyed by his concern for his subjects and his country. Edmund's speech to Hinguar's messenger outlined his qualities as king, chief of which was that he did not want to outlive his subjects and fail in his duty. Furthermore, the importance of the nation was tied to the land, as he exclaimed: 'if only those who presently lament living, lest they perish in bloody slaughter, might be preserved amid the sweet fields of their homeland, even if I should fall in death'.[35] Although Edmund had been king of East Anglia only, Abbo extended the significance of his words and sanctity to include all the English people. For Abbo, East Anglia was merely the

---

[31] Abbo, p. 72: '…quae antichristum, [ut legimus,] secuturae sunt ante omnes gentes…'; '…maxime Dani, occidentis regionibus nimium uicini, quoniam circa eas piratycam exercent frequentibus latrociniis'.

[32] Abbo, p. 72: 'ut absque ulla miseratione pascantur hominum cruciatibus qui caracterem bestiae noluerint circumferre in frontibus'; Coupland, 'The Rod of God's Wrath?', pp. 546–7.

[33] Abbo, p. 80: 'quod alienae sectae cultores, inuidendo nostrae fidei, sustullisent caput martyris'.

[34] Mostert, *Political Theology*, pp. 157, 165–7, 170–1, 173.

[35] Abbo, p. 75: 'Et utinam inpresentiarum uiuendo quique gemerent ne cruenta cede perirent, quatinus patriae dulcibus aruis, etiam me occumbente, superstites fierent…'

'orientalis pars' of a larger whole.[36] If Abbo gave the region any special identity in his geographical preface, it was as a wilderness that housed monastic communities like Ramsey, not as the home of a separate people.[37] Moreover, at no point does he refer to a distinct East Anglian people, but always to the *Angli*, and has Edmund present himself as the leader of 'Anglorum reipublicae'.[38] His version was not specific to East Anglia, but presented the region as one province in the unified land of the English people. Abbo glossed over the fact that East Anglia was a separate kingdom from Wessex and the rest of England – and this was done far more easily when Edmund was placed in opposition not to other English kings, but to 'a barbarian foreigner with drawn sword [who] threatens the old occupants of our kingdom'.[39]

In these depictions, Abbo appealed to the shared experience of Christians as victims of the vikings, 'as those who have experienced the savagery of the northern peoples have learned all too well, having suffered to their cost the throw of the falling die against them'.[40] This passage would have grown in relevance in the years following the text's composition, as Danish attacks increased in severity. Abbo's words reminded those Christians who suffered or feared Danish attack in the decades around 1000 that they were enduring the same process as the people in the *Passio Eadmundi*. Christians, in Abbo's text, were English, and the *Passio* solicited their identification with Edmund and his people.

Ælfric of Eynsham continued the process of moulding Edmund into a pan-English saint by rewriting the *Passio* in Old English rhythmical prose. This act of translation defined the audience more narrowly as English speakers. The Life of Edmund formed part of Ælfric's *Lives of Saints* collection, which was composed probably in the 990s, and was prefaced with his aim of spreading knowledge of these saints to the laity of 'angel-cynn'.[41]

---

[36] Abbo, pp. 69, 72.

[37] Abbo, p. 70: 'Quae paludes praebent pluribus monachorum gregibus optatos solitariae conversationis sinus, quibus inclusi non indigeant solitudine eremi, ex quibus sunt sancti monachorum patris Benedicti caelibes coenobitae, in loco celebri hac tempestate.'

[38] Abbo, p. 76.

[39] Abbo, p. 75: 'Ecce barbarus aduena districto ense ueteribus nostri regni colonis imminet'. In making the above argument, I disagree with Pinner, *Cult of Edmund*, pp. 42–4, that the regional aspect is emphasized; her statements about the English language, in particular, surely apply to the Anglo-Saxon kingdom/people as a whole.

[40] Abbo, p. 72: 'sicut plus aequo didicere, perperam passi aduersos iactus cadentis tesserae, qui aquilonalium gentium experti sunt seuitiam'.

[41] *Ælfric's Lives of Saints: being a set of sermons on saints' days formerly observed by the English church*, ed. W. Skeat, 2 vols. (London, 1881–1900), I, 4. P. Clemoes, 'The Chronology of Ælfric's Works', in *The Anglo-Saxons*, ed. Clemoes, pp. 212–47 (p. 244). H. Gittos, 'The Audience for Old English Texts: Ælfric, Rhetoric, and "the

Ælfric developed Abbo's appeal to Englishness, upholding Edmund as one example, alongside Cuthbert and Æthelthryth, of how 'the English nation is not deprived of the Lord's saints'.[42] Indeed, he used Edmund to demonstrate God's favour on the English.[43]

Ælfric considerably abbreviated the narrative and, noticeably, he omitted Abbo's vitriolic description of the background of the vikings. Rather than discuss their devilish heritage and northern origins, Ælfric restricted his explanation to the fact that the vikings, in harrying and slaying, were acting 'as their custom is'.[44] In employing this phrase, he, like Abbo, expected his audience to have experienced such behaviour, thus relating Hingwar and Hubba to the forces assailing England in the 990s. Furthermore, he presented the Danes as a group distinct in custom from his English audience. Although in cases like this Ælfric's text was less explicit than the Latin *passio*, by placing the Danes in the same roles of judges, torturers and tempters he implied that they were the devil's representatives. His description of Hingwar and Hubba as 'associated by the devil' is made comprehensible in this context: they were both carrying out the work of the devil in their separate raids.[45] The opposition between Christian English and pagan viking remained essential to the narrative.

In many ways, the approach of these hagiographical texts to writing about conflict with viking invaders differs from earlier representations. Abbo's depiction of the viking enemy at first appears to have more in common with continental than with insular traditions. The only writer who had used similar ideas and language previously in relation to England was Alcuin, in his letters of the 790s. In these letters, Alcuin expressed his concern for the fate of Lindisfarne through heightened emotion, and the presentation of events as a pagan attack on Christianity:

> Now I am away your tragic sufferings daily bring me sorrow, since the pagans have desecrated God's sanctuary, shed the blood of saints around the altar, laid waste the house of our hope and trampled the bodies of the saints like dung in the street.[46]

---

edification of the simple"', *ASE* 43 (2014), 231–66, argues that Ælfric also wrote for a monastic audience.

[42] Ælfric, *Life of St Edmund*, in *Ælfric's Lives of Saints*, ed. Skeat, II, 314–35 (pp. 332–3): 'Nis angel-cynn bedæled drihtnes halgena.'

[43] M. Godden, 'Apocalypse and Invasion in Late Anglo-Saxon England', in *From Anglo-Saxon to Early Middle English: Studies Presented to E. G. Stanley*, ed. M. Godden, D. Gray and T. Hoad (Oxford, 1995), pp. 130–62 (p. 138).

[44] Ælfric, *Life of St Edmund*, pp. 316–17: 'swa swa heora gewuna is'.

[45] *Ibid.*: 'geanlæhte þurh deofol'.

[46] *Alcuin of York*, p. 36; *Alcuini Epistolae*, p. 57: 'Sed versa vice vestrae tribulationis calamitas licet absentem multum me cotidie contristat, quando pagani contami-naverunt sanctuaria Dei et fuderunt sanguinem sanctorum in circuitu altaris,

In this respect, it is noteworthy that Alcuin wrote from the court of Charlemagne, rather than his home kingdom of Northumbria. His view of the situation was therefore conditioned by an imperial Frankish experience of paganism. He viewed the viking attacks as a punishment for the sins of the English as a whole.[47] Similarly, the Carolingians placed the vikings within a wider framework of barbarian attacks on their Christian empire.

Alcuin may have directly influenced Abbo, or at least they were following similar ideas concerning viking attack. Abbo used the same biblical verse quoted by Alcuin on the arrival of the vikings:[48]

> In us is fulfilled what once the prophet foretold: 'From the North evil breaks forth, and a terrible glory will come from the Lord'.[49]

Abbo, however, adapted the verse slightly, so that Edmund's viking perse-cutors appeared to be the authors of evil themselves. Now, instead of God sending evil from the north, he claimed that 'from the north comes all evil', indicating that Edmund was being tried by the devil's instruments rather than punished by God.[50] This change was necessary for a text glorifying a dead king – he could not be held responsible for his fate. Edmund, as a martyr, achieved a moral victory, refusing the temptation to submit to Hinguar despite the urging of his bishop and the extremities of his torture. These hagiographies transformed defeat into victory, showing Edmund as having responded correctly to the devil's challenge.

Through its dissemination and Ælfric's translation, Abbo's text became the standard narrative of Edmund's death and the origin of his cult. Numerous manuscripts of the *Passio* survive, from France as well as from England, predominantly dating from the eleventh to the thirteenth centuries.[51] While the hagiographic tradition was repeatedly elaborated throughout the Middle Ages, with subsequent writers adding miracles, a backstory to the Danish

---

vastaverunt domum spei nostre, calcaverunt corpora sanctorum in templo Dei quasi sterquilinium in platea'.

[47] Coupland, 'Rod of God's Wrath'; on Alcuin's development of this view, see M. Garrison, 'Divine Election for Nations – a Difficult Rhetoric for Medieval Scholars?', in *The Making of Christian Myths in the Periphery of Latin Christendom (c.1000–1300)*, ed. L. Boje Mortensen (Copenhagen, 2006), pp. 275–314 (pp. 300–7).

[48] See Coupland, 'Rod of God's Wrath', p. 537 for further usages of this scriptural quotation.

[49] *Alcuin of York*, p. 40; *Alcuini Epistolae*, p. 55: 'In nobis impletum est, quod olim per prophetam praedictum est: "Ab aquilone inardescunt mala et a Domino formi-dolosa laudatio veniet" (Jeremiah 1.14; Job 37.22)'.

[50] Abbo, p. 72: 'ab aquilone uenit omne malum'; Coupland, 'Rod of God's Wrath', pp. 537–8.

[51] There has been no thorough examination of the manuscripts of the *Passio Eadmundi*, but details of the most important manuscripts and the main lines of transmission are given in Abbo, pp. 8–10, and Pinner, *Cult of Edmund*, pp. 46–7.

invasion and an account of Edmund's childhood, Abbo's narrative continued to be read and always provided the base of the legend.[52] Inevitably, Ælfric's Old English account had a slightly shorter lifespan, but its inclusion in twelfth-century compilations as well as eleventh-century copies indicates ongoing interest.[53] The texts are included in passionals and preaching collections, and often marked up into lessons for reading: they testify to the vitality of Edmund's cult and the central role these texts played within it. Ælfric explicitly intended his Life of Edmund, as part of the *Lives of Saints*, to spread devotion beyond monastic celebration to an elite secular audience: he sent his work to ealdorman Æthelweard and his son Æthelmær at their request.[54] We know from Æthelweard's *Chronicon* that he could read and write Latin, so he may have requested a vernacular text for the purpose of reading to his entire household, as Jonathan Wilcox has suggested. Indeed, Wilcox posits a wide range of circumstances in which the *Lives of Saints* were read, reaching a varied religious and secular audience, including non-elites.[55]

Moreover, later writers used Edmund's hagiographies as historical sources for describing the events of the ninth century, so that their influence was felt beyond the sphere of saintly veneration. Since the Anglo-Saxon Chronicle's accounts generally lacked drama or detail, and there were few alternatives, Ælfric's and particularly Abbo's accounts of Hinguar's activities and Edmund's death were applied by post-Conquest historians to narrate the viking presence in East Anglia – or even England – more generally.[56] Indeed, Ælfric's Life of Edmund remains one of the most read Old English texts, and thus continues to shape historians' views of the vikings in England.

However, Abbo not only introduced a new discourse for describing the viking past, but also made significant changes to previous traditions about Edmund. Earlier mentions of his death in West Saxon sources, such as the Anglo-Saxon Chronicle, imply that he was killed in battle, rather than suffering the martyr's death described by Abbo.[57] Æthelweard, writing

---

[52] On the subsequent hagiographic texts, see Pinner, *Cult of Edmund*, esp. pp. 48–111.

[53] *Ælfric's Lives of Saints*, ed. Skeat, II, vii–xxi; J. Hill, 'The Dissemination of Ælfric's *Lives of Saints*: A Preliminary Survey', in *Holy Men and Holy Women: Old English Prose Saints' Lives and Their Contexts*, ed. P. E. Szarmach (Albany, 1996), pp. 235–59 (esp. pp. 248–9); E. Treharne, 'Making Their Presence Felt: Readers of Ælfric, *c.* 1050–1350', in *A Companion to Ælfric*, ed. H. Magennis and M. Swan (Leiden, 2009), pp. 398–422.

[54] *Ælfric's Lives of Saints*, ed. Skeat, I, 4.

[55] J. Wilcox, 'The Audience of Ælfric's *Lives of Saints* and the Face of Cotton Caligula A. XIV, fols. 93–130', in *Beatus Vir: Studies in Early English and Norse Manuscripts in Memory of Phillip Pulsiano*, ed. A. N. Doane and K. Wolf (Tempe, 2006), pp. 228–63 (pp. 248–9; 258–9).

[56] Barrow, 'Danish Ferocity and Abandoned Monasteries', pp. 92–3.

[57] ASC A 870 [869]: 'þy wintra Eadmund cyning him wiþ feaht, 7 þa Deniscan sige namon, 7 þone cyning ofslogon' ('that winter King Edmund fought against them, and the Danish took the victory, and killed the king').

only a few years before Abbo, adapted this Chronicle passage to recognize Edmund's sanctity, but not to expand on the circumstances of his death. These references suggest that the story told by Abbo was not yet known at the West Saxon court. Of course, Abbo's preface stated that the story had been told to King Æthelstan but, even if we accept his reported chain of oral transmission (which should not necessarily be dismissed, despite its clear rhetorical purpose),[58] then it was still 'unknown to many, written by no one', his account implies it was not repeated within the royal court, and there is no evidence that the story was yet considered the martyrdom of a saintly figure.[59] Veneration of Edmund seems originally to have been restricted to East Anglia, his own kingdom. The earliest evidence of a cult is the 'St Edmund memorial coinage', which was minted in East Anglia in the period between Danish settlement in 880 and the West Saxon conquest in 917. There were several different issues of these coins, all bearing a variant of the inscription SCE EADMUNDUS REX.[60] This inscription, in the vocative, indicates Edmund's acceptance as a powerful intercessor, calling upon his status as king. Parallels may be drawn by coins minted by Scandinavians elsewhere in England, especially the St Peter coinage of York and the St Martin coins from Lincoln. That St Edmund would be chosen in East Anglia suggests that he was already perceived as particularly powerful in the area, given the high status locally of the saints chosen elsewhere (they were the patrons of the cathedral and a major church of the city, respectively). This veneration, however, may have had more to do with his status as king of East Anglia than his death at the hands of the vikings – after all, there was a significant Anglo-Saxon tradition of royal saints.[61]

Furthermore, the fact that veneration for Edmund arose when the East Anglian kingdom was under Danish rule implies that his cult had not yet acquired the anti-Danish connotations emphasized by Abbo. It is important to remember that those Danes in power in East Anglia, led by Guthrum and then Eohric, were not the same group who had been responsible for Edmund's death, and their seizure of power did not occur until a decade after he had been killed. Abbo and Ælfric's parallels between the Danes led by Hinguar and the vikings contemporary with their texts were thus an important re-interpretation of events that overwrote the earlier history of the cult.

Moreover, crucially, Abbo stated that Hinguar and his vikings went back to their ships and left East Anglia after the death of Edmund, as pirates rather than conquerors. He made no mention of Guthrum and the other

---

[58] Pinner, *Cult of Edmund*, pp. 35–7.

[59] Abbo, p. 67: 'pluribus ignotam, a nemine scriptam'.

[60] C. Blunt, 'The St Edmund Memorial Coinage', *Proceedings of the Suffolk Institute of Archaeology* 31 (1969), 234–55.

[61] Cf. the category of saints described in D. Rollason, 'The Cults of Murdered Royal Saints in Anglo-Saxon England', *ASE* 11 (1983), 1–22.

Danish rulers of the region. Abbo's simplistic construction of Danes and English as enemies completely bypassed those Danes who may have had the greatest impact on East Anglia. The chronology given by the Chronicle, coupled with archaeological and place-name evidence, suggests that a reasonably large population of Danes settled in East Anglia; that the region was under Danish control for at least 47 years, from 870 to 917; and that these circumstances caused significant disruption to ecclesiastical life.[62] Abbo and Ælfric, however, remained vague about any specific towns or churches that may have been destroyed, made no mention of viking settlement or rule, and presented the local inhabitants as restoring the earlier situation. The aftermath of viking destruction led to a revival for the Christian people, a calm after the storm. Abbo related how, 'with however small a peace having been restored to the churches, the Christians began to rise up from their hiding-places', and the community could then rebuild and re-establish itself.[63] The viking period was presented as a temporary interruption to Christian life in England, which was then reconstructed by the Christian community who lived there.

Edmund's role as a representative of the English in Abbo's and Ælfric's texts reflected the view from Wessex, not East Anglia and the cult's origins. Although he referred to the role of the local people in the early stages of the cult, Abbo seems not to have used local East Anglian information. He reported that his story came from the Wessex court, told to 'gloriosissimo regi Anglorum Aethelstano' and preserved by Archbishop Dunstan.[64] Abbo wrote while staying at Ramsey, Bishop Oswald's Benedictine foundation, and not at the cult centre of Bury St Edmunds. In fact, there was no real attempt in the text to promote Bury as the holders of the relics. Abbo depicted Edmund's sanctity as applying to all of the English people, not tied to one place. As discussed above, the relevance of the text to the English was apparent from the beginning, where Abbo set the scene by recounting the Anglo-Saxon origin myth.[65] This passage contains Abbo's first of only two references to the name 'Eastengle', but he stated that it was the Saxons who settled this 'orientalem ipsius insulae partem', thus associating its people with the West Saxons (invoking the name for a second time at the introduction of Edmund,

---

[62] Hadley, *Vikings in England*, pp. 11–12, 29–37; Kershaw, 'Culture and Gender in the Danelaw'; J. Barrow, 'Survival and Mutation: Ecclesiastical Institutions in the Danelaw in the Ninth and Tenth Centuries', in *Cultures in Contact*, ed. Hadley and Richards, pp. 155–76 (pp. 157–9).

[63] Abbo, p. 80: 'quantulacumque reddita aecclesiis pace, coeperunt Christiani de latibulis consurgere'. Ælfric included similar statements in *Life of St Edmund*, pp. 324, 326.

[64] Abbo, p. 67.

[65] Just as Fulbert's *Vita Romani* opened with a history of the Franks, discussed below, so Abbo's *Passio Eadmundi* opened with a brief history of the Anglo-Saxons, thereby implicitly comparing the events it described with that earlier invasion.

he added that the king came from a Saxon lineage).[66] Ælfric, though he does introduce the saint as 'Eastengla Cyncincg', made an explicit connection to the West Saxon dynasty, by situating the events 'in the year when Ælfred the ætheling was one and twenty years old, he who afterward became the renowned king of the West-Saxons'.[67] Indeed, this chronological relationship implies that Alfred was Edmund's successor.

The contexts in which Abbo and Ælfric wrote may explain their focus on a single English kingdom under the West Saxon kings. Both wrote while living at monasteries patronized by West Saxon elites and associated with the tenth-century monastic reform. (On the other hand, although Bury St Edmunds was granted land by West Saxon kings of England during the tenth and eleventh centuries, it was not reformed until the 1020s, under Cnut).[68] Ælfric trained as a monk and masspriest in the heart of Wessex, at the Old Minster, Winchester, under the reforming bishop Æthelwold;[69] Æthelwold, in turn, had been taught by Dunstan, to whom Abbo addressed his work. Abbo's home institution of Fleury was where Oswald had been sent for his training, and thus the Frankish monk's background had much in common with Anglo-Saxon monastic reform culture.[70] Taking into account also Oswald's central role in the foundation of Ramsey, where Abbo wrote his *Passio*, the major three figures in the tenth-century Benedictine monastic movement may all be seen to have exerted considerable influence on the two writers and the institutions at which they worked.

These institutions, and the monastic networks in which Abbo and Ælfric operated, depended on strong links to West Saxon kings and aristocracy. Oswald established Ramsey, with royal support, on a gift of land from Æthelwine, ealdorman of East Anglia. Despite Æthelwine's local importance, he was no less powerful in the West Saxon royal court, perhaps because Edgar had been raised as his foster-brother; under Æthelred, he became the foremost ealdorman in the kingdom, from 983.[71] Ælfric's transfer to Cerne

---

[66] Abbo, pp. 69, 70: 'Eadmundus, ex antiquorum Saxonum nobili prosapia oriundus'.

[67] Ælfric, pp. 314, 316–17: 'on þam geare þe ælfred æðelincg . an and twentig geare wæs . / se þe west-sexena cynincg siþþan wearð mære'.

[68] A. Gransden, 'Traditionalism and Continuity during the Last Century of Anglo-Saxon Monasticism', in A. Gransden, *Legends, Traditions and History in Medieval England* (London, 1992), pp. 31–79 (at pp. 46, 77). Dumville surveys the evidence more thoroughly, and suggests that reform may have taken place in the 970s or 980s, but this remains at most a possibility: D. N. Dumville, *English Caroline Script and Monastic History: Studies in Benedictinism, A.D. 950–1030* (Woodbridge, 1993), pp. 35–48.

[69] J. Hill, 'Ælfric: His Life and Works', in *A Companion to Ælfric*, ed. H. Magennis and M. Swan (Leiden, 2009), pp. 35–65 (pp. 35–6).

[70] J. Nightingale, 'Oswald, Fleury and Continental Reform', in *St Oswald of Worcester: Life and Influence*, ed. N. Brooks and C. Cubitt (Leicester and London, 1996), pp. 23–45.

[71] C. Hart, 'Æthelwine (d. 992)', *Oxford Dictionary of National Biography*, Oxford,

Abbas, meanwhile, was carried out at the request of its founder, the nobleman Æthelmær, an influential figure at the royal court in the 990s, a member of the West Saxon dynasty and the son of Ealdorman Æthelweard, whose close relationship to the royal family has been discussed in Chapters 1 and 2.[72] Indeed, Ælfric dedicated the *Lives of Saints* to Æthelweard and Æthelmær, stating that they had requested it from him.[73] Catherine Cubitt has proposed that Ælfric was supported by Æthelweard and Æthelmær from a young age, perhaps because he originated from their estates or served in their households: their influence may thus have shaped his entire life.[74] Intellectual, political and practical influences on Abbo and Ælfric derived overwhelmingly from the same milieu, which promoted partnership between West Saxon kings of England, their leading ealdormen and the monastic church in order to ensure the success of the monastic movement. These influences are apparent in the two writers' works more generally, in which they often dwelt on the duties and virtues of kingship.[75] In writing of Edmund, both could present idealized visions of an English king, which reflected their own experiences, perspectives and political theologies.

Abbo may have been a visitor from Francia, but the popularity and influence of his work show that his interpretation of the past was approved of in England. Ælfric's Old English version of the Life of Edmund, while significantly adapted in some ways, maintained the binary divide of good and evil between Christian and viking. Each demonstrates that equating vikings with hagiographic villains was a credible and potent technique. The hagiographies clearly distinguished the two groups and demonstrated that allegiance to a Danish heritage excluded the possibility of being a good Christian. Being a good Christian, conversely, was in each of these texts equated with loyalty to England and its West Saxon kings. The adoption of Edmund's cult by the West Saxon kings and monks, therefore, encouraged an interpretation of the

---

2004; online edn, Oct. 2005 <http://www.oxforddnb.com/view/article/8919> [accessed 8 Sept. 2016].

[72] Hill, 'Ælfric: His Life and Works', pp. 43, 51; C. Cubitt, 'Ælfric's Lay Patrons', in *A Companion to Ælfric*, ed. Magennis and Swan, pp. 165–92 (pp. 171–2). Æthelmær became Ealdorman of the Western Provinces after his father's death.

[73] *Ælfric's Lives of Saints*, ed. Skeat, I, 4: 'Non mihi inputetur quod diuinam scripturam nostrae lingue infero, quia arguet me praecatus multorum fidelium et maxime æþelwerdi ducis et æðelmeri nostri, qui ardentissime nostras interpretationes Amplectuntur lectitando'; 'Ælfric gret eadmodlice Æðelwerd ealdorman and ic secge þe leof . þæt ic hæbbe nu gegaderod on þyssere béc þæra halgena þrowunga þe me to onhagode on englisc to awendene . for þan þe ðu leof swiðost and æðelmær swylcera gewrita me bædon . and of handum gelæhton eowerne geleafan to getrymmenne . mid þære gerecednysse . þe ge on eowrum gereorde næfdon ǽr.'

[74] Cubitt, 'Ælfric's lay patrons', p. 177.

[75] M. Clayton, 'Ælfric and Æthelred', in *Essays on Anglo-Saxon and Related Themes in Memory of Lynne Grundy*, ed. J. Roberts and J. Nelson (London, 2000), pp. 65–88; Mostert, *Political Theology*.

Danes in England focused solely on conflict, and which maintained a binary division between native English Christians and foreign Danish invaders, a century after Scandinavian settlement in East Anglia.

Normandy: Dudo and the Fécamp Chronicle

The decades either side of the year 1000 were formative in Normandy, just as in England, in the creation of a lasting narrative of the viking past. Dudo of St-Quentin's *De moribus et actis primorum Normanniae ducum*, discussed in Chapters 1 and 2, is usually seen as the starting point of Normandy's strong tradition of historical writing.[76] All other medieval histories of Normandy's origins and tenth-century development to some extent drew upon Dudo's account. Even when later historians were sceptical of some of Dudo's claims, they lacked an alternative source of information.[77] Although reworked and adapted several times, Dudo's history established the basic narrative of Norman origins that persisted throughout the duchy's existence and beyond.

Norman identity has been viewed primarily as a construction of this influential Norman historiography.[78] Yet, until recently, the role of Dudo's *De moribus* in the historiographical development has been somewhat under-played. In recent years, historians have emphasized the uses of Dudo's rich history as a witness to the view of the past in Normandy around the year 1000.[79] He described the viking past in unabashed detail, as an essential part of the Normans' ethnic inheritance. Moreover, he positioned the Normans in relation to other peoples: the Franks, the Bretons and even the English.[80]

---

[76] Davis, *Normans and their Myth*; Albu, *Normans in their Histories*; L. Shopkow, *History and Community: Norman Historical Writing in the Eleventh and Twelfth Centuries* (Washington, DC, 1997); Webber, *Evolution of Norman Identity*. For later adaptations, see *Gesta Normannorum Ducum*, ed. van Houts.

[77] Note the comments of William of Jumièges in the *Gesta Normannorum Ducum*, ed. van Houts, pp. 4–7: 'Principium namque narrationis usque ad Ricardum secundum a Dudonis, periti uiri, hystoria collegi... Sane genealogiam Rollonis... necnon somnium eius cum pluribus id generis ab hystorica serie desecui, animaduertens ea penitus adulatoria, nec speciem honesti uel utilis pretendere'; 'I have drawn the first part of the narrative down to Richard II from the history of Dudo, a skilled man... I have, however, cut out from my history the genealogy of Rollo... as well as his dream and many other matters of that kind, for I consider that they are merely flattering, and do not offer a model of what is honourable or edifying.' See further Pohl, *Dudo of St-Quentin's* Historia Normannorum, pp. 129–31.

[78] Davis, *Normans and their Myth*, pp. 49–67.

[79] Searle, 'Fact and Pattern'; Shopkow, *History and Community*, pp. 68–83, 174–89; E. Albu, 'Dudo of Saint-Quentin: The Heroic Past Imagined', *HSJ* 6 (1994), 111–18; Pohl, *Dudo's* Historia Normannorum, pp. 113–24 (and see pp. 2–5 on Dudo's ongoing contribution to Norman historiographic tradition).

[80] It is unclear exactly which English kings Dudo referred to in the episodes concerning Rollo in England. Christiansen suggested that some passages discussing

Dudo's history testified to and moulded the identification of the Norman ethnic group as a people who emerged from Scandinavian roots through conflict and co-operation with those around them in northern France.

Dudo's history was shaped by and for the ducal family. Much of the material may well have been told directly to Dudo by Richard I, Gunnor, Archbishop Robert and Count Rodulf, stories moulded into shape by oral circulation between generations. Dudo's history had to please Duke Richard II, and so we can be sure that it is the ducal view we are hearing. Dudo did have considerable literary pretensions, however, and much of the *De moribus* is literary invention and embellishment. Moreover, as Albu has pointed out, the lifetime of Dudo's informants is actually the period which he rather neglects, suggesting that he did not rely on them as much as he implied.[81] Whatever their level of input, these informants seem to have narrated their collective family history rather than their own lived memories.

However, the historical narrative of the *De moribus* was not the only historical text produced in early Normandy, nor did it take a radical new line.[82] The dukes did not commission Dudo, who originated from the Vermandois, because Normandy was devoid of historians.[83] There may well have been oral historians at the time: Searle has emphasized the similarities of Dudo's history to Norse sagas, and we know that both Norse skalds and Latin poets were present in Rouen.[84] Monks living in Normandy also recorded the events of the early principality. In the years around the publication of the *De moribus*, several restored monastic houses in and near Rouen produced historical texts dealing with both the distant Merovingian past and also more recent events. These texts show (sometimes very strong) similarities to Dudo's narrative. In a number of cases, this was due to direct influence from Dudo, and all these texts demonstrate the evolution and dominance of a similar view of the past.

All historical writing in the century after 911, other than the *De moribus*, emerged from a few monastic houses closely associated with the Norman

---

Alstemus Æthelstan were actually referring to Guthrum using his baptismal name. Certainly, this would make more sense in terms of chronology, but Dudo's dates are notoriously flexible. The *De moribus* presents us with an unfamiliar external view of the English; it also provides evidence that the Norman dukes laid claim to England from the very beginning of the eleventh century.

[81] Albu, *Normans in their Histories*, p. 21.

[82] Arnoux, 'Before the *Gesta Normannorum*', p. 30.

[83] Pohl, *Dudo's* Historia Normannorum, pp. 115–20, suggests reasons why Dudo was commissioned, as an official, non-monastic voice.

[84] Searle, 'Fact and Pattern'. The Icelandic poet Sigvatr Þórðarson refers to his time in Rouen in his *Vestrfararvísur* (dating probably from the 1020s): ed. J. Jesch, in *Poetry from the Kings' Sagas 1*, ed. Whaley, II, 617. The poet Warner wrote Latin poetry at the court of the archbishop in the 990s: see Warner of Rouen, *Moriuht: A Norman Latin Poem from the Early Eleventh Century*, ed. C. McDonough (Toronto, 1995), pp. 5–6.

dukes. The earliest monastery to be refounded was at St-Ouen in Rouen, in the time of Rollo, whom later tradition credited with a central role in the return of the monks. His son, William Longsword, re-established Jumièges before 943, and such was his association with the monastery that the *Planctus* composed on his death implied he had wished to become a monk there.[85] St-Wandrille at Fontenelle was rebuilt in 960 by a monk of Ghent, Mainard, with the aid of Richard I, who then sent him to complete a similar task at Mont-Saint-Michel.[86] An earlier attempt in 944–53 by Gerard of Brogne had failed because of aristocratic opposition: the eleventh-century *Miracula Sancti Vulfranni* report that the Norman nobles were unwilling to return the land they had taken from the monastery.[87] The support of the dukes was necessary in re-establishing the monasteries, not least to coerce their followers into restoring the patrimony. Richard I also built a great church at Fécamp next to the ducal residence, and established a house of canons there in 990.[88] These communities began to produce various kinds of records of their foundations.

Apart from Dudo's *De moribus*, historical writing in Normandy was generally hagiographical, and related to the history of the institutions in which it was composed. Like Abbo in his *Passio Eadmundi*, writers in Normandy, many of whom were monks originating elsewhere in Francia, drew on existing ideas about vikings from continental hagiography more generally. The equivalent hagiographies and chronicles of Normandy's ninth- and tenth-century neighbours presented an image of viking destruction that was catastrophic to ecclesiastical life.[89] Although the veracity of this narrative of mass monastic exodus in the face of viking terror has been disputed, tenta-tively by Lucien Musset and, more recently and more assertively, by Felice Lifshitz, it was already well established in the tenth century.[90] This was the narrative which the inhabitants of the Norman duchy inherited in monastic texts and historical memory. Thus, looking back at the histories of its institu-tions and people, the Church confronted the new Norman dukes and people with their viking past in their earliest encounters.

It is worth briefly considering Dudo's narrative again, since the monastic narratives examined in more detail in this chapter and the next contain similar themes. Dudo, like the hagiographers, employed prevalent Frankish ideas

---

[85] *The Planctus for William Longsword*, ed. R. Helmerichs (1999–2002), <http://vlib.iue. it/carrie/documents/planctus/planctus/> [accessed 21 June 2013], verses 5 and 6.

[86] Musset, 'Monachisme d'Époque Franque', p. 57.

[87] *Inventio et Miracula Vulfranni*, ed. Laporte, pp. 28–30. See p. 192 below.

[88] F4, F9.

[89] Planavergne, 'Les Normands avant la Normandie', pp. 39–40.

[90] L. Musset, 'L'Exode des Reliques du Diocèse de Sées au Temps des Invasions Normandes', *Société Historique et Archéologique de l'Orne*, 88 (1970), 3–22; F. Lifshitz, 'The "Exodus of Holy Bodies" Reconsidered: The Translation of the Relics of St. Gildard of Rouen to Soissons', *Analecta Bollandiana* 110 (1992), 329–40.

about vikings. In his *De moribus*, Dudo used the lives of two vikings, Hasting and Rollo, to describe the impact of viking raiders in detail. He narrated damage suffered both by secular communities, which left land uncultivated, and by ecclesiastical institutions, which he listed by name.[91] However, Dudo carefully presented Rollo as protector, rather than destroyer, of churches in Normandy. On reaching Jumièges, he reported, Rollo realized that it was a holy place, and left it alone; Dudo then included a puzzling detail about Rollo's translation of the body of a virgin saint, Hameltrude, to the nearby chapel of St Vedast. Rollo proceeded to Rouen, where he made peace with the bishop, finding the churches already in ruins.[92] All this occurred before Rollo's official conversion, but indicated his future destiny. In addition, Dudo claimed that Rollo, in the midst of a campaign of ravaging along the Saône and Loire, respected the monastery of St Benedict at Fleury, and thereby implied that it suffered only from other viking groups.[93] Thus he did not avoid or deny the sources of Frankish hostility, but used them to distinguish positively the Norman ducal line alone among vikings.

Dudo also turned the Frankish interpretation of vikings as God's punishment to the service of the Norman dukes. Firstly, he emphasized that the people of Francia were deserving of this punishment, so that, in a sense, the vikings were God's instrument.[94] Secondly, his narrative presented the conversion of the vikings – under Rollo – as the only respite and solution to this punishment and, indeed, the desired outcome. As discussed in Chapter 2, Rollo's prophetic dream became an origin myth for the Norman people: it was an allegory of how diverse individuals were combined into one ethnicity under the rulers of Rollo's dynasty. But the primary significance of the dream within Dudo's history, as interpreted by Rollo's Christian prisoner, was that before this could happen, Rollo and his followers needed to convert to Christianity and reconstruct the Norman church. The vision presented the Norman future as a divinely ordained plan.

As part of this divine plan, Rollo's vision emphasized the restoration of the places which the vikings had destroyed. Introducing Rollo, at the beginning

---

[91] Lair, pp. 131–2, 149–50, 156–7, 161–2; Christiansen, pp. 17, 32–3, 38, 42–3.

[92] Lair, pp. 152–3; Christiansen, p. 35.

[93] Lair, p. 161; Christiansen, pp. 42, 193.

[94] Lair, p. 137: 'Contrita est namque gens, ultore Alstigno, Francigena, quae spurcaminum erat sorde nimium plena. Perfidi perjurique merito sunt damnati, increduli infidelesque juste puniti... quae nutu Dei gesta sunt...'; p. 141: 'non desistit illi [*sc. superna Deificae Trinitatis providentia*] salutifera praebere suffragia, ex ferocitate saevae gentilitatis Dacigena'; Christiansen, p. 22: 'For the Frankish nation was crushed because it was overflowing with foul indecencies, and Alstignus was the punisher. Traitors and perjurers deserve to be condemned, and unbelievers and infidels are justly punished... what was done, with God's approval...'; p. 25: 'It [the godly Trinity] did not cease to offer that church wholesome counsel by reason of the ferocity of the savage Dacian-born gentiles.'

of the second book of the *De moribus*, Dudo was explicit that this primarily meant the church. He stated that God, seeing the terror waged on the church by the Danish heathens, ordained that they should be the ones to save it:

> ...that where it had been lamentably afflicted, there it should vigorously come to life; and by those who had prostrated it headlong, it should be raised up to heaven; and by those whose actions made it of no account, by their gifts it would be restored; and by those whose hordes had trampled it down it should be adorned with gold and gems; and by those who had robbed them down to their rags, it should be elegantly decked with robes.[95]

Norman benefactors, led by Rollo, were in this way equated with viking pillagers, exemplified by Hasting. Usually, Dudo portrayed Hasting as the heathen ravager of churches, in contrast to Rollo as a 'good' pagan, who instinctively respected holy places (such as Jumièges), even before his conversion.[96] However, this passage made explicit the underlying logic of the *De moribus* and the inclusion of Hasting. Hasting and Rollo were not opposites, but part of the same people-group: the Normans could trace their heritage to Hasting just as to Rollo. The attacks on Francia and its church, exemplified by Hasting, were as necessary as the restoration that would take place under Rollo, his successors and their followers.

In his emphasis on the refoundation of churches and monasteries, Dudo linked ducal patronage very closely to conversion. Upon his baptism, Rollo asked the bishop Franco which churches and saints were the most powerful and held in greatest reverence. The churches which Dudo had Franco name correspond to those which had enjoyed ducal patronage and support: the churches of Rouen, Bayeux and Évreux, and the monasteries of Mont-Saint-Michel, St-Ouen and Jumièges. The gift to St-Denis, meanwhile, demonstrated to their new neighbours as well as their subjects that the Normans were now Christian benefactors.[97] St-Denis was well chosen: it was closely associated with the Carolingian, and later the Capetian, monarchs.

These narratives of refoundation tied Norman Christianity to the viking past. It was common in Francia for endowments of monasteries to be presented as restorations, since a history of there being a church in a given location assured the sanctity of the site.[98] Likewise, English kings and nobles, in particular King Edgar, patronized the restoration of monasteries

---

[95] Christiansen, p. 25; Lair, p. 141: 'ut unde fuerat flebiliter afflicta, inde esset viriliter vegetata; et quibus in praeceps lapsa, his coelo tenus exaltata: quorumque actu floccipensa, horum munere refecta: quorum frequentia conculcata, horum auro gemmisque ornata: quorum praedatu pannosa, horum dono compte palliata'.

[96] Christiansen, p. 35; Lair, p. 152.

[97] This gift was confirmed by Richard I in a charter of 968 (F3).

[98] A. Remensnyder, *Remembering Kings Past: Monastic Foundation Legends in Medieval Southern France* (Ithaca, 1995), pp. 45–50.

which had been abandoned during the previous century. In Francia, it was increasingly common to attribute destruction to viking raiders, and writers in Normandy followed this pattern. Anglo-Saxon monastic writers, on the other hand, did not refer to viking destruction when narrating refoundations, although post-Conquest accounts regularly attribute the state of monasteries in the mid-tenth century to viking attack in the ninth.[99] However, it was less common for those who presented themselves as the architects of the restoration also to align themselves with the original seizers of church land, as they did in Normandy.

This narrative was applied to a particular institution most clearly in the case of Fécamp. The dukes of Normandy built a palace at Fécamp, alongside which Richard I added a large church dedicated to the Holy Trinity and a house of canons.[100] The strength of the connection with the ducal family explains the space devoted to Fécamp by Dudo, who included verses addressed to the site in the *De moribus*, celebrating it first as the birthplace and then as the resting-place of Richard I.[101] Dudo's account of Richard I's construction of Fécamp abbey is found in a contemporary chronicle from the monastery itself. This chronicle recounts the history of the monastery from its foundation as a Merovingian nunnery to the grants of property made to the new house of canons by Richard I in 990. However, the Chronicle was not composed immediately after Richard's foundation of Fécamp, as it refers to him as 'Richard of pious memory' ('pie memorie Richardus', ch.8) and he died in 996. Because it makes no reference to the Benedictine reform of the house under William of Volpiano in 1001, it is safe to conclude that the Chronicle was composed before this date.[102]

The foundation chronicle was composed to emphasize continuity with the previous religious houses at Fécamp. The first three chapters of the Chronicle are derived from three associated saints' lives, which were culled for information about the Merovingian nunnery. Thus from the beginning the new male house, built by Richard I on the same site, traced its continuity with the Merovingian foundation. After explaining the origins of religious

---

[99] K. Cross, '"And that will not be the end of the calamity": Why Emphasise Viking Disruption?', in *Stasis in the Medieval World*, ed. M. Bintley, M. Locker, V. Symons and M. Wellesley (London, 2016), pp. 155–78.

[100] P. Bouet, 'Dudo de Saint-Quentin et Fécamp', *Tabularia* 2 (2002), 57–70.

[101] Lair, pp. 219–20, 299; Christiansen, pp. 95–6, 173.

[102] Arnoux, 'Before the *Gesta Normannorum*', p. 31. The text is edited at pp. 43–6. See further M. Arnoux, 'Les premières chroniques de Fécamp: de l'hagiographie à l'histoire', in *Les Saints dans la Normandie médiévale*, ed. Bouet et Neveux, pp. 72–82. Dudo's second set of verses addressed to Fécamp (Lair, p. 299; Christiansen, p. 173) presents the history of the monastery in a similar way to the Fécamp Chronicle, but does include reference to the reformed monastic life there, indicating that these were written later (Christiansen, pp. 227–8).

life at Fécamp, the author of the Chronicle began to describe the viking raids in the Seine valley: this section set up the need for restoration by Richard I. The chronicler stated that the activities of the 'most savage Danish people' ('seuissima Danorum gens'), directed against Christians, caused the nuns to flee and Fécamp to fall into ruin. As noted above, Dudo's lengthy narrative in the *De moribus* develops a contrast between Hasting, the violent viking who desecrates churches, and Rollo, warlike but with an innate respect for Jumièges as a place of God. The Fécamp Chronicle, in common with other brief accounts of translations and foundations, does not mention Hasting at all but lays all the blame with the Northmen in general and Rollo in particular. The same message is condensed into one character, who stood for the past of the Norman people as a whole.

The ruin of Fécamp is described in a manner familiar from hagiographical accounts: 'it became a habitation of wild animals, where formerly it had been an ornament of Christians'.[103] The pitiable state of the place is said to have continued throughout the reign of William Longsword, with walls overtaken by trees. This description was conventional: Dudo used similar phrases in his description of Rollo's first view of Rouen's 'walls broken down everywhere', and the eleventh-century *Translatio Severi* gives a comparable account of Sever's church in western Normandy: 'it was in the middle of the forest undergrowth and near the haunts of wild beasts'.[104] These descriptions used a language shared with other areas supposedly devastated by the viking invasions: the Chronicle of Nantes, for example, describes the city, 'for many years deserted, devastated and overgrown with briars and thorns'.[105]

However, the Fécamp Chronicle emphasized that the memory of the monastery, embodied in its altar, was preserved by the local people.[106] Here we find echoes of the English reconstruction of churches in the *Passio Eadmundi* – the difference being that, in Normandy, restoration was always dependent on the Norman dukes. Using a popular origin story, the Fécamp chronicler said that God himself had indicated the site destined to serve him by the presence of a beautiful stag.[107] After mentioning the murder of William

---

[103] Ch. 4: 'fieret ferarum habitatio qui fuerat prius christicolarum ornamentum'.

[104] Christiansen, p. 35; Lair, p. 153: 'murosque hinc inde disruptos'; *Translatio Severi*, ed. Pigeon, p. 57: 'inter silvarum fruteta ferarumque latibula'.

[105] *EHD*, ed. Whitelock, p. 345. William of Jumièges's description of his own monastery after viking attack is so similar that it seems likely he took inspiration from the Fécamp Chronicle: *Gesta Normannorum Ducum*, ed. van Houts, pp. 18–20.

[106] Ch. 8: 'in ipso autem loco coloni ipsius uille repertum altare ex uirgultis quantum ualuerunt ad presens cooperuerunt'.

[107] See Remensnyder, *Remembering Kings Past*, pp. 57–65 for foundation legends concerning divine revelation of a future site through animals, and pp. 60–3 for deer specifically. Fécamp Chronicle, ch. 5: 'de cuius initio sicut ab antiquis audiuimus ipse auctor et redemptor humani generis prescius sibi in ipso loco futuri seruitii grande miraculum ostendere est dignatus in forma cuiusdam spetiosissimi cerui'.

Longsword, the chronicler inserted a long extract from Dudo's *De moribus* on Richard I's resolve to build a great church on the site. Thus, the narrative of Scandinavian desecration and subsequent reconstruction by the Norman dukes was built into the community's history.

The section taken from Dudo's *De moribus* contains a reference to Rollo's prophetic dream, in which Richard explained his desire to build a grand church on the site, stating, 'for indeed here is the mount on which my grandfather Rollo saw himself standing and washing himself in the fount of salvation, in his prayer of divine vision, and he saw himself to be healed from the leprosy of his sins which infected him greatly'.[108] Incidentally, this reference provides conclusive evidence that this section was taken from Dudo's history for the Fécamp Chronicle, and not the other way around, as it harks back to the earlier passage.[109] It also provides us with evidence for knowledge of Rollo's dream outside of Dudo's history, perhaps even before that history was finished. The author of the Fécamp Chronicle may have been Dudo himself, as Arnoux has argued, or – perhaps more likely – it may have been a canon at Fécamp working contemporaneously with the ducal chaplain (since the Chronicle seems to have been finished before Dudo's history).[110] It gives just enough information that the Chronicle's author need not have assumed knowledge of the story of Rollo's dream among his readers. In the Fécamp Chronicle, the reference to the prophecy is included in order to link Richard I's actions back to the desecration wreaked by Rollo. Both the abandonment of Fécamp and its glorious restoration connect in this way to the Norman ducal family. Moreover, the repeated reference to the prophecy further embedded the idea that Scandinavian raiders were destined by God to conquer Normandy.

An emphasis on restoration was a key part of the Norman dukes' early ecclesiastical policy. All of the early monastic foundations were built on the sites of previous houses, and attempts were made to restore their original patrimonies. Moreover, there were even attempts to rebuild according to Carolingian fashions and plans. Musset's investigation into this phenomenon considered it a matter of continuity between the Carolingian province and the Norman principality.[111] But the attendant point is that this restoration was carried out deliberately by the Norman dukes, aristocracy and religious communities. They emphasized, rather than understated, viking disruption, and deliberately presented each foundation as a repair to the damage done in this period. Similar narratives could be found throughout Francia, where the

---

[108] Ch. 8: 'hic namque mons est in quo meus auus Rollo se stantem seque ablui fonte salutifero diuine uisionis oraculo conspexit et a lepra uiciorum qua infectum se sommo cernebat expiari'. Cf. Christiansen, pp. 164–6; Lair, pp. 290–1.

[109] Arnoux, 'Before the *Gesta Normannorum*', p. 31.

[110] Arnoux, 'Before the *Gesta Normannorum*', p. 41.

[111] Musset, 'Monachisme d'Époque Franque'.

destruction of churches was frequently blamed on pagans, be they Northmen or Saracens, or merely on abandonment by the dissolute and disinterested Christians of a former age. In many cases, as perhaps for some religious houses in Normandy, the narratives of destruction were dreamt up as a way of explaining movement to a new site, translations of relics or connection to a powerful new patron.[112]

The difference in Normandy was that these pagan destroyers were not invoked as faceless monsters, but as the close ancestors of the restorers. The act of restoration required the preceding ruin – and foundation narratives such as that composed at Fécamp attributed both to the same people. These writers explicitly stated that the Normans were restoring what they themselves had destroyed. As Cassandra Potts has explored, the Normans emphasized the dramatic nature of their conversion through these actions.[113] In doing so, they created a collective history for the people of Normandy aligned with the viking conquerors. The dukes promulgated this idea in texts commemorating their gifts and foundations, and thereby reiterated the connection of their people to the vikings who were said to have devastated the region.

The viking prophecies of St Romanus

A slightly different narrative is found in another early Norman monastic text, the *Vita Sancti Romani*, written by a certain Fulbert. Romanus was a Merovingian bishop of Rouen, whose cult seems to have appeared for the first time in the new Norman province. He was mentioned briefly as the predecessor of Rouen's patron saint, Audoenus, in the eleventh-century Fontenelle episcopal list, but he does not appear in a ninth-century copy from St Aubin.[114] In the 840s, the people of Rouen convinced the monks of St Medard of Soissons to accept Romanus's head in place of St Gildard's: Romanus was clearly not so dear to them at this time.[115] However, by the mid-tenth century he was receiving much greater reverence. A series of coins bearing his name gives an indication of his exalted status in tenth-century Rouen. Duke Richard I had conceded the right to mint coin to Archbishop Hugh, though not to his successors.[116] The St Romanus coins are from this same period, and produced in the same workshop as those of the duke. Because of the similarity with the ducal coinage, the earliest types of these coins can be reliably dated to *c.*970

---

[112] Remensnyder, *Remembering Kings Past*, pp. 48–50.

[113] C. Potts, *Monastic Revival and Regional Identity in Early Normandy* (Woodbridge, 1997), pp. 14–35.

[114] Lifshitz, *Pious Neustria*, p. 115, n. 38.

[115] Lifshitz, 'The "Exodus of Holy Bodies" Reconsidered'; Lifshitz, *Pious Neustria*, p. 117; the text of the *Translatio* is in Lifshitz, 'The Dossier of Romanus', pp. 349–55.

[116] Bates, *Normandy Before 1066*, p. 31.

and *c*.980, respectively.[117] Some of these bear the legend 'SCE ROMANE', in the vocative, which seems to indicate that they were made in the name of the saint, rather than of an institution as Dumas implies. Jens Christian Moesgaard has proposed on numismatic grounds that the Norman dukes, rather than ecclesiastical institutions, issued and controlled the Romanus coinage (and also the earlier St Audoenus coinage).[118] Such an interpretation is reinforced by comparison to the East Anglian St Edmund Memorial Coinage, discussed above, as well as those coins issued in the name of St Peter and St Martin at York and Lincoln. The parallel cases reveal similarity in action: the viking rulers of Rouen, like the viking rulers in England, sought to legitimize their rule through an alliance with the Church and a saint who was their special associate. From evidence summarized here, it appears that St Romanus had risen from obscurity to prominence as a result of this strategy, and thus perhaps the best parallel is the case of St Edmund: in both East Anglia and Normandy, a new saint emerged as a source of local authority.

The first *Vita Romani* seems to have been composed as part of the promotion of St Romanus in the middle of the tenth century. As we shall see, it is likely that this first hagiography is that written by Fulbert and preserved in two manuscripts of the late eleventh and mid-twelfth centuries.[119] It is Fulbert's *Vita* which builds into the narrative references to the viking conquest of Normandy – other hagiographies of Romanus refer exclusively to the Merovingian context of the bishop's life.

Fulbert's *Vita Romani* opens with a lengthy preface, which is addressed to 'Dominis et confratribus suis sancte Rothomagensis ecclesie matris filiis', implying that Fulbert was a clerk of the cathedral, or perhaps a monk of St-Ouen (pp. 234–6). Fulbert's desire that his work should not be spread outside the community ('extra domesticos parietes'), lest his poor work reflect badly on them all, suggests the latter. The *Vita* begins by describing the advent of doctors of the church, followed by a brief history of the Frankish people and their conversion (pp. 237–9). Romanus's aged parents were both informed of their son's forthcoming birth by an angel, and his mother foresaw Romanus's influence spreading light across Neustria (pp. 240–2). When he had grown, Romanus reluctantly became bishop of Rouen at the king's command and the election of the people after an angelic oracle instructed them (pp. 243–7). After this, the narrative is occupied with Romanus's miracles in Rouen. Many

---

[117] F. Dumas, *Le Trésor de Fécamp et le Monnayage en Francie Occidentale Pendant le Seconde Moitié du Xe siècle* (Paris, 1971), pp. 98–100.

[118] J. C. Moesgaard, 'Saints, Dukes and Bishops: Coinage in Ducal Normandy, c. 930–c. 1150', in *Money and the Church in Medieval Europe, 1000–1200*, ed. G. E. M. Gasper and S. H. Gullbekk (Farnham, 2015), pp. 197–207.

[119] Lifshitz, *Pious Neustria*, pp. 229–30: Paris Bibliothèque Nationale MS lat. 13090, ff. 112v–124v (mid-12th c.) and Evreux Bibliothèque Municipale MS 101, ff. 17v–29v (11th c.).

of these involved expelling the demons of paganism: first, he drove demons out of an ancient amphitheatre (pp. 248–52); then he sent back a flood into the Seine (pp. 252–3); and later he cast evil spirits out of a pagan temple (pp. 254–5). Thereafter follow miracles which occurred in Romanus's monastery and in his personal hermitage (pp. 256–63). The *Vita* finishes with Romanus's death, and records that he was buried on 23 October in his own oratory, one milestone from the city in the church of St Gildard (p. 267).

Fulbert's *Vita Romani* deals with the exodus of holy bodies from Normandy in a unique way. Although Fulbert reported that Romanus lived under Clothar I (*c*.511–61), he referred to the viking invasions in two prophetic passages in the middle of the narrative. The first of these dealt with saints fleeing from the future Normandy, while the second predicted the subjugation of the inhabitants of Rouen to pagan overlords.

It is noteworthy that the *Vita Romani* mentions this exodus at all, since Romanus's body remained in Rouen throughout the period. Romanus's head was taken to Soissons in the 840s, and kept there until 1090, when it was returned to Rouen. However, at no time was this translation associated with the Northmen.[120] Moreover, Fulbert did not mention it in his *Vita*. Rather, he implied that the intact body of Romanus remained in its original resting-place, in the church of St Gildard just outside Rouen. Seemingly in contradiction to this, however, in the prophetic passages, Fulbert invoked the familiar connection between the departures of the saints in the ninth century and the coming of the vikings, and he explicitly included the bones of Romanus within this mass exodus – and eventual return. The explanation for this may be that the alternative, to admit that Romanus's relics had been left behind because he had not been considered sufficiently important to save, would have greatly undermined his hagiography. The mention of the departure of saints' bones before advancing viking raiders demonstrates how widespread and conventional such connections had become by the mid-tenth century.

The first prophetic passage occurs during Romanus's first great miracle: expelling the demons from a pagan temple in an ancient amphitheatre outside Rouen, which also doubled as brothel. As Romanus cast out the demons, Fulbert made their leader threaten the saint with retaliation:

> Indeed on this day of iniquity you cast us forth from our seats. So will I also rouse against you a nation from the extreme ends of the sea and the unknown islands, which will compel your people, ejected as well from their own dwellings, to seek seats in an outer region, or to serve foreign lords in their own homes. But that will not be the end of the calamity. For I will also bring it about that your bones and those of other slaves of God, removed from their own seats for fear of that overcoming nation, will assume an

---

[120] Lifshitz, 'The "Exodus of Holy Bodies" Reconsidered'.

unwilling pilgrimage of exile and, carried all through alien territories, seek new seats for themselves.[121]

In characterizing the invading vikings as tools of supernatural forces, this passage is typical of the general Frankish interpretation of these events. However, there is a significant difference: Fulbert presented the vikings not as the scourge of God, but as a diabolical attack. This removed the blame which other narratives placed on the inhabitants of Francia and their sins. The vikings were no longer presented as a divine punishment, but received a new demonic guise. This would hardly have been flattering to the Christian Norman elites who traced their ancestry to vikings. Romanus's response to the demon addressed that problem by subverting the demon's prediction, which matched the narratives of earlier *translationes* and external chronicles. By placing these narratives in the mouth of a demon, Fulbert to a certain extent devalued them. The man of God, Romanus, was the one who knew the full story, and those who did not recognize it were by implication as blind to the truth as the demon. He responded:

And even though that nation first hasten to penetrate lands that do not belong to them, nevertheless by its own will shall it finish with a better end, since it will soon renounce you and your world and be imbued with lordly sacraments. Moreover, that place which that nation will pervade with barbaric cruelty will be for it the effective cause of that hoped-for salvation, since the name of Christ which it would otherwise never have heard will it soon hear there, and having heard it, will faithfully believe, and having believed will magnificently worship, and thus will it become a chosen lineage, from an adulterous nation, a holy nation, a purchased people, announcing the virtues of him who called it out of the darkness into his marvellous light, who at one time were not a people, but are now a people of God, who once had not obtained mercy, now however have obtained mercy...[122]

---

[121] Lifshitz, *Pious Neustria*, p. 250: 'Tu quidem inique hodie a sedibus nostris exturbas, suscitabo et ego tibi gentem aduersam ab extremis finibus maris et ignotis insulis, que tuos quoque a propriis laribus eiectos, externe regionis sedes querere, aut certe intra proprios lares externis Dominis famulari compellet. Sed ne in hoc calamitatis terminus herebit. Nam et ego ossa tua et aliorum seruorum Dei pro metu superuenture gentis a sedibus propriis remota, inuitam exilii peregrinationem assumere, et girouaga deportatione faciam per alienas regiones sedes sibi querere'; trans. in Lifshitz, 'Dossier of Romanus', pp. 257–8.

[122] Lifshitz, *Pious Neustria*, p. 250: 'Et ut cumque erratica intentio ipsius festinet ad peruadendas sedes aliene hereditatis, hec ipsa tamen ipsius intentio meliori exitu consummabitur, quia tibi a seculo tuo renuntiatura mox dominicis imbuetur sacramentis. Locus autem quem barbarica feritate peruasura est illi erit effectiua causa insperate salutis, quia Christi nomen quod alias necdum audierat ibi mox audiet, auditumque fideliter credet, et creditum magnifice recolet, et ita fiet de gente adultera genus electum, gens sancta, populus adquisitionis, annuntians uirtutes

Romanus's response presented a history which privileged the Scandinavian ruling elite of the new Norman province. In reaching their new position, they became 'a chosen lineage... a holy nation, a purchased people' (that is, purchased by the blood of Christ). Essentially, however, Fulbert stressed that they came to this new position on their own terms. It was not the Frankish inhabitants of Neustria, their conquered subjects, who converted them, but the land itself: 'that place', said Romanus, 'will be for it the effective cause of that hoped-for salvation', because there the vikings would hear about Christianity. Fulbert glossed over the fact that they must have received the faith from the Franks, laying the emphasis on the land alone.[123] Thus the connection between the Norman people and the land of Normandy was presented as part of the divine plan, ordained from long ago.[124] Furthermore, Fulbert wrote that the Norman people would convert and morph into 'a chosen people' not by the imposition of Christianity, but by 'its own will'. This stands in contrast to Fulbert's brief introductory history of the Franks at the beginning of the *Vita*, wherein he stated that 'military force compelled [Clovis] to become, from a pagan, a Christian'.[125] A number of parallels appear between the origins of the Franks and the prophecy of Norman origins, but in this respect the Normans emerged not only as independent, but also as superior.

Fulbert's view of history was shaped around ethnic groups. This was established early on in the *Vita Romani* by his recounting of Frankish origins – just as Abbo opened his *Passio Eadmundi* with the Anglo-Saxon origin myth.[126] Given the considerations necessary for interpreting origin myths discussed in Chapter 2, in both cases we may conclude that these writers considered Franks and Anglo-Saxons to be contemporary, distinct peoples at the time

eius qui eum de tenebris uocauit in ammirabile lumen suum, qui aliquando non populus, nunc autem populus Dei, qui non consecutus misericordiam, nunc autem misericordiam consecutus'; trans. in Lifshitz, 'Dossier of Romanus', pp. 258–9. I have slightly adapted Lifshitz's translation to reflect the fact that this passage (*gens sancta... misericordiam consecutus*) is a quotation from I Peter 2. 9–10.

[123] On the silence of eleventh-century historians about Frankish evangelism to the Normans, see O. Guillot, 'La conversion des Normands peu après 911: Des reflets contemporains à l'historiographie ultérieure (Xe–XIe s.)', *Cahiers de Civilisation Médiévale* 24 (1981), 101–16, 181–219 (p. 219).

[124] The parallels between this passage and the early eleventh-century *Vita Taurini* suggest that Fulbert's text was known to its author, Deodatus. In this text, Taurinus argues with a demon which he casts out from a pagan temple in Evreux; the area is devastated, but an angel predicts its restoration; this devastation means that the people lose knowledge of the place of the tomb. Herrick reads this as foretelling the arrival of the vikings: S. K. Herrick, *Imagining the Sacred Past: Hagiography and Power in Early Normandy* (Cambridge, MA, 2007), pp. 60–1, 63–6, 73.

[125] Lifshitz, *Pious Neustria*, p. 238: 'quem de pagano christianum fieri fors bellica coegit'; trans in Lifshitz, 'Dossier of Romanus', p. 239.

[126] This is another aspect of the text which is particular to Fulbert: it is not present in Gerard's abridgement (Lifshitz, *Pious Neustria*, p. 238).

of writing. Fulbert recounted that 'a certain folk came out of Sicambria', the Franks, and described their characteristics through their conflict with the Romans.[127] These two groups were then placed in relation to 'violent peoples' and 'unknown peoples' outside the Roman Empire. Fulbert's view of these various peoples was hierarchical: the Franks and Romans joined in 'the friendship and society of the kingdom', and it was by the military superiority of the Franks that the Empire could be extended; the Franks subjugated the 'violent peoples', on the other hand, 'on whom they imposed rights and laws, with indomitable fierceness', while the 'unknown peoples' were also placed in a power relationship as 'their tributaries and subject to their imposts'.[128] Fulbert was surprisingly vague about Romanus's ethnic background, merely saying that he came from 'the royal blood of those peoples', but the impression given is of an individual born into an ethnically diverse society.[129]

Fulbert presented the origins of the Norman people in a similar way. Unlike the other narratives produced in Normandy, Fulbert's *Vita Romani* described the actions of an entire people, rather than its leaders. Unusually, he did not mention the dukes at all, but ascribed all the actions he recounted – even the return of relics – to the Norman people as a whole. He described the result of the arrival of the vikings as an ethnic conflict between two distinct peoples – the Scandinavians, 'that nation whom you say will be the exterminator of our people', and 'our people', the Neustrian Franks.[130] Those Franks were the direct descendants of the sixth-century inhabitants of Neustria, and Fulbert's demon seems intended to provoke his listeners through their emotional connection with their descendants. Even after the conversion of the newcomers, in Fulbert's view, the distinction between peoples was maintained. Ethnic distinctions would be reproduced in the stratification of society, with Scandinavian conquerors continuing to rule over the subjugated Neustrians. Conversion did make a difference, but it was simply that these 'foreign lords' began to rule justly, rather than continuing to oppress their subject people. Fulbert made this clear in the second prophetic passage, in which Romanus again prophesied the coming of the vikings to the people of Rouen. After driving back the waters of a terrible flood, he explained:

---

[127] Lifshitz, *Pious Neustria*, p. 238: 'a Sicambrie partibus gentem quandam aduenisse'; trans. in Lifshitz, 'Dossier of Romanus', p. 239.

[128] Lifshitz, *Pious Neustria*, p. 238: '...composito federe in amicitiam et regni societatem ex senatus consulto receperunt... Nam gentes indomita feritate tumentes perdomuerunt, quibus iura et leges imposuerunt... hos inquam uectigales et tributarios sibi fecerunt, atque ita sociis signis adiuti, gentibus ignotis Romane potentie terrorem infuderunt'; trans. in Lifshitz, 'Dossier of Romanus', p. 239.

[129] Lifshitz, *Pious Neustria*, p. 238: 'horum regio sanguine'; trans. in Lifshitz, 'Dossier of Romanus', p. 239.

[130] Lifshitz, *Pious Neustria*, p. 250: '[Sed quid tibi et] gente huic de qua futurum gentis nostre exterminium [tanto faustu comminaris?]'; trans. in Lifshitz, 'Dossier of Romanus', p. 258.

> Those waters are merely a foretelling of the piratical army of enemy nations
> that will one day come against you, who will completely subjugate with
> an unheard-of savageness the occupied boundaries of your territory, and
> subject your descendants to their dominion for a while... that nation about
> which we are speaking, until now still in the grip of the error of heathendom,
> as soon as it shall hear the name of Christ, will take up the worship of the
> Catholic faith, and go on to foster its subjects in great peace.[131]

In this passage, the ethnic distinction was maintained between conquerors
and subjects. Fulbert saw the society around him as one people's triumph
over another. The Frankish ethnicity of the subject people was reinforced by
the connection drawn with the distant, Merovingian past: Fulbert's contemporaries were the descendants of Romanus's flock. Likewise, the Scandinavian
conquerors ruled over them as a separate group, who had grown peaceful
through their conversion. Fulbert employed the viking association with the
sea, but the waters in this prophecy seem to represent the paganism of the
vikings rather than the viking people themselves, who did not retreat.[132]
Moreover, Fulbert again emphasized the link with the land of Normandy, 'the
occupied boundaries of your territory' implying that the province had been a
distinct unit already, just waiting for the Normans to arrive.

This image of 'a chosen people', become just rulers through conversion,
was powerfully employed to counter the demonic narrative of the exodus of
holy bodies. In his response to the demon in the amphitheatre, Fulbert made
Romanus retort:

> Truly as soon as that nation, reborn in Christ, has been imbued with
> lordly sacraments, it will bring back our bones with highest veneration
> to the proper seat, from whatever lands it shall hear they have been
> translated to.[133]

The viking conquerors were thus presented as the saviours of the saints, and
the agents of their return to Normandy. Through two passages of prophecy,
Fulbert transformed the familiar narrative of vikings driving the saints from

---

[131] Lifshitz, *Pious Neustria*, p. 253: 'Aque iste prelocuntur uobis aduersarum gentium
quandoque piraticum superuenturum exercitum, qui uestre huius regionis fines
occupatos, inaudita feritate perdomabit, et posteros uestros per tempus et per
spatium temporis, suo subiugabit dominio... quoniam gens illa de qua loquimur
gentilitatis errore adhuc detenta, mox ut Christi nomen audierit, catholice fidei
cultum arripiet, et populum sibi subiectum multa in pace confouere persistet';
trans. in Lifshitz, 'Dossier of Romanus', pp. 264–5.

[132] Cf. discussion of the associations of vikings, Anglo-Saxons and the sea in *The Battle
of Maldon* in Harris, *Race and Ethnicity*, pp. 158–9, 171–2, 178–84.

[133] Lifshitz, *Pious Neustria*, p. 250: 'Gens sane ista mox ut in Christo regenerata
dominicis fuerit imbuta sacramentis, ossa nostra de cunctis terre partibus ad quas
translata esse audierit, summa cum ueneratione ad sedem propriam reportabit';
trans. in Lifshitz, 'Dossier of Romanus', p. 259.

Normandy. The original fault was made to appear with the forces of evil, embodied in a demon, rather than with the vikings themselves or with the sins of the Franks. The arrival of the vikings was part of God's plan, but it was for the sake of the salvation of the Scandinavian raiders themselves, rather than for the good of Frankish souls. The new people, the Normans, in Fulbert's narrative were the 'chosen people' who assured the saints of the 'highest veneration' in their own lands. They were no longer the enemies of the saints, but their rightful patrons and supporters.

The prophetic passages in the *Vita Romani* convey an understanding of ethnicity in Normandy that privileged the new settlers, but was not hostile to those who traced their roots back to Frankish origins. In their superior position, the vikings were shown as a ruling elite, who steered the destiny of the principality through their good government. The previous – Frankish – inhabitants were shown as subordinate, but not in conflict with the newcomers. This narrative, therefore, distinguished between settlers and natives of Normandy, and related this ethnic distinction to the stratification of society. The Scandinavian migrants' association with Romanus justified their authority over the conquered Neustrians, and so the *Vita* presented a narrative of reconciliation, though not ethnic integration.

The lack of reference to viking leaders and the ducal dynasty further distinguishes Fulbert's vision from other early hagiographical and historical texts: the dominant narrative established by Dudo and reflected in the Fécamp Chronicle foregrounds Rollo's family, whereas Fulbert referred to a broader class of viking conquerors. Other iterations of Romanus's hagiography – notably the very similar, but briefer, version written by a certain Gerard (BHL 7313) – do not contain the prophetic passages referring to viking invasions. The date at which Fulbert wrote his *Vita Romani* (and its relationship to Gerard's text) is, therefore, important to our understanding of ethnic narratives in Normandy. Does the *Vita Romani* represent one of the earliest interpretations of viking settlement in Rouen, a contemporary alternative to the dominant discourse, or a later development?

Considerable disagreement arises concerning the date of Fulbert's *Vita Romani*. Lifshitz, in her detailed study of the cult, proposed that this was the earliest version of the hagiography, and that it was written in the 940s or 950s (she suggested 943). The shorter *Vita*, written by Gerard, she believed to be an abbreviation made before 959.[134] Jacques Le Maho, however, has challenged this view and proposed that Fulbert's text was not written until the mid-eleventh century.[135] His interpretation thus implies that Fulbert

---

[134] Lifshitz, 'Dossier of Romanus', pp. 76, 80; Lifshitz, *Pious Neustria*, p. 179. See also J. Howe, 'The Hagiography of Jumièges (Province of Haute-Normandie)', in *L'Hagiographie du Haut Moyen Âge en Gaule du Nord: Manuscrits, textes et centres de production*, ed. M. Heinzelmann (Stuttgart, 2001), pp. 91–125 (pp. 105–7).

[135] J. Le Maho, 'La production éditoriale à Jumièges vers le milieu du Xe siècle',

developed Gerard's text, and the original *Vita Romani* is now lost entirely. Because of the statements made by Fulbert in his opening preface, the relationship of his writings to other texts and the nature of the textual correspondences between Fulbert's and Gerard's *Vitae Romani*, Lifshitz's proposed dating of the mid-tenth century is most plausible. Appendix 1 expands on the evidence and respective arguments in more detail: I conclude that Fulbert wrote the first version of the *Vita Romani* between 940 and 959, and that it was abridged by Gerard not long after its composition. The prophetic passages in Fulbert's *Vita Romani* are, therefore, evidence of a very early vision of ethnic relations in Normandy, presented before the ducal family of Rollo began to play such an essential part in its historical narratives. Potentially, it reflects the presence of several other viking leaders.[136]

Although the actions of successive dukes and archbishops made Romanus into a popular saint in Rouen, the prophetic passages referring to the viking invasions did not become an essential part of Romanus's cult. The various texts adapted from Fulbert's *Vita* – the metrical version and abbreviation made by Gerard, and the offices from Rouen and Fécamp – were all produced swiftly after the original composition, and further texts were added to the dossier in the later Middle Ages. However, none of these adaptations contains the prophecies examined here. Lifshitz suggested that Gerard omitted the mention of Romanus's resting place at Rouen, which is found in the original text, because he knew of the claim of the monks of Soissons to Romanus's head, and sought to be diplomatic.[137] We may apply similar reasoning to his omission of the prophetic passages from his abbreviation and metrical *vita*: they state that relics such as Romanus's head would be sought out and returned to their rightful home of Rouen. Moreover, Gerard of Brogne, if he was the author of these texts, was himself responsible for the continued absence of the Fontenelle saints from Normandy, as he was the force behind their 944 translation to Ghent.[138] Once the anxiety over the loss of Normandy's saints had passed, these prophecies were no longer promoted. Moreover, the image of a stratified ethnic distinction did not last long, but was replaced by the unity described by Dudo and popularized especially in the story of Rollo's dream.

It was by fully acknowledging the past as found in Frankish monastic narratives that the Norman dukes were able to assert their control over the church in their new province. These texts recall how viking raiders without internal

Tabularia 'Études' 1 (2001), 11–32 (pp. 31–2).

[136] See Abrams, 'Early Normandy', p. 64.

[137] Lifshitz, 'Dossier of Romanus', p. 57.

[138] *Une Translation de Reliques à Gand en 944: Le Sermo de Adventu Sanctorum Wandregisili, Ansberti et Vulframni in Blandinium*, ed. N.-N. Huyghebaert (Brussels, 1978), esp. pp. cvi–cxxx, 24–6.

distinctions attacked the Frankish people and church. In Normandy, these raiders became conquerors, who subjugated the people of Rouen and the surrounding area through force of arms. For most of this characterization, the authors of these texts took their lead from previous traditions and accounts written elsewhere in Francia. However, it was only in Normandy that vikings were seen as restorers as well as destroyers. No texts produced in Normandy after 911 presented vikings primarily as the scourge of the Church. References to viking destruction were always matched by narratives of Norman restoration.

Hagiographical accounts such as these provided a historical narrative with which readers could identify. They told a story of local significance, whether focused on one monastery such as Fécamp or a wider community like the city of Rouen. The local audience was drawn to empathize with the followers of the saints, both the inhabitants of Rouen in the distant past under Romanus, and the dukes who patronized Fécamp in more recent years. Elsewhere in Francia, turmoil at the hands of the vikings was presented as divine punishment for Frankish sins. Although Dudo (and the author of the *Translatio Prima Sancti Audoeni*, discussed in the next chapter) confirmed this view, they did not develop it in the same direction. Rather, the process of ruin and restoration, in these texts, benefited the vikings themselves. God called them to Normandy in order that they would hear the name of Christ and be saved. The process also aided those over whom they ruled. The people of Rouen were provided with God-fearing rulers who were also formidable warriors, ready to protect their interests.

These narratives presented the dukes at the head of a Norman people. The earliest of them, the *Vita Romani*, distinguished that *gens* from the Neustrians who already inhabited the area around Rouen. The prophecy spoken by Romanus describes the Scandinavian people as enemies and rulers of the citizens of Rouen. Christianity brought about their transformation into good rulers, but they continued to be distinguished from those over whom they ruled. This kind of narrative was also implicit in the Fécamp foundation chronicle, which employed monastic commonplaces about a violent conquering people persecuting the 'Christian people'. Again, Rollo's conversion changed things in his ruling style rather than his ethnic identity. However, this narrative focused primarily on the ducal family and so the role of other Scandinavian settlers was left unelucidated. As in Dudo's *De moribus*, the trajectory of the Norman leaders represented an entire people.

Consensus around this narrative emerged through the production of texts linked to the ducal family. The ducal palace was situated at Fécamp, and the monastic church there, built by Richard I in his birthplace, would become the family mausoleum. The textual borrowing between Dudo and the author of the Fécamp Chronicle identifies the latter text as similarly a product of ducal propaganda. The narrative of destruction and restoration found in these texts may therefore confidently be identified as emanating from the ducal household. The earlier text of Fulbert's *Vita Romani*, however, presents a slightly different narrative, with no emphasis on any ruling dynasty, and no concept of ethnic integration. If the early date of composition for Fulbert's *Vita Romani* is accepted, then this text provides evidence that ethnic narratives of the relationship between Scandinavian immigrants and native inhabitants were in flux during the tenth century, only coming to crystallize around Rollo's dynasty at the very end of the tenth century.[139]

In the narrative that then came to dominate, presented by Dudo and the Fécamp Chronicler, the dukes presented themselves as viking descendants, and thus as destroyers of the church, but ultimately responsible for the peace that enabled its reconstruction. Because of the prevalence of viking destruction in monastic narratives and, especially, translations, this period could not be ignored. But neither did the dukes disassociate from it: they deliberately identified with the viking past. Emily Albu has suggested that this maintenance of a Scandinavian character was designed to convey a threat to the Normans' neighbours.[140] Their association with vikings of the past meant Normans were believed to be innately ferocious and able to summon Scandinavian reinforcements. Within the monastic narratives of ruin and restoration this viking heritage had a more immediate force. The peace the Norman dukes established was shown to have removed vikings from Francia completely, and enabled the restoration of the saints, their patrimonies, monastic communities and the buildings of the church.

Conclusion

Hagiographical writing was especially suitable for the crystallization of group identities in opposition to each other.[141] Hagiography provided a predefined dichotomy of good and evil, represented by the saint and his demonic or human persecutor.[142] Because these texts were intended to recruit

---

[139] Cf. Pohl, *Dudo's* Historia Normannorum, p. 73; F. McNair, 'The Politics of Being Norman in the Reign of Richard the Fearless, Duke of Normandy (r. 942–996)', *EME* 23 (2015), 308–28.

[140] Albu, *Normans in Their Histories*, pp. 7–9.

[141] I. H. Garipzanov, 'Introduction: History Writing and Christian Identity on a European Periphery', in *Historical Narratives and Christian Identity on a European Periphery: Early History Writing in Northern, East-Central and Eastern Europe (c. 1070–1200)*, ed. I. H. Garipzanov (Turnhout, 2011), pp. 1–11 (pp. 1–2).

[142] A summary of methodological approaches and recent work can be found in C. Watson, 'Old English Hagiography: Recent and Future Research', *Literature Compass* 1 (2004) ME 100, 1–14; E. G. Whatley, 'An Introduction to the Study of Old English Prose Hagiography: Sources and Resources', in *Holy Men and Holy Women: Old English Prose Saints' Lives and Their Contexts*, ed. P. Szarmach (Albany, 1996), pp. 3–32. For Latin saints' lives, see L. Coon, *Sacred Fictions: Holy Women and Hagiography in Late Antiquity* (Philadelphia, 1997), pp. 1–25. F. Lifshitz, 'Beyond

adherents to the cults they supported, they encouraged their audiences to relate to their saintly protagonists and their followers. Hagiographical texts exhorted devotees to protect the rights and possessions of the saint against enemies who might encroach upon them, thus continuing the dichotomy of good and evil into their contemporary relations.

Thus hagiographies not only provide evidence of changing ethnic relations, but they also *shaped* ethnic relations by depicting a certain view of the past. Their narratives led readers and listeners to identify the effects of the viking wars and conquests in their own relationships. Just as origin myths represented contemporary political and social entities, so the history of the recent past was written to explain the situations of its readers.

Episodes of conflict hardened these distinctions. Representations and commemorations of conflicts are an integral part of giving violence its meaning. This is certainly true of supposedly 'ethnic conflict' which, Brubaker has argued, should rather be considered 'ethnically framed conflict'.[143] As he has demonstrated, violent dispute only becomes 'ethnic' when it is interpreted as such, whether this is by participants, victims, observers – or historians. Interpretations of conflict as 'ethnic' not only impose meaning on a past event, but may mobilize belief in group identity and even lead to further conflict. In an early medieval context, research into feud has highlighted the importance of narrating events as an integral part of the dispute, and a way to keep the temporarily dormant feud alive. Hagiographies and histories presented conflict from the viewpoint of one side, in contrast to the enemy. Audiences were thus led to identify two sides of a past conflict with significant cultural and social distinctions. Accounts of viking raids and wars, therefore, presented Scandinavian raiders in opposition to existing inhabitants of England and Normandy. Historians led their readers to identify with either the victorious conquerors or the humble and wronged victims of violence. Hagiography provided models for either, in the form of Christian victory or Christian martyrdom.

Furthermore, hagiography had the potential to spread these narratives widely. The deeds and miracles of the saints were celebrated on their feast days, and the laity seems to have attended some of these occasions. Pilgrims came to visit the shrines of the saints and benefit from the *virtus* of their relics. The saints became the subjects for sermons and homilies, which were delivered to laypeople as well as religious.[144] In the case of

---

Positivism and Genre: "Hagiographical" Texts as Historical Narrative', *Viator* 25 (1994), 95–114, emphasizes the historiographical nature of hagiographical texts; however, I believe it is useful to retain the distinction.

M. Gretsch, *Ælfric and the Cult of the Saints in Late Anglo-Saxon England* (Cambridge, 2005), pp. 71–4.

[143] Brubaker, *Ethnicity Without Groups*, p. 9.

[144] On the cult of saints generally, see P. Brown, *The Cult of Saints: Its Rise and Function in Latin Christianity* (Chicago, 1981); S. Yarrow, *Saints and Their Communities: Miracle Stories in Twelfth Century England* (Oxford, 2006); J. Blair, *The Church in Anglo-Saxon*

vernacular hagiography, these texts themselves may have been read aloud to lay audiences. Ecclesiastical networks and their patrons thus exerted the strongest influence over how the past was interpreted and applied to ethnic relations. In Normandy, the dukes took the lead in patronizing monasteries; in England, the kings of the West Saxon dynasty, often in partnership with politically powerful members of the monastic party, supported key religious institutions. Monastic interests and secular rulers combined in each region to produce very different narratives of the viking past.

Continuing to investigate hagiographical writing, the next chapter provides further evidence of these dominant narratives. Moreover, all of the institutions and cults discussed in these two chapters held a further factor in common: the support of secular powers. In England, the West Saxon kings favoured the cult of St Edmund, and patronized the monastic reformers who wrote about him. In Normandy, the ducal lineage made Fécamp its home and family monastery, while the cathedral monastery of St-Ouen sat right at the heart of its power base in Rouen; both were re-established in the tenth century by the support of the ducal dynasty. The histories that came to dominate perceptions of the viking past, therefore, not only reflected monastic viewpoints but also promoted the narratives approved by secular rulers. The texts investigated in the next chapter place those secular rulers at centre stage.

Society (Oxford, 2005), pp. 141–9. On sermons and their audiences, *The Old English Homily and its Backgrounds*, ed. P. Szarmach and B. Huppé (Albany, 1978), esp. M. McC. Gatch, 'The Achievement of Ælfric and his Colleagues in European Perspective', pp. 43–63; C. Wright, 'Old English Homilies and Latin Sources', in *The Old English Homily: Precedent, Practice, and Appropriation*, ed. A. Kleist (Turnhout, 2007), pp. 15–66 (pp. 37–42); D. d'Avray, 'Method in the Study of Medieval Sermons', in *Modern Questions about Medieval Sermons*, ed. N. Bériou and D. d'Avray (Spoleto, 1994), pp. 3–29 (pp. 8–17).

4

Hagiography II: Saintly Patronage

Norman dukes and English kings not only influenced hagiographical narratives, but on occasion acted as protagonists within them, interacting directly with the saints. In the hagiographies examined in this chapter, the bonds between rulers and saints are in each case made explicit and central to the narrative. The Fécamp Chronicle and the *Vita Romani*, discussed in the previous chapter, both used prophecies and visions to connect past and present to the crucial moment of viking invasion. In the texts discussed here, the device of saintly visions was used to even more direct effect. Two *Translationes Sancti Audoeni*, composed in early eleventh-century Normandy, defined the relationship of Rouen's patron saint with the ducal dynasty – a reciprocal relationship, in that the saint demanded devotion from his ducal patrons through posthumous interactions. In tenth- and eleventh-century England, two similar narratives related the appearance of saints Cuthbert and Neot to King Alfred, leading to his victory in battle over the Danes, and thus placed the West Saxon dynasty in these saints' debt. The Latin *Vita Prima Sancti Neoti* and the Old English Life of St Neot reflect the influence of the West Saxon dynasty in eastern and south-western England, respectively; the *Historia de Sancto Cuthberto* presents the dynasty's more gradual establishment of authority in the north. In all three cases, a narrative of personal relationship between saint and ruling dynasty reinforced a dominant perspective on the viking past. Moreover, these vision narratives presented the partnership between ecclesiastical institution (and, by extension, divine approval) and secular power as forged in that viking past.

It emerges that English kings and Norman dukes used saints' cults to establish their authority in comparable ways. Both presented their dynasties as the special devotees of existing cults, and at the same time associated those cults with narratives of the viking past. These similar strategies raise the question of how viking rulers in England interacted with ecclesiastical institutions and saints' cults and so, after analysing these texts, I turn to the slight evidence for such interactions. Courting saintly patronage was clearly a successful strategy for secular rulers in promoting their own ideological agendas, and hagiographical narrative provided a means for shaping the recent past to support their authority.

Normandy: the translations of St Audoenus

The absence of the saints posed a pressing problem when re-establishing the Church in Normandy. During the viking disruptions, many communities, especially those along the Seine at St-Ouen, St-Wandrille and Jumièges, had fled elsewhere to safety, along with their most holy relics. Relics provided a centralizing sense of community for the scattered monks: we find a distinct community of St-Wandrille present in their sheltering monastery of St-Pierre of Ghent as late as 952.[1] The monks carrying the saints' bodies produced texts authenticating the relics and recording their miracles. They narrated the travels of the saints in translation narratives, some of which are corroborated by similar initiatives from those who housed them on their travels, and which used a shared language to describe the Norman terror from which they were fleeing.[2] The vikings fitted into the tradition of pagan destruction found in such *translationes*. Texts from across northern Francia and Aquitaine contained similar descriptions, but their conventional nature meant that, in southern Francia, these roles were filled just as often by Muslims.[3] The image of viking persecutors of the saints was transmitted throughout Normandy and the surrounding regions by these narratives of transportation. Moreover, these translation accounts provided information about the past across the 'caesura' of the viking conquest. In their search for saints, the Norman conquerors encountered a well-travelled image of themselves as the enemy.

The Norman dukes, engaged in a process of re-foundation and reinvigoration of the Church, needed to deal with this problem. The cult of the saints was an important aspect of the Neustrian Church in the Carolingian period, among both ecclesiastics and laity. Venerating the saintly patrons of their monasteries bound monastic communities together. Miracle collections testify to the popularity of the saints among the laity, and their reliance on particular institutions to facilitate access to that holy power. The aristocracy, in particular, displayed their piety through gifts to those saints whom they particularly favoured – or who favoured them. For the main reason that the ducal family were eager to restore the saints to Normandy was surely their belief in the power of saintly patronage. St-Denis's relationship with

---

[1] Musset, 'Monachisme d'Époque Franque', p. 57.

[2] Canon Legris, 'L'Exode des Corps Saints', *Revue Catholique de Normandie* 28 (1919), 125–36, 168–75, 209–21, provides an overview of the translations; A. Trumbore-Jones, 'Pitying the Desolation of Such a Place: Rebuilding Religious Houses and Constructing Memory in Aquitaine in the Wake of the Viking Incursions', *Viator* 37 (2006), 85–102, considers similar narratives written for Aquitaine.

[3] P. Geary, *Furta Sacra: Thefts of Relics in the Central Middle Ages* (Princeton, 1978; rev. edn 1990), pp. 10–15 on *translationes*, and pp. 84–5, 131 on the pervasiveness of vikings and Muslims as the background to translations; pp. 75, 114 for the translation of Mary Magdalene to Vézelay, which demonstrates the interchangeability of Normans and Saracens in many such texts.

the Carolingian kings provided a powerful example, and one with which Archbishop Hugh, who came to Rouen from St-Denis, would have been very familiar.[4] Doubtless strongly encouraged by the monks and clergy of Rouen, Rollo and his descendants wanted to harness the power of the saints by restoring them to their city. They also recognized the political advantage lent by partnership with the church. Rollo probably embarked on this partnership very soon after his conversion; Dudo certainly saw it as an essential part of the process. He presented Rollo taking the initiative, asking Archbishop Franco 'which churches within his land were held in greater respect, and which should be called the more powerful for the merit and protection afforded by the saints'.[5] The historical Rollo did not take much longer than this to recognize the power of the saints.

We encountered one strategy for tackling the problem of absent saints in the previous chapter. While the most distinguished saints were missing from Normandy, the relics of several more insignificant saints, such as Romanus, had been left behind when the monks departed. The settlers – apparently now Christians – used these saints to assert continuity with the region's past, and to lend spiritual authority to their nascent rule over the region's inhabitants. Originally they may have been of lesser status than saints such as St Audoenus, the focus of this chapter, but they held the advantage of being physically present in the principality. The issue of status, after all, could be dealt with through the promotion of these saints by ecclesiastical institutions and their writers of hagiography. As discussed in the previous chapter, and in greater detail by Felice Lifshitz, ecclesiastics at Rouen cathedral seem to have promoted the cult of Romanus in just such a context.[6]

However, St Audoenus, another early Merovingian bishop of Rouen and patron of the episcopal monastery of St-Ouen, was the first saint whose support the Norman dukes cultivated. Through possession of his important position, he was considered the patron of Rouen in general. Audoenus was also one of the few saints of Rouen who was well-known further across Francia.[7] The monks of St-Ouen had fled, with the relics of their patron and four other saints, during the viking invasions. The initial flight probably occurred in the face of a viking attack in 872, according to a charter of Riculf, archbishop of Rouen.[8] The *translatio* examined below states that

---

[4] '*Acta Archiepiscoporum Rotomagensium*: Study and Edition', ed. R. Allen, *Tabularia* 'Documents' 9 (2009), 1–66 (p. 38); see G. Spiegel, 'The Cult of St Denis and Capetian Kingship', *Journal of Medieval History* 1 (1975), 43–69, for the alliance of St-Denis with Frankish royalty throughout the medieval period.

[5] Christiansen, p. 50; Lair, p. 170: 'quae ecclesiae veneratiores in sua terra haberentur [sciscitatur], et quae potentiores merito et patrocinio sanctorum dicerentur'.

[6] F. Lifshitz, 'Eight Men In: Rouennais Traditions of Archiepiscopal Sanctity', *HSJ* 2 (1990), 63–74 (pp. 66–7).

[7] Legris, 'L'Exode des Corps Saints', p. 129.

[8] *Translatio Secunda Sancti Audoeni* (BHL 757), *AASS*, August IV (1752), pp. 823–4,

Audoenus returned to Rouen in 918. Guillot has questioned whether this date is accurate, proposing that his relics were returned some years later, but the monastery of St-Ouen seems to have been re-inhabited early in the tenth century.[9] Coins were being struck in the name of St Audoenus by the 940s, which indicates that the monastery was functioning by this point.[10] If the monks had returned, they had undoubtedly brought their patron with them.

Two *translationes* of St Audoenus recounting these events were written in the early eleventh century.[11] They appear to have been written by two different authors, at different times: the second summarizes the first at its opening, indicating that it was conceived as a separate text rather than a continuation (chs.17–19). This summary differs in an important matter of detail. The first *translatio* follows the relics of St Audoenus, St Nicasius and his companions on their enforced exile from Rouen, stating that St Audoenus was taken to Condé-sur-l'Escaut while Nicasius and his companions went to 'Wanbasio'.[12] The second *translatio*, however, states that Audoenus went to 'Wadiniacum' (Gasny, a detail taken from the 872 charter), and that all four saints' bodies were then taken to Condé. The difference in accounts reveals that the *translationes* were written by two separate authors, party to different information. The second *translatio* refers back to the time of Richard I, so it was written after his death; Arnoux suggests before 1001.[13]

---

ch. 18; Legris, 'L'Exode des Corps Saints', p. 133, thought the relics were taken to Gasny in 841; P. Lauer, 'Les Translations des Reliques de Saint Ouen et de Saint Leufroy du IXe au Xe siècle, et les deux abbayes de la Croix-Saint-Ouen', *Bulletin Philologique et Historique du Comité des Travaux Historiques et Scientifiques* (1921), pp. 119–36 (p. 127), used the Rouen annals to claim that the relics were taken from Rouen twice during the ninth century (in 841 and in the 870s), but this seems to be based on a misreading of the *translatio*; this is corrected by F. Lifshitz, 'The Migration of Neustrian Relics in the Viking Age: the Myth of Voluntary Exodus, the Reality of Coercion and Theft', *EME* 4 (1995), 175–92 (p. 179), to show that they were at Gasny in 872, but returned by 876, and were taken to Condé at some point after this; a charter of Riculf, archbishop of Rouen, dating from 872 records that the relics had been removed to Gasny 'causa metus Nordmannici': it is printed in J.-F. Pommeraye, *Histoire de l'abbaye royale de St-Ouen de Rouen* (Rouen, 1662), pp. 399–400 and see further Potts, *Monastic Revival and Regional Identity*, p. 21.

[9] Guillot, 'La conversion des Normands', pp. 216–17; Lauer, 'Les Translations de Saint Ouen et de Saint Leufroy', pp. 130–2; but for an argument in favour of 918, see Lifshitz, 'Migration of Neustrian relics', pp. 179–81.

[10] Dumas, *Le Trésor de Fécamp*, p. 100, n. 2.

[11] *Translatio Prima Sancti Audoeni* (BHL 756), *AASS*, August IV (1752), pp. 820–2; *Translatio Secunda Audoeni*.

[12] Pommeraye, *Histoire de l'abbaye de Saint-Ouen*, pp. 379–80 notes that the Livre Noir of St-Ouen identifies Wanbasio as Vanbase, in Luxembourg, a priory of the abbey, given by St Audoenus during his lifetime. It was from here that St Nicasius's relics were recovered by a monk of St-Ouen in 1032 (Herrick, *Imagining the Sacred Past*, pp. 17–18).

[13] *Translatio Secunda Audoeni*, ch. 20; Arnoux, 'Before the *Gesta Normannorum*', p. 36.

However, the reference to 'Robert the Dane', who was deceased at the time of writing, provides a further clue. Although van Houts has identified him as an unknown son of Richard I and Gunnor, he was probably their son Robert who became archbishop of Rouen in 989, and died in 1037.[14] Thus the second *translatio* is more likely to date from the period after 1037. It continues the same narrative as the first *translatio*, but we can see that the monastery's sphere of influence had enlarged by this point.

The *translationes* claim that it was Rollo himself who was the prime mover in recovering the relics of St Audoenus. The second *translatio*, summarizing, states that Rollo, having converted and restored peace, restored Audoenus to 'propriae ecclesiae Rothomagensi'. The first *translatio* took this restoration as its main theme. Firstly, it states that it was Rollo's action which motivated and legitimized the transfer of the relics back into Normandy. The desire came from the people of Rouen, who missed their saint and needed him to combat the drought they were suffering (ch.4); the information required was passed on to Rollo by Archbishop Franco (ch.5); but it was Rollo himself who persuaded the king, somewhat aggressively, that the relics should be returned to Rouen, 'ad propria' (ch.6). Secondly, it was Rollo who physically brought the relics back into the city – an action which the saint himself endorsed and required. At a certain place one mile outside the city, the bier on which the saint's body lay became immovable (ch.8). It was only once Rollo had given a gift of land, had restored the rights and properties of the saint and had pledged himself as the monastery's protector, that the body could again be moved (ch.10). Rollo bowed his neck and took the bier upon his shoulders, becoming the first to bear Audoenus into the city (ch.11). Rollo's conversion and absolution was completed through this action, for Rollo's particular sins were outrages against the saints themselves, and had caused the exile of Audoenus in the first place. The rest of the Danes followed Rollo's lead in converting (ch.12), and the presence of the saint duly put an end to the drought (chs.13–14).

In emphasizing Rollo's central role, the text dealt directly with the problem facing the Norman dukes in their encounters with the saints: the fact that their activities and those of their ancestors were responsible for the exodus of holy bodies to begin with. The first *translatio* opens with an account of the viking desecrations (ch.1). The author, in common with his contemporaries and predecessors, described an invasion of a people: 'an army of the faithless and most cruel people of the Danes' ('perfidae ac crudelissimae gentis Danorum exercitus'). It appears at first that the author identified with the Franks, stating

[14] *Gesta Normannorum Ducum*, I, 130, n. 1; J. Le Maho, 'Après les Invasions Normandes', in *L'abbaye Saint-Ouen de Rouen, des origines à nos jours*, ed. J.-P. Chaline (Rouen, 2009), pp. 25–32 (p. 32, n. 9). Robert's close association with St Peter of Chartres makes it likely that he was buried there, as the *Translatio* states 'Robert the Dane' was.

that the Danes devastated 'the neighbouring places of our home' ('finitima... habitationis nostrae loca'). However, this could rather be read as referring to the places which the Normans would later inhabit as their own, since the author generally referred to the Franks as 'Galliae populum' in his narrative, as opposed to the inhabitants of Normandy. Nevertheless, he did not vilify the Franks, despite claiming that the viking invasions were a punishment for their sins. Instead, he likened them as a people to Israel (ch.2), a comparison he later also drew for the Normans (ch.9). The account established that the Danes were responsible for destruction in Francia generally (ch.1), and Normandy specifically (ch.2): the monastery of Jumièges and the city of Rouen were singled out as having been attacked. Thus it was the Danes who caused the monks to flee with St Audoenus, 'rabiem metuentes gentilium', a phrase which echoes the 'causa metus Nordmannici' of the earlier charter.[15]

The *Translationes Sancti Audoeni* made no attempt to disassociate the Norman dukes from this past. The first *translatio* claimed that Rollo took part in the worst of these activities, and explicitly stated that he destroyed churches and massacred Christians (ch.2). The characterization of Rollo as 'trusting in his warlike strength... just like a lightning-bolt invading the borders of Gaul' would not have been wholly negative, however: it presented the Norman leader as heroic and strong, a formidable force against the Franks (or Gauls).[16] Once he had become a Christian, Rollo's activities related to the destruction he had wrought (ch.3). The writer of the *translatio* stated that the newly baptized Rollo, 'regretting all of his past evils', dedicated himself to 'the restoration of the churches of God which he had destroyed'.[17] The heathen destruction of Rollo's past could not be ignored, so instead it was used to emphasize the completeness of his conversion. Rollo at the moment of conversion was described as 'just like Constantine' ('uti Constantinus'), an association made implicitly by Dudo in his account of Rollo's dream.[18] Just like Constantine's, Rollo's leadership was successful because of his conversion to Christianity, and like the Roman emperor he brought about peace and unity through that conversion. Rollo's ferocity only helped in this image: his demands to the king threatened a disturbance to the peace which

---

[15] Pommeraye, *Histoire de l'abbaye de St-Ouen*, p. 399; the author of the second *translatio* explains that the body was moved once more 'ob metum infandorum gentilium'.

[16] *Translatio Prima Audoeni*, ch. 2: 'bellicosa fretus virtute... velut fulgur fines irrumpens Galliae'.

[17] *Translatio Prima Audoeni*, ch. 3: 'praeteritorum poenitens malorum totum se contulit ad ecclesiarum Dei, quas destruxerat, restaurationem'.

[18] Christiansen, pp. 29–30, Lair, p. 146. B. Pohl, 'Translatio imperii Constantini ad Normannos', makes the argument that Dudo modelled Rollo's entire life-story on Constantine; see also Pohl, *Dudo of St-Quentin's Historia Normannorum*, pp. 197–223. Although Dudo makes no explicit comparison with Constantine, the use of this phrase in the *Translatio Prima Audoeni* seems to support Pohl's argument and imply that at least one contemporary read his work in this way.

he had created. In this way, the *translatio* transformed Rollo and the Normans from the cause of saints' exodus to the facilitators of their return home.

The narrative of Rollo's conversion, and the importance ascribed to it here, strongly recall Dudo's account. As well as the comparison to Constantine, there are points of similarity in factual detail (such as his marriage to Gisla) and in the characterization of baptism. As Olivier Guillot has demonstrated, it appears that Dudo's text influenced the writer of the *translatio*.[19] However, it is far more than simply a copy – there are few direct borrowings – and thus it demonstrates the currency of Dudo's view at the turn of the eleventh century. It is a further example of how a single dominant narrative of the viking past became accepted in Normandy, as discussed in the previous chapter.

A key development beyond Dudo's narrative is the emphasis in this *translatio* on Rollo's followers as well as the viking leader himself. The author stated that God took pity on the Franks and subdued 'the fury of the raving heathens' ('debacchantium furorem... gentilium') through the conversion of Rollo; he was baptized alongside his army; and Christians rejoiced not only at 'the conversion of so great a duke' but also for 'the salvation of the heathen people'.[20] The conversion of the Danes who accompanied Rollo was described at length (ch.12). The author invoked the words familiar from ecclesiastical accounts of viking attacks as the characteristics of the Danes in the past. Now converted, the Danes were said to turn from vicious, heathen enemies into the opposite, virtuous and peaceful Christians:

> And the Danes who were now there were turned from wolves into lambs, not, as formerly, gaping with bloody jaws at their prey but, together with the others, venerating the precious relics of the saint, just as the prophet said, the lion will eat chaff with the ox. And no longer did they thirst for human blood in bestial madness, or in the manner of heathen sorcerers seek divination in the entrails of sheep; but they embraced brotherly love from the heart, and, detesting foolish playthings and incantations of idols, they willingly requested intervention from the saints.[21]

The transformation of the Danes bonded them with the Christians around them. By juxtaposing their previous pagan state with their new Christian identity, the author dramatized the conversion of the Norman people and stressed its completeness. There is an unusually direct reference to

---

[19] Guillot, 'La conversion des Normands', pp. 208–17.

[20] *Translatio Prima Audoeni*, ch. 3: 'pro tanti ducis conversione & gentilium salute'.

[21] *Translatio Prima Audoeni*, ch. 12: 'Aderant ibi & Dani jam ex lupis facti agni, nec ut olim praedae cruentis rictibus inhiantes; sed una cum aliis pretiosas Sancti reliquias venerantes, juxta quod propheta, Leo, inquit, & bos simul comedent paleas. Nec enim ulterius belluina rabie humanum sitiunt cruorem, nec more gentilium sortilegorum, vel in extis pecudum rimantur divinationem; sed geminam ex animo complectuntur dilectionem, & inepta execrantes ludicra, & idolorum naenias, sanctorum pronixe expetunt interventionem'.

their previous religion, but this was now replaced by the veneration of St Audoenus.[22] Moreover, this account of the Danes' conversion melded them with the other inhabitants of Rouen, who had requested the return of St Audoenus. It depicted the converted Danes worshipping 'together with the others', and in doing so they fulfilled the prophecy that the lion of Danish fury would live peacefully alongside the ox of the frightened Rouennais; furthermore, their rejection of paganism was coupled with 'brotherly love'. The text took the general point that it was Christianity which bonded the new Danish people with the previous inhabitants of the Seine valley, and applied it more specifically to St Audoenus.

The *Translatio Secunda Sancti Audoeni*, written slightly later in the reign of Richard II, presents the other side of the relationship between Audoenus and the Norman dukes. Whereas, in the first *translatio*, Rollo had pledged to be the saint's benefactor and special protector, in this second account it was the saint himself who insisted on the connection. The *translatio* relates how Audoenus appeared to Richard I in a dream and castigated the duke, physically and verbally, for protecting his sanctuary in Rouen insufficiently. In doing so, he reminded Richard of his people's viking past and Christian conversion. At the time of the vision, Richard was building himself a stronghold in Bayeux. Audoenus accused him of growing in wealth at the expense of the church: 'your ancestors, erupting from outside and barbarian nations, had gained these spoils and resources by burning and despoiling…'.[23] Audoenus's words to the duke explicitly recalled the translations of saints out of Normandy during the viking period, and laid the blame for this squarely at the Norman dukes' feet. He said,

> My monks, forced by hunger, even stripped off my golden vestments, and they endured the hardship of much need, carrying me off with them on their pilgrimage and flight, on account of their fear and the rapacity of the cruel pagans.[24]

Audoenus's message to Richard was clear: he must guard and honour the saint appropriately, for he and his ancestors had sinned greatly against him. Audoenus even threatened him with 'the torments of eternal hell'

---

[22] The contemporary Norman poet Warner refers to vikings divining using the entrails of animals (Warner of Rouen, *Moriuht*, ll. 147–8 and 190–4, with comments on pp. 150–1).

[23] *Translatio Secunda Audoeni*, ch. 22: 'tui vero antecessores ab exteris & barbaris nationibus erumpentes, praedia & facultates… depraedando & incendendo abstulerunt'.

[24] *Translatio Secunda Audoeni*, ch. 23: 'Insuper etiam vestimentum meum aureum monachi mei, famis compellente inedia, detraxerunt, & multarum incommoda egestatum in sua peregrinatione & fuga me secum ferentes ob metum & rapacitatem crudelium paganorum pertulerunt'.

('aeternae... tormenta gehennae') unless he built an appropriate church for him and his companion saints. In response, Richard granted two properties to St-Ouen and promised lights for the two altars in the church. The preceding story acted as an explanation and a record for these gifts.[25] Furthermore, the stated connection between Audoenus and Duke Richard also applied to successive Norman dukes. The community at St-Ouen was just as invested in the narrative of viking conversion as the dukes were: it allowed them to emphasize the obligations of the dukes towards their saint and church.

These obligations were raised when the monks felt under threat. In this text, the threat appeared from outside Normandy, in the shape of the Franks. The reason that Audoenus appeared to Richard was an attempt at *furta sacra* by two Frankish monks.[26] The *translatio* clearly defined Franks against Normans, as an alien presence in Rouen. Had their attempt at theft been successful, the author stated, it would have been 'an irretrievable loss and an insufferable sorrow to us, or rather, a national calamity (*iustitium*) for the entire Norman people'.[27] This passage demonstrates that Audoenus's relics were more than a possession of the monks of Rouen. Their presence in the duchy linked the saint with the whole population, the Normans. They therefore needed to be defended from Franks who came to steal them and now posed the threat in place of the vikings. The passage set up 'the entire Norman people' in opposition to the Franks, united through the patronage of St Audoenus and the protection of the dukes.

Together, the *translationes* show how the viking past was used in the reciprocal relationship of duke and Church. Successive Norman leaders courted the support of St Audoenus and presented themselves as his primary protectors, who had redirected the ferocity which had caused him to flee. The monks of St-Ouen repeated the same narrative, reminding the dukes that their power in Normandy was the gift of Audoenus. This partnership deflected challenges to the central authority of the dukes and Rouen from divisions within Normandy: the shared devotion of ducal subjects to Audoenus cohered Danes and natives, inhabitants of Rouen and Bayeux. Moreover, this devotion defined Normans against outsiders – Franks – who threatened to deprive them of their patron.

The transformation of Danes and natives into Normans, therefore, was negotiated through the contrast with the Frankish people. This contrast between

---

[25] The text functioned in this sense like a charter, and even mimicked one in some respects: the threat of hell worked like the *sanctio* clause. See further M. Chibnall, 'Charter and Chronicle: The Use of Archive Sources by Norman Historians', in *Church and Government in the Middle Ages: Essays Presented to C. R. Cheney on his 70th Birthday*, ed. C. N. L. Brooke and others (Cambridge, 1976), pp. 1–17.

[26] See generally Geary, *Furta Sacra*.

[27] *Translatio Secunda Audoeni*, ch. 20: 'nobis irreparabile damnum & intolerabilem luctum, immo potius totius Normanniae genti justitium'.

in-group and out-group overrode distinctions internal to the population of Normandy and acted as the motor that drove ethnic narratives. Yet it seems likely that the focus on the relationship with Franks reflected high-level ducal anxieties, rather than the concerns of ordinary people in Rouen or in lower Normandy. Ducal authority in these texts was limited by the king and other Frankish nobles, not the duke's subjects, whether Scandinavian immigrants or long-term inhabitants. Moreover, while the narratives hint at enmity – the second *translatio* of Audoenus, in particular, contrasts the interests of Frankish monks to those of the Normans – it seems that these identities were formed as much through allegiance to princes as to places of origin. Most of the monasteries which the Norman dukes re-founded were peopled by monks from elsewhere in Francia. While the Norman dukes were demonstrably interested in the restoration of the churches which had been destroyed or vacated in the ninth century, they do not seem to have been concerned with restoring the original communities. Fécamp was established as a male house where previously there had been a nunnery, and was reformed by William of Volpiano from 1001. After this, William became the abbot of Jumièges but, even at its 942 re-foundation, Jumièges had been populated by Martin of St-Cyprian, Poitiers, and his monks. It has been suggested that Fulbert, the author of the *Vita Romani*, was one such monk. Like Dudo, these monastic authors wrote for the Norman dukes but may also have had Frankish allegiances.

This complex relationship between the Normans and Franks is reflected in the production of Norman hagiography concerned with the distant past. The *Vita Romani*, discussed in the previous chapter, is one example of this: the *Vita Aichardi* by the same author, and the *Vitae* of Vigor, Taurinus and Nicasius, were also concerned with the era of the conversion of the Merovingian Franks.[28] The production of these texts emphasized the similarities of the contemporary situation with the distant past, although only the *Vita Romani* made these comparisons explicit. Parallels with the Franks arriving in Gaul and their conversion through the agency of these saints suggested the innate similarity of these peoples' histories. The Normans in this view were, in a sense, the successors of the Franks and their superiors, who inherited the land which the Franks had been too sinful to retain.

Internally to Normandy, the combination of peoples forged together into one ethnic group also appeared to result from the dukes themselves. As in the *De moribus*, the *translationes* focused on the ducal family as rulers, who cohered their subjects into one Norman people. The author of the first *Translatio Audoeni* devoted more attention to Norman subjects than Dudo had done, describing the conversion of Rollo's Danish followers, who became one with the existing citizens of Rouen through their veneration of St Audoenus. This solution may have been suggested by the language of the earliest

---

[28] For the latter three Lives, see Herrick, *Imagining the Sacred Past*.

monastic accounts of vikings despoiling the church: they contrasted the barbarian Northmen with the 'Christian people' of the lands they attacked. In becoming Christian, therefore, the Northmen could be seen to unite with those they conquered. Nevertheless, Rollo led the way, and the Danes' and natives' joint devotion to Audoenus could also be seen as joint submission to the new viking leader.

The two *Translationes Audoeni*, like the texts examined in the previous chapter, reflect the influence of Rollo's dynasty on the ecclesiastical institutions they supported. The monasteries where literary activity took place were those restored and patronized by successive Norman leaders: St-Ouen, Fécamp, Jumièges. We also find evidence that the dukes promoted the cults of these saints: the mint established in Rouen to produce ducal coinage was responsible for the production of coins in the names of saints Audoenus and Romanus.[29] Institutional links further testify to the closeness between the ducal family and the writers of these texts. As the dukes gained a firmer hold on the Rouen see, one of their own family, Robert, became archbishop. It was during his episcopate that the first *translatio* of Audoenus was composed. The hagiographical texts produced at these institutions in and around Rouen, closely associated with the dukes, must therefore have presented narratives approved and promoted by these rulers. Yet, as the second *Translatio Audoeni* demonstrates, production of textual histories was also a means by which ecclesiastics held the dukes accountable and defended their own interests. Their viking heritage had been transformed into a positive history and source of authority for the Norman dukes, through their partnership with the Church; but it never became neutral, and this transformation depended upon the rulers fulfilling their obligations to the institutions that supported them.

England: King Alfred's saintly visitors

Hagiographical writers in England used similar strategies to connect the West Saxon kings to saintly patrons. A particularly close comparison may be seen in the employment of visions in hagiographical narratives. Just as the Norman ducal dynasty's relationship to Audoenus was negotiated and emphasized through the saint's appearances to Duke Richard I in a vision, so were relationships constructed between the West Saxon dynasty and saints Neot and Cuthbert through the saints' posthumous appearance to King Alfred. Texts reporting these visions were composed in the mid-tenth to early eleventh century: perhaps it is in the nature of this category of narrative that visions are situated in the past, since the passing of time

---

[29] Moesgaard, 'Saints, Dukes and Bishops: Coinage in Ducal Normandy', p. 205 and above, pp. 110–11, 126.

makes it difficult to assail the credibility of the episode, and also allows the inclusion of prophecies. In these cases, however, the appearance of the saints to earlier generations reinforced the connection with the dynasty, rather than the individual ruler. Just as Audoenus referred to Richard's viking ancestors and ducal successors, so Neot and Cuthbert's words to Alfred reflected the continuing interests of the West Saxon dynasty. The rest of this chapter investigates how these episodes constructed political and ethnic relations in late Viking Age England.

Defending the kingdom: St Neot

Similarly to the hagiographies of St Edmund, the cult of St Neot at Eynesbury (Huntingdonshire) established a narrative of one English kingdom attacked by vikings. Like nearby Ramsey, where Abbo composed his *Passio Eadmundi*, Eynesbury was a monastic house newly founded by one of the most prominent Benedictine reformers, in this case Æthelwold.[30] The hagiography produced there displayed a view of the viking past in many ways similar to that of the *Passio Eadmundi*, but which concentrated instead on King Alfred's victory over the viking force led by Guthrum.

The two earliest surviving hagiographies of St Neot, one in Latin and one in Old English, both contain the saint's admonitions to King Alfred, including a prophecy that his kingdom would be overrun by vikings; and they contain an account of Neot's appearance to Alfred before battle, promising that he would lead the English to victory. They also relate the story of Alfred burning the cakes, which would later become famous because of its interpolation by Matthew Parker into Asser's *Life of Alfred*; the earlier of the two is the first witness to this legend.[31] Both texts were written in the late tenth or early eleventh century, but their relationship is not clear.

Both hagiographies were long considered post-Conquest productions, until research by Michael Lapidge on the Latin *Vita Prima Sancti Neoti* and Malcolm Godden on the Old English Life of St Neot established that each of them was written in the late tenth or eleventh century.[32] Appendix 2 explores the composition of these texts more thoroughly; as discussed there, the relationship between the Latin and Old English Lives suggests that the *Vita Prima Sancti Neoti* should in fact be situated early in Lapidge's suggested window for composition, and thus probably before the end of Æthelred's reign. The *Vita Prima Sancti Neoti* must have been written following the foundation of the priory at Eynesbury (modern St Neots) sometime after 975. Although

---

[30] VPSN, p. lxxvii: according to the Liber Eliensis, Eynesbury was founded with monks from Ely and Thorney between 975 and 984 by St Æthelwold.

[31] *Alfred the Great*, ed. Keynes and Lapidge, pp. 197–202, presents discussion and translations of all the earliest records of this legend.

[32] VPSN, pp. lxxv–cxxiv; M. Godden, 'The Old English Life of St Neot and the Legends of King Alfred', *ASE* 39 (2010), 193–225.

Neot lived in Cornwall, the *Translatio* which follows the *Vita Neoti* (probably by the same author) tells of the translation of his relics to Huntingdonshire.[33] The Old English Life, on the other hand, was probably composed closer to the original cult site; perhaps at one of the institutions where Neot's festival was celebrated in the West Country, such as Glastonbury, Exeter, Crediton or Sherborne, as Godden has suggested.[34]

The different narratives found in the two early texts may most usefully be viewed in relation to their places of composition. The differing depictions of Neot's interactions with viking forces in England, in particular, display the different concerns of hagiographers in eastern and western England during Æthelred's reign.

These different concerns are particularly clear regarding the characterization of the conflict between Alfred and the vikings. The Old English Life is more critical of Alfred: it contains a passage emphasizing that 'he immediately took to flight in terror and abandoned all his soldiers and his chieftains, and all his people, his treasures and treasure-chests, and looked to his own safety'.[35] The hint of criticism in the Old English Life of Neot may be contrasted with the favourable picture Abbo painted of Edmund, who was willing to die for his people and country. The issue of the king's role in defending his kingdom was clearly topical.[36] However, the author of the Old English Life of St Neot was largely unconcerned with the viking enemies of King Alfred, describing them briefly as 'Guthrum, the heathen king, with his bloodthirsty army'.[37] The *Vita Prima* author, on the other hand, spent considerable effort elaborating on their characteristics. The conflict between Alfred and Guthrum, the viking leader, is the main theme of the *Vita Prima Sancti Neoti*. In devoting the majority of the text to the development of this conflict, the hagiographer emphasized the distinction between Christian English and pagan Dane, and encouraged his audience to identify with the former group.

---

[33] VPSN, p. cii.

[34] The Old English Life was written for delivery on Neot's feast day: it opens by referring to 'þyssen halgen, þe we todæig wurðigeð': 'The Old English Life of Seinte Neote', in *Early English Homilies from the Twelfth Century MS Vesp.D.xiv*, ed. R. D. N. Warner, EETS os 152 (London, 1917 for 1915), 129–34 (p. 129). Godden, 'Old English Life of St Neot', p. 211.

[35] 'Old English Life of Seinte Neote', p. 132: 'he sone forfyrht fleames cepte, 7 his cæmpen ealle forlet, 7 his hertogen, 7 eall his þeode, madmes 7 madmfaten, 7 his life gebearh'. This passage (translated in *Alfred the Great*, ed. Keynes and Lapidge, pp. 198–9) contradicts the reference in the *Vita Prima* to Alfred's treasures being with him in hiding: VPSN, p. 125: 'thesaurorumque locula custodiri locupletaria'. On the depiction of Alfred, see Godden, pp. 212–13.

[36] See further K. Cross, 'Byrhtferth's *Historia regum* and the Transformation of the Alfredian Past', *HSJ* 27 (2015), 55–78 (pp. 76–8).

[37] 'Old English Life of Seinte Neote', p. 132: 'Guðrum, se hæðene king, mid his wælreowen here'.

The *Vita* begins with an account of the early life of Neot in Glastonbury abbey (chs.1–4) and then as an anchorite in Cornwall, where he ultimately founded a monastery (chs.5–7). According to the *Vita*, King Alfred heard of Neot's reputation and visited him in Cornwall, where he received admonition from the living Neot on two occasions. As a result, Alfred sent alms to Rome for the *schola Anglorum*. Neot also prophesied his own death and the arrival of the pagan armies (chs.8–9). After Neot's death (ch.10), the narrative moves to the invasion of the pagan king Guthrum. Guthrum's army was so vicious and successful in conquest that Alfred was forced to flee to Athelney, where he stayed with a swineherd and was scolded by the swineherd's wife for allowing the bread to burn (chs.11–12). The rest of the *Vita* concerns Alfred and the English regaining power at the battle of Edington in 878. Alfred reassembled his troops and, after two nocturnal visions of Neot, succeeded in defeating and converting the pagan forces (chs.13–17). The *Vita* ends with the peaceful completion of Alfred's reign (ch.17). It is followed by a *Translatio* explaining the presence of the saint's relics in East Anglia, and a miracle collection, probably by the same author (chs.18–23).[38]

The earliest mention of Neot occurs in Asser's *Life of Alfred*, which suggests that the saint's connection with the West Saxon king was a long-standing one.[39] Although there are a few chapters in the *Vita Neoti* describing the life of Neot at Glastonbury and in Cornwall, the major part of this text was concerned with the saint's relationship with Alfred, during life and after death. In fact, the *Vita* ends with the death of Alfred, rather than that of Neot. However, although Alfred was a central focus of the text, Neot's spiritual superiority was clearly demonstrated. Neot not only exhorted Alfred to good, but rebuked him for sinful behaviour. Mary Richards attributed this aspect of Neot's hagiography to Celtic influence.[40] The text developed Alfred's role to an unusual degree, while his reputation would have enhanced that of Neot.

The *Vita* describes how, when Neot's prophecies came to pass, Alfred had to learn patience and humility before being given aid to overcome his enemies.[41] The tale of Alfred burning the cakes while staying with a swineherd, which later became a popular legend about the king, appears at

---

[38] VPSN, p. cii.

[39] *Asser's Life of Alfred*, p. 55; see VPSN, p. lxxxvi. A section of the *Annals of St Neots*, derived from the *Vita Neoti*, was interpolated into Asser's Life of Alfred by Matthew Parker, but this reference appears to be genuine, and probably inspired the insertion: see *Alfred the Great*, ed. Keynes and Lapidge, p. 201.

[40] M. Richards, 'The Medieval Hagiography of St Neot', *Analecta Bollandiana* 99 (1981), 259–78 (pp. 266, 274).

[41] The emphasis on royal humility resembles a similar emphasis in Æthelred's diplomas, discussed in C. Insley, 'Charters, Ritual and Late Tenth-Century English Kingship', in *Gender and Historiography: studies in the history of the early middle ages in honour of Pauline Stafford*, ed. J. Nelson and S. Reynolds with S. Johns (London, 2012), pp. 75–89.

this point in the *Vita*. This legend laid emphasis on the moral and spiritual improvement of Alfred through Neot's intervention. However, the activities of the Danes were not depicted as a punishment on a sinful king. Alfred was always shown as receiving God's favour, and his sufferings were evidence of God's care:

> For from him [Neot] he had received what he held faithfully in his grateful heart: for the apostle says, 'He whom the Lord loves, he chastises; and he scourges every one of the sons whom he receives'.[42]

Just as Edmund's death had been transformed into martyrdom, part of the divine plan, so Alfred's defeat and suffering were depicted hagiographically as evidence that Alfred had a special importance to God and St Neot.

After these sufferings had been recounted, the author narrated Alfred's recovery and defeat of the Danes, in which he was directed and led at every stage by Neot. The focus was on Alfred's vision before the battle of Edington in 878, an incident which is better known from its inclusion in the *Historia de Sancto Cuthberto*, discussed below. This episode is more developed in the *Vita Prima Sancti Neoti*, however, in which Neot is said to have made two appearances to Alfred, in addition to his original prophecy during his life.

The hagiographical context again provided models for the *Vita Neoti*. Guthrum, the viking leader and Alfred's enemy, took on the role of villain. Guthrum was depicted in the text as a vicious pagan, in the same florid language used in Abbo's *Passio Eadmundi*. Like Hinguar, he was characterized as 'tyrannus'.[43] This typical description of a persecutor in martyrological literature was particularly appropriate in texts composed in East Anglia, an area of previous viking rule, or at a time of external Danish threat such as Æthelred's reign – it implied that Danish leaders had no right to rule any part of Britain. The paganism of the vikings was also emphasized – although in this case, Guthrum was eventually converted. Guthrum was introduced as one 'cruelly tangled in the deception of idols', who 'pulled down all the holy places, he trampled on them', and in his actions 'blasphemed everything holy'. He was identified as an enemy of God, 'with his soul hastening to perpetual destruction'.[44] Guthrum's conversion fulfilled Neot's earlier prophecy to Alfred, in which he predicted that his victory over the pagans would be so

---

[42] VPSN, p. 126: 'Ab ipso enim conceperat memori quod pectore credens tenebat: 'Quem,' namque inquit apostolus, "Dominus diligit, castigat; flagellat autem omnem filium quem recipit" (Hebrews 12.6)'. Alcuin also evoked this verse in two letters to Higbald, bishop of Lindisfarne in 793: *Alcuini Epistolae*, pp. 57, 59.

[43] VPSN, p. 124.

[44] VPSN, p. 124: 'idolorum crudeliter irretitus errore'; p. 125: 'sancta omnia loca destruxit, conculcauit' (compare Alcuin's description of the sack of Lindisfarne, pp. 95–6); pp. 128–9: 'cunctaque sancta blasphemare; quippe animo ad perpetuum festinanti'.

complete that he would restore them to God.[45] The extent of their paganism was emphasized in order that this appeared a striking measure of Alfred's success. Alfred achieved saintly qualities through Guthrum's conversion. He was compared to the martyr Stephen, 'entreating the Lord for his stoners – by whose prayers even Saul was changed into Paul'.[46]

Guthrum played a prominent role as leader of the Danes in the legend of St Neot. One chapter of the *Vita Neoti* even reported the speech Guthrum made to his army before battle. The demonization of Guthrum would have had special relevance to the eastern audience of the *Vita Prima Neoti* and the community at Eynesbury. Alfred and Guthrum's 878 agreement, which saw Guthrum placed as ruler over East Anglia, is not mentioned in the *Vita Neoti*. Rather, Guthrum's conversion was described as the condition that meant Alfred allowed him to go home. The hagiographer followed the Anglo-Saxon Chronicle for the events of this chapter, and so the change must have been a deliberate one. The *Vita Neoti*'s details of Guthrum's surrender and conversion match those given in the Chronicle – that Guthrum came to Alfred at Athelney, three weeks after his defeat, and brought thirty companions for baptism.[47] However, rather than following the Chronicle's account of Guthrum's settlement and rule in East Anglia, the *Vita Neoti* stated that, on their surrender, the Danes 'promised by swearing oaths that their prince would be a worshipper of the holy and indivisible Trinity, and likewise that they would cross over the sea to their own country from where they had landed'.[48] The hagiographer emphasized this again later in the same chapter, describing how the newly Christian Guthrum 'went over the sea to his own kingdom with his companions', in contrast to King Alfred, who held 'the throne of the kingdom'.[49] The hagiographer chose to ignore the Chronicle entry for the year 880, which stated that 'the raiding-army went from Cirencester into East Anglia, and settled that land, and divided it up'.[50] The claim that the Danes went back to their own kingdom appears in the Old English Life and the (post-Conquest) *Vita Secunda* as well.[51] East Anglia and

---

[45] VPSN, p. 128.

[46] VPSN, p. 132: 'quasi alter Stephanus pro suis exorans Dominum lapidatoribus – cuius etiam precatibus Saulus commutatus est Paulus...'

[47] The Old English Life contains 'thirteen' in error for 'thirty' in this passage (p. 133), which suggests that the author did not consult the Chronicle directly, but misunderstood his or her Latin source. However, it does contain the detail that Guthrum stayed twelve days with the king, found in the Chronicle but neither of the two Latin *vitae*.

[48] VPSN, p. 132: '...iureiurando spoponderunt eorum principem sancte et indiuidue Trinitatis fore cultorem, et perinde ad propria unde huc appulerant se transfretaturos'.

[49] VPSN, p. 133: 'ad propria transfretauit regna cum sociis'; 'regni solio'.

[50] ASC A: 'Her for se here of Cirenceastre on Eastengle 7 gesæt þæt lond 7 gedelde'.

[51] 'Old English Life of Seinte Neote', p. 133: '7 he twelf dages æfter þan her on lande wunede mid mycelre blisse, 7 syððen gesund gewende mid his herelafe to his agenen earde mid ealre sibbe'; Vita II, ch. 65: 'suam cum suis recessit in patriam'.

the northern provinces of England are not mentioned in any of these texts; they all implied that the Danes departed back to Denmark, and that Alfred united the English peoples under his rule.

English and Danish in the North: St Cuthbert

A very similar episode occurs in the *Historia de Sancto Cuthberto*, a text produced by the community of St Cuthbert in northern England. This text, while including a summary of St Cuthbert's life, deals with the patrimony of the community before and after his death. The descriptions of gifts and thefts of land are supplemented by miracle accounts which explain the circumstances of the transactions and indicate the severe consequences of disrespecting the property of St Cuthbert. Like the *Translationes Audoeni*, the *Historia de Sancto Cuthberto* presents the acquisition and maintenance of property as intimately connected to devotion to the saint. The miracles and transactions are generally presented chronologically, with some inconsistency, covering the period from the time of Cuthbert to King Cnut. The narrative is at times disjointed, and the latter parts of the text (from chapter 26 onwards) mimic charters. Finally, a miracle account concerning King Guthred has been added at the end, out of place chronologically.

The unusual nature of the text has led to considerable discussion about its dating and composition. The *Historia de Sancto Cuthberto* was clearly drawn together from a diverse range of sources, including Bede's *Historia ecclesiastica*, land charters and probably oral tradition. However, the disagreement lies in whether this compilation occurred at one time, in two stages or over a long period. The different models are outlined by the *Historia*'s editor, Ted Johnson South, and also by Sally Crumplin.[52] Johnson South argues for a later, eleventh-century date of composition for the text; however, Crumplin has argued effectively against this model of composition, which is based largely on the thematic unity of the text. As she has demonstrated, this unity does not require a single author, but is a reflection of the ongoing concerns of the Cuthbertine community. A continuous process of composition explains the disjointed narrative (resulting in repetitions and chronological inconsistencies) and changes in style, as well as the evolving attitudes to the Danes and West Saxons found in the text. Crumplin's theory suits the structure of the text, and also helps to explain the move from Danes as protectors in the early part of the text, to enemies in the later sections, as a reflection of the changing loyalties of the community in the mid-tenth century.

The *Historia* shows a definite moment of change, as the community was adopted by West Saxon patrons after having previously benefited from the

---

[52] HSC, pp. 25–36; S. Crumplin, 'Rewriting History in the Cult of St Cuthbert from the Ninth to the Twelfth Centuries' (unpublished doctoral thesis, University of St Andrews, 2005), pp. 34–41, 61–70.

support of the Danes.[53] From chapter 15 onwards, the focus of the *Historia* was no longer solely on the Cuthbertine community, but expanded to include the West Saxon dynasty. Local history was now contextualized by connections to the West Saxon kings, whose deaths and successions were carefully recorded. The text identified support for the West Saxon kings with support for Cuthbert: for example, Ealdred son of Eadwulf allied with Elfred, a 'faithful [man] of St Cuthbert' because he 'was a favourite of King Edward, just as his father Eadwulf had been a favourite of King Alfred'.[54] The *Historia* particularly emphasized the devotion of Alfred as the king who first pledged loyalty and protection to Cuthbert. By the time of the *Historia's* composition, Alfred's reputation as the vanquisher of the Danes appears to have been already well developed.

The *Historia's* transfer of allegiance to the West Saxon kings was effected by Cuthbert's appearance to Alfred before the battle of Edington in 878. This episode bears great similarity to the parallel episode in the *Vita Prima Sancti Neoti* and the Old English *Life of St Neot*. In the *Historia de Sancto Cuthberto*, Cuthbert promised in the vision to help Alfred against the Danes, and in return Alfred and all his descendants pledged devotion to the saint. This section of the text has been regarded by some as an interpolation made after 1016, since the extant manuscripts mistakenly name the battle-site as *Assandune*, the site of Cnut's 1016 victory. However, Crumplin has argued that the confusion was in fact with Alfred's 871 battle at Ashdowne, and there are sufficient references to the episode later in the text for the idea that this section was added later to be dismissed.[55] Luisella Simpson has also demonstrated the likely mid-tenth century context for the miracle.[56] Furthermore, the miracle is referred to in the early sections of the *Historia regum*, composed by Byrhtferth of Ramsey around 1000.[57] For all these reasons, it is safer to assume the mistake of a later copyist than a later date for composition.

There are numerous similarities between the accounts found in the *Historia de Sancto Cuthberto* and the *Vita Prima Sancti Neoti*: in each case, the saint is said to appear to Alfred one night while the king cannot sleep, to reveal his

---

[53] For a historical narrative of the community's relationship with Danish and West Saxon patrons, see W. M. Aird, *St Cuthbert and the Normans: The Church of Durham, 1071–1153* (Woodbridge, 1998), pp. 24–49.

[54] HSC, pp. 60–1: 'Elfredum sancti Cuthberti fidelem'; 'erat dilectus regi Eadwardo sicut et pater suus Eadulfus dilectus fuit regi Elfredo'.

[55] Crumplin, 'Rewriting History', p. 40.

[56] L. Simpson, 'The King Alfred/St Cuthbert Episode in the *Historia de Sancto Cuthberto*: its significance for mid-tenth century English history', in *St Cuthbert, His Cult and His Community to AD 1200*, ed. G. Bonner, D. Rollason and C. Stancliffe (Woodbridge, 1989), pp. 397–411; HSC, pp. 90–4.

[57] *Symeonis monachi opera omnia*, II, 83. Cross, 'Byrhtferth *Historia regum*', pp. 73–4: it is possible that Symeon, knowing the *Historia de Sancto Cuthberto*, interpolated this passage into the *Historia regum*.

identity to a doubtful Alfred and then to predict Alfred's victory in battle against the pagans. However, there are considerable differences of emphasis in the two texts, and there do not appear to be any textual parallels. The only clear written source for this section of the *Vita Neoti* is the Anglo-Saxon Chronicle, and there is no textual precursor for the Cuthbert episode.[58] Yet it stretches credibility to believe that two such similar episodes arose independently. Roger of Wendover, writing his *Flores Historiarum* in the thirteenth century, certainly saw the two as one incident: he combined the *Vita Prima Sancti Neoti* with William of Malmesbury's account of Alfred's vision of Cuthbert, and so both saints appear in his version of the episode.[59]

The incidents' similarities in content, but differences in style and presentation, might best be explained by a common, perhaps orally transmitted, source for the narrative. Because the *Vita Prima Sancti Neoti* was previously considered an eleventh-century text, the episode has usually been presented as secondary to, if not derivative of, the *Historia de Sancto Cuthberto*.[60] Johnson South considers both stories to have originated in the West Saxon court in the tenth century, perhaps with Æthelstan, as the West Saxon kings attempted to consolidate their rule in the North and East of England.[61] This theory explains the emphasis on Alfred and his descendants, and the presence of a similar narrative in two separate areas, associated with two different cults. Furthermore, both saints were also associated with the kings of Wessex in other ways: the legend of Neot developed to make him a brother of Alfred, while the community of Cuthbert created links of patronage with successive West Saxon kings. However, the Alfred incident, though similar in essence, developed independently for Neot and for Cuthbert. When each text was composed, the narrative changed to reflect local concerns as well as those of the West Saxon kings. But both emphasized that the West Saxon kings, represented by Alfred, were the rightful Christian rulers, and associated the Danish leaders with paganism and destruction.

Many of the differences can be explained by the incident's role in each text. The *Vita Neoti*'s concern was to demonstrate the victory of Christianity against the forces of paganism. In the *Historia de Sancto Cuthberto*, the appearance of Cuthbert facilitated a bargain between king and saint which established new, reliable protectors for the community. In return for victory in battle, Cuthbert demanded the loyalty of Alfred and urged him, 'be faithful to me and to my people'.[62] Cuthbert explicitly granted Alfred power over 'tota Albion' and

---

[58] VPSN, pp. cv–cviii.

[59] Roger of Wendover, *Chronica sive Flores Historiarum*, ed. H. Coxe, 5 vols. (London, 1841–44), I, 330–3; William of Malmesbury, *Gesta Pontificum*, I, 312–13, 408–11 (and cf. *Gesta Regum*, I, 182–3); VPSN, pp. cxix–cxx.

[60] E.g. Gretsch, *Ælfric and the Cult of Saints*, p. 78.

[61] HSC, pp. 90–4.

[62] HSC, pp. 54–5: 'Esto fidelis mihi et populo meo'.

made him 'rex totius Britanniae', titles which Æthelstan and his successors used in their charters.[63] It was a hereditary right. From that moment forth, the West Saxon kings became Cuthbert's protectors, and their enemies the Danes were now Cuthbert's enemies too.

The compilers of the *Historia de Sancto Cuthberto* used miracles several times to demonstrate who currently received St Cuthbert's favour. Earlier sections of the text, before Alfred's vision, are ambivalent about the Danes (or Scaldings, as they are sometimes called), and demonstrate the co-operation and negotiation that took place between them and the community.[64] In an early section, Ælle, an Anglo-Saxon king of Northumbria, 'made good promises to the holy confessor but acted badly' in taking the possessions of St Cuthbert.[65] In this episode, Ubba, the 'duke of the Frisians... with a great army of Danes' ('dux Fresciorum cum magno Danorum exercitu'), was the instrument of God and St Cuthbert, and exerted revenge on the Northumbrian king. But he was not exempt from Cuthbert's anger, for, although he was permitted to ravage all England, he received divine revenge when he finally devastated the lands of St Cuthbert.[66] Co-operation with the Danes could go further: the community received oaths and engineered the placement of Guthred as king.[67] In these earlier sections, there was no mention of the kings of Wessex, and the ethnic origins of the various kings appear to have made little difference to how they were depicted. If anything, the Danes were presented as Cuthbert's best protectors. However, from the time of Alfred onwards, the kings of Wessex were shown as the rightful rulers of all England (or even Britain), and the Danes as the pagan enemy. As we have seen, at no point in the *Passio Eadmundi* or *Vita Neoti* was the settlement of the Danes acknowledged. The *Historia de Sancto Cuthberto*, on the other hand, dealt extensively with the settlement and land-ownership of the vikings, and the army which settled in Northumbria was contrasted positively with those who settled in Mercia and Sussex.[68] However, in Alfred's vision of Cuthbert, the West Saxon king gained 'all Albion', and the following chapters detail the community's recuperation of the land which they had lost to the Danes, 'sicut iustum erat'.[69]

The change in presentation of viking leaders is starkest in a miracle said to occur during the reign of Edward the Elder (899–924).[70] The compiler presented Onlafbald, a warrior of king Rægnald, unambiguously as the

---

[63] Simpson, 'The King Alfred/St Cuthbert Episode', pp. 400–2; HSC, p. 93.
[64] See pp. 34–5 for discussion of 'Scaldings'.
[65] HSC, pp. 50–1: '...bene promisit sancto confessori sed male egit'.
[66] HSC, pp. 50–3.
[67] HSC, pp. 52–3.
[68] *Ibid.*
[69] *Ibid.*
[70] HSC, pp. 60–3.

enemy of the community of St Cuthbert.[71] He was associated with the devil, exactly like Hinguar in the *Passio Eadmundi*: he was called 'son of the devil' ('filius diaboli') twice in this short passage, while he had a 'diabolical heart' ('diabolicum eius cor') and, finally, it was the devil who dragged him into Hell. Onlafbald's wickedness was displayed through his paganism, which caused him to blaspheme St Cuthbert. The author of the *Historia* even included the names of the pagan deities, having Onlafbald pronounce: 'I swear by my powerful gods Thor and Odin that from this hour I will be the bitterest enemy to you all.'[72] As in Abbo's *Passio*, religion was presented as an uncrossable divide between the community and the pagan Danes. Furthermore, the pagan enemy was depicted as receiving divine revenge for his actions. At the end of this chapter, the compiler recorded that Onlafbald died after the community begged God and Cuthbert to seek revenge. At the end of the next chapter, king Rægnald was similarly said to have received divine revenge for his outrages against St Cuthbert, dying in battle against the English, 'and of the things that he had stolen from St Cuthbert he took away with him nothing except [his] sin'.[73] The reader was left in no doubt that the arrogant, blasphemous pagan king and his followers were enemies to the Christian community, in contrast to the pious, protective kings of Wessex.

The divide between Christian and viking was depicted in a way appropriate to the hagiographical context, but there are noticeable differences from the narratives of Abbo and the anonymous author of the *Vita Prima Neoti*. Most importantly, the association of Alfred and the West Saxon kings with the community is not depicted as a natural connection, but one earned through the patronage of the saint. Cuthbert helped them because they supported him, not because they were the natural rulers of Northumbria. Indeed, the title 'rex totius Britanniae' implied that this new realm included several peoples.[74]

A sense of Christian community against the Danes, rather than explicitly English ethnicity, emerges from the *Historia de Sancto Cuthberto*. The differences from the presentation of the English in the *Vita Prima Sancti Neoti* (and in Abbo's *Passio Eadmundi*) may be explained by the likely earlier date of the *Historia*'s compilation, but they also reflected the different situations of East Anglia and Northumbria. The Northumbrians maintained political independence from the rest of England for a much longer time, and the *Historia de Sancto Cuthberto* reflects the West Saxon kings' respect for their

---

[71] HSC, pp. 60–1: 'Et hic filius diaboli inimicus fuit quibuscunque modis potuit Deo et sancto Cuthberto' ('And this son of the devil was an enemy, in whatever ways he was able, of God and St Cuthbert').

[72] HSC, pp. 62–3: 'Iuro per meos potentes deos Thor et Othan, quod ab hac hora inimicissimus ero omnibus uobis'.

[73] *Ibid.*: 'nichilque de his quae sancto confessori abstulerat secum praetor peccatum tulit'.

[74] Simpson, 'The King Alfred/St Cuthbert Episode', pp. 401–2. See pp. 171–5.

identity: however, they clearly rejected any Danish elements through the intercession of St Cuthbert.

In each case, the texts considered here rewrote ninth- and early tenth-century events and attached them to the cults of saints who were already venerated. Cuthbert was commemorated by three existing Lives when the *Historia* was compiled, and was venerated on the Continent as well as in northern England.[75] Although Neot and Edmund both died in the ninth century, these texts appear to be the first hagiographical works concerning them. However, they had both been the subjects of cults of some sort for around a century before the texts were composed. The emphasis on viking aggression found in these hagiographies was an added focus to existing cults. Even in the case of Edmund, who was killed by vikings, there is evidence to suggest that other qualities, such as his royal status, had been equally important in the early stages of his cult.[76]

Similarly, most accounts of relics being moved through fear of viking attack were written in a later period. It is well known that the community of St Cuthbert left Lindisfarne with the relics of their saint and travelled around northern England during the late ninth century, until settling at Chester-le-Street (and eventually Durham in 995). This period of wandering is generally seen as a flight from viking attackers, who raided Lindisfarne in 793 and perhaps again in 875, and thus equivalent to those reported in Normandy. However, the earliest record of this wandering, which comes from the community itself (in the *Historia de Sancto Cuthberto*), does not mention the viking invasions. It was not until the twelfth century that this connection was made explicit.[77] Unlike in Francia, where the viking threat to saints rapidly became a hagiographical commonplace, the desecration of shrines in England was a much later narrative development.[78] There is no contemporary equivalent to the *Translationes Audoeni* from England. In pre-Conquest texts from England, the posthumous interaction of saints with viking invaders was limited to the activities of Cuthbert and Neot.

Thus the viking connection was not a general feature of late Anglo-Saxon hagiography. The two cases considered here, along with the texts concerning St Edmund discussed in the previous chapter, are the only ones to deal with

---

[75] Gretsch, *Ælfric and the Cult of Saints*, pp. 71–4.

[76] Cf. those described in Rollason, 'Cults of Murdered Royal Saints'.

[77] HSC, p. 99; T. Johnson-South, 'The Norman Conquest of Durham', *Journal of the Charles Homer Haskins Society* 4 (1992), 85–95. There are examples of contemporary fear, however: a 1001 charter of Æthelred to Shaftesbury abbey (S899) granted the *cenobium* of Bradford-on-Avon for the protection of the relics of the saints (including his brother, Edward the Martyr), so that 'aduersus barbarorum insidias ipsa religiosa congregacio cum beati martiris ceterorumque sanctorum reliquiis ibidem Deo seruiendi impenetrabile optineat confugium'.

[78] Cross, '"And that will not be the end of the calamity"'.

this aspect of the past. The unity of the depictions of vikings as the adversaries of Edmund, Cuthbert and Neot, and their roles within the hagiographies, arose from the geographical and institutional contexts in which they were written. In particular, the West Saxon dynasty influenced these narratives of the viking past and therefore the presentation of ethnic identities.

These hagiographies all presented a West Saxon viewpoint. In the cases of Cuthbert and Neot, Alfred and his descendants were given central importance. Even the texts describing the martyrdom of Edmund emphasized the community of the English promoted by the West Saxon dynasty. It seems likely that the West Saxon kings encouraged and transmitted these narratives associated with cults they patronized.[79] The interest of the kings in Cuthbert can be traced most clearly, from Æthelstan onwards, and the success of the connection is demonstrated by Abbo's reference to Cuthbert in his preface to the *Passio Eadmundi*. The partnership of the West Saxon kings with these communities was not a one-sided process. Simpson has shown that locating the origins of patronage in the past, with Alfred, legitimized the connection for the Cuthbertine community.[80] Half a century later, a similar narrative was used by the author of the *Vita Neoti* to establish a local cult for his saint, benefiting from and contributing to the developing reputation of Alfred. This formulation of the past implied that these areas had been loyal to the West Saxons since the time of Alfred, rather than the actual conquests of Edward the Elder and Æthelstan.

These were not the only saints patronized by the West Saxon kings, but they all had specific qualities that suited them for association with the viking past. Most importantly, they were venerated in specific areas: those which had been under Scandinavian rule and which had been most affected by Danish settlement. The rightful exercise of power around Durham, and the competition between various claimants, including Scandinavians, is one of the main themes of the *Historia de Sancto Cuthberto*. Whereas this text negotiated the transfer of authority and allegiance, the hagiographies of Edmund and Neot denied that the Danes ever wielded significant power in England. This may be because East Anglia, where these cults were based, was not ruled by Danes for such a long time. Furthermore, West Saxon influence and then conquest of the area occurred much earlier in the tenth century. Overwriting the viking history of East Anglia may therefore have been a more rapid process than in

---

[79] D. Rollason, 'Relic-cults as an Instrument of Royal Policy c.900-c.1050', *ASE* 15 (1986), 91–103, esp. pp. 95–6, deals with the acquisition of northern saints' relics by West Saxon kings as an expression of political dominance.

[80] Simpson, 'The King Alfred/St Cuthbert Episode', p. 407. D. Rollason, 'St Cuthbert and Wessex: The Evidence of Cambridge, Corpus Christi College Ms. 183', in *St Cuthbert, His Cult and Community*, ed. Bonner, Rollason and Stancliffe, pp. 413–24 (p. 417) emphasizes, however, that the impetus for the connection came primarily from the West Saxon monarchs.

the North. West Saxon interest in all of these cults, however, responded to their earlier histories of Danish rule and settlement. These narratives were aimed specifically at those communities likely to present an alternative to the West Saxon view of ethnic conflict.

Viking rulers in England

The similarity between the strategies of Norman dukes and English kings in employing saints' cults as supports to their expanding authority raises the question of whether viking rulers in England attempted anything similar.

No comparable texts commissioned or patronized by viking rulers in England survive. It is unlikely that this is merely a matter of survival: rather, they seem to have operated in a predominantly oral culture. The lack of a textual literary culture at viking courts, and a broad lack of textual production in ecclesiastical institutions within viking polities (including the production of charters), inevitably meant no new hagiographical written texts were produced. However, viking rulers in England may well have patronized and co-operated with saints' cults in other ways. The *Historia de Sancto Cuthberto*, as a rare text composed within the sphere of viking political influence, provides hints that this was the case. The most relevant is the story of King Guthred's election, in which Eadred, abbot of Carlisle, redeemed and appointed a slave as the king of the Danish army at the instruction of St Cuthbert; the Danish army then proceeded to swear on Cuthbert's relics, with the community receiving gifts of land and lifelong fidelity from them.[81] Appended to the end of the *Historia* is an account of Guthred's own vision of Cuthbert, in which the saint promised Guthred victory in the next day's battle against the Scots – an incident of striking similarity with the King Alfred episode discussed above.[82] Yet, in other ways, the accounts of the Community of St Cuthbert's relationship with Guthred and the Danes seem fundamentally different from the presentation of its relationship with the West Saxon kings. The episode concerning Guthred's election credits Cuthbert with all the power, and records how he elevated a slave to authority over the Danes, thus neutralizing their own leadership. Moreover, the *Historia* makes no mention of Guthred's successors or ongoing legacy, key features of the West Saxon sections. Because of their oral culture, the production of texts was not of paramount interest to these viking rulers, and so they exerted little influence over the representations which have survived.

Viking kings, *jarls* and *holds* were far more interested in other forms of cultural production. Although we have relatively little evidence for oral

---

[81] HSC, ch. 13, pp. 52–3.
[82] HSC, ch. 33, pp. 68–71; but for the possibility that this is a later interpolation, see pp. 116–17.

literature from ninth- and tenth-century viking England, a few extant verses reveal that skalds produced praise-poetry for local rulers.[83] These poems seem to have emerged from court contexts, and contain pagan mythological allusions rather than references to saints. However, passing references in the two earliest Old Norse prose texts, written in Iceland, are highly suggestive of storytelling about St Edmund within a Norse milieu. Firstly, one genealogy in the twelfth-century Icelandic *Landnámabók* traces ancestry back to Úlfrún, 'dótt[i]r Játmundar Englakonungs' (Wulfrun, daughter of Edmund king of England).[84] Clearly, this reference indicates a strikingly different image of Edmund than that promoted by Abbo and Ælfric. While they emphasized Edmund's virginity, the Old Norse tradition indicated that Edmund had children. Virginity was a highly prized virtue for a Christian saint, so Abbo's insistence on this point does not require further explanation in itself but, in light of this reference, it is possible that he sought to counter claims to descent from Edmund that may have existed in East Anglia.[85] The second set of references appear in *Íslendingabók*, also written in the first half of the twelfth century, by Ari Thorgilsson (who was probably at least partly responsible for *Landnámabók*). *Íslendingabók* dates the settlement of Iceland to the year in which 'Ívarr, son of Ragnarr Loðbrók, had St Edmund, king of the Angles, killed', giving the date 870, said to be from Edmund's 'saga'.[86] The reference may allude to a now-lost saga of Edmund separate from the hagiographical tradition, a suggestion reinforced by the fact that neither the date nor 'Ragnarr Loðbrók' (a name found only in Scandinavian sources) is actually mentioned by Abbo or Ælfric.[87]

---

[83] Townend, 'Whatever Happened to York Viking Poetry?', pp. 51–8; J. Jesch, 'Skaldic verse in Scandinavian England', in *Vikings and the Danelaw: Papers from the Proceedings of the Thirteenth Viking Congress*, ed. J. Graham-Campbell and others (Oxford, 2001), pp. 313–25.

[84] *Landnámabók*, ed. J. Benediktsson, Íslenzk Fornrit 1, 2 vols. (Reykjavik, 1968), I, 49; II, 312. *Landnámabók*, trans. Pálsson and Edwards, pp. 22, 119 (here the translator is following the *Sturlubók* version of the text, which does not include Edmund's title; but *Hauksbók* does, and also specifies that Wulfrun was illegitimate). See Abrams, 'Flegg, Norfolk', p. 313 for a possible East Anglian relevance. For the deployment of this genealogy in Icelandic sagas, see Townend, 'Whatever Happened to York Viking Poetry?', p. 72.

[85] Ridyard, *Royal Saints*, p. 226.

[86] *Íslendingabók*, ed. J. Benediktsson, Íslenzk Fornrit 1, 2 vols. (Reykjavik, 1968), I, 4: 'es Ívarr Ragnarssonr loðbrókar lét drepa Eadmund enn helga Englakonung; en þat vas sjau tegum <vetra> ens níunda hundraðs eptir burð Krists, at því es ritit es í sǫgu hans'; pp. 9, 18, 25–6; *Íslendingabok / Kristni Saga: The Book of the Icelanders / The Story of the Conversion*, trans. S. Grønlie (London, 2006), p. 3; pp. 5, 9, 13.

[87] R. McTurk, *Studies in Ragnars Saga Loðbrókar and its Major Scandinavian Analogues* (Oxford, 1991), p. 7. Smyth, *Scandinavian Kings in the British Isles*, pp. 52–5, suggests that a Ragnarr Loðbrók tradition involving Edmund flourished in East Anglia, providing material involving 'Lodbroch' for later English chroniclers such as Geoffrey of Wells and Matthew Paris.

That our evidence for viking patronage relates to Cuthbert and Edmund, two of the same saints whose West Saxon-influenced hagiographies we have been examining, is no coincidence. Their esteem and influence in these regions made them obvious focuses for the conquering West Saxon rulers; moreover, their histories of viking patronage probably prompted West Saxon rewriting of their cults, in order to produce narratives that supported the claims of the expanding kingdom of England.

The evidence of coinage produced in regions of Scandinavian settlement, encountered several times in these two chapters, also reveals patronage of saints' cults by viking rulers. Indeed, *Landnámabók*'s hint at a narrative tradition relating to Edmund reinforces the argument that the St Edmund Memorial Coinage was minted for viking rulers. The St Peter coins, minted in York *c.* 905–*c.* 919 and during the 920s, and the St Martin coins from Lincoln, which probably also date from the 920s and show a familial relationship to the York coinage, reveal that viking rulers also associated themselves with other powerful saints.[88] St Peter and St Martin were, of course, widely popular saints in early medieval Europe, but it was probably their local significance that attracted conquering rulers to them: St Peter was the patron of York minster, while a church in Lincoln was dedicated to St Martin. The choice of St Martin still requires explanation since, in ninth-century Lincoln, the church of St Mary seems to have been more prestigious.[89] It is perhaps noteworthy that all the saints discussed in connection to viking rulers are male; moreover, the later St Peter and the St Martin coins each use a sword to represent their saint, presumably since both had specific associations with the weapon. This military aspect may have appealed to their new viking devotees. The St Peter coins are particularly intriguing, since in some cases they also display, unmistakably, a Thor's hammer, either on the same side of the coin as the saint's name or on the reverse.[90] Without further evidence, explanations for this combination remain speculative, but it suggests that viking rulers of York imbued the local cult of St Peter with their own meanings and symbols, relating to existing Scandinavian traditions.

These scattered pieces of evidence reveal that viking rulers in England did pursue similar strategies both to viking rulers in Normandy – the ducal dynasty of Rollo – and also to the West Saxon kings of England. They, too, connected themselves to powerful saints of local significance, whether through partnership with ecclesiastical communities, the promotion of new

---

[88] M. Blackburn, 'Expansion and Control: Aspects of Anglo-Scandinavian Minting South of the Humber', in *Vikings and the Danelaw*, ed. Graham-Campbell, pp. 125–42 (pp. 126, 135–8).

[89] C. E. Blunt, B. H. I H. Stewart and C. S. S. Lyon, *Coinage in Tenth-Century England* (Oxford, 1989), p. 106; I. Stewart, 'The St Martin Coins of Lincoln', *British Numismatic Journal* 36 (1967), 46–54 (pp. 46–7).

[90] Blunt, Stewart and Lyon, *Coinage in Tenth-Century England*, pp. 105–6.

cults or the association of local patrons with Scandinavian mythology and symbols. Each strategy, we may surmise, enhanced the conquering rulers' acceptance in their region, among Christian inhabitants and Scandinavian newcomers, through its mobilization of existing traditions of legitimate authority. However, because of the lack of textual production their interpretations of these cults remained temporary and malleable. This lack also suggests a more fundamental drawback, in that they did not provide financial or organizational support to ecclesiastical institutions and networks that would have promoted their messages more widely.

Conclusion

The evidence presented in this chapter indicates the similarities in the strategies employed by English kings and Norman dukes in the mid-tenth to early eleventh centuries. Both dynasties courted saintly patronage as a means to bolster their authority. The saints whose favour they sought, whose institutions they supported and whose relics they collected had particular attributes that attracted secular rulers.[91] In the cases examined here, it is notable that these rulers linked themselves to existing cults of significance: St Audoenus was the patron of Rouen, a well-established saint with the cathedral monastery as his seat and his roots deep in the history of the city; St Cuthbert alone of Northumbrian saints had survived the Viking Age as the focal point of a strong monastic community, and through them he commanded significant power and property; St Neot, previously recognized only in the south-west and Cornwall, found a new context and connection with a prominent ecclesiastical network in the reformed fenland monastery of Eynesbury. Of course, the cases of Edmund and Romanus examined in the previous chapter demonstrate that rulers in both England and Normandy did promote new or uncelebrated cults in the service of their authority.[92] However, it was with established, powerful saints connected to significant institutions, such as Audoenus, Neot and Cuthbert, that secular rulers gained the most through personal association.

These personal associations were constructed in several ways, including ritual performance such as visits to the saint's shrine and material reminders

---

[91] Rollason, 'Relic Cults as an Instrument of Royal Policy'; C. Potts, 'When the Saints Go Marching: Religious Connections and the Political Culture of Early Normandy', in *Anglo-Norman Political Culture and the 12th-Century Renaissance*, ed. C. W. Hollister (Woodbridge, 1997), pp. 17–31.

[92] And, in addition, they promoted cults that had little direct relevance to the viking past and so are not examined here, including Merovingian-era ecclesiastics in Normandy (see Herrick, *Imagining the Sacred Past*) and royal saints and tenth-century reformers in England (see D. Rollason, *Saints and Relics in Anglo-Saxon England* (1989), pp. 133–63, 173–89; Ridyard, *Royal Saints*, pp. 235–7).

such as donations of luxury textiles and illuminated books – one manuscript donated by Æthelstan to the shrine of St Cuthbert contained a picture of the king bowing before the saint, presenting that very book to him.[93] Such actions were the equivalents of the narratives discussed above, which created bonds between saint and ruler through accounts of their direct, personal interactions. In sponsoring narratives, performing actions and commissioning donations, rulers presented themselves and their dynasties as the special devotees of these existing cults. Indeed, in the narratives at least (which, as we have seen, were frequently linked to the performance of pious donation), English kings and Norman dukes also demonstrated that these relationships were reciprocal: they enjoyed the support of the saints, too. Clearly, this support was more valuable, in terms of impressing the local populace, when it emanated from saints widely known and revered in the regions concerned.

Regional significance may hold a further clue to the interest of rulers in these particular saints. The geographical locations of the communities associated with Audoenus, Neot and Cuthbert (and, indeed, Edmund, Romanus and the abbey at Fécamp) reflect two different patterns of expanding authority. The Norman dukes concentrated closely on Rouen (and nearby Fécamp), the centre of their power base, only extending their saintly connections as their authority grew in western Normandy – a process reflected in the *Translatio Secunda Audoeni*. The West Saxon kings of England, on the other hand, concentrated on the borders of regions of Scandinavian settlement, in the fenland area of East Anglia (where Edmund's and Neot's shrines could be found) and north of the viking kingdom of York (where Cuthbert held sway). These two alternatives to some degree reflect the broader patterns of ecclesiastical patronage by both dynasties, but they may also be associated with the specific links created between these cults and the viking past.

Stories of the viking past were particularly relevant in these regions and in the establishment of each dynasty's power within them. The Norman ducal dynasty built up a centre at Rouen, founded on its viking identity – and this is reflected in the hagiographical texts produced there. As the Norman dukes eliminated rival Scandinavian leaders settled nearby, not only did they commandeer the entire viking past for their own lineage, but they also presented lower Normandy's growing attachments to their dynasty, Rouen and Audoenus. West Saxon power in England, on the other hand, centred on Winchester and a strongly Anglo-Saxon heritage, and we find little mention of the viking past in the hagiographies composed in the English heartland. It was only at the frontiers of West Saxon authority, abutting regions of Scandinavian settlement, that the viking past became a focus of hagiographical writing.

---

[93] Rollason, 'Cuthbert and Wessex'; S. Keynes, 'King Æthelstan's Books', in *Learning and Literature in Anglo-Saxon England*, ed. M. Lapidge and H. Gneuss (Cambridge, 1985), pp. 143–201 (pp. 180–5; this article includes a reproduction of the frontispiece).

These texts present a West Saxon appropriation of cults that seem previously to have interacted with local powers – including Danes.

The ruling dynasties in both England and Normandy aligned themselves with saints' cults as a means of dynastic promotion and in order to underpin their authority ideologically. To do so, they used similar methods of personal association – particularly through accounts of visions – but where and how they concentrated their efforts related primarily to the specific demographic and political situations. West Saxon patronage of saints' cults was strategic, and negotiated the ethnic boundary between English and Dane by eliding regional distinctions and loyalties; Norman patronage was more focused, and asserted the distinction between Normans and Franks. The ethnic narratives presented thus arose from a combination of hagiographical construction and local power relationships.

The main difference in these narratives, of course, was that Norman dukes encouraged identification with viking converts, while English kings aligned themselves with Alfred the Great as victor over the viking Guthrum. In so doing, they framed the viking past in each region in ethnic terms relevant to their contemporary audiences. By attributing significance to these narratives as evidence for ethnic relations, and identifying ruling families as their source, this model places considerable emphasis on the actions of political elites in shaping ethnic identities. As such, it may seem to have echoes of the ethnogenesis theory popular – though controversial – in explaining the formation of 'barbarian' peoples in Late Antiquity. This discussion hinges on the transition from the universal aims of the Roman Empire to the language of ethnicity that prevailed in the following centuries. Students of the 'ethnogenesis' school proposed that barbarian war leaders and elites constituted the 'Traditionskern', as holders of ethnic traditions; their followers, from disparate backgrounds, then associated themselves with these ethnic traditions.[94] However, among the various problems with this theory, evidence from the period shows that ethnic identities among non-elites could be maintained while fighting in a different group: the ethnogenesis model makes little allowance for minority or oppressed groups.[95] The idea that elite groups determined ethnic identity in the early Middle Ages, whether in the fourth and fifth centuries or in the Viking Age, has justly received criticism, and I shall clarify how the argument proposed here should be distinguished from such a claim.

Firstly, the narratives created in these hagiographies, although revolving around elite figures and interests, cannot be considered 'traditional', but were newly constructed. In some cases, they may reflect a prior process of

---

[94] Wolfram, '*Origo et religio*'; *Strategies of Distinction*, ed. Pohl and Reimitz. These historians draw on ideas from Wenskus, *Stammesbildung und Verfassung*.

[95] Gillett, 'Ethnogenesis: A Contested Model', pp. 247–52; Heather, 'Disappearing and Reappearing Tribes'.

oral transmission: Abbo claims as much in his preface, while the similarities between the episodes in the Latin and Old English *Lives* of Neot and the *Historia de Sancto Cuthberto* are most credibly explained through a looser process of oral storytelling. Yet these connections merely represent the texts' position within a more general system of historical storytelling: the *Historia de Sancto Cuthberto* and the *Translationes Audoeni* also display links to charters, while their narrative links to place-names were surely intended for future oral repetition. The flexibility of these narratives in the texts that survive demonstrates that they were not closely guarded ethnic traditions but adaptable, depending on the teller and the situation.

Moreover, these narratives cannot be considered reflections of a deeply embedded ethnic tradition among either Rollo's or Alfred's descendants. Instead, they were appropriated: Cornish, Northumbrian and East Anglian saints became West Saxon supporters, while Frankish Merovingian bishops found themselves on the side of the Normans against the Franks. Similarly, the presentation of the narratives, so essential to how ethnic identities were conveyed, reflected hagiographic conventions and the educational backgrounds of the writers – Abbo drew on the *Miracula Sancti Benedicti* from Fleury, the *Vita Neoti* reflected Cornish traditions, the *Translatio Prima Audoeni* presented biblical parallels and Dudo seems to have derived his style, pretensions and some of his material from his Carolingian education and hagiographical models. Thus neither narratives nor identities were 'traditional'. They were created at a certain moment in time, not passed down, and are certainly not evidence of ethnic continuity.

Secondly, it was not merely elite groups who were represented within these texts. While the narratives explored in this chapter focus on elite dynasties and their actions, they do reflect the concerns of a wider group of people. As discussed in the previous chapter, monastic institutions, the immediate creators of these texts, used hagiographical writing as one instrument in their own formulations of community identity, the promotion of institutional interests and the assertion of their relationships to power. Norman dukes and English kings, in associating themselves with the saints, in practice recognized the authority of the institutions and communities who were those saints' worldly representatives.

Furthermore, the audiences of the texts had demands and expectations. The *Historia de Sancto Cuthberto* and the *Translationes Audoeni* were likely received by local monastic and ecclesiastical audiences whose interests revolved around their institutions, but they contain narratives associated with feast days and celebrations attended by wider local populations. Moreover, the clear indications of oral storytelling found in these texts suggest lay interest at elite (the royal court) and non-elite (by vernacular preaching) levels. Subjects did not merely adopt their rulers' ethnic identities. After all, once Cnut had conquered all England in 1016, he continued to refer to his subjects as English *and* Danes. Rulers responded to their subjects' affections and memories in order to provoke feelings of identity. Most clearly, local variations reflect the adaptation of narratives to their audiences. The English hagiographies seem intended for areas of Danish settlement. Therefore, they encouraged inhabitants of these areas to identify with the English, rather than the Danes. Similarly, the Norman hagiographies appealed to the inhabitants of Rouen and emphasized their regional identity in distinction to the Franks.

English and Norman rulers required their subjects to identify with their interests, and consequently they promoted their ethnic narratives through saints' cults, dynastic propaganda and rituals of property transfer (as discussed in the next chapter). In this way, they operated as 'ethno-political entrepreneurs': in pursuit of political goals, and working primarily in their own interests as leaders, they evoked feelings of ethnic affinity and conflict among their subjects, and treated those over whom they held power as if they were members of the ethnic groups described.[96] The narratives that English and Norman rulers promoted were not determined by their biological characteristics or family backgrounds. Presenting themselves and their people in these ways suited their political relationships and the loyalties of their audiences. A successful narrative of ethnic identity could not simply be imposed, but needed to respond to a complex web of existing relationships and ideas about social groups – thus, the Normans had to accept existing stereotypes and understandings of the vikings before they could subvert them in their own interests.

Rulers were the primary ethno-political entrepreneurs because they possessed the mechanisms for disseminating ideological messages widely. In partnership with members of the Church and aristocracies, they had considerably greater influence over the manipulation of identity than anyone else. This was not because ethnic identity was an elite attribute, but because elites had access to the wealth and expertise necessary for the production of cultural artefacts such as the hagiographies discussed here. In fact, in doing so, they clearly responded to perceptions of ethnic relations among different social and regional groups. The promotion of ethnic narratives was usually a process of overriding competing alternatives.

---

[96] Brubaker, *Ethnicity Without Groups*, p. 10. Historical investigations such as this one provide a useful complement and corrective to the 'elite theory' of ethnicity discussed by Malešević, *Sociology of Ethnicity*, esp. p. 125.

5

Charter Narratives: Normans, Northumbrians and Northmen

The regional significance of the saints' cults highlighted in the previous chapter points towards a crucial perspective on viking heritage both sides of the Channel: territorial and geographical distinctions. Different regions responded in varied ways to Scandinavian, English and Norman rulers, and were affected differently by the viking past. In modern historiography, the duchy of Normandy – and with it, the Norman people – is frequently presented as the direct outcome of the actions of Rollo's viking army and the territorial agreement made in 911. Likewise, modern historical accounts of Scandinavian influence in England employ numerous maps revealing the distribution of Old Norse place-names, 'viking' artefacts and Anglo-Scandinavian sculpture across the so-called 'Danelaw'. Yet tenth-century developments, by which the political boundaries of the Norman duchy and the English kingdom were reshaped, proceeded gradually, as Norman rulers received land from the French king and English kings expanded their territory into areas dominated by Norse leaders. Contemporaries did not always attribute the same significance to these developments as modern historians have done. Moreover, existing regional loyalties continued to attract allegiance.

This final chapter compares the historical consciousness represented in Norman ducal charters and English royal diplomas, with particular emphasis on how it related to ethnic identity in different regions. Geographical identity is frequently identified as a focus of ethnicity: Handelman views 'permanent territorial boundaries' as the force which makes ethnicity into a community, and Hutchinson and Smith include 'a link with a homeland' as one of their six main features of ethnic groups.[1] We encountered medieval manifestations of these views in the emphasis on migration myths in Chapter 2, while the idea of the 'homeland', or *patria*, appeared as a strong motivation, full of emotional ties, in many of the historical and hagiographical texts explored in earlier chapters. On a local scale, regional identities were particularly strong in the early medieval world, in societies in which long-distance communication was slow and mass communication infrequent. The various levels of geographical identities illustrate particularly clearly how individuals perceived themselves

---

[1] D. Handelman, 'The Organization of Ethnicity', *Ethnic Groups* 1 (1977), 187–200 (p. 197); *Ethnicity*, ed. J. Hutchinson and A. D. Smith (Oxford, 1996), pp. 6–7.

to be members of several ethnic groups, which were employed in different situations. Among the overlapping geographical identities present in England and Normandy, this chapter explores the perceived effects of viking raids and conquests on geographical boundaries between peoples.

In order to investigate the development of these territorial identities, we need to turn to the documents which dealt with land: charters. Charters reveal how the Normans, the English and their neighbours perceived and negotiated land ownership and occupation. They demonstrated authority over territory in wide and narrow terms. Moreover, ownership of cultivated land included authority over the person who maintained it and the peasants who resided there. Charters also had to justify the process of land transfer in legal terms. This often entailed a narrative explaining the history of a property's ownership, or it might be a more general account of how the property was held. These explanations defined the legal and acceptable terms by which land was owned and inhabited, and thus how it shaped communal identities.

Charters utilized a specific rhetoric of authority, which is the element that will tell us most about identity.[2] I therefore take a primarily literary approach to these documents, rather than following the structuralist analyses of social relations employed by social historians, or more recent investigations into legal history, ritual and literacy.[3] Knowledge of charters' social contexts resulting from such studies has enabled new attempts at literary analyses of these documents, although there is still work to do to integrate the different approaches.[4] The literary choices of charter draftsmen have further potential to increase our understanding of social relations.

The language, concepts and narratives employed in documents reflected and constructed ethnicity no less than did literary texts. Firstly, draftsmen employed formulaic terms for land, the people who lived there and those who held authority over it. These terms, often repeated, defined communities legally. However, they were not inflexible, but changed according to the

---

[2] On the definition and legal expansion of the territory of Normandy, see Bauduin, *La Première Normandie*.

[3] See in particular *Property and Power in the Early Middle Ages*, ed. W. Davies and P. Fouracre (Cambridge, 1995), esp. C. Wickham, 'Property Ownership and Signorial Power in Twelfth-Century Tuscany', pp. 221–44; *Documentary Culture and the Laity in the Early Middle Ages*, ed. W. Brown, M. Costambeys, M. Innes and A. Kosto (Cambridge, 2013); S. Kelly, 'Anglo-Saxon Lay Society and the Written Word', in *The Uses of Literacy in Early Medieval Europe*, ed. R. McKitterick (Cambridge, 1990), pp. 36–62; C. Insley, 'Rhetoric and Ritual in Late Anglo-Saxon Charters', in *Medieval Legal Process: Physical, Spoken and Written Performance in the Middle Ages*, ed. M. Mostert and P. S. Barnwell (Turnhout, 2011), pp. 109–21.

[4] E.g. P. Hofmann, 'Infernal Imagery in Anglo-Saxon Charters' (unpublished doctoral thesis, University of St Andrews, 2008); D. Johnson, 'The Fall of Lucifer in "Genesis A" and Two Anglo-Latin Royal Charters', *The Journal of English and Germanic Philology* 97 (1998), 500–21.

draftsman's preference, the particular situation and current fashion. Moreover, they reflected local differences in terminology and custom. Therefore, the language of charters reproduced various perceptions of regional communities, but also played a role in the definition and maintenance of group identities. Secondly, charter draftsmen interpreted land transactions in general terms. The charters of the Norman Duke Richard II and the English royal diplomas of King Æthelred II included lengthy preambles, or *arengae*, which established the origin and nature of their jurisdiction over the land concerned.[5] The royal and ducal administrations used these preambles, and occasionally the more specific *narrationes*, to impose particular interpretations of their actions, which would be preserved and replicated by the beneficiaries. Therefore, charters promoted the kings' and dukes' views of ethnic relations in the regions under their jurisdiction.

From these aspects of the charters – the terminology of ethnicity, and the *arengae* and *narrationes* – we may trace the development of the idea of a unified 'Normandy', on the one hand, and the recognition of ethnic diversity and a north–south divide within the kingdom of England, on the other. But neither body of evidence makes any significant reference to the viking past. We have to place charters in the context of narratives and law codes to understand the place of the Viking Age in the construction of concepts of Normandy and the Danelaw – which do not turn out to be as analogous as often assumed.

In this final chapter, I focus on the texts of charters, which were surely approved by the benefactors in whose voices they were written, and by the named witnesses. In addition, through associated rituals, the views of geographical identities contained in these charters were presented to a wider audience. There is some evidence that the texts of charters were spoken during rituals of property transfer. Tabuteau notes the example of a Norman charter from the late eleventh century, which states that it was read aloud before being signed.[6] This may well have been more common: given that a charter must have already been written before being read, it is scarcely surprising that few of them record this action.[7] Alternatively, a charter might detail the content of speeches made during the ritual of transfer or privilege. Various narrative accounts indicate that speeches were made before and as part of the issuing of the charter.[8] In a passage of the *Vita Sancti Ecgwini*, Byrhtferth of Ramsey

---

[5] H. Fichtenau, *Arenga: Spätantike und Mittelalter im Spiegel von Urkundenformeln* (Graz-Cologne, 1957), is the classic study of preambles; see more generally H. Wolfram, 'Political Theory and Narrative in Charters', *Viator* 26 (1995), 39–51.

[6] E. Z. Tabuteau, *Transfers of Property in Eleventh-Century Norman Law* (Chapel Hill and London, 1988), p. 131. See also M. Hagger, *Norman Rule in Normandy, 911–1144* (Woodbridge, 2017), p. 37.

[7] Similarly, several charters record that they were placed on the altar during the act of donation: it is unclear at what point the charter was written in relation to this act. Tabuteau, *Transfers of Property*, pp. 130–1.

[8] Tabuteau, *Transfers of Property*, pp. 136–9.

imagined the issuing of a diploma for Evesham abbey at an eighth-century Mercian council in Alcester; it appears he represented it as an assembly of his own time, the early eleventh century.[9] Byrhtferth reported that the king made a speech explaining his intention before the witan. After a diploma had been drawn up and ratified, it was then taken to Evesham, and placed in the altar with speeches including an anathema. It seems likely that the words spoken in Evesham, and perhaps also in Alcester, represented the diploma text.[10] The episode reveals that not only those present at the royal assembly, but also an audience local to the recipient, heard the text of the charter – there is even some suggestion that the congregation of the church may have been present.[11] Whether many could have understood the more elaborate *arengae* is questionable, but the practice of writing the bounds of the property granted in Old English suggests that a non-clerical and local audience had an interest in the text of these documents.

Charter evidence in comparison

This chapter investigates two comparable bodies of evidence: the earliest documents from Normandy, the majority of which were ducal charters issued by Richards I, II and III, up to the year 1027; and the royal diplomas of King Æthelred 'the Unready' of England (978–1016). Although arising from slightly different diplomatic traditions and holding varied legal status, these two sets of documents resemble each other in format, production and the ideas expressed within them.

The series of Norman charters began with Richard I. According to Dudo, Rollo's first actions as Christian ruler of Normandy were to bestow estates from his new land on churches and counts. Dudo specified that he carried this out 'by word of mouth'.[12] Under the earliest dukes – Rollo and William Longsword – there was no tradition of recording property grants in writing. Their descendants found it necessary to formalize their gifts to churches in written charters. Indeed, a 1025 charter of Richard II, which confirmed all the gifts that his ancestors and followers had given to Jumièges, emphasized that previous grants had been oral because his predecessors had not been

---

[9] Byrhtferth of Ramsey, *Vita Ecgwini*, in *Byrhtferth of Ramsey*, ed. Lapidge, pp. 258–67; L. Roach, *Kingship and Consent in Anglo-Saxon England, 871–978: Assemblies and the State in the Early Middle Ages* (Cambridge, 2013), p. 86.

[10] Just as the text of the *Translationes Sancti Audoeni*, examined in Chapter 4 above, may be considered the dramatization of a charter text.

[11] Roach, *Kingship and Consent*, p. 86. Byrthferth records the departure of the people (*populus*/*uulgus*) twice, so it is unclear whether this happened before or after the charter's placement in the altar.

[12] Christiansen, p. 51; Lair, p. 171 : 'coepit metiri terram verbis suis comitibus, atque largiri fidelibus...'.

accustomed to write down such actions.[13] The first written documents were produced under Richard I, who was also the first of the Normans to attest the charters of the French king. The process of writing the charter and having it marked by witnesses probably became familiar to him in this way.

For this comparison, I have analysed all the extant charters produced in Normandy before 1027. This includes fifty-five charters of the reigns of Richards I, II and III, in which the dukes donated or confirmed property transfers, gave concessions or influenced the government of a religious house, or simply attested a charter as witnesses.[14] These documents are supplemented by a small number of charters which did not involve the dukes, but related to properties or beneficiaries within Normandy. Cassandra Potts, building on the analysis in Marie Fauroux's edition of the early ducal charters, established that Richard II's charters, with which we are primarily concerned here, display a number of characteristics that those produced under later Norman dukes no longer contained.[15] In particular, many of Richard II's charters resembled public diplomas, enacted simply by the cross of the duke. Other documents of this period were more akin to private charters, with full witness lists.[16] The variety of forms stemmed from the experimental nature of the first Norman documents.

These Norman charters are placed in comparison with diplomas of King Æthelred from England ('diploma' refers to the formal Latin documents recording gifts and judgements of the Anglo-Saxon king; these are a subset of the term 'charters'). These diplomas recorded judgments of the witan, and included witness lists of those present. According to the Electronic Sawyer database, 117 texts survive which purport to be charters of Æthelred.[17] Two of these are vernacular writs, rather than Latin diplomas, and are not

---

[13] F36 (1025): 'Hec consensu et astipulatione genitoris mei supra nominato loco data sunt, sed minime propriis cartulis descripta'; cf. F53 (1025–26): Rollo 'sed propriis cartulis ad notitiam futurorum minime descripsit'; William Longsword 'simili modo absque cartarum notamine concessit'.

[14] All of these charters are published in *Recueil des Actes des Ducs de Normandie (911–1066)*, ed. M. Fauroux, Mémoires de la Société des Antiquaires de Normandie, 36 (Caen, 1961): references are given in the form 'F36'. Dates are given where available, but most are undated – further details on the dates of individual charters can be found in the *Recueil*.

[15] C. Potts, 'The Early Norman Charters: a New Perspective on an Old Debate', in *England in the Eleventh Century: Proceedings of the 1990 Harlaxton Symposium*, ed. C. Hicks (Stamford, 1992), 25–40 (p. 29).

[16] On public and private acts generally, see O. Guyotjeannin, J. Pycke and B.-M. Tock, *Diplomatique Médiévale* (Turnhout, 1993), pp. 103–4; L. Genicot, *Les Actes Publics*, Typologie des Sources de Moyen Âge Occidental 3 (Turnhout, 1972).

[17] *The Electronic Sawyer: Online Catalogue of Anglo-Saxon Charters* <http://www.esawyer.org.uk/> [accessed 19 May 2013]. Charter references are given by their number in this handlist/database (hereafter S).

considered here.[18] Other documents can be dismissed as spurious. Slightly over half of Æthelred's diplomas have been newly edited in the British Academy Anglo-Saxon Charters series, and in general I have followed the opinions of their editors regarding these charters' authenticity.[19] In addition, Simon Keynes included many valuable comments on the authenticity – or otherwise – of Æthelred's diplomas in his monograph on the subject.[20] For those charters yet to be edited, I have taken Keynes's opinions as my principal guide, but references to further discussion of each document may be found in the relevant entries of the Electronic Sawyer. After dismissing those texts which either are spurious or show signs of later interpolation, ninety-three diplomas remain.[21] Of course, this corpus constitutes a fraction of the diplomas produced during Æthelred's reign, as they are only those which were preserved in the archives of a few religious institutions.[22] However, they survive in sufficient quantity and variety for an analysis of their key features and content. Although some other types of document are extant, such as vernacular wills and leases, and a few charters modelled on royal diplomas but in which the benefactor is a bishop or lay magnate, these had a much lower rate and less representative pattern of survival.[23] Here I concentrate analysis on the royal diplomas, which form a more cohesive group.

Among Anglo-Saxon charters, the character of the diplomas produced for Æthelred makes them particularly suitable for an analysis of this kind. Unlike the Norman examples, Æthelred's charters followed a long, largely unbroken diplomatic tradition in Anglo-Saxon England, dating back at least to 675 (the date of the earliest extant text, S7, although it is not an original

---

[18] S. Keynes, *The Diplomas of King Æthelred 'The Unready': A Study in Their Use as Historical Evidence* (Cambridge, 1980), pp. 140, 145, suggests that writs may have been produced in this period, although the two surviving examples are unlikely to be authentic.

[19] *Anglo-Saxon Charters* series (Oxford, 1973–).

[20] Keynes, *Diplomas*, esp. pp. 237–68.

[21] In the cases of S866 and S912, there are signs of later interpolation in the dispositive or immunity clauses, but their editors argue that the rest of the diplomas are authentic. Therefore these texts have been included in my analyses of royal styles and proems. In this selection of material, I aim not to be reductive, which necessitates using documents which do not survive as originals. Productive answers may be found by restricting analysis to original documents: see J. Crick, 'Edgar, Albion and Insular Dominion', in *Edgar, King of the English 959–975: New Interpretations*, ed. D. Scragg (Woodbridge, 2008), pp. 158–70. However, I follow an approach more similar to that of S. Foot, 'Reading Anglo-Saxon Charters: Memory, Record, or Story?', in *Narrative and History in the Early Medieval West*, ed. E. Tyler and R. Balzaretti (Turnhout, 2006), 39–65 (p. 46).

[22] Keynes, *Diplomas*, pp. 1–4.

[23] See C. Insley, 'Archives and Lay Documentary Practice in the Anglo-Saxon World', in *Documentary Culture*, ed. Brown, Costambeys, Innes and Kosto, pp. 336–62 (pp. 341–2, 362).

copy) and probably to the Augustinian mission of 597.[24] Charter production peaked in Edgar's reign, from which 164 diplomas survive. After this explosion in production, Æthelred's diplomas represent the final height of the Anglo-Saxon Latin royal diploma, soon to be superseded in large part by the writ.[25] Towards the end of Æthelred's reign, fewer charters seem to have been produced, but those that were composed were longer and more considered.[26] They include new and distinctive features, notably short narratives describing the history of an estate and lengthy, often unique, preambles.[27] These features mean that the corpus of Æthelred's diplomas, more than that of any other tenth-century king, describe contemporary perceptions of land ownership and its significance.[28]

Moreover, Æthelred's reign provides special interest since, as we have seen in previous chapters, narrative texts composed in this period showed renewed interest in the ancient Danish heritage of the English (Chapters 1 and 2) and in the historical events of the First Viking Age (Chapter 3 and 4). A focus on Æthelred's charters allows us to investigate the presentation of territorial identity in this same period of renewed viking threat.[29] Likewise, the period 996–1027 that the Norman charters cover saw the production of the majority of the narrative texts from Normandy examined in the rest of this book.

---

[24] P. Chaplais, 'Who Introduced Charters into England? The Case for Augustine', in *Prisca Munimenta. Studies in Archival and Administrative History Presented to Dr A. E. J. Hollaender*, ed. F. Ranger (London, 1973), pp. 88–107, and P. Chaplais, 'The Origin and Authenticity of the Royal Anglo-Saxon Diploma', in *Prisca Munimenta*, ed. Ranger, pp. 28–42; S. Thompson, *Anglo-Saxon Royal Diplomas: A Palaeography* (Woodbridge, 2006), p. 3.

[25] C. Insley, 'Where Did All the Charters Go? Anglo-Saxon Charters and the New Politics of the Eleventh Century', *ANS* 24 (2002), 109–27 (pp. 120–2); Keynes, *Diplomas*, pp. 140–2; P. Chaplais, 'The Anglo-Saxon Chancery: from the Diploma to the Writ', in *Prisca Munimenta*, ed. Ranger, pp. 43–62.

[26] Susan Kelly points out in *Charters of Abingdon Abbey*, Anglo-Saxon Charters 7–8, 2 vols. (Oxford, 2000–1) II, 460: 'If fewer charters were being drawn up, then the draftsmen could spend more time on each text.'

[27] Keynes, *Diplomas*, pp. 95–8.

[28] P. Stafford, 'Political Ideas in Late Tenth-Century England: Charters as Evidence', in *Law, laity and solidarities: Essays in honour of Susan Reynolds*, ed. P. Stafford, J. Nelson and J. Martindale (Manchester, 2001), pp. 68–82 (p. 79): these diplomas 'became more discursive in the (post)-modern sense, that is, more rhetorical, more ideologically charged. Thus we can read from them statements of beliefs and values, hitherto less articulated, which justified political claims in tenth- and early eleventh-century English culture'. See also F. Stenton, *The Latin Charters of the Anglo-Saxon Period* (Oxford, 1955), pp. 74–5.

[29] On Æthelred's charters, see Keynes, *Diplomas*. On the reign of Æthelred, see most recently L. Roach, *Æthelred the Unready* (New Haven and London, 2016); R. Lavelle, *Aethelred II: King of the English 978–1016* (Stroud, 2002); A. Williams, *Æthelred the Unready: the Ill-Counselled King* (London, 2003).

All of these charters were produced under royal or ducal influence, and therefore reflect the views of the ruler in whose voice they were written. However, the practicalities of this system, and the degree of royal or ducal involvement, have been a matter of debate in both cases.

Although Potts determined that, in Normandy, it was 'almost always' the case that documents were produced by the clergy of beneficiary institutions, resulting in considerable diversity, exceptions may be found in the charters of Richard II's reign.[30] Some charters produced under Richard II seem to have been drafted by individuals within the ducal retinue. Of the eight occasions on which notaries were named in grants from Norman benefactors, one notary is already known to us: Dudo of St-Quentin. In one charter (F13) he described himself as Richard II's *capellanus*, indicating a formal position within the ducal household. Witnesses appear in some documents identified with various other offices of the household such as *cubicularius* and *procurator* (F15), *camberarius* and *hostiarius* (F44). In another charter (F18), Dudo described himself as *cancellarius*, as did another notary, Hugo, in 1025 (F34). The use of *cancellarius* suggests that the Norman notaries may have followed the practice of the royal household. Many of Richard II's charters contain common elements: from such evidence, it has been adduced that he began to cultivate a chancery, perhaps in imitation of the royal chancery.[31] The degree of organization is not clear, however, and between Richard's death and the reign of William the Conqueror the duty of producing charters passed back to beneficiary monasteries. Nevertheless, Richard II oversaw the production of a considerable number of his own charters, and in this respect these documents resemble the Anglo-Saxon diplomas.

In England, the diplomas of King Æthelstan display the first clear evidence of centralized production. Most would agree that charters were produced by the same draftsmen throughout Æthelstan's reign, although Pierre Chaplais argued that they were monks rather than royal officials. Indeed, Chaplais claimed that diplomas were always produced in ecclesiastical scriptoria, but that royal authority at various points delegated this duty to particular institutions. Opinions diverge further over the fate of the 'chancery' after Æthelstan's reign. Richard Drögereit thought the chancery ceased to function under Edgar. Simon Keynes, on the other hand, maintains that the degree of correspondence between diplomas for different beneficiaries indicates that a

---

[30] Potts, 'Early Norman Charters', p. 29. See clear indications in F42, F14, and the 'house style' of the Mont-St-Michel charters (*The Cartulary of the Abbey of Mont-Saint-Michel*, ed. K. Keats-Rohan (Donington, 2006), p. 39).

[31] Fauroux (*Recueil*, pp. 41–3) proposed this idea, which has been developed by Potts ('Early Norman Charters', p. 33) despite Tabuteau's claim (*Transfers of Property*, p. 8) that it is 'beyond dispute' that there was not an 'organized chancery' before 1066. Yet it must at least be recognized that Richard II produced charters as donor, and that they were not all produced by beneficiary institutions during his reign.

royal chancery remained in existence throughout the tenth century and into Æthelred's reign.[32] Ultimately, those of both viewpoints agree that there was a considerable degree of centralization and royal control in the production of tenth-century diplomas. The question left unresolved is whether tenth-century kings entrusted this production to favoured ecclesiastical houses or to their own officials. Both positions require a degree of flexibility, as there are clearly charters which are outside of the 'diplomatic mainstream' and were produced by beneficiaries.[33]

Although the royal chancery may not have been a developed institution, we can identify the involvement of Æthelred and his counsellors in the composition of diplomas. Diplomas recorded decisions made at the meeting of the witan, and their witness lists were (largely) accurate records of those present.[34] As was the case for Norman ducal involvement, the king must have agreed the general sentiments and the details of the disposition to which he put his name, even though Anglo-Saxon subscriptions were not autographs.[35] Although the English king or Norman duke himself may not have specified the points he wished to be made, the charter was written in his voice, and the thoughts of the *arenga* were ascribed to him. In Duke Richard II's reign, these links often took the form of a discussion of his own internal considerations and reflections, thus making the sentiments of the *arengae* personal to the duke. Similarly, a number of Æthelred's diplomas deal explicitly with the king's personal motivations. A group of charters expressing the king's remorse for the actions of 'the ignorance of my youth' ('meae iuuentutis ignorantia', S876) has been most intensely studied.[36] Discussion of this group of charters has also led to greater consideration

---

[32] Chaplais, 'Anglo-Saxon Chancery'; Keynes, *Diplomas*, pp. 14–83 on pre-Æthelred centralized production, and at pp. 134–53 argues for a 'central writing office' under Æthelred. Chaplais upheld his view, arguing further that 'Athelstan A' was a monastic draftsman, in 'The Royal Anglo-Saxon "Chancery" of the Tenth Century Revisited', in *Studies in Medieval History Presented to R. H. C. Davis*, ed. H. Mayr-Harting and R. I. Moore (London, 1985), pp. 41–51. R. Drögereit, 'Gab es eine angelsächsische Königskanzlei?' *Archiv für Urkundenforschung* 13 (1935), 335–436; *Abingdon Abbey*, I, lxxiii.

[33] Some charters include phrases in the subscriptions that imply a particular ecclesiastic was responsible for the charter's drafting: Thompson, *Anglo-Saxon Royal Diplomas*, p. 15; Keynes, *Diplomas*, pp. 26–8.

[34] Keynes, *Diplomas*, p. 37.

[35] Kelly, 'Anglo-Saxon Lay Society and the Written Word', p. 42. On the role of the king, see Chaplais, 'Anglo-Saxon Chancery Revisited', p. 42; E. John, '"Orbis Britanniae" and the Anglo-Saxon Kings', in E. John, *'Orbis Britanniae' and Other Studies* (Leicester, 1966), pp. 1–63 (p. 3).

[36] S876 (AD 993), S893 (AD 998), S891 (AD 997), S885 (AD 995) and S937 (AD 990x1006); S838 (AD 981) may be considered in addition, though the relevant passage must have been interpolated later. Keynes, *Diplomas*, pp. 176–80; Stafford, 'Political Ideas in Late Tenth-Century England'; Insley, 'Where Did All the Charters Go?', pp. 112–14.

of rituals and demonstrative behaviour associated with land grants.[37] Such practices fortified the relationship between the actions of the king and the texts of the diplomas. However, in rituals and in documents, the king was constrained in his displays of power. Produced by king, witan and ecclesiastical draftsmen, charters were a negotiation of authority between several parties.[38] They show Æthelred's ambitions, which were themselves shaped by the real limits of his power, but they also indicate the pressures from his supporters and rivals.

Each document, therefore, was more than a straightforward record of a transaction that had taken place. Norman charters, Tabuteau has argued, were aids to memory that contained the names of witnesses and were accompanied by actions to be recalled.[39] However, since memories are often contested, charters containing long narrative descriptions of the circumstances of a transaction acted as normative accounts. Narratives contained in charters might be expected to outclass contrary recollections: over the course of time the documents' narratives would become embedded in memory, too.[40] Documentary evidence in this form bolstered claims to land by asserting a single view of events.

Thus charters were also political statements.[41] In his recent study of late Carolingian royal diplomas, Geoffrey Koziol proposed that 'any given diploma was issued in order to institute, publicize, and memorialize a crucial alteration in the political regime'.[42] Similarly, documents produced in ducal Normandy and Anglo-Saxon England recorded acts which embodied new political realities and relationships. One of the very earliest Norman charters, which records Richard I's 990 donation to Fécamp, provides a suitable example (F4).[43] This document recorded the ceremony by which Richard not only gave a donation of property to the monastery he had constructed, but also cemented the new relationship between duke and church. It represented the ceremony for future readers, expounding Richard's Christian duty as duke and the heavenly reinforcement of his authority. But it also introduced the episcopal hierarchy of Normandy, including the role of the new archbishop of Rouen, Richard's son Robert. Thus this charter – the first of a Norman donor for a Norman beneficiary – established ducal influence over the entire

---

[37] Insley, 'Rhetoric and Ritual', pp. 117–19.

[38] S. Foot, *Æthelstan: the First King of England* (New Haven, 2011), pp. 133–4 discusses the relationship between the witan and the text of a diploma.

[39] Tabuteau, *Transfers of Property*, pp. 211–20.

[40] Foot, 'Reading Anglo-Saxon Charters', pp. 63–5.

[41] Wolfram, 'Political Theory and Narrative', p. 42: diplomas were 'total symbols of lordship'.

[42] G. Koziol, *The Politics of Memory and Identity in Carolingian Royal Diplomas: The West Frankish Kingdom (840–987)* (Turnhout, 2012), p. 3.

[43] On this charter, see D. Douglas, 'The First Ducal Charter for Fecamp', in *L'abbaye Benedictine de Fecamp* (Fécamp, 1959), pp. 45–56; Koziol, *Politics of Memory*, p. 46.

archdiocese of Rouen in partnership with the monastic and episcopal church. In a similar manner, the witness lists of Anglo-Saxon royal diplomas not only recorded the presence of members of the witan, but repeatedly reinforced political hierarchies and the importance of consent to the king's actions. We cannot read any of these documents as passive reflections of group identities: they served political purposes in their presentations of ethnic relations and the sources of royal or ducal authority.

Terminology of ethnicity and authority

Normandy

The Norman dukes expressed the extent of their authority through various formal components of the charter. The most direct were the titles they used in the *intitulatio* at the beginning and signature at the end of the document. The title – *dux, comes, marchio, princeps* – showed the nature of the benefactor's authority in his and his subjects' eyes.[44] However, the titles used by Richard I, Richard II and Richard III for themselves and their predecessors varied not only between charters but even within the same documents. For example, in a 1006 charter for Fécamp (F9) Richard II was introduced as 'comes and patritius' and later in the document referred to as 'comes' and 'dux'; various combinations of these titles were used in many documents (see for example F24, F47, F49). Although there has been much debate about the Normans' early use of titles, Helmerichs' detailed study has concluded that they do not reflect clear-cut legal definitions.[45] The choice of title may well have been down to the context of the individual transaction and other parties involved. Often, it seems that the notary preferred to use a combination of titles (in one of his charters, Dudo spoke of 'ducis et marchionis praepotentissimi, et patricii almiflui', F13), presumably to emphasize Richard's status.[46]

The most common title was simply *comes*, without a demographic or territorial identifier. In discussions of this title, it has been assumed that it referred to the county of Rouen. Certainly, this was one of the ways in which the Normans' neighbours perceived their authority. Raoul Glaber called Richard

---

[44] I. Garipzanov, *The Symbolic Language of Authority in the Carolingian World (c.751–877)* (Leiden, 2008), pp. 102–3 reflects on Wolfram's concept of the *intitulatio* as both *Selbstaussage* (self-statement) and *Fremdaussage* (external statement): H. Wolfram, *Intitulatio I: Lateinische Königs- und Fürstentitel bis zum Ende des 8. Jahrhunderts* (Vienna, 1967), pp. 12–25.

[45] R. Helmerichs, '*Princeps, Comes, Dux Normannorum*: Early Rollonid Designators and their Significance', *HSJ* 9 (2001), 57–77; K. Werner, 'Quelques observations au sujet des débuts du "duché" de Normandie', in *Droit privé et institutions régionales: Études historiques offertes à Jean Yver* (Paris, 1976), pp. 691–709.

[46] Cf. the titles Dudo used in the *De moribus* (Lair, p. 276): 'Marchio duxque, comes mirabilis…'.

II 'christianissimum comitem eiusdem ciuitatis' and William Longsword 'Rothomagorum ducem'.[47] However, no Norman charter includes the title *comes Rotomagensis*, even used retrospectively. The closest any of them come is F14bis, which refers back to William Longsword. The document notes that he lived in 'Rotomagensis civitate', but it does not make this his title.[48] On the other hand, the *Planctus* of the 940s called William 'Rodomensis' in opposition to William of Aquitaine as 'Pictavensis', and in its final stanza addressed Richard I as 'comes Rodomensis, o Ricarde, comitatus princeps atque pater'.[49] Richard I's coins associated his name with the city of Rouen, where they were struck.[50] From this evidence, it seems likely that Richard I, and before him Rollo and William Longsword did use this title during their lifetimes. However, dukes Richard I and Richard II began to produce charters as a mark of a broader authority. In the *pagus* of Rouen, by this time, the authority of the descendants of Rollo was unquestioned. The complete absence of the title *comes Rotomagensis* from Norman charters resulted from a deliberate decision: not to reject the use of the title *comes* which, as Helmerichs has shown, continued alongside *dux*,[51] but to present themselves as possessing authority across the wider principality of Normandy.

Titles contributed to this assertion by emphasising that these were the leaders of a people, the *Normanni*. Unlike the diversity of titles employed in early Norman charters, the associated identifiers were remarkably stable. In the case of Richards I, II and III, the identifier *Nor(th)mannorum* appears added to titles in almost half of the charters dating from their reigns – thirty different documents. It presented them as rulers of a single people. No charter refers to any other people under their authority. This stands in contrast to Dudo's frequent claims in the *De moribus* that Rollo and his descendants were rulers of both Normans and Bretons.[52] The designation as rulers 'of the Normans', however, was not restrictive. There was no other term used for the people who inhabited Normandy, and no one else claimed jurisdiction over them. Using such titles in charters reinforced the extension of *Normanni* to include everyone within the regions under discussion in a given transaction.

---

[47] *Rodulfi Glabri Historiarum libri quinque/ Rodulfus Glaber, The Five Books of the Histories*, ed. J. France (Oxford, 1989), pp. 138, 162.

[48] F14bis: 'Igitur, post multa curricula annorum, extitit nobilissimus comes Vuillemus Rotomagensis civitate, qui uxorem habuit nomine Leyardam...'. Werner, 'Quelques observations', p. 697, treats this as William's formal title of count of Rouen, but I read this as 'the most noble count William lived in the city of Rouen'.

[49] *Planctus*, ed. Helmerichs, v. 15, v. 17.

[50] Dumas, *Trésor de Fécamp*, pp. 71–5. M. Dolley and J. Yvon, 'A Group of Tenth-Century Coins Found at Mont-Saint-Michel', *British Numismatic Journal* 40 (1971), 7–11, reports a single example of a coin minted by William Longsword as duke of Brittany, but his son and grandson were not so ambitious in this respect.

[51] Helmerichs, 'Early Rollonid Designators'.

[52] See Christiansen, pp. 49, 58–9, 60–3, 84; Lair, pp. 168–9, 181, 182–5, 208–9.

Thus, *Normanni* may originally have derived from the settler Scandinavian elite but, by the early eleventh century, it had extended to all the subjects of the Norman duke or all the inhabitants of the area the dukes ruled.

A small number of charters refer to the dukes as leaders of a territory rather than a people: *Normannia* or *Normannica*. These are some of the first occurrences of this name for the principality.[53] In some cases, it may be a later emendation, added when 'Normandy' had become a more commonly used name.[54] However, 'Normannia' is included twice in an original 1014 charter for Notre Dame de Chartres (F15). In his charter of 1015 (F18), Dudo used the title 'dux Normanniae' in opposition to 'rex Francorum': 'Normannorum' would have been a more obvious parallel, and thus we may assume that the geographical designation was well understood, if not already in common usage. *Normannorum* and *Normanniae* were attached to titles seemingly interchangeably. Richard I's charter for the monastery he founded at St-Taurin (F5) uses both 'dux Normannie' and 'Normannorum princeps'.[55] In this sense, people and territory were treated as coterminous.[56]

Normannia appears as a geographic term in two further documents (F14 and F52). The original copy of Richard II's confirmation audit for St-Wandrille (F52) describes the monastery as 'in Normannica provintia'. Similarly, a document recording the exchange of properties between Jumièges and Bourgueil describes Longueville, the property acquired by Jumièges, as 'in Normannia sita' (F14). This record of the exchange was preserved in the cartulary of Bourgueil: thus, *Normanni(c)a* was a geographical term understood and used within and outside the area to which it referred. The title *Dux Normanniae* did not refer simply to Richard's personal identity, but to the region he ruled over . A charter of Drogo, count of the Vexin, from 1024, recalled that St Wandregislus had founded St-Wandrille 'in Normannorum prouincia'.[57] The Northmen were now so closely linked to the region that their identity was projected back into the period before they arrived.

The perception of *Normannia* as the territory and people under ducal authority was created by the transactions themselves, as well as the terms of

---

[53] *Nortmannia* appeared on the ducal coinage in the second half of the eleventh century: Bates, *Normandy Before 1066*, p. 57.

[54] e.g. F11; the title in F1 is probably also late.

[55] However, this document is preserved only in copies dating from the thirteenth century and later, so the phrasing may not be entirely original.

[56] Exceptionally, in F12, a charter of 1009, Richard II was entitled 'princeps et marchio totius Neustrie provinciae cunctis religionis christiane fidelibus'. Richard's claim to rule all Neustria was an unrealistic assertion of authority over Brittany and Maine, presumably deployed to justify his intervention in the affairs of Mont-Saint-Michel. By the end of the eleventh century, this connection had developed to the extent that 'Neustria' was used as a poetic synonym for Normandy: Davis, *Normans and their Myth*, p. 58.

[57] F. Lot, *Études critiques sur l'Abbaye de Saint-Wandrille* (Paris, 1913), no. 7.

description. Exchanges of property as in F14 show the collection of abbatial land within Normandy. In 1024, Jumièges again took part in an exchange, this time with Saint-Vaast (F26). Jumièges gave Haspres, 'quia vicinior nobis erat', in the words of the abbot of Saint-Vaast, who returned the favour by giving Angicourt to Jumièges, because it was 'viciniorem sibi'. However, this policy was not purely for convenience: properties which were located at a distance, but within Normandy, were retained by these abbeys. As Tabuteau has suggested, Jumièges and perhaps other Norman abbeys may have striven to concentrate their possessions within the borders of the region ruled over by the duke.[58] Moreover, in the early eleventh century, it seems to have been a deliberate policy of the dukes to grant property in western Normandy to the abbeys of Rouen. Arnoux has shown how three early eleventh-century narratives, the *Translatio Secunda Audoeni*, the Fécamp Chronicle and the *Translatio Severi*, which use the conventions of charters and performance of land transactions, all established ties between ecclesiastical institutions in and around Rouen and properties in the Cotentin, Bessin and Avranchin.[59] In doing so, they created ties between the ducal capital and centre of support at Rouen, and the less secure areas in the west.

Ecclesiastical networks were essential to the extension of ducal authority westwards. Indeed, the final borders of Normandy mapped almost exactly onto the archdiocese of Rouen (only the French Vexin lay outside Norman borders). Richer of Rheims saw the province and the archdiocese as equivalent, stating that 'Rouen is the metropolitan see of this province, and its authority extends over just six cities: Bayeux, Avranches, Évreux, Sées, Coutances, and Lisieux. It is clear, then, that the pirates have held this territory from the distant past.'[60] As the vikings had taken control of Rouen, he saw their dominance of the rest of the region as a logical extension. Moreover, by supporting Benedictine reform, the dukes could exert direct authority over monasteries outside the jurisdiction of the bishop. Their influence over monastic life emanated from their family monastery at Fécamp, where in 1001 Richard II established the reformer William of Volpiano as abbot. William's reforms, instituted by himself or one of his pupils, were then introduced at the other monasteries in Normandy.[61]

---

[58] Tabuteau, *Transfers of Property*, pp. 35–6.

[59] Arnoux, 'Before the *Gesta Normannorum*'. For practices such as the transfer by knife and staff in Normandy, see Tabuteau, *Transfers of Property*, pp. 127–9. The property which the *Translatio Secunda Audoeni* claimed Richard I gave to St-Ouen, Rots in the Bessin, is recorded as a gift of Richard II in a charter of 1017–24 (F44).

[60] Richer of St-Rémi, *Histories*, I, 16–17: 'Huius provinciae metropolis Rhodomum esse dinoscitur, sex tantum urbibus, Baiocis videlicet, Abrincanto, Ebrocis, Sagio, Constantiae, Lisioio vim suae dominationis intendens. Hanc itaque ex antiquo a piratis possessam esse manifestum est'.

[61] R. Herval, 'Un Moine de l'An Mille: Guillame de Volpiano, 1er abbe de Fecamp (962–1031)', in *L'abbaye Benedictine de Fécamp*, pp. 27–44.

The public authority of the king was acknowledged in the occasional use of dating clauses, which generally employed the regnal year of the Frankish king alongside the year since the incarnation. In one case, a charter composed for St-Ouen by the monk Bernerius, the dating clause is filled with extravagant language, introducing the king as 'Robert, with his glorious right hand happily bearing the sceptre of the shining peoples of the Gauls... the true catholic king sitting on the most exalted throne of all the noblest peoples of the Franks'.[62] Yet the notary carefully distinguished the two figures – king and duke – by the peoples they ruled. Bernerius emphasized that Robert was the king of 'gentium Galliarum' or 'Francorum cuntarum gentium nobilissimorum'; his fulsome praise of Duke Richard created a parallel role for him as leader of 'nobilium valde Normannorum gentium'. In this way, Bernerius differentiated the peoples over whom the two rulers held authority and thereby claimed separate spheres of jurisdiction, equivalent in their leadership of ethnic groups.

While external authorities make infrequent appearances in the charters, the dukes themselves frequently confirmed donations to Norman monasteries. The audits of Jumièges, Fécamp, St-Ouen and Bernay were composed for precisely this purpose. Firstly, they confirmed the gifts of Richard's predecessors – Rollo, William Longsword and Richard I. Richard never looked further back than this: all gifts stemmed from their dynasty. By confirming these gifts, he re-enacted his ancestors' generosity and reaffirmed his relationship with the beneficiary monasteries. Richard also confirmed the donations of his nobles in these charters, thereby demonstrating that these gifts were made under his authority.

Confirming the gifts of earlier Norman rulers was an act of succession, by which Richard emphasized that his authority over the land was inherited.[63] The dukes were identified by their fathers as well as by territorial designations. Richard I was referred to as 'son of William' a number of times; although he had been a child when William was killed, he retained the rulership of the Normans purely through their relationship. In emphasizing their descent, the dukes also asserted dynastic rights and the heritable nature of their authority following the model of kingship. The charters contain frequent references to the patronage of their fathers and grandfathers, demonstrating the continuity of earlier plans and relationships. Richard II's installation of William of Volpiano at Fécamp (F9) was justified by his assertion that monasticism had been his father's design for the place, while the confirmation charters of the great ducal monasteries essentially re-enacted the donations of Richard II's father and grandfather.

---

[62] F42: 'Rodbertus stringens gloriosa dextera candentium gentium Galliarum feliciter sceptrum... sedens sublimissimo solio Francorum cuntarum gentium nobilissimorum vere catholicus rex'.
[63] Koziol, *Politics of Memory*, pp. 5, 97–118.

In the language of charters, Norman people and the geographical unit of Normandy became coterminous. Richard I and Richard II began to produce charters to create this definition. Their charters show the dukes exercising inherited authority in their own territory largely independent of the French king. In doing so, they distinguished their subjects in Normandy from the Franks outside their borders.

England

Tenth-century English kings from Æthelstan onwards, taking charter composition into centralized control, also used various titles in their diplomas – in dispositives and in subscriptions – as a means of expressing relationships with their subjects and neighbours and their own changing spheres of authority. These styles were political statements, which reflected ambition but also responded to neighbouring authorities. Although expressed in a number of forms, Æthelred's charters contained a clear concept of the region and peoples over which he ruled.

Æthelred's primary title was *rex Anglorum*. This title appears alone in eleven dispositive phrases, but was more common in subscriptions: he subscribed thirty-six diplomas with this simple phrase. *Rex Anglorum* also usually constituted the base of more developed royal styles, such as the thirteen diplomas dating from 983–90 which include in addition the phrase 'regni totius fastigium tenens'.[64] It was also the title that appeared on Æthelred's coins.[65] *Anglorum* was the most frequent qualifier of *rex*, appearing alongside it a little under two-thirds of the time. Four charters use the term 'Anglo-Saxons', which was perhaps derived from earlier models, but apparently held a similar meaning.[66] Thus, in his most widely used title, Æthelred was king of a people, the English.

'English' (*Angli*) by this point had become a relatively stable term. Earlier tenth-century kings had often divided their realm into Wessex and Mercia (and East Anglia and Northumbria when they were under English control). Æthelred's father, Edgar, went by *rex Merciorum* from 957–59, while his brother Eadwig, ruling Wessex, was called *rex Anglorum*.[67] But Æthelred, having been crowned king of both parts of the kingdom, never used the separate title of *rex Merciorum*: this was included within *rex Anglorum*. Although Mercia

---

[64] Keynes, *Diplomas*, p. 85.

[65] M. Dolley, 'An Introduction to the Coinage of Æthelraed II', in *Ethelred the Unready*, ed. Hill, pp. 115–33.

[66] S931 (AD 1013); S911 (AD 1005); S890 (AD 997); S898 (AD 1001). '*Rex Anglo Saxonum*' was used relatively frequently up to the end of Eadwig's reign, but thereafter appears only in one charter of Edward the Martyr (S830, AD 976) and one of Edgar (S810, AD 961x963).

[67] Edgar used the title *rex Merciorum* or a variation in S667, S675, S678, S676, S676a, all AD 958. Edgar used *rex Anglorum* in three charters of this period: S674, S679 and S673, all AD 958.

appeared as a distinct administrative unit well into Cnut's reign, its inhabitants were no less English for that. Moreover, the *Angli* were identified as the primary audience of Æthelred's charters. The English language was used for essential details, such as descriptions of bounds and, in a few documents, a brief history of the estate's ownership. Place names given in the vernacular were identified as being in English, or in the speech of the place's inhabitants. Language was not an exclusive guide, however, since it sometimes indicated regional diversity, as in a Kentish charter of 995.[68] But, although the regional difference could be expressed in terms of *gens*, the inhabitants of Kent still came under the authority of Æthelred as *rex Anglorum*, implying simultaneous membership of a wider *gens Anglorum*.

Thus Æthelred, like his tenth-century forebears, was king of an ethnic group rather than a geographical region. His claims over particular territories stemmed from his status as king of the English people. Geographical terms for England were rare in these diplomas. In one, Æthelred is called 'king of the land of the English' (S900: 'rex Anglorum telluris gubernator et rector'), and in another 'king of the territory of the English people' (S850: 'regionis Angligenarum rex') without this land being defined in either case. But there was no use of *Anglia*, *Englalond* or similar in Latin royal diplomas. In contrast to the Norman presentation, people and territory were separate concepts in Æthelred's charters.

Rather than *Englalond*, the most frequent geographical designator for the area Æthelred ruled was *Britannia*: royal styles feature this term or the similar *Britannica* twenty-five times. The term *Britannia* had been used since the Roman occupation, and did not retain a close connection with the British/Welsh population. When invoking *Britannia*, therefore, Æthelred's charters were not referring particularly to land inhabited by Britons, but to the whole island. Indeed, in a few examples he was called ruler of 'the entire island of Britain'; in one this was expanded to include 'the islands lying around it'.[69] Æthelred's notaries' use of the term *Britannia* stemmed from their knowledge

---

[68] E.g. S885 (AD 995): '...sex quidem mansas. quas Cantuarii. syx sulunga nominare solent. illo scilicet in loco. cui iamdudum gentis eiusdem indigene uocabulum. æt Wuldaham indiderunt. Unam quoque mansam. solita Anglorum uocitatione. æt Lytlanbroce celebriter appellatam...' Precursors from the 940s include S489, S512, S497, S510, S535.

[69] 'Totius Britannicae insulae' or similar in S866 (AD 987), S874 and S942 (both AD 990), S898 (AD 1001), S904 (AD 1002/1008), S933 (AD 1014). S904: 'gentis gubernator Angligenae totiusque insulae coregulus Britannicae et caeterarum insularum in circuitu adiacentium'. S914 is a late-eleventh-century forgery, which calls him 'gratia Dei summitonantis Angligenum Orcadarum necne in gyro iacentium monarchus': M. Lapidge, 'B and the Vita S. Dunstani', in *St Dunstan: his Life, Times and Cult*, ed. N. Ramsay, M. Sparks and T. Tatton-Brown (Woodbridge, 1992), pp. 247–59 (pp. 258–9). Cf. IV Edgar 14.2, which makes a command applying 'to all of us who dwell in these islands' ('us eallum gemæne, þe on ðissum iglandum wuniað': *Die Gesetze der Angelsachsen*, ed. F. Liebermann, 3 vols. (Halle, 1898–1916), I, 214).

of Bede's *Historia ecclesiastica*, which began with a description of the island and the peoples who inhabited it. Britain was conceived as a geographical unit that might be governed from a single centre, although it contained a diversity of peoples.

Æthelred's territory was also called 'Albion'. As Julia Crick has discussed regarding the use of the term in Edgar's charters, this too referred to the whole island of Britain and seems to have been derived also from the pages of Bede's *Historia ecclesiastica*, which begins with the words 'Britain, formerly known as Albion, is an island in the ocean...' ('Britannia Oceani insula, cui quondam Albion nomen fuit...').[70] Crick has shown the preference for the term among the monks of the Benedictine movement; the narrative sources composed during Æthelred's reign, and the proportion of his diplomas that employ 'Albion', demonstrate its continuing currency.[71] The presentation of a king with authority over all Britain, or all Albion, although it originated with Æthelstan, was promoted primarily by the Benedictine monks throughout the second half of the tenth century.

Supporting these ambitious claims to rule all Britain, Æthelred's draftsmen deployed titles with imperial connotations. The most common title used by Æthelred after *rex* was *basileus*, a Greek word for emperor, which appears in thirty-seven charters (while S923 uses the Greek word *archos*).[72] Draftsmen used *imperator* in six charters, and referred to Æthelred's *imperium*, although this seems to have referred more generally to his authority. Previous kings had applied *imperator* only when they asserted rule over several named peoples, but Æthelred used *basileus* and *imperator* more or less interchangeably with *rex*.[73] In one subscription, Æthelred was even called 'rex Anglorum rite dicatus basileus' (S861).[74] These titles suggested that the position of king of the English brought imperial power with it.

However, Æthelred's claims to rule all Britain are barely substantiated by the evidence within his surviving diplomas. Witness lists contain predominantly Mercian and West Saxon ecclesiastics and officials, and most beneficiary institutions were located in Mercia and Wessex, too. These were

---

[70] *Baedae Opera Historica*, ed. J. E. King (London, 1930), pp. 10–11.

[71] Crick, 'Edgar, Albion and Insular Dominion', esp. p. 164. Albion is mentioned in 28% of Edgar's authentic diplomas, and 23% of Æthelred's.

[72] G. Molyneaux, 'Why Were Some Tenth-Century English Kings Presented as Rulers of Britain?', *TRHS* 21 (2011), 59–91 (p. 63) suggests this term was employed for its sense of grandeur.

[73] '*Imperator*' appears only in the 'alliterative' charters of Eadred, and one of Eadwig; and Edgar used it twice (S751, S775 – this latter resembles Æthelred's styles instead).

[74] Drögereit reached the same conclusion for Edgar's use of the title. See H. Loyn, 'The Imperial Style of the Tenth-Century Anglo-Saxon Kings', *History* 40 (1955), 111–15 (p. 111) and R. Drögereit, 'Kaiseridee under Kaisertitel bei den Angelsachsen', *Zeitschrift der Savigny-Stiftung für Rechtsgeschichte, Germanistische Abteilung* 69 (1952), 24–73.

the heartlands of royal authority and regions where people may be assumed to be most receptive to Æthelred's view of English identity; his claims to imperial rule over the rest of Britain were safely made here. Moreover, from the 990s, Æthelred was keen to patronize religious houses, but these were almost all located in southern England.[75] We are left without comparable source material for areas of ninth-century Danish settlement, where alternative perceptions of geographical identity may have flourished. While the concentration of diplomas concerning the south is partly a result of the pattern of survival, it seems that this disparity results from more than chance in the preservation of Anglo-Saxon material.[76] The available sources suggest that Æthelred did not issue charters or give land so frequently in the regions most affected by Scandinavian settlement.[77] The viking invasions were one cause of destruction to documents, and subsequent pagan Scandinavian settlement had severely disrupted ecclesiastical life, which meant fewer charters were produced in these areas.[78]

The few northern ecclesiastical foundations which survived in the tenth century – York minster, St John at Beverley, and the community of St Cuthbert at Chester-le-Street – developed their own ways of recording and protecting landed property.[79] English kings therefore had much less control over the representation of their authority in northern England. However, in giving gifts to St Cuthbert and York, they made their influence felt, and attempted to impress upon these institutions the sphere of that influence. As Æthelstan travelled north in 934, he aimed to cultivate the support of the community of St Cuthbert through the giving of gifts. However, the record of his gifts was produced entirely by the beneficiary community, either as notes in important

---

[75] Keynes, *Diplomas*, pp. 198–9.

[76] *Abingdon Abbey*, I, lxxviii: most surviving charters relate to Wessex, Kent and Sussex, the Abingdon region and the West Midlands, there are a scattering from Essex and the East Midlands, and 'virtually nothing' from East Anglia and north of Trent. There remains, however, a substantial number of charters relating to Devon, which do indicate alternative strategies: C. Insley, 'Charters and Episcopal Scriptoria in the Anglo-Saxon South-West', *EME* 7 (1998), 173–97.

[77] P. Stafford, 'The Reign of Æthelred II, a Study in the Limitations on Royal Policy and Action', in *Ethelred the Unready*, ed. Hill, pp. 15–46 (pp. 25, 28, 32) maps Æthelred's land grants.

[78] *Charters of Northern Houses*, ed. D. Woodman, Anglo-Saxon Charters 16 (Oxford, 2012), pp. 5–6. Other causes of destruction include the harrying of the north in 1069 and Eadred's burning of Ripon in 948: the archives of York minster were burned in 1069, and only eleven Anglo-Saxon documents survive, two in pre-Conquest copies: *Northern Houses*, p. 68. The archive of St John of Beverley contains two writs of Edward the Confessor (p. 187), while there are no genuine documents from Ripon (p. 249). The community of St Cuthbert at Durham is in a different situation again – there are four pre-Conquest notes in Woodman's edition (pp. 316–23).

[79] D. Hadley, *The Northern Danelaw: Its Social Structure, c.800–1100* (London and New York, 2000), pp. 216–97, surveys smaller churches in the region; *Northern Houses*, pp. 8–9.

books, such as the community's *Liber Vitae*, or in the narrative *Historia de Sancto Cuthberto*. Both reflect charter formulae and contemporary diplomatic practice in several ways, but were clearly produced entirely separately from the diplomas examined above.[80] The titles applied to Alfred in the *Historia de Sancto Cuthberto* are those of tenth-century kings: 'rex totius Britanniae', ruler of 'tota Albion' and 'regnum Brytanniae'.[81] The compiler of the *Historia* represented the extension of West Saxon authority over Northumbria in the same imperial terms as the royal draftsmen.

In eastern England, the small number of charters is probably more a question of documentary survival, since the borderlands of this region of Scandinavian settlement were the site of a number of reformed houses, such as Peterborough, Ely and Ramsey. However, West Saxon influence can also be seen in their narratives. The *Vita Prima Sancti Neoti*, apparently composed in this region bordering on East Anglia, shows a view of English rule over Britain similar to that in Æthelred's royal styles. Several times, the text refers to 'in Britannie Anglice partibus', but the viking invasion was said to affect 'Brittannie Anglice insulam'.[82] While there was awareness that the English inhabited only some parts of Britain, they were represented as the dominant nation on the island. Thus, the documents and practices of religious communities in northern (and, to a lesser extent, eastern) England reveal considerable regional difference. Nevertheless, they accepted royal authority at a distance and reflected the rhetoric of power found in the charters of tenth-century kings.

Claims to rule all Britain also made a statement in relation to British kingdoms. No other king was mentioned in the same diploma as Æthelred, and so his status as the ultimate authority in the territory concerned was reinforced.[83] Æthelred's charters, although similarly calling him 'steersman' (*gubernator*) of other peoples of Britain, did not follow those of his mid-tenth-century predecessors in including British kings.[84] However, he may have

---

[80] *Northern Houses*, pp. 301, 316–23.

[81] HSC, pp. 54–6.

[82] VPSN, pp. 112, 118, 124–5. See further the *Libellus Æthelwoldi* in the *Liber Eliensis*, ed. Blake, pp. 72–117, 395–9.

[83] S904 (AD 1002) refers to Æthelred as 'coregulus' of Britain, which at first seems to complicate the picture, but this was probably intended as *curagulus*, 'guardian', since this title was used in a number of Æthelstan's charters (S430, AD 935; S438, AD 937; S440, AD 938; S446, S447, S449, all AD 939) and one of Edmund's (S466, AD 940).

[84] J. Barrow, 'Chester's Earliest Regatta? Edgar's Dee-rowing Revisited', *EME* 10 (2001), 81–93 (p. 88). S. Keynes, *An Atlas of Attestations in Anglo-Saxon Charters, c.670–1066* (Cambridge, 2002), Tables XXXVI and XXVIII, shows the subscriptions of British 'sub-kings' in the diplomas of Æthelstan (928–35) and in 'alliterative' charters between c. 946 and 956. In Æthelstan's charters (S400, 407, 413, 416, 417, 418a, 425, 426, 434), they attest as '*subreguli*'; in Eadred's (S520, 550, 552a, 566) and Eadwig's (S633), they are each called '*rex*' or '*regulus*'.

174

claimed his overlordship in other ways. In the year 1000 he engaged in a northern campaign which seems to have been designed as a show of superiority over the kingdoms of Strathclyde and Man.[85] While tenth-century kings, including Æthelred, were ambitious in asserting their authority over the whole of Britain, they did refer to areas where their influence was felt.[86]

Æthelred's claims to imperial authority thus extended over several peoples within Britain. The English were always singled out as the principal ethnic group, but it was often specified that he was also ruler of 'ceterarum[que] gentium in circuitu persistentium'.[87] Æthelred was described as king *caeterarum gentium* or *nationum* in nineteen authentic diplomas, and 'caeterarum provinciarum imperator' in another (S931). His usage of this formulation reflects its popularity throughout the tenth century: this phrase or similar occurs in nearly a third of the extant authentic diplomas from Æthelstan's reign to Edgar's. It asserted that Æthelred ruled the people-groups who inhabited his territory: his authority over them was dictated by where they lived. Æthelred's position at the head of the English people gave him power and authority, but that power was not limited to the English. This assertion made clear that Æthelred's land-grants and rulings over territorial possessions were to be respected by all those under his authority, regardless of ethnicity. Æthelred borrowed this phrase from his predecessors' imperial rhetoric, which rarely specified precisely which peoples tenth-century kings ruled. The phrase was inclusive, and its content was determined by the geographical limits of Britain.

Æthelred did not explicitly lay claim to authority over any people other than the English, except in one document, S931. This charter of 1013 gave Æthelred the title 'rex Anglosaxonie atque Norðhymbrensis gubernator monarchie, paganorumque propugnator, ac Brettonum ceterarumque prouinciarum imperator'. The draftsman of this charter, in using this style, relied on models from the mid-tenth century.[88] Seven such 'alliterative' diplomas of Eadred and Eadwig divided the king's subjects into the same four peoples (although *Anglorum* was more usual than *Anglosaxonie*). These titles recognized a distinction between the Northumbrians and the rest of the English, but the two peoples were always grouped together. In Æthelred's charter S931, the pagans and Britons were placed at a greater distance by the use of titles implying less direct rule. The only surviving charter of Edgar that

---

[85] ASC E, 1001; Lavelle, *Æthelred*, pp. 101–2.

[86] Molyneaux, 'Rulers of Britain', pp. 64, 75.

[87] Two earlier charters defined the English against the 'barbarian' other peoples of Britain: Eadwig (S632) claimed rule of 'huius insule barbarorum' as well as of the English, and a diploma of Edgar (S725) distinguished the English from 'barbarorum atque gentilium'.

[88] C. Hart, 'Danelaw and Mercian Charters of the Mid Tenth Century', in Hart, *Danelaw*, pp. 431–53 (p. 435), on earlier models. Cf. S548, 549, 550, 569, 572 and 633; S520 uses a similar phrase in the dating clause.

divided the inhabitants of Britain into these same peoples followed the same groupings by calling him 'rex Anglorum cum Nordhymbra regimine, ac progenie Paganorum Brettonumque prosapia sublimiter roboratus' (S766, AD 968).[89] This fourfold division seems to have been devised by the draftsmen of the 'alliterative' charters in the 940s, but it remained sufficiently familiar to be redeployed in 968 and again in 1013.

The fourfold division also separated 'Northumbrians' from 'pagans'. Regardless of their religious belief, the label 'pagans' was probably intended to apply to Scandinavians – as noted above, writers such as Asser and Æthelweard used the terms 'Dane' and 'pagan' interchangeably. These styles are therefore evidence that English kings throughout the tenth century did identify a Danish element in their subject populations. However, this Danish element was presented as a group distinct from the Northumbrians and not necessarily geographically determined. No tenth-century styles referred to the East Angles as a separate people, so it is possible that 'pagans' referred to Danish settlers in the east as well as the north. The idea of the 'fourfold kingdoms' ('regna quadripertiti', S520, AD 946) probably derived from Bede's similar idea of four peoples within Britain in the first chapter of the *Historia ecclesiastica*. Draftsmen may have striven to fit the peoples they perceived in Britain into four categories in order to continue this pattern.[90]

Despite the ongoing use of 'imperial styles' delineating subject peoples, the key issue is their changing contemporary meanings.[91] Eadred seems to have been the first to name distinct peoples in this way in his diplomas.[92] In doing so, he responded to the actions of the Northumbrians in choosing the Norse king Eric, and asserted his imperial rule not only by force but also in his royal styles.[93] The use of a similar style in Æthelred's charter of 1013, which was issued before the Northumbrians' submission to Swein, seems to have served

---

[89] This division hints at the distinction between the king's 'extensive' and 'intensive' power in different regions that Molyneaux sees emerging in this period: 'Rulers of Britain', pp. 87–91. In addition, S677 (AD 958) called Edgar 'rex Merciorum et Norðanhymbrorum atque Brettonum', during the period in which Eadwig was styled *rex Anglorum*. This apparent original implies consciousness of a similar fourfold division which would include the *Angli*.

[90] One 'alliterative' diploma of Eadred, S636 (AD 956), used the unusual royal style 'gentis Geuuisorum orientaliumque nec non occidentalium simul etiam aquilonalium Saxonum archons': the Gewissae was an archaic name for the West Saxons, while the other labels were probably meant to imply rule of all the peoples of Britain, rather than referring specifically to the Saxons. See Molyneaux, 'Rulers of Britain', pp. 63–4 for lists of subject peoples in non-charter contexts.

[91] John, 'Orbis Britanniae', p. 46.

[92] S404 (AD 930) is unlikely to be preserved in its original form.

[93] John, 'Orbis Britanniae', pp. 46, 50–2, 55. The relevant charters of Eadred are S520 (AD 946), S544, S548, S549, S550 (all AD 949), S552a (AD 950), S569 (AD 955), S572 (956 for 954x955). The popularity of these titles in 949, the year after Eadred carried out a punitive raid in Northumbria, is striking.

a different purpose. Innes has drawn attention to this charter as the only (surviving) occasion on which Æthelred acknowledged the distinct identity of the Northumbrians, arguing that Æthelred was trying to gather support in 'Danish' areas.[94] However, closer examination of the diploma suggests that the phrasing was not a deliberate strategy from the king, but an exception to Æthelred's main diplomatic tradition.

The charter of 1013 probably owed more to the influence of the draftsman and expressed regional interests. It was overseen, perhaps even personally drafted, by the diocesan bishop of the grant in Northamptonshire, Bishop Eadnoth of Dorchester. Bishop Eadnoth subscribed the diploma with the phrase 'Ego Eadnoð episcopus hanc scedulam dictitans. rege suisque praecipientibus perscribere iussi'.[95] The bishop of this northern diocese chose a royal style which emphasized the separate nature of the Northumbrians and their 'monarchia' as a geographical region, looking back to the mid-tenth century when they enjoyed more independence. This charter implies that the distinction between the Northumbrian kingdom and the rest of England suited the interests of the northern bishop. Yet Eadnoth used an outmoded style which distinguished, rather than equated, Northumbrians and pagans.

A few references in contemporary narrative sources suggest that this north–south geographical distinction had a widely perceived ethnic significance. In the *Life of St Æthelwold*, composed in the 990s, the Northumbrian thegns who accompanied King Eadred to Abingdon were singled out as a different people ('ex gente Northanhimbrorum'), with the characteristic habit of drinking: 'The Northumbrians became drunk, as they tend to, and very cheerful they were when they left at evening.'[96] Byrhtferth of Ramsey distinguished Northumbrians and Danes in his description of York, although he drew a connection between them. He described the city as 'metropolis totius gentis Northanimbrorum', which was filled with merchants from Denmark.[97] The *Vita Prima Sancti Neoti* provides a rare view of East Anglia. It refers to this area as in 'aquilonarium partium', although this perspective may relate to Neot's journey from Cornwall.[98] However, those who lived in the north and east were never referred to as 'Danes' in narrative texts: their distinctiveness was not equated with Scandinavian heritage. In this sense, the narrative texts reflect the same perception as these few charters which distinguish northerners from the southern English.

---

[94] Innes, 'Danelaw Identities', pp. 75–6.

[95] On Eadnoth's role, see Keynes, *Diplomas*, pp. 124–5.

[96] Wulfstan of Winchester, *The Life of St Æthelwold*, ed. M. Lapidge and M. Winterbottom (Oxford, 1991), pp. 24–5: 'inebriatis suatim Northanimbris et uesperi cum laetitia recedentibus'.

[97] *Byrhtferth of Ramsey*, ed. Lapidge, pp. 150–1: 'Que inedicibiliter est repleta et mercatorum gazis locupletata, qui undique adueniunt, maxime ex Danorum gente'.

[98] VPSN, p. 135.

In fact, when diplomas did refer to Danes, they were never speaking of the inhabitants of Northumbria. Several charters made allusions to the money paid by Archbishop Sigeric to the Danes from 994 onwards.[99] In these cases, 'Danes' applied to foreign invaders: they were a 'gens pagana', called 'hostes' (S882, AD 995 for 994). However, Danes were friends and allies as well. One diploma even records 'quidam Danus nomine Toti' as the beneficiary and his 'propinquus' Celi as intermediary; the land granted was in Oxfordshire (S943, AD 1006x1011). None of the references to Danes in Æthelred's diplomas seems to have had any specific connection to northern England.

A vernacular charter in which Æthelred confirmed the will of Æthelric of Bocking hints at a division of *ceterarum gentium* which included Danes (S939, 995x999). At the end of the witness list, rather than listing the names of the thegns, the draftsman simply referred to 'all the thegns who were gathered there from far, both West Saxons and Mercians, and Danes and English' ('ealle ða ðegnas ðe þær widan gegæderode wæron ægðer. ge of Westsexan. ge of Myrcean. ge of Denon. ge of Englon'). The division is intriguing. Conceivably it is a fourfold division, in which 'Denon' referred to Northumbrians and 'Englon' to East Angles; however, in this period 'Englon' usually referred to the English people generally, and in that case should surely *include* 'Westsexan' and 'Myrcean'. It seems more likely that the draftsman had categorized the thegns in two different ways: firstly, they came either from Wessex or Mercia, in terms of their regional origin; and secondly, they were either Danish or English in terms of an ethnic origin not based on regional identity. He probably referred to this additional division because of the content of the charter, which discusses the accusation that Æthelric was involved in a conspiracy to receive Swein in Essex. The draftsman drew a distinction between 'native' English and 'foreign' Danes, who lived side by side. Although England had been under attack by Swein, Æthelred still counted Danes among his thegns, and so did not assume their disloyalty based on their ethnic identity.

'Danes' refers to a similar group in a charter of 1004, although by this time Æthelred's viewpoint had drastically changed. This detailed account of Danish–English interaction in the charter for St Frideswide's, Oxford, (S909) is one of unbridled ethnic hostility. This diploma restored privileges and territories to the monastery after the people of the town had burned a group of Danes alive in the church. This action was explained as a response to Æthelred's command on St Brice's Day 1002 'that all the Danes who had sprung up in this island, sprouting like cockle amongst the wheat, were to be destroyed by a most just extermination'.[100] While post-Conquest historians such as William of Malmesbury believed this applied to the descendants

---

[99] S882 (AD 995 for 994); S912 (AD 1005); S919 (AD 1008).

[100] '…ut cuncti Dani qui in hac insula uelut lolium inter triticum pullulando emerserant, iustissima examinatione necarentur'; trans. in *EHD*, ed. Whitelock, p. 591.

of ninth-century Danish settlers, modern historical opinion has tended to agree with Susan Reynolds's claim that the command was aimed at 'recent immigrants', perhaps merchants who had come via northern England, or mercenaries paid by Æthelred in agreements such as that represented by II Æthelred.[101] If so, Æthelred's application of the phrase 'cuncti Dani qui in hac insula' in this context clarified that he did not consider his northern subjects to be 'Danes'. The description of Danes 'sprouting like cockles among the wheat' implies that this was not a geographical distinction, but that the people to whom the draftsman referred were mixed everywhere among the English. In the *narratio* of this charter, Æthelred maintained his claim to rule the entire *insula* of Britain – not just the English – but identified the Danish element as an alien force.

Origins of authority in *arengae* and *narrationes*

To understand the lack of reference to the viking past in these charters, let us take a brief excursus to consider the visions of ethnicity and political community that they do contain. In the majority of Æthelred's and Richard II's charters, lengthy *arengae*, or preambles, explain and justify in general terms the gifts of land or concessions which they record. The *narrationes* which follow link the general motivations found in the *arengae* to the specific circumstances of the particular transaction.

Despite containing conventional sentiments, preambles reveal the attitudes to land and donations which were to be found among the royal or ducal family, monks, clergy and secular elites. Norman notaries drew upon existing charters, recently composed or from the Carolingian period, and apparently a *florilegium* which provided appropriate quotations from scripture and the Church Fathers, but the considerable variation in wording, length and content suggests that they did not use a formulary.[102] They shared elements, but the *arengae* are all unique (although there are a few examples which are very similar, notably the charters from Mont-Saint-Michel and those drafted by Dudo). Likewise, the proems of Æthelred's charters, after the 980s at least, were composed especially for the occasions on which they were used.[103] The uniqueness of the *arengae* is such that a repeated proem is cause for

---

[101] William of Malmesbury, *Gesta Regum*, I, 276–7. Innes, 'Danelaw Identities', p. 65; Reynolds, 'What Do We Mean by "Anglo-Saxon"?', p. 412.

[102] Potts, 'Early Norman Charters', pp. 31–2, 37; Tabuteau, *Transfers of Property*, pp. 11–12.

[103] *Abingdon Abbey*, II, 460. For the creativity of the proems, see the extended metaphors presented in S858 (AD 985, body as boat), S874 (AD 990, military) and S875 (AD 990, gladiatorial combat).

suspicion.[104] Despite their unique formulations, Æthelred's *arengae* display themes shared with each other and with proems composed earlier in the tenth century (they rarely relied on texts earlier than this for their models). In both cases, shared themes provided contexts for the king's or duke's authority over the land he granted to churches and laymen. *Arengae* were therefore expressions of contemporary political thought, applied to specific situations.[105]

Thus, while they drew inspiration from their models, notaries certainly engaged with the meaning of the pious sentiments they produced. The content of a preamble was chosen to correspond to the transactions recorded in each charter. For instance, the preambles for dowries describe and explain the institution of marriage (F11, F58). The notary did not have complete freedom, as the other parties in a transaction were also concerned with the content of the charter. They exerted different degrees of influence: it may well be the case that charters produced in a monastery included the sentiments favoured by that institution, whereas those produced in an official chancery would have reflected the interests of the duke or king more closely. However, both parties, as well as those consenting to the transaction, needed to approve the text. The *arengae* exhibit principles which contented donors and recipients alike.

Moreover, sentiments preserved in the *arengae* continued to exert an influence on the donor's behaviour after the texts were produced. The principles which are contained in the charters had a degree of binding force. They cannot be dismissed as pious platitudes, even if they do not necessarily reveal 'true' motives. While rulers did follow political strategies in their monastic patronage, their stated religious motivations were important components of their actions. Once they had justified actions using an ideological principle, the dukes' or kings' future behaviour was then constrained by this principle. The ideological justification was convincing only while the ruler appeared to act consistently according to principle; he needed to continue behaving appropriately in order that others would believe the original profession of motivation.[106]

External neighbours, as well as internal political pressures, required such maintenance of credible ideological justifications. A later charter of William the Conqueror gives an indication of how the Normans needed to convince

---

[104] E.g. *Charters of Burton Abbey*, ed. P. Sawyer, Anglo-Saxon Charters 2 (Oxford, 1979), p. 72: S920 (1008) and S930 (AD 1012).

[105] The potential of Anglo-Saxon charters, especially *arengae*, to illuminate aspects of political thought has been established by C. Insley ('Where Did All the Charters Go?', esp. pp. 113–18; 'Rhetoric and Ritual', p. 118), and P. Stafford ('Political Ideas').

[106] Q. Skinner, *Visions of Politics I: Regarding Method* (Cambridge, 2002), p. 155, expresses this idea most clearly: '...even if they were not motivated by any such principle, they will find themselves committed to behaving in such a way that their actions *remain compatible* with the claim that their professed principles genuinely motivated them'.

those around them. The charter records the following exchange, which took place on the occasion of William's donation to St-Florent of Saumur:

> When the monks said that alms ought to be given purely, he, as a most prudent man, replied, 'Although we may be Normans, we know well that it ought to be done in this way, and thus, if it is pleasing to God, we will do it.'[107]

This incident reveals the expectation, even in the 1050s (Fauroux dated the charter, which survives in an original, to between 1051 and 1066), that Normans would not follow Christian traditions and principles – and it also reveals that they were aware of this expectation. Land donations, particularly to external recipients, were opportunities to demonstrate their Christian credentials, but their motives needed to appear impeccable. The principles found in the *arengae* of these charters constituted a programme which the Norman dukes, English kings and their nobles pursued in combination with the monasteries they patronized.

Many charters open with a statement concerning the practice of producing such documents. Norman *arengae* presented the custom of recording transactions in charters as a long-standing institution, which in itself gave justification. However, as already noted, the predecessors of Richard I in Normandy did *not* follow this custom. The *antecessores* mentioned in several charters cannot therefore be understood to mean the dukes' immediate ancestors.[108] Rather, the Norman notaries referred to their *antecessores* in the Christian religion, as one *arenga* made clear when addressing the custom of giving land to the Church. The origins of the custom were located within Christian history, which was said to have arisen 'In the beginning of the birth of the church, with the examples of the holy apostles having spread throughout the earth'.[109] Likewise, notaries situated the origins of the custom of producing charters vaguely in the Christian past, with 'the authority of the holy fathers' ('sanctorum patrum auctoritate', F33). The antiquity of the custom linked the practice of the Norman participants to the long-standing tradition of the Christian community. A lengthy preamble in a donation to the chapter of Lisieux described how these practices were created in the earliest history of the Church, when it began to own property and construct buildings (F48). This *arenga* seems to make a parallel between the new Norman Church and the early days of Christianity: both had the same need for securing that

---

[107] F199: 'Monachis enim dicentibus helemosinam mundam debere dari, ipse, ut vir prudentissius, respondit: "Licet Normanni simus, bene tamen novimus quia sic oportet fieri, et ita, si Deo placuerit, faciemus".'

[108] F49, F17, F16; *Cartulary of Mont-Saint-Michel*, ed. Keats-Rohan, no. 47, p. 131.

[109] F43: 'In exordio nascentis aecclesie, per omnem terram documentis sanctorum apostolorum diffusae.'

which was given 'because many people, having abandoned heathen idolatry, surrendered themselves by the profession of Christianity, and they bestowed their inheritance, which had earlier been emptiness, to the use of the Church, for the cure of their souls'.[110] The Normans' pagan past was substituted for a wider history of the Church, which they adopted for themselves.

Like the *arengae* of Norman charters, the proems of Æthelred's charters occasionally deal with the practice of charter-writing itself (nine charters discuss this theme). It was common for Anglo-Saxon diplomas to claim the superiority of writing over memory, and the institution of the practice might be ascribed to their forefathers.[111] The concern for continuity across generations was clear: the deeds of the forefathers were intended to be known by their descendants.[112] However, discussion of Christian history in this context was more limited than in Norman charters. The few references to Church history in Æthelred's charters concerned the English, rather than the universal Church. This is most apparent in the charters of St Albans, which refer to the monastery's patron saint, 'the proto-martyr of the English people'.[113] An *arenga* of 1007 proclaimed that 'the glorious victory of the blessed martyr Alban is to be honoured especially by the population of the English placed in the circumference of Britain; who was subjected to martyrdom for Christ and consecrated that people with the outpouring of his rose-red blood'.[114] It was known from Bede's *Historia ecclesiastica* that Alban was a Briton martyred under the Romans, before the Anglo-Saxons arrived in Britain. His sanctification of the English people was thus transmitted through the land they inhabited, rather than genetic connection, as the charter's draftsman indicated in the phrase 'ambitum Britanniae'.[115] The St Albans charters claimed their saint for the English people precisely because they were defined through their inhabitation of the island of Britain.

Draftsmen also united the histories and dynasties of Mercia and Wessex. Diplomas for St Albans referred to King Offa of Mercia, the abbey's original

---

[110] '...quia plurimi, relicta gentilitatis idolatria, se christianae professioni manciparunt, et patrimonia, quae prius vanitati, pro animarum remedio, ecclesiae utilitati contulerunt'.

[111] See e.g. on memory S883: 'quia hominum fragilis memoria moriendo obliuiscitur quod scriptura litterarum seruando retinet' ('because the fragile memory of men forgets in dying what the writing of letters retains in preserving'); Foot, 'Reading Anglo-Saxon Charters', p. 40.

[112] S888 (AD 996), S842 (AD 982).

[113] S888, AD 996: 'gentis Anglorum protomartyri'; S912, AD 1005: 'huius patriae protomartyris'.

[114] S916: 'Anglorum tamen populis intra ambitum Britanniae constitutis specialiter est honoranda beati martyris Albani gloriosa uictoria; qui et ipse pro Christo martyrium subiit; et hanc gentem rosei sanguinis effusione consecrauit.'

[115] Ælfric went further and called the land in which Alban died 'engla lande' (*Ælfric's Lives of Saints*, I, 414): see Wormald, '*Engla Lond*: The Making of an Allegiance', p. 11.

benefactor, emphasizing the abbey's royal origins.[116] Similarly, charters from Abingdon recounted its foundation and the privileges conferred by King Coenwulf of Mercia and Pope Leo III, while charters from the Old Minster at Winchester looked back to that monastery's foundation by King Cenwalh of Wessex.[117] Although only the last of these was of the West Saxon royal line, Æthelred claimed connection to all of these kings. A St Albans diploma of 1005 linked Offa directly to Æthelred by having the king refer to him as 'my ancestor and predecessor Offa, princely king' and connect himself to Offa through his similar benefaction.[118] In references to his predecessors, Æthelred stressed the continuation of the family line, the transfer of kingship and the similar relationship of patronage to the recipient monasteries. In his charters of restitution of the 990s, Æthelred emphasized that his action connected him with his immediate predecessors as king, to whom he was also joined by family relationship. In S891 (AD 997), a restoration of lands to the Old Minster, Winchester, Æthelred presented his gift:

> just as in the beginning of Christianity it was decided by king Cenwalh, and afterwards signed by Cynewulf; then indeed it was restored by Ecgbyrht, and reached its former heights; at last, by Eadred, that is uncle of my father Edgar, it was renewed in a similar way with the certain stipulation of letters to the above-mentioned holy place; most recently it was restored by my father...[119]

The reference in this charter to 'in the beginning of Christianity' alludes to the establishment of Christianity among the Anglo-Saxons, and more specifically the conversion of the first West Saxon kings.[120] The Norman dukes concentrated narrowly on their own immediate lineage by name, as discussed above, and then positioned themselves as part of the worldwide Christian community. Æthelred, on the other hand, aligned himself not only with the West Saxons but with all prior Anglo-Saxon royal lines. The concern was with the English as Christians, rather than membership of any wider community.

---

[116] S916, AD 1007; S912, AD 1005. See *Charters of St Albans*, ed. J. Crick, Anglo-Saxon Charters 12 (Oxford, 2007), pp. 171, 185.

[117] S876 (AD 993); S891 (AD 997).

[118] S912: 'abauus praedecessor meus Offa, scilicet, rex inclitus'; 'ipsum coenobium rex beneuolus Offa ditauit, et egomet nunc confirmando renouaui'.

[119] S891 (AD 997): 'uti in inchoatione christianitatis a Kynewalho rege deliberatum est; ac postmodum a Kynewulfo praetitulatum est; dein uero ab Ecgbyrhto restauratum, ac apicibus recuperatum est; ad ultimum autem ab Eadredo patruo scilicet patris mei Eadgari simili modo cum certa litterarum adstipulatione redintegratum est eidem suprascripto sancto loco; nouissime uero ab ipso patre meo satis clara demonstratione renouatum est...'

[120] S914 refers to Augustine, Gregory and Æthelberht, because of its Canterbury origin, but this is a forgery from later in the eleventh century (n. 53, above).

In fact, in Æthelred's diplomas, Christian faith was presented as equivalent to the rule of the English kings. Although gifts were presented in terms of eternal possession and heavenly reward, a number of charters substitute *perpetualiter* with a phrase such as 'so long as the torch of faith shines out on the *patria* of the English'.[121] Narrative sections indicate that the king could and did deprive people of their lands in punishment, but the commands and sanctions of the charters were purely spiritual. The injunction that property given by the king should be respected was strengthened by recourse to Christian principles and beliefs, and thus cohered with the instruction that it should last as long as the faith itself.[122] Moreover, this phrase aligned the persistence of Christianity in the land of the English with civilization and the accepted order.

The rest of the *arengae* concern the motivations of donors in making transactions, and the custom of giving away land in gift more generally. The most common sentiment is the idea, which was popular in charters across medieval Europe, that giving lands to the Church will lead to the donor receiving a place in heaven. This principle established that the donors' acts were more significant than they appeared to be.

Several Norman *arengae* emphasize the idea that all possessions are held from God. A charter of Richard II and Gunnor to Mont-Saint-Michel expresses this most directly, stating that they gave gifts not of their own property, but of God's: 'For do we think we have anything except that which we have received from him?', a sentiment echoed in another charter of Gunnor to the same monastery (F17).[123] Elsewhere it is more briefly stated that 'these possessions were given to us in this world by God' or that the Church should be served 'out of these good things given to us by God'.[124] A charter recording the assumption of the monastic habit by Richard II's brothers-in-law foregrounded this concept by opening with the assertion that 'all earthly possession is a gift of merciful God' ('terrena possidere ex dono est clementis Dei', F46bis). These motivations were not restricted to the ducal family, but also ascribed to

---

[121] S925, AD 1012: 'quamdiu Anglorum patriae facula eluxerit fidei'.

[122] Chaplais, 'Origin and Authenticity', p. 33 highlighted the purely ecclesiastical nature of sanctions and authenticity in Anglo-Saxon diplomas. However, Norman charters provide a comparable system in this respect. Hadley notes that such phrases indicated the threat felt to be posed by pagan vikings: *Northern Danelaw*, p. 36, n. 126. Variants linking the English people to Britain include a will of the ninth century, in which the donor hopes his gifts will last 'as long as there be baptism on the English people's island' (S1508), and a charter of Eadwig (S610): 'quamdiu Christianitas in hac Albionis insula uiguerit'.

[123] F49: 'Detur igitur Deo non nostrum, sed suum. Quid enim aliud nos habere putamus quam quod ab eo accepimus?'

[124] F4 (Richard I): 'ipsis in hoc mundo a Deo tribuuntur bonis'; *Chartes de l'Abbaye de Jumièges (v.825 à 1204) conservées aux Archives de la Seine-Inférieure*, ed. J. Vernier, 2 vols. (Rouen, 1916), I, 20 (no. VIII, Hugh d'Ivry): 'ex bonis a Deo nobis attributis'.

Rainaldus, viscount of Arques, as he donated to Fécamp, explaining that 'it is right that it is returned to him by whom all things are given' ('quia justum est ut ei reddantur a quo omnia tribuuntur', F54). The idea is even found in a charter of a certain Imma, which cites the biblical injunction to honour your father and mother – here interpreted as the Church – so that 'you will live long upon the land which the Lord your God will give to you'.[125] *Arengae* thus emphasized that possessions, particularly land, were given directly by God to the Norman dukes, ecclesiastics and wealthy individuals.

Just as earthly possession was seen to have come from God, so was earthly power. A charter of 1021–25 which records the gifts of Duke Richard II to St Peter of Chartres elaborated on this theme at length. Unusually, in this document, there is no distinct *arenga*, but the principles were applied directly to Richard. The text reads as a discussion of Richard's power specifically, rather than the more common general axioms.

> ...Next, by a similar reasoning, it is openly certain that I am elevated to such dominion of power, not by human but rather by divine grant, and for no other reason than for the defence of holy mother church and the necessary establishment of the rule of public law. Having considered these things through this inquiry of reason, I feared lest that saying in the Gospels: 'every tree that does not bear good fruit should be cut down and thrown in the fire' [Matt. 7.19], should be ascribed to me as unfruitful, if I did not deserve to become the holder of heavenly property through the fruitfulness of good deeds, or if I could not recall the community of the holy church to better things by an example of honesty. And remembering what is said of this: 'having gifts according to the grace which is given to you' [Romans 12.6], I decided to give to God a portion of the possessions divinely given to me, because he who lays up treasure in Christ does not forget for whom he shall gather these things [Matt. 6/Psalm 38(39)].[126]

This passage describes how Richard's authority, wealth and power was given by God – but could also be taken away by God. The reasoning, presumably

---

[125] F55: 'Honora patrem tuum et matrem, ut sis longevus super terram quam Dominus Deus tuus daturus est tibi' (Deuteronomy 5. 16). On this charter, see Potts, 'Une charte de Saint-Wandrille'; Imma appears in *Inventio et Miracula Vulfranni*, pp. 43–4.

[126] F32: 'Deinde, simili ratione, in propatulo constitit non humane sed potius divine esse concessionis me tante imperiositatis dominio sublimari, nec ob aliud nisi ad sanctae matris aecclesie defensionem et constituendam juris publici normalitatem. His ita per rationis indagationem cognitis, veritus sum ne illud ewangelicum: "omnis arbor que non facit fructum bonum excidatur et in ignem mittatur" mihi infructuoso deputaretur, si non per bonorum emolumentorum fructificationem celestis adquisionis consecutor fieri meruissem, nec sancte ecclesiae congregationem, probitatis exemplo, ad meliora revocarem. Ac memor illius quod dicitur: "Habentes donationes secundum gratiam que data est vobis" possessionis mihi divinitus concesse Deo portionem dare decrevi, quia qui in Christo thesaurizat non ignorat cui congregabit ea.'

written by a cleric at St Peter of Chartres, may be read as a reminder to Richard that he was reliant on the Church in legitimizing his rule, and that the Church possessed powerful spiritual sanctions if he forgot this. Conversely, the charter was an opportunity for Richard to assert that he ruled with the favour of God – the evidence was in the very exercise of authority and the ability to donate to the Church. In the 1009 charter by which he replaced the abbot of Mont-Saint-Michel, Richard offered similar sentiments (F12). This charter was probably composed by the ducal chancery and presented Richard's own interests. Richard asserted that he acted in the care of the monks 'laid under our excellent dignity' ('nostrae subditam excellentiae dignitatis') and, more generally, for 'the security of the people entrusted to us by God' ('stabilitate plebis a Deo nobis delegatę'). Thus, in recognising that the land they possessed was granted by God, the Norman dukes demonstrated also that God had appointed them to the rulership of the people who lived in that land.

Narrative texts also exploited this concept. The idea that Normandy was given to the Normans by God was a powerful element of their ethnic myth, found in the pages of the *De moribus*. Dudo reassured his readers that the vikings assailed Francia 'with God's approval' because of the wickedness of the Franks.[127] He continued this theme by stating that it was 'the high providence of the godly Trinity' who directed Rollo towards Francia, in order that those who afflicted it would save the Church.[128] Rollo's dream firmly rooted this prophecy in Normandy: his Christian prisoner interpreted 'the mountain in Francia' as 'the church of that land', while the Dacian men indicated to Rollo that they believed 'the interpretation of your vision directs us to this very country' – the Seine valley, and Rouen.[129] The vision included the diverse people of the land who were united under the rule of Rollo. Towards the end of the *De moribus*, Dudo recounted how it was God who restored Richard I to his rightful place in Normandy because this was the Christian desire of the people: 'the Lord who is the King of Kings was placated by the continual prayers and fasting most devoutly engaged in by the Normans and Bretons with a single mind, and He snatched Richard, the boy of inestimable promise, from the king's hands'.[130] People, land and ruler were united through God's plan for them.

More than merely pious posturing, this viewpoint distanced the Normans from the French king. The dukes presented their power and possessions as

---

[127] Christiansen, p. 22; Lair, p. 137: 'nutu Dei'.

[128] Christiansen, p. 25; Lair, pp. 140–1: 'superna Deificae Trinitatis providentia'.

[129] Christiansen, pp. 30, 36 (and p. 47); Lair, p. 146: 'Mons Franciae quo stare videbaris, Ecclesia illius designatur'; p. 153: 'Forsan interpretatio tuae visionis vertetur in finibus istius' (and p. 167).

[130] Christiansen, p. 105; Lair, p. 230: 'Northmannorum et Britonum precibus continuis jejuniisque singulis mensibus devotissime exercitatis placatus, regum rex Dominus, eripuit Ricardum, inaestimabilis incrementationis puerum, taliter de regis manibus.' I have slightly added to Christiansen's translation.

the direct gift of God, rather than a superior territorial lord. The dukes, and increasingly the Norman elites, did this using the tools, network and ideology of the Church. The partnership between secular powers and the Church created a discourse in which fidelity to God was also fidelity to the Norman rulers. People in the province were thus strongly encouraged to identify as Normans.

Æthelred's charters also linked royal and divine authority. Firstly, they did so by creating parallels between the English king's rule in Britain and God's rule of the universe: like Æthelred, God was called *gubernator* and *rector*.[131] Moreover, the terms of his power reflected those Æthelred used: *monarchia* (S884, AD 995), *imperium* (S882, AD 995 for 994) and *regnum* (S893, AD 998); he too sat on a throne ('residente solio', S901, AD 1002). The comparison was most directly stated in a proem of 988, which created a neat parallel between God as heavenly governor and the government of earthly kings (S869: 'All positioning of worldly things is governed by the heavenly moderator... and the lineages of kings and princes rule over the summit of the world through renowned government').[132]

From 984 (which Keynes saw as the end of Æthelred's 'period of tutelage'), draftsmen began to reflect on the idea that God granted worldly authority directly.[133] New *arengae* were composed expanding on this theme and specifically applying it to the king.[134] A rare repeated proem (used in S856 and S860, both AD 985) described how God established the world after the Fall, and 'conceded that diverse monarchies of nations should be dominated by various rectors'.[135] These statements established that Æthelred ruled by the will of God, and therefore should be obeyed in his decisions, for 'the laws of the kingdoms are governed by the dispensation of providence'.[136] In particular, the theme of Creation, which features in seventeen diplomas, provided scope for further reflection on God's role as governor and on his delegation of earthly authority. Draftsmen emphasized God's bestowal of worldly authority, rather than physical possessions as in Norman *arengae*. God's gift of wealth separate from authority appears in three charters only, spread across the period in 985, 1011 and 1015. This may reflect the fact that Æthelred claimed authority over the whole of Britain, but royal possessions were concentrated primarily in the south.

---

[131] Insley, 'Where Did All the Charters Go?', pp. 117–18. E.g. S869 (AD 988), S880 (AD 994).

[132] 'Omnis status mundanarum rerum superno gubernatur moderatore... regum satrapumque prosapia mundi iam iamque principantur fastigio precluenti moderamine'.

[133] Keynes, *Diplomas*, pp. 176–7.

[134] See the comment by S. Miller in *Charters of the New Minster, Winchester*, Anglo-Saxon Charters 9 (Oxford, 2001), p. 137.

[135] S856: '...diuersas nationum monarchias uariis concessit dominari rectoribus...'

[136] S886, AD 995: 'regnorum iura prouida dispensatione gubernatur'.

The relationship between ruler and subjects was more prominent. Although the royal styles of these diplomas presented the king as ruler of many peoples, the rhetoric of the *arengae* framed the nation with reference to the English past and the Christian community, and Æthelred's responsibility was to them. Charters from later in the reign refer to specific troubles from which Æthelred sought to defend his people, which has led various editors and commenters to ascribe such statements to the viking invasions of Æthelred's reign.[137] Indeed, the openings of two charters of 1005 (S911) and 1016 (S935) specifically referred to viking attackers, characterizing them as *piratae, hostes barbari* and *paganae gentes*. Diplomas presented these troubles as assailing the English land ('the dreadful roars of obscene and horrible death warn us that we are not safe in our own land of acquired peace'), and the king claimed he acted in the interests of his nation, to gain favour with God ('on account of the cure of my soul and the stability of the kingdom conceded to me from heaven').[138] The *arengae* of Æthelred's charters emphasized unity among his subjects, referring to the Mercian and West Saxon royal pasts and to the Christian history of Britain as the legacy of all the English people. Æthelred's authority, however, did not come from this heritage alone but from God's delegation. The 'English' were those who obeyed his authority, as Christian subjects should. The ideology of authority in both Norman and Anglo-Saxon charters linked ethnicity to Christian duty and obedience.

Viking heritage

These brief and allusive mentions of contemporary viking attackers in Æthelred's later charters highlight the complete absence of any reference to the viking or Scandinavian past in the diplomas of his reign. As discussed above, the Danes who appear in a few charters were foreign visitors or contemporary threats, not inhabitants of the English kingdom. In line with the hagiographical evidence discussed in Chapters 3 and 4, English diplomas stressed continuity with the pre-viking period. However, even Edgar's charters associated with the Benedictine reform and the re-establishment of fenland monasteries, which we might expect to relate to earlier viking destruction, make no mention of Scandinavian raiders. Late tenth- and early eleventh-century English royal diplomas emphasize unity and continuity, and any disruption or conflict was strictly contemporary. If Danes or vikings were a threat, there was no hint in the diplomas that this had any deeper roots in the history or demography of the English kingdom.

---

[137] E.g. *Abingdon Abbey*, II, 516.

[138] S928, AD 1012: 'diris obcene horrendeque mortalitatis circumsepta latratibus. non nos propria indepte pacis securos'; S912, AD 1005: 'ob meae remedium animulae et ob stabilimentum regni coelitus mihimet concessi'.

Perhaps more surprisingly, neither did Norman charters refer to the viking past which, as we have seen, the Norman dukes emphasized in other contexts. The only Norman charter to refer to viking destruction was the confirmation for Jumièges, in which Richard II recalled William Longsword's restoration of the monastery. He stated that Jumièges had been 'once torn down to the ground by the raving sword of evildoers' (F36: 'quondam perversorum bacante gladio ad solum usque diruto'). Even in this reference, the destroyers were not identified as vikings specifically, although the identification would probably have been assumed. Nor were they identified as the ancestors of the Norman nobles, as they were in narrative texts. The focus was firmly on William Longsword's restoration, and no connection was drawn between his action and the previous destruction. In all other charters, Richard I and Richard II presented their donations as given purely from pious generosity, and out of concern for the growth of monastic life ('ad augendam igitur vitam inibi Domino militantium', F31).

The charters of the Normans' neighbours in the West Frankish kingdom, in contrast, did identify viking destruction as a reason for their donations and restitutions. This was even the case at monasteries patronized by the Norman dukes. The Mont-Saint-Michel cartulary records the gift of Ivo fitz Fulcoin on 12 October 997–1003/04, who restored eight villas which were lost during the viking invasions. He made no distinction between his contemporary Christian Normans and the pagan invaders of the ninth century, simply stating that 'irruente Normannorum infestatione locus ipse per multorum curricula annorum amiserat'.[139]

The Norman charters very rarely referred to any events that far in the past. Recompense was made for more recent injuries: for example, Richard II gave to Notre-Dame de Chartres so that 'the cause of immoderate injury which I had carried out grievously in their neighbourhood was placated to anyone's satisfaction'. But such charters only ever refer to the events of recent years, rather than viking activities of the past.[140]

This omission of all reference to the viking past from charters requires explanation. Musset and Potts have shown that the dukes pursued a

---

[139] *Cartulary of Mont-Saint-Michel*, ed. Keats-Rohan, no. 26 (p. 109). Further examples: *Cartulaire de l'Abbaye de Saint-Père de Chartres*, ed. B. Guérard, 2 vols. (Paris, 1840), I, no. 1 (c. 930), no. 4 (c. 954); *Cartulaire de l'Abbaye de Redon en Bretagne*, ed. A. de Courson (Paris, 1863), no. 283 (924); *Recueil des Actes de Louis IV, Roi de France (936–984)*, ed. P. Lauer (Paris, 1914), no. 2 (936).

[140] F15: 'tum injuriae causa non modicae quam in vicinia ejus graviter exercueram, quatenus aliquantula satisfactione placata'. See also his attestation of William of Bellême's donation to the church of Sées, F33: 'reminiscens plurimarum injuriarum quas ego et praedecessores mei Salariensi intuleramus ecclesiae, decrevi boni compensatione male acta delere'. Fauroux (*Recueil*, p. 93, n. 1) suggests that Richard II was atoning for injuries sustained in war *c.* 1013 during his conflict with Odo II of Chartres over the dowry of his sister: see *Gesta Normannorum Ducum*, pp. 22–7.

deliberate policy of restoration, choosing to re-found houses dating from the Merovingian or Carolingian period rather than establish completely new sites. Much of the land which they gave to these houses consisted of estates which the monasteries had held during the ninth century.[141] Moreover, the histories and hagiographies produced in these houses and for the dukes explicitly referred to the viking destruction of their ancestors as the reason why the Normans restored them to a new glory. Yet the charters examined in this chapter were produced by the same people as these longer historical texts, including Dudo, the dukes' own historian. Many documents were written by clerics and monks of beneficiary houses, and their language and proprietary concerns are echoed in the other texts they produced, notably in the case of the *Translationes Audoeni*. The difference in emphasis cannot, therefore, be explained by a different authorship or purpose.

In their charters, the Normans did not refer to any claims from before the establishment of their principality. They might refer to the original foundation of a monastery by its saintly father, but they did not recall the original acquisition of its property.[142] The grand confirmation charters of St-Ouen (F53), Jumièges (F36), St-Wandrille (F52), Bernay (F35), Fécamp (F34) and Mont-Saint-Michel (F49) trace all their possessions back to the gifts of one of the dukes, or of their followers: they do not include any properties granted to them before the viking conquest. The immediate effect of this was that all grants of land and other concessions now stemmed ultimately from one of the dukes or Norman conquerors. Frequent reference was made to the restoration of property given in gift by ducal predecessors. Even a very early charter for St-Denis (F3) claimed the gift had originally been given by Rollo and William Longsword, a claim reinforced in Dudo's *De moribus*.[143] Other charters traced the past ownership of properties to inheritance or gifts in dowry from previous dukes, and the origins of monasteries to the work of predecessors, but only ever as far back as Rollo.[144] The more general effect was that the idea of Normandy as a unit was maintained. No recourse to the region's previous existence – when it had not been a discrete unit – was required.

The exception, again, was the confirmation charter for Jumièges (F36). This document, as the other confirmation charters, focused on the ducal lineage by emphasizing the current duke's continuation of his father's and grandfather's work. When recalling the gifts of William Longsword, however, Richard II

---

[141] Potts, *Monastic Revival*, pp. 38–9; Musset, 'Monachisme d'Époque Franque'.

[142] F52 notes that St-Wandrille was built by St Wandregislus and later dedicated to him. F59 refers to Jumièges's claim to land that it had held 'ex sanctę Batildis tempore', but this was a judgment of the king, heard in the king's court at Senlis, and concerned with property outside Norman borders. Nevertheless, the example highlights the fact that equivalent claims were never made for property within Normandy.

[143] Christiansen, p. 51; Lair, p. 171.

[144] E.g. F3, F9, F14bis, F17.

explicitly framed them as a restoration of property that had been lost in the viking period, repeatedly using the word '*restituit*'. He stated that:

> I give... the farms, possessions and tithes listed below, which by these precepts had once belonged to that place by right but, after the ravaging of the place made way for the domination and the uses of certain evil men, and had been restored to the use of the servants of God by the zeal and care of that most pious restorer.[145]

As suggested above, it may well be that the tradition of destruction and restoration at Jumièges was too strong to be ignored.[146] William Longsword had held a special attachment to the monastery and probably did present himself primarily as a restorer. The later donations confirmed in the charter, however, the gifts of Richard I, Richard II and their nobility, were not considered to be restorations. The charter thus drew a line under the process of restitution, indicating that it was complete. Moreover, the actual claims to property from the pre-viking period were not rehearsed. William Longsword's action remained the origin of all future claims.[147]

Therefore, although it was not mentioned in charters, the viking past was a vital part of the Normans' legal claim to Normandy. In narrative texts, the Norman dukes promoted their viking seizure of the land in order to show that their ancestors had conquered the land of Normandy themselves, rather than merely receiving it in gift or benefice from the French kings. In the *De moribus*, Dudo presented Rollo at the advantage in his meeting with Charles the Simple at St-Clair-sur-Epte. Dudo stated clearly that Rollo and his vikings had already taken Normandy by conquest.[148] The *Translatio Prima Audoeni*, discussing the agreement with the king and Rollo's baptism, emphasized that Rollo had subjugated Normandy by force of arms himself.[149] Rollo's claim

---

[145] 'Concedo... subnotata predia et possessiones sive decimas, prescriptis his que quondam ipsius loci juris fuerant, sed post loci devastacionem quorumdam malignorum usibus et dominationi cesserant, ipsius vero piissimi restauratoris studio et diligencia in usus servorum Dei fuere restituta.'

[146] In addition, it seems that the monks of Jumièges retained a number of their pre-viking conquest charters, unlike most other monasteries. See *Jumièges*, ed. Vernier, I, 1–14 (nos. I–IV).

[147] A later example from St-Wandrille did call on claims from a more distant past: the monks received the island of *Belcinnaca* from William, count of Arques (Richard II's son), as the result of a claim based on the ninth-century *Vita Condedi*, from which they forged a charter. However, this took place between 1032 and 1047, a time of weakened ducal authority and, moreover, it did not refer to the viking past but the life of the saint. See Chibnall, 'Charter and Chronicle', p. 3; F234 (p. 452) and Lot, *Saint-Wandrille*, no. 1 and no. 15.

[148] Christiansen, p. 60; Lair, p. 182: 'the kingdom won by laborious contests and by the sweat of battle'; 'regnum, labore certaminum sudoreque praeliorum adeptum'.

[149] *Translatio Prima Audoeni*, ch. 3: 'totiusque Normanniae provinciam, quam sibi isdem Rollo debellando subegerat, regali munere liberaliter concessit.'

on Normandy passed down to his successors, giving them the province as a rightful inheritance, independent of the king.

An episode from the mid-eleventh century *Inventio et Miracula Sancti Vulfranni* dramatized this issue. The text, written at St-Wandrille in 1053, records an early attempt at restoration of the abbey by Gerard of Brogne in the 940s.[150] Gerard came to Richard I at Rouen bearing the relics of St Wandregisilus, who had been evacuated from the monastery of St-Wandrille during the viking invasions. Gerard requested that the land of St-Wandrille should be restored, and produced charters (*cartarum priuilegia*) proving the monastic community's ownership of various properties. The Norman nobles, however, disputed Gerard's claims – not because they did not believe the charters, but because they considered themselves to have stronger claims on the land. They regarded these properties as their own possessions, 'which the warlike strength of their predecessors had gained for them by arms and blood, or which they had obtained for themselves through long service and much effort'.[151] Gerard had come up against a society which did not share his views of what constituted a binding claim to land ownership. No charters had yet been produced in Normandy, so it is not surprising if the Norman elites remained unimpressed by the documentary record of ownership or claims to the perpetual possession of Church land. They had their own claims on the land they inhabited, justified by history, inheritance and experience.

This episode is often interpreted as a comment on past attitudes of the mid-tenth century.[152] However, the narrator did not criticize the Norman nobles. In fact, in the very same text, he continued their attitude, demonstrating how Normandy had been won by viking conquest. The text described how Rollo, the greatest viking leader, had divided the province among his army, with no reference to the king.[153] The early Scandinavian elite's claim by conquest was shown to trump Gerard's charters dating from before their arrival. Even in the Jumièges confirmation charter, when William Longsword restored land held by one of his followers, it was stated that it was done 'consensu et voluntate' of the owner: the property was not the church's by right. The origins of Norman ownership were based in the events of the viking conquest, and these were the most ancient claims that would be recognized. In this way, charters demonstrated that all Norman monasteries, churches and individuals were indebted to the family of Rollo.

---

[150] E. van Houts, 'Historiography and Hagiography at Saint-Wandrille: The *Inventio et Miracula Sancti Vulfranni*', ANS 12 (1990), 233–51 (p. 238); *Inventio et Miracula Vulfranni*, pp. 29–30.

[151] *Inventio et Miracula Vulfranni*, p. 30: '...propriis honoribus quos sibi armis et sanguine predecessorum suorum pepererat bellicosa uirtus, siue quos sibi ipsi diuturno adquisierant seruitio multisque sudoribus'.

[152] Potts, *Monastic Revival*, p. 25; Tabuteau, *Transfers of Property*, pp. 213–14.

[153] *Inventio et Miracula Vulfranni*, pp. 26–7.

This conquest involved the violent seizure or destruction of churches and their properties. Charters, delineating the lawful transfer of specific pieces of land, could not legitimize such behaviour as a legal means of taking possession. It would certainly not have been acceptable to repeat this conquest. The *arengae* of these documents established the special status of the viking conquest of Normandy: it had been God's plan. As in the narrative texts, conquest and Christianity combined to underpin the origins of Normandy, and of Norman ducal authority.

We can, therefore, trace the emergence of Normandy through charter evidence. Charters show a developed concept of land and population under the authority of Rollo's dynasty, reflected in the increasingly consistent terminology of a single Norman people and a Norman territory. Although the viking past was rarely explicitly referred to within these charters, the viking conquest of the region by the dukes' ancestors formed an essential basis of ducal authority and a moment of origin for Normandy.

The 'Danelaw'

The English Danelaw is often considered as an equivalent to Normandy. However, the complete absence of reference to the term or concept in Anglo-Saxon charters indicates that its development was considerably different. Modern scholars often use the term 'Danelaw' to refer to regions of Scandinavian settlement in northern and eastern England, and thus identify its origins similarly in the viking past.[154] However, the uniform use of the term 'Danelaw' for the whole area throughout the later ninth to eleventh centuries masks the changing political structures and relationships within the region and with the rest of England.[155] The situation under Edgar, Edward the Martyr and Æthelred was very different from that of their predecessors. Areas of Danish settlement, which had previously been under various states of Scandinavian rule, were all now incorporated into one kingdom under the West Saxon king's direct authority. It was this situation of formerly Danish regions within a united English kingdom that led to the creation of the term 'Danelaw', which first appeared in the legislation – but not the charters – of Æthelred.

Æthelred's tenth-century predecessors had referred to regional distinctions directly, albeit briefly, also in legal contexts. Edward the Elder's law code made a general distinction between the customs of his own kingdom, and those 'in the east and the north'.[156] Only once these areas were combined in one kingdom did an English king concern himself with the specific differences

---

[154] E.g. Hadley, *Northern Danelaw*; K. Holman, 'Defining the Danelaw', in *Vikings and the Danelaw*, ed. Graham-Campbell, pp. 1–11.

[155] Abrams, 'Edward the Elder's Danelaw', pp. 128–33, on definitions.

[156] II Eadweard 5.2: *Die Gesetze* ed. Liebermann, I, 144: 'gif hit sy east inne, gif hit sy norð inne'.

between them. The first considerable references to legal distinctions between English and Danes appeared in IV Edgar, Edgar's law code promulgated at *Wihtbordesstan*, which was perhaps written around 970 and certainly after Edgar's accession to the kingdom of England in 959.[157] IV Edgar drew the distinction between 'mid Denum' and 'mid Englum', legislating directly for the English and stating several times that, in general, the Danes should follow 'the best constitution which they can determine upon'.[158] But the term 'Danelaw' was first used in the early eleventh century, in Archbishop Wulfstan's legislation for Æthelred.[159] The Danelaw was thus a creation of the English kings after they had conquered these areas and removed the final Norse-speaking king of York in 954. It was an expression of the accommodation of previously independent communities into the kingdom of England under the authority of the West Saxon dynasty.

Both the term and the concept of the 'Danelaw' are usually interpreted geographically; in general, historians have taken Edgar's legislation 'mid Denum' and Æthelred's references to 'Dena lage' to refer to a defined region in which a different law applied to all inhabitants, rather than as the expression of 'personal law' (the practice by which different laws applied to different ethnicities in the same geographical region).[160] In his law codes, Edgar recognized that local custom endured even after the removal of 'Danish' rulers and the appointment of ealdormen and bishops by the English king, and he explained the difference ethnically.[161] How Scandinavian in character the laws and customs of northern England really were continues to be a matter of considerable debate – after all, Northumbrian custom may well have been different to West Saxon custom, regardless of Danish input. However, in a legal context, this difference was labelled as stemming from Danish tradition.

Those who see the Danelaw as a geographical entity have often considered the Treaty of Alfred and Guthrum of 886 to be the foundation document of the Danelaw.[162] The text of the treaty opens with a clear delineation of geographical boundaries between the two kings' realms:

---

[157] P. Wormald, *The Making of English Law: King Alfred to the Twelfth Century. Volume I: Legislation and its Limits* (Oxford, 2001), pp. 441–2.

[158] IV Edgar 12: *The Laws of the Kings of England from Edmund to Henry I*, trans. A. J. Robertson (Cambridge, 1925), p. 37; *Die Gesetze*, ed. Liebermann, I, 212: 'swa gode laga swa hy betste geceosan'.

[159] Edward-Guthrum 7.2: *Die Gesetze*, ed. Liebermann, I, 132: 'on Deone lage'; VI Æthelred 37: *ibid*, p. 256: 'on Dena lage'.

[160] Discussion of this issue in Abrams, 'Edward the Elder's Danelaw', p. 133; Reynolds, 'What Do We Mean by "Anglo-Saxon"?', p. 406.

[161] For a particularly influential interpretation, see N. Lund, 'King Edgar and the Danelaw', *Mediaeval Scandinavia* 9 (1976), 181–95.

[162] P. Kershaw, 'The Alfred-Guthrum Treaty: Scripting Accommodation and Interaction in Viking Age England', in *Cultures in Contact*, ed. Hadley and Richards, pp. 43–64 (p. 45). The dating of the treaty depends on the status of London. Whitelock (*EHD*, p. 416) thought it was probably written after Alfred took London in 886.

First as to the boundaries between us. [They shall run] up the Thames, and then up the Lea, and along the Lea to its source, then in a straight line to Bedford, and then up the Ouse to Watling Street.[163]

The Alfred–Guthrum Treaty might thus be seen as comparable to the Treaty of St-Clair-sur-Epte, which has played a similar role as a foundation document in the historiography of Normandy. It was a political agreement with a 'native' ruler which established the Danes in a permanent settlement in a defined region.

However, just as the tradition of Normandy's foundation in 911 owed a significant amount to Dudo's interpretation, so the status of Alfred–Guthrum was developed by a later interpreter, Dudo's contemporary Wulfstan II, archbishop of York. In an important article of 1941, Dorothy Whitelock showed that the so-called 'Laws of Edward and Guthrum', which appear in one manuscript after the 'Peace of Alfred and Guthrum', were in fact written in the early eleventh century by Archbishop Wulfstan.[164] These laws are prefaced by a short note, apparently contemporary, claiming that they represent the agreements made between Edward (the Elder) and Guthrum, the viking ruler of East Anglia:[165]

This also is the legislation which King Alfred and King Guthrum, and afterwards King Edward and King Guthrum, enacted and agreed upon, when the English and the Danes unreservedly entered into relations of peace and friendship. The councillors also who have been [in office] since then, frequently and often have re-enacted the same, and added improvements thereto.[166]

In producing the 'Laws of Edward and Guthrum', Wulfstan aligned the regional difference in law with an ethnic boundary between English and Danes. He dated the origin of this distinction precisely to the treaty between Alfred and Guthrum which drew a linear boundary between English and

---

[163] Alfred-Guthrum 1, *The Laws of the Earliest English Kings*, trans. F. L. Attenborough (Cambridge, 1922), p. 99. *Die Gesetze*, ed. Liebermann, I, 126: 'Ærest ymbe heora landgemæra: andlang Témese, þ[onne] up on Ligean, andlang Ligean oð hire æwylm, ðanon on gerihta to Bedaforda, þanon upon on Usan oð Wætlingastræt'.

[164] D. Whitelock, 'Wulfstan and the So-called Laws of Edward and Guthrum', *EHR* 56 (1941), 1–21.

[165] The identities of Edward and Guthrum have been disputed because they were not contemporaries, but now the text is known to be a forgery, the error may be attributed to Wulfstan.

[166] *Laws*, trans. Attenborough, p. 103; *Die Gesetze*, ed. Liebermann, I, 128: 'And ðis is seo ge'rædnyss eac, ðe Ælfred cyng 7 Guðrum cyng 7 eft Eadward cyng (7 Gyþrum cyng) gecuran 7 gecwædon, ða ða Engle 7 Dene to friðe 7 to freondscipe fullice fengon; 7 ða witan eac, ðe syððan wæron, oft 7 unseldan þæt seolfe geniwodon 7 mid gode gehuhtan.'

Danish kingdoms along Watling Street.[167] In fact, this ninth-century document was not a law code, but a peace treaty between kings, which agreed their separate spheres of influence. However, Wulfstan interpreted it, as many historians after him have done, as the establishment of the geographical and legal entity of the Danelaw, which later became subject directly to English kings.

The 'Laws of Edward and Guthrum' attributed differences between north and south to the ninth-century viking settlement, rather than the specific character of the historical kingdoms of Northumbria and East Anglia. Moreover, in this document Wulfstan stated that the division had been maintained in subsequent generations through inter-ethnic dialogue. Something of this process is hinted at in Edward the Elder's law code from Exeter (II Edward 5.2), which referred to 'treaties' between his kingdom and those in the east and north. By claiming that this was an ongoing process, Wulfstan implied that Anglo-Saxons and Danes survived as distinct groups either side of the border.

Wulfstan's interpretation seems to have reflected wider perceptions of the symbolic importance of Watling Street as a boundary between two regions of England. The Anglo-Saxon Chronicle records that in 1013, Swein received the submission of 'all the raiding-army to the north of Watling Street', and then proceeded to raid 'after he came over Watling Street'.[168] The passage implied that those to the north of the boundary submitted to Swein because of their Danish identity (alluded to in the use of the word *here*), and that he waited to cross Watling Street before raiding for a similar reason.[169]

Wulfstan's emphasis on Guthrum derived from the text of the 'Peace of Alfred and Guthrum', which he was effectively updating. Historical sources would have shown him that Edward and Guthrum were not contemporaries. According to the Anglo-Saxon Chronicle, Guthrum died before Alfred and was succeeded by a certain Eohric, who was killed in 904. Edward the Elder's contemporary would therefore have been Eohric's successor.[170] Moreover, Wulfstan's laws were clearly meant to apply to the entire 'Danelaw', including Northumbria, whereas Guthrum was only king of East Anglia. Wulfstan's choice reflects an interest parallel to that found in the narrative texts discussed in Chapter 4. Guthrum appeared as a fleshed-out character in the early eleventh-century *Vita Prima Sancti Neoti* (and to a lesser degree in the *Historia de Sancto Cuthberto*), which implies that he was better known as Alfred's viking adversary.

---

[167] F. Curta, 'Linear Frontiers in the 9th Century: Bulgaria and Wessex', *Quaestiones Medii Aevi Novae* (2011), pp. 15–32.

[168] ASC E 1013: 'þæs eall here be norðan Wætlingastræte'; 'syððan he com ofer Wæclingastræte'.

[169] Innes, 'Danelaw Identities', p. 74.

[170] ASC A 904.

Whitelock suggested that Wulfstan's interest in these laws arose from his appointment as archbishop of York and Worcester in 1002. Although Wormald labelled the text 'a forgery', Wulfstan may well have written it from genuine belief in the need for a textual record of a long-standing tradition of customary law.[171] Whitelock and Wormald both determined that Wulfstan, in this text as in his later legislation, was striving for the best interests of the northern diocese. The 'Laws of Edward and Guthrum' were produced between 1002 and 1008, and shortly afterwards Wulfstan began to draft laws for the king which accounted for the same divide in the same terms.[172] The archbishop of York used his 'forgery' to convince Æthelred to legislate according to a geographical Danish–English distinction. It was, however, a dangerous strategy: Wulfstan composed a text which stressed 'peace and friendship' between English and Danes, but events of the following decade showed that the distinction was more likely to bring discord.

The silence of both charters and narrative texts about 'Danish' regions of England, or any concept of the 'Danelaw', raises questions about Wulfstan's legal distinctions. The hundreds of royal diplomas surviving from tenth-century England provide a different perspective on divisions among inhabitants of the English kingdom. They suggest that regional divides on the lines demarcated by Wulfstan were recognized at an earlier date, but that they were employed by West Saxon kings and northern authorities for different political reasons. Moreover, they were not usually expressed in terms of English and Danish heritage.

The divide between north and south was only expressed in terms of English–Danish interaction in legal texts. In charters, northern ecclesiastics called their people 'Northumbrians' or 'northerners', and sometimes referred to 'pagans' as another group. They did not identify themselves as Danes – but neither, in general, did the king, the witan or royal draftsmen. The Danes in royal charters were attackers, visitors and inhabitants of Wessex and Mercia. They were involved in political life, even though they were perceived as alien; at other times, they were enemies of the nation. For these reasons, the divide between English and Danish was a matter of contemporary concern.

Perhaps it was the legal context that led Wulfstan, and the draftsmen of Edgar's laws, to ascribe a Danish character to the regional distinction. Early medieval understandings of what constituted a *gens* included law and, conversely, non-Roman law was seen to apply to a people-group rather than a territory. The 'Danish' explanation of difference was therefore readily understandable. Moreover, this explanation avoided distinctions among the English, such as Northumbrian and West Saxon: by attributing difference to the Danes, the fiction that the English were one people legally, customarily

---

[171] Wormald, *Making of English Law*, p. 391.
[172] Wormald, *Making of English Law*, pp. 330–45; P. Wormald, 'Æthelred the Lawmaker', in *Ethelred the Unready*, ed. Hill, pp. 47–80.

and ethnically could be maintained. But the 'Danelaw', a geographical and legal entity and an area ruled directly by the English monarch, was a creation of the West Saxon kings and their advisors (principally Wulfstan); in this it differed significantly from the Norman dukes' creation of their semi-independent principality of Normandy.

Conclusion

The essential comparability of Norman and Anglo-Saxon charters from this period extends into their presentation of ducal and royal authority. In each case, Norman dukes and English kings asserted their legal and territorial rights by presenting themselves as leaders of a single people: the *Normanni* and the *Angli* respectively. It was from their leadership of these ethnic groups that they derived their positions, and so their charters repeatedly reinforced the existence and importance of these peoples.

The geographical claims of English kings and Norman dukes differed in scope; so, too, did their perceptions of their subjects' identities. Norman dukes seem to have treated *Normanni* and the inhabitants of *Normannia* – the geographical area under their authority – as equivalent: thus they defined their subjects as a single group, created by the combination of place and obedience to ducal authority. Æthelred and the English kings of the tenth century, however, asserted imperial ambitions across all Britain. They saw the *Angli* as the principal group among several peoples inhabiting *Britannia* – over all of whom they laid claim to authority (although perhaps with differing degrees of influence).

Viking conquests and past rulers were conspicuously absent from both rhetorical programmes. However, the viking past underpinned the Norman case for a people defined as inhabitants and subjects of *Normannia*. The ducal dynasty's authority originated with Rollo, and was reinforced by his descendants; their charters made no reference to earlier claims or events. The viking conquest thus acted as a crucial backdrop to Norman claims to authority, independent of Frankish kings, making a case that complemented historical texts such as Dudo's *De moribus*. Moreover, Norman dukes situated their actions within a Christian historical tradition, thereby invoking the second essential component of Dudo's narrative: their conversion to Christianity.

In England, kings not only acknowledged the diversity of peoples and regions within *Britannia*, but also recognized a north–south divide under their more direct authority in the kingdom of England. However, their charters did not attribute this north–south divide to the viking past or to histories of Scandinavian settlement. Invocation of a Northumbrian identity distinct from that of other *Angli* – West Saxons and Mercians – remained a more likely explanation. When charters did include Danes, they identified them as one of several elements in Æthelred's multi-ethnic realm, but in these cases they referred to contemporary migrants with no special association with northern regions of England.

It was Wulfstan who attributed the north–south divide to Danish heritage and the viking past, in the early eleventh century, and in legal writings rather than land charters. This important fact highlights how ethnic terms and relationships were mobilized differently according to the context. The contemporary political context of an English kingdom threatened by Danes and divided under Æthelred's rule was certainly significant in this new development; but so, too, were the conventions, considerations and generic constraints of normative law codes and legal ideals. Furthermore, Wulfstan, as archbishop of York, represented the interests of the northern diocese as much as those of his West Saxon king – a perspective rarely encountered in land charters. Thus his creation of the 'Danelaw' emerges as a manifestation of ideas about and perceptions of ethnic relations that suited the current political, social and legal context, and relied on a new interpretation of the viking past.

The narratives of ethnic relations deployed in charters by Norman dukes and English kings are far from replications of those found in narrative texts. And the presentation in law codes, such as those by Wulfstan, provides a new angle again. Despite the differences in emphasis in Norman texts, and inherent contradictions in English sources, the major influences can always be traced back to the ruling secular and ecclesiastical elites. Yet the impossibility of fully reconciling the multiplicity of ethnic narratives from Viking Age England and Normandy should not pose a problem. In these different texts and contexts, we are encountering the strategic deployment of narratives of ethnicity: they were always invoked *for* something, and every presentation of ethnic relations shaped the social situation as much as reflecting it. The evidence presented in this chapter, when viewed alongside the previous chapters, reinforces an understanding of early medieval ethnicity as situational. Presenting a view on the viking past, and its effects on ethnic relationships, was always a political act.

Conclusion: Viking Age Narratives and Ethnic Identities

The evidence of genealogies, histories, hagiographies, charters and law codes reveals how Viking Age writers deployed diverse visions of ethnic relations in different texts and contexts. In some instances, vikings of the ninth century were depicted as the enemies of Christians and even equated with contemporary Danish attackers, while in others viking heritage or distant Scandinavian origins were drawn on as a source of pride and power. Dudo's *De moribus* evoked both perspectives at once. Yet such apparent contradictions should not pose a problem for the historian. Rather than attempting to reconcile these varied accounts into a single vision of ethnic relations in either England or Normandy, we must engage with the purposes and impact of each ethnic narrative and its propagation. The varied depictions of ethnic relations in both societies provide evidence that early medieval ethnicity was indeed 'situational': not an innate and unchanging feeling but a flexible expression of perceived social relations, formulated in response to immediate needs and political concerns.[1]

The diversity of ethnic narratives in the various texts discussed in this book add significantly to our understanding of 'situational' ethnicity because, in Viking Age England and Normandy, they stem from the same individuals. The same elites have been identified as patrons of diverse texts and divergent narratives. The Norman dukes commissioned Dudo to write the *De moribus* as an account of their dynastic origins, patronized monastic houses where hagiographical accounts of their ancestors were produced, and controlled the production of charters that presented their authority as interlinked with people and territory. These representations of the past may all be identified as promoting the Norman ducal family's interests, but their emphases – and the significance of viking identity – differed in each one. In England, the situation was even more diverse, involving conflicting claims as well as differences in emphasis. In their genealogies, West Saxon monarchs presented their dynasty as stemming from Scandinavian kings and heroes; they influenced hagiographical narratives to associate Anglo-Saxon Christian resistance to viking pagans with their more immediate ancestors; and charters and law codes provided them with varied means of responding to regional differences, only occasionally attributed to Scandinavian settlement. That multiple narratives of the Viking Age and its contemporary significance emanated

---

[1] See Introduction, and Geary, 'Ethnic Identity as a Situational Construct'.

from the same political centres and even individual rulers underlines the situational nature of ethnic identities. Firstly, in line with the concept as Geary has elucidated it, an individual might present himself or herself differently according to circumstance and apparent advantage, just as the West Saxon royal family sometimes claimed Scandinavian heritage and sometimes rejected it. Secondly, and crucially, an individual's membership of a particular group meant something different in each situation. A Dane or Dacian as presented by Dudo to an educated Frankish audience was not the same Dane ascribed different legal rights from the English by Wulfstan. These texts were not representations of an external reality but political statements appropriate to different audiences and historical moments.

In each chapter of this book, it has been established that the West Saxon kings of England are a better comparator to the Norman dukes than are any Anglo-Scandinavian rulers. Of course, on the whole, the ethnic narratives they used differed in that the Norman dynasty expressly identified as 'viking', while the West Saxon kings positioned themselves as the enemies of vikings. However, both ruling elites employed similar techniques of successful rule and ideological dominance. Separation of the *content* of ethnic narratives from the means by which they were constructed allows us to identify these parallels, and to trace how divergent historical narratives became established in the two regions.

Norman narratives about the Viking Age

As immigrants to Francia, establishing a new society within a shifting power structure, the Norman rulers engaged with presentations of themselves, their authority and their relationship with their subjects. Strong identification with vikings of the past constituted a key part of such engagement by the ruling house. Some narrative texts extended this identification to their leading families, as well, presenting the new Norman elite as descendants of a viking army led by Rollo. Both positive and negative aspects of viking activity were incorporated into this vision, which Dudo split into the two vikings Rollo and Hasting. However, crucially, the historiographic production sponsored by the Norman ducal family associated all viking activity with their dynasty alone, capitalising on the distinctiveness this heritage lent them.[2]

Viking ancestry provided a means of demonstrating independence from Frankish royal power and neighbouring counts. These neighbours presented the major threats to Norman ducal power. Conflict with Arnulf, count of Flanders, resulted in William Longsword's assassination in 943. Afterwards,

---

[2] Abrams, 'Early Normandy', p. 64, on the disappearance of other viking leaders from the historical record.

the future of Normandy must have looked very uncertain, as King Louis IV and Hugh the Great attempted to wrest direct control of the region from the young Richard I. Once Richard, as an adult, had re-asserted ducal authority, he and his successors were eager to defend their position against such attempts in the future. They built up Normandy as a distinct unit, ruled separately from the rest of France by right. Therefore, the dukes employed the viking heritage of their dynasty to define their people against the Franks.

The earliest texts presented the subjects of the Norman dukes as two groups: the existing inhabitants of Rouen, and the new viking elite. Very rapidly, however, this internal distinction disappeared. The construction of a boundary between Normans and Franks led to the coherence of all the inhabitants of Normandy into one people, defined by their difference from their neighbours.

Likewise, Norman writers occasionally employed links to the Scandinavian past, but only in order to negotiate the relationship with the Franks. Presentations of Scandinavia seem to have derived from Frankish or western Christian conceptions of the North, rather than memories carried by Norse immigrants and their descendants. In Norman historical consciousness, a Scandinavian background served as a means of creating origins for the Normans that were parallel to those of the Franks and set them up as a people equivalent to – related, but distinct from – the Franks.

In various contexts, different emphases served to distinguish the Norman people from the Franks and promote the dominance of the ducal family of Rollo: viking conquest, Christian conversion and the support of local saints provided claims on a defined territory, independent from royal power, with their roots in the late ninth and early tenth centuries. However, the various visions of ethnic relations and the viking past produced in Normandy were more consistent than those from England. The Normans were consistently defined against the same boundaries, distinguishing the people under ducal authority from the Franks. Ethnic relations in terms of genealogical, historical and geographical identity operated across analogous boundaries between Normans and Franks. This threefold interpretation of ethnicity reinforced the strength of the distinction.

West Saxon-influenced narratives about the Viking Age

The West Saxon dynasty capitalized on its status as the only remaining Anglo-Saxon kings after the viking conquests, and thus began to define its role against the Scandinavian presence in England. The majority of narratives told from a West Saxon viewpoint were vehemently anti-Scandinavian. They associated Christians and the *Angli* with the victims and enemies of ninth-century viking invaders; in so doing, they encouraged their readers to identify as a cohesive ethnic and religious group against the outsiders.

These texts, predominantly written in hagiographical genres, represented vikings as inherently pagan, in part because of their Scandinavian origins. Such narratives were shaped by hagiographical conventions, and responded to different local contexts, but the influence of the West Saxon kings can be identified both in the roles they played within the texts – either in their focus on Alfred and his descendants, or in the presentation of Edmund as a king of the English, associated with the West Saxon dynasty – and in their patronage of the authors and their institutions.

Yet in their expansion of what it meant to be *rex Anglorum*, the West Saxon kings not only appropriated the pasts of other Anglo-Saxon dynasties, but also incorporated a distant Scandinavian past by including Danish royal ancestors in their genealogy and, perhaps, celebrating a shared heritage in the North. West Saxon elites promoted identification with this remote past and vilification of more recent vikings, including their Scandinavian origins at the same time. Other inconsistencies between texts have emerged in the preceding discussion. In different contexts, the impact of Scandinavian settlement in England was ignored (as was usually the case in hagiography), superseded (as in the *Historia de Sancto Cuthberto*), subsumed in a 'Northumbrian' identity (in charters and in some narratives) or given the significance of a legal distinction (in Wulfstan's law codes). All of the texts examined here therefore broadly defined 'English' against Scandinavians, Norse or vikings – but they did so in a variety of different ways that we cannot easily reconcile. Indeed, there was no contemporary attempt to reconcile these different visions of ethnic relations: they served different purposes.

Anglo-Scandinavian narratives about the Viking Age

These narratives of Scandinavian heritage, viking enmity and regional distinction, emanating in the main from the West Saxon royal house and their associated monastic institutions, came to dominate understandings of Viking Age England. In doing so, they responded to and overwrote alternative understandings of conflicts and interactions between viking armies and native inhabitants of England.

A few pieces of evidence provide hints that Anglo-Scandinavian rulers had promoted their own narratives of Viking Age England. The majority of evidence relates to the viking leader Ívarr (Hinguar, killer of St Edmund). Irish sources refer to the dynasty of Ívarr, suggesting that subsequent viking rulers drew on his reputation; several of the same individuals operated in England and may possibly have promoted their dynasty in a similar way there.[3] Conflicting narratives in England and Ireland about Ívarr's demise

---

[3] Downham, *Viking Kings*; and above, pp. 55–6, 146–9.

perhaps reflect competition over his memory. In the early eleventh century, Cnut's skalds referred to the exploits of Ívarr in England – again, suggesting that narratives circulated about the viking leader, and demonstrating again their employment by a Norse ruler in England. Later narratives found in Old Norse literature (especially the sagas of Ragnarr Loðbrók and his sons), Middle English and Anglo-Norman literature (such as Gaimar's *Estoire des Engleis*) could well stem from traditions originating in an Anglo-Scandinavian or Insular viking milieu.[4]

Later medieval texts such as these also suggest the possibility that further narratives negotiating relationships between English and Scandinavian ethnic groups emerged during the Viking Age. The story of Haveloc the Dane, for example, which occurs in various forms, is fundamentally concerned with the relationship between rulers of England and Denmark, and how these might be represented by personal or familial relationships. Ninth-century Anglo-Saxon and twelfth-century Old Norse references to St Edmund the Martyr, meanwhile, which suggest that he died in battle and had children, hint at a stock of narrative distinct from the main hagiographic tradition. While the St Edmund memorial coinage produced in the viking kingdom of East Anglia does suggest a degree of 'official' interest, these different narratives, which emerged in later texts, were not necessarily promoted by rulers but may have had other means of transmission that contributed to their pattern of survival.

In addition, it is not possible to pinpoint the origins of these traditions: while they may have first emerged in the ninth- and tenth-century viking polities of northern and eastern England, it is just as likely that they originated in the time of Cnut, later in the eleventh century or even after the Norman Conquest. Moreover, the lack of chronological grounding makes it difficult to determine the level of cross-fertilisation from West Saxon narrative traditions after they became dominant: Edmund's reputation in Iceland may have continued directly from his celebration in an Old Norse milieu in Anglo-Scandinavian East Anglia, for example, but it could just as well have developed later through contact with his more established cult in the kingdom of England.

Apart from in hagiographies of Edmund, West Saxon-influenced narratives produced in the Viking Age focused not on Ívarr and his brothers, nor on Haveloc, but on the figure of Guthrum. Guthrum was associated with – and, crucially, subdued by – Alfred, and so appeared as a figure amenable to celebrations of the West Saxon dynasty. In addition, histories involving Guthrum may have been more open to West Saxon interpretations because of the short-lived nature of the East Anglian viking kingdom, and the apparent lack of dynastic counter-narratives featuring the viking king. There is no

---

[4] See above, pp. 80–3; and Parker, 'Anglo-Scandinavian Literature and the Post-Conquest Period', pp. 160–71.

evidence for attempts to re-establish Scandinavian rule in East Anglia after Edward the Elder's conquest, in contrast to the turbulent events and multiple viking rulers in northern regions of England. As a consequence, unlike Ívarr and his dynasty, Guthrum does not appear in Old Norse literary tradition. Yet, most intriguingly, he may appear in Dudo's *De moribus*, as the English king Alstemus, or Æthelstan (which was Guthrum's baptismal name).[5] What does this connection mean? Without further research into Dudo's sources, we cannot be certain that Alstemus really represents Guthrum, nor whence Dudo derived his information. Potentially, Dudo's Alstemus is an indication of connection between early viking rulers in Normandy and East Anglia. Alternatively, it may be a reflection of the developing relationship between Norman dukes and West Saxon kings of England in the early eleventh century.

Similar strategies

This brief recap highlights the comparable success of Norman ducal and West Saxon narratives of the viking and Scandinavian pasts, despite the dissimilarity in how those ruling houses identified themselves with or against viking ancestors. The broad acceptance of the visions of the past promoted by the two ruling dynasties had significant influence on ethnic relations either side of the Channel, apparently driving them in opposite directions in terms of ethnic framing. However, such acceptance related to the similar strategies pursued by these ruling elites. Anglo-Scandinavian rulers in some cases began similar processes, but their influence never became established and their narratives never became dominant – partly because of the short-lived nature of viking polities within England (and the lack of continuity between viking rulers), and partly because Anglo-Scandinavian elites did not pursue those strategies that most influenced wider social groups and encouraged the longevity of historical narratives.

Four broad elements may be distinguished within these strategies, identified in both England and Normandy. Firstly, both dukes and kings, and their aristocracies, pursued partnerships with monastic institutions and sponsored the production of narrative texts by monastic writers. This strategy not only employed the talents and resources of ideologically and fiscally powerful institutions, but also provided an institutional basis for the ongoing transmission of historical narratives. Similar narrative devices appeared in monastic texts in England and Normandy, such as the use of conversion from Norse paganism to Christianity as a means of ethnic adaptation.

Secondly, in a connected strategy, Norman dukes and West Saxon kings courted saintly patronage for their dynasties. This promoted similarly useful

---

[5] Lair, pp. 149–51, 158–9; Christiansen, pp. 32–3, 39–40.

institutional links, and it also encouraged the dissemination of ethnic narratives and dynastic propaganda to a wider audience, through their association with saints' cults, celebrations, miracle stories and hagiographical representations. Thus these narratives reached ordinary men and women, lay and religious, through the mediation of clerical and secular elites. Again, narrative devices such as visions linked saints' cults to ruling elites and the viking past in both regions. There is some evidence that Anglo-Scandinavian rulers began to pursue partnerships with the saints, too. Their restricted influence in this regard may testify to a lack of institutional basis for such partnerships, and, crucially, the absence of written texts.

Thirdly, interpretations of viking identities in England and Normandy were intimately connected with the dynastic promotion of the ruling houses. As a result, greater resources and secular institutional continuities allowed 'official' narratives to become dominant. Norman dukes and West Saxon kings appear to have been interested in the reputation of their own dynasties as a means of asserting contemporary authority. The dominance of 'official' narratives meant that roles played by past members of their dynasties began to stand as figureheads for an entire ethnic group.

Finally, within these ethnic narratives, both sets of elites situated the origins of their authority in the viking past of the late ninth and early tenth centuries. The turbulence and confusion associated with this period permitted both to identify it as the historical moment that established their authority, placing its roots further back chronologically. Anglo-Scandinavian rulers, on the other hand, suffered from a lack of dynastic continuity, although there may have been similar attempts to locate their authority in the actions of Ívarr and his killing of King Ælle.

We have at several points encountered hints of regional traditions and non-elite narratives that differed from those promoted by Norman dukes and English kings. The earliest texts – including the Anglo-Saxon Chronicle and Fulbert's *Vita Romani* – present slightly different visions of the events of the Viking Age, while post-Conquest and high medieval literature include more varied stories concerned with ethnic relations between immigrants and natives. These hints should remind us that alternative narrative traditions often operate in parallel to textual transmission and, particularly on a local level, more varied means of dissemination will have been available which we cannot now trace.

Ethnicity and its implications

Throughout this investigation, we have repeatedly encountered the dominant role of ruling elites in identity formation. Viking Age England and Normandy thus provide a fresh perspective on the 'ethnogenesis' debate which has been prevalent in early medieval studies. Ethnogenesis theory, as discussed in

Chapter 4, has presented ruling elites as the guardians of ethnic traditions (especially genealogies and origin myths). However, as the narratives investigated here reveal, the influence of elites on ethnic relations may be attributed to their political and economic power, and thus their patronage of cultural production. Norman texts primarily reflected ducal interests and viewpoints, either because they were directly commissioned by the dukes (as in the case of the most influential, Dudo's *De moribus*), or because their monastic authors relied on ducal patronage of their monasteries, and themselves may have arrived in Normandy as a result of the dukes' repopulation of their foundations. The relative unity of the narratives they contain is a result, not of complete consensus within Normandy, but of the dominance of the ducal family in textual production. Likewise, textual production in tenth-century England was often the result of a partnership of secular authority, in the person of the king and his witan, and monastic reformers. Dominant interpretations of the viking past were apparently promoted by the royal court in conjunction with monasteries that enjoyed royal patronage. Elites, in this context, should not be envisaged as holders of memory, but as 'ethno-political entrepreneurs', able to use ethnic narratives to their own advantages. Of course, others could act similarly on a reduced or local scale, but those in positions of power held the advantage in terms of ideological dominance.

The actual content of ethnic narratives remained situational and strategically determined. Thus, although produced or influenced primarily by those in positions of power, these visions of ethnic relations responded to contemporary political and social contexts and to a much wider demographic. Monastic narratives also promoted the interests of ecclesiastical institutions and their associated cults, as evidenced by the threatening words of St Audoenus to Duke Richard I in the *Translatio Secunda Audoeni*, or those of St Neot to King Alfred in the *Vita Prima Neoti*. Charters were at least some of the time produced, and most commonly archived, at beneficiary institutions, in which cases monastic scribes or the diocesan bishop could present matters in their own interests. In Northumbria, especially Bernicia, beneficiaries seem to have had complete control over how royal gifts were recorded.[6] Even in the case of centralized charter production in the English kingdom, the majority of these documents represented the viewpoint not only of the king, but also of the governing elite, and his West Saxon and Mercian thegns in particular.

Moreover, narratives developed in new forms and beyond the written word. Although the tales of Alfred's interaction with saints Cuthbert and Neot probably originated at the royal court, they developed local versions in Chester-le-Street, Eynesbury and the South-West, not all of which were completely complimentary to the king. Especially in England (perhaps because the English kings laid claim to a much larger geographical area than

---

[6] *Northern Houses*, pp. 11–16.

the Norman dukes), regional differences were a major concern and prevented the West Saxon kings exercising a monopoly on anything other than genealogical production. Yet, even in Norman narratives and charters, there was considerable difference between the treatment of Rouen, the dukes' power base, and Lower Normandy, where their authority began to extend much later. In constructing ethnic narratives, elites had to respond to divisions and tensions among their subjects.

In each case, religious and secular authorities combined familiar elements into very different creations in order to negotiate, define and manipulate ethnicity. They faced similar past events and used similar methods, but their interpretations differed according to their purposes. The Norman dukes integrated themselves into Frankish political life, and focused on the creation of a polity that held the greatest independence from royal power. In support of these aims, their ethnic narratives emphasized their people's separation and interaction with the Franks across a multiply reinforced boundary. The English kings, on the other hand, attempted to unify several societies into a single kingdom, but continually faced various Scandinavian threats. Their ethnic narratives, therefore, balanced inclusive unity with opposition to these threats, and the boundaries they constructed were fluid and permeable.

In making such a comparative argument, this book has developed a historical model from Fredrik Barth's distinction between 'ethnic boundary' and 'cultural stuff'. It was possible for Norman elites to assert a viking identity without demonstrating particular aspects of Norse culture, but they could use Frankish Christian ideas to do so. Conversely, Scandinavian language, art and material culture displayed by communities in England did not necessarily map onto expressions of distinctive ethnic identities. An ethnic significance was only attached to such 'cultural stuff' when historical actors chose to use it as a means of distinction in a given situation.[7] Therefore, we cannot simply trace Scandinavian influence as an index of ethnic identity, but need to remain sensitive to the varied and evolving meanings of the viking past, Scandinavian heritage and Old Norse culture in their new contexts.

Scandinavian contact

Most significantly, in these societies, viking identity did not relate simply to contact with Scandinavia. Norman texts consistently defined 'viking' identity within a Frankish context. Genealogical, historical and geographical boundaries were constructed between the vikings of Normandy and the neighbouring Franks. These ethnic narratives were not aimed at the rest of

---

[7] Eriksen, *Ethnicity and Nationalism*, p. 12, makes a similar point: 'Only in so far as cultural differences are perceived as being important, and are made socially relevant, do social relationships have an ethnic element.'

the Old Norse world. In England, on the other hand, viking and Scandinavian heritage were employed in the negotiation of various relationships. Sometimes they were used to construct boundaries within England, and sometimes they were used for boundaries between the inhabitants of the English kingdom and external forces. Continued contact between England and Scandinavia meant that the meanings of 'Danish' and of the viking past remained ambiguous and context dependent. The lack of such contact between Francia and Scandinavia allowed the Normans and their neighbours to impose a consistent meaning on viking identity.

Dudo, like the writers of hagiographies and charters, wrote for an audience based in Francia and Normandy. There is no evidence that Dudo's Scandinavian contemporaries had any knowledge of his work: Saxo Grammaticus referred to Dudo's work in the beginning of his *Gesta Danorum*, but he wrote over 150 years later.[8] Old Norse references to Normandy are generally late, and still scarce. *Landnámabók* contains a reference to Rollo, as 'Ganger-Hrolf', but again this dates from the twelfth century at the earliest.[9] There is record of a skaldic poet's presence in Rouen in 1025: Sigvatr Þorðarson, Óláfr Haraldsson's skald, mentioned the city in his *Vestrfararvísur*, but there is no evidence that Old Norse poetry was composed in Normandy at this time.[10] Richard II and his brother Archbishop Robert seem to have confined their literary patronage to the production of Latin texts for an audience within the Frankish world.[11] The ducal family concerned themselves with mediating the ethnic relations between their people and their Frankish neighbours.

Their lack of concern for the Old Norse world reflects dwindling relations with Scandinavia. Although Norman dukes occasionally called upon viking armies to assist them against their neighbours, in 945 and 962 and perhaps again in 1013, it was increasingly rare for them to resort to this policy. The dukes were content to allow viking armies raiding England in the 980s to use their ports, and to enrich their markets with booty from the raids. Yet it became clear that the Church authorities would not permit the Normans to maintain this double loyalty for long. In 991, Pope John XV brokered an agreement between Richard I and Æthelred, in which Richard swore not to assist Æthelred's enemies any longer.[12] Richard II flouted this treaty in the year 1000, but Normandy's Scandinavian alliances did not have long

---

[8] Saxo Grammaticus, *Gesta Danorum*, I, 10.

[9] *Landnámabók*, trans. Pálsson and Edwards, pp. 119–20; Hartmann, *The Göngu-Hrólfssaga*, pp. 53–5. For an overview of Normandy's Old Norse connections, see Abrams, 'England, Normandy and Scandinavia'.

[10] Sigvatr, *Vestrfararvísur*, p. 617.

[11] L. Musset, 'Le satiriste Garnier de Rouen et son Milieu (Début du XIe siècle)', *Revue du Moyen Âge Latin* 10 (1954), 237–58.

[12] *Memorials of St Dunstan*, ed. W. Stubbs (London, 1874), pp. 397–8.

to live.[13] Similarly, the French King Robert II negotiated peace between the Normans and Bretons in 1013, in order to remove the viking armies.[14] Although Sigvatr's presence in Rouen testifies to some ongoing connections, by the second decade of the eleventh century, Scandinavian visitors came to Normandy only in the course of trade and travel. Even economic connections diminished considerably, and quite abruptly: the evidence of coinage found in Normandy, Scandinavia and along viking trade routes suggests a sudden rupture in the second decade of the eleventh century.[15]

Norman dukes were exclusively concerned with ethnic relations within the Frankish world because of the nature of these contacts. Essentially, Scandinavian forces never seriously threatened them; after the mid-tenth century, they did not threaten the Franks, either. On the other hand, the Norman dukes and their subjects engaged in a process of constant negotiation with their Frankish and Flemish neighbours, which frequently erupted into conflict. The Norman dukes created ethnic narratives that assisted them in these conflicts. The writers they patronized were free to use the viking past and the imagined world of Scandinavia in the service of these ethnic narratives, precisely because they did not need to engage with contemporary Scandinavians. At the same time as these histories and hagiographies were composed – the second half of the tenth and early eleventh centuries – contacts with Scandinavia and viking forces stopped. Counter-intuitively, it was the *cessation* of Scandinavian connections that enabled the creation of Norman viking identity.

Conversely, in England, continuing links with Denmark and the resumption of viking raids led to fluctuating connotations of viking identity. English writers identified several different contemporary groups with Danes: inhabitants of north-east England, who had previously been subject to Scandinavian rulers; merchants and thegns recently arrived from Scandinavia; and the raiders who attacked England throughout Æthelred's reign. Boundaries between English and Danish were constructed in different ways in different regions of England and depending on the situation. Sometimes ethnic narratives were used to construct boundaries within England, and sometimes between the inhabitants of England and external forces. These overlapping visions of ethnic relations resulted in identities that were fluid and open to political manipulation.

English interest in the Scandinavian past intensified in response to the resurgence of viking attacks in the 980s, which posed a significant threat to the kingdom from 991 onwards. It was only in this period that writers turned their gaze back to the viking wars of the ninth century, as if searching for solutions

---

[13] L. W. Breese, 'The Persistence of Scandinavian Connections in Normandy in the Tenth and Early Eleventh Centuries', *Viator* 8 (1977), 47–61.

[14] *Gesta Normannorum Ducum*, II, 24–7.

[15] Bates, *Normandy Before 1066*, p. 36.

and reassurance for their current problems. Abbo of Fleury and Ælfric of Eynsham, the author of the *Vita Neoti* and the homilist of the Life of St Neot, Byrhtferth of Ramsey and Ealdorman Æthelweard all produced reinterpretations of the events of the 860s to 890s. The *Historia de Sancto Cuthberto* is the only tenth-century text dealing with these events that is likely to have been written earlier than Æthelred's reign. These writers imposed their presentations of ethnic conflict on the inhabitants of England, and especially those in the north and east. Their visions of ethnic relations were political creations, which were intended to inspire allegiance to the West Saxon king against Danish invaders. However, conflict was not the only paradigm. Æthelweard in particular also considered the Scandinavian origins of the English, apparently inspired by Norse-speaking inhabitants of England.

English kings seem to have been uneasy about the possibility of 'Danish' elements among their subjects sympathizing or aligning themselves with foreigners and enemies from Scandinavia. As a result, their presentation of English–Danish relations was very changeable and context dependent. Æthelred in particular worried about treason. He ordered the St Brice's Day massacre of 1002 in response to rumours that the 'Danes' in England were planning to kill him and take over the kingdom. This was not the first time that Æthelred had heard of such a plot. The charter which confirmed the will of Æthelric of Bocking recorded the accusation that Æthelric 'was in the plot that Swein would be received in Essex when he first came there with a fleet'.[16] However, this same charter documented the presence of Danish thegns at the meeting. Ethnic simplification was not possible in these situations.

Moreover, texts such as *Beowulf* and Æthelweard's *Chronicon* reveal that interaction with Norse-speakers persisted as an element in the English creation of ethnic narratives. A degree of contact continued between England and Scandinavia throughout the tenth century. Danish thegns attested at the *witenagemot* and Danish merchants traded in York. In addition, English missionaries seem to have travelled to Denmark and Norway to evangelize.[17] Nevertheless, the principal mode of contact was conflictual. Danish and Norwegian vikings attacked England from the 980s until 1016. Vikings living in Ireland also participated in the earliest of these raids; although the English identified them as 'Norsemen', they may have originated far from Scandinavia. These continuing contacts influenced and fed into ethnic narratives about the settlement of Danes in England. Unlike in Normandy, English writers were not able to define 'viking' or 'Danish' heritage purely by their internal ethnic relations. However, 'Danish' ethnicity still remained a means of expressing internal divisions. Wulfstan found it useful in the early eleventh century, when he legislated for northern distinctiveness according to 'Danish law'.

---

[16] S939, AD 995x999: 'he wære on þam unræde þæt man sceolde on Eastsexon Swegen underfon ða he ærest þyder mid flotan com'.

[17] Abrams, 'Anglo-Saxons and the Christianization of Scandinavia', pp. 216–20.

Thus, despite facing numerous different ethnic boundaries within England, across the British Isles and against Scandinavian invaders, English writers did not develop an ethnic vocabulary to distinguish them. The Anglo-Saxon Chronicle hints at such distinctions when it states that 'earlier the Danes were under Northmen'.[18] But this is a rare example. Modern historians have developed distinctions such as 'Hiberno-Norse' and 'Anglo-Scandinavian' in order to define different groups, dynasties, polities and cultures active in the British Isles.[19] When medieval writers created narratives about ethnic relations in England, they were not engaged in an act of classification. Ethnicity was a means of manipulating people's political loyalties, not a taxonomy.

The West Saxon kings of England faced various threats: they worried about separatism within their kingdom, or the return of Norse rule in the north, or the acceptance of Danish rulers in their stead (as in fact took place). One of the weapons they used to assert themselves across the new English kingdom was the ideology of ethnicity. Rather than distinguishing between their Scandinavian enemies as different cultural groups or political leaders, they employed existing ideas about English–Danish relations in new ways. Grand ethnic generalizations affect loyalties at a deeper level than would the decisions of mere political pragmatism.

Continuing contacts, friendly and conflictual, with Scandinavians meant that 'Danes' never held a stable meaning for the inhabitants of England. English kings conducted relationships with political actors of various Scandinavian backgrounds – Eric Bloodaxe, Olaf Tryggvasson, Swein Forkbeard – and groups within their kingdom that they considered to hold Danish loyalties. Because of these constantly changing relationships, ethnic relations between English and Danes always operated across more than a single boundary.

Significance of this research

Throughout this book, I have called upon sociological and anthropological theories of ethnicity in order to illuminate the processes at work in Viking Age Europe. But the comparative nature and chronological scope of this historical research mean that it can speak back to work in the social sciences, and contribute a different perspective. A central question raised by Barth in 1969 – 'what is needed to make ethnic distinctions *emerge* in an area?' – has been neglected because of the need for large-scale, longitudinal research to answer it, such that historical study can provide.[20] Insights from modern

---

[18] ASC A 942: 'Dæne wæran ær under Norðmannum'.

[19] Downham ('"Hiberno-Norse" and "Anglo-Danes"') argues against the usefulness of these terms.

[20] Barth, *Ethnic Groups and Boundaries*, p. 17; Eriksen, *Ethnicity and Nationalism*, p. 79; Wimmer, *Ethnic Boundary Making*, p. 210.

social-scientific studies emphasizing the political nature of ethnicity and its framing have contributed a crucial perspective to the arguments of this book. Their application to the pre-modern world demonstrates the broader definition that may be applied to concepts such as 'ethno-political entrepreneurs', the culturally variable manifestations of ethnicity in contexts with markedly different terminology and understanding from that of the researcher, and the significance of longer processes of identity formation. With regard to the latter point, the focus of this book on the consciousness of the past in Viking Age England and Normandy reveals the role of history in ethnic relations: how the sense of a shared past may be created, used to define groups and maintained.

The comparison of two societies in similar demographic situations, responding to the same meeting of Old Norse and Western Christian cultures, also highlights a point which has been underplayed in recent social-scientific literature, despite its recognition of the 'virtual' or unbounded nature of ethnic groups: ethnic identities and boundaries do not emerge for their own reasons, develop according to internal narrative logic or follow their own trajectories. In his recent book on *Ethnic Boundary Making*, Andreas Wimmer sought to investigate the question of why ethnicity appears to be a stronger or more political force at certain moments, also by employing a comparative perspective.[21] This comparison of Viking Age societies indicates that the answer to his question, in any historical context, cannot be found by focusing purely on an 'ethnic group' or the strength of assertion of ethnic identities. It is not because some identities are somehow inherently more powerful than others that they achieve political significance. There is no evidence that those who settled in Normandy were any more or less 'viking' than those who made new homes in England, nor that England's native inhabitants were more committed to an emergent Anglo-Saxon/English identity than the people of Rouen and Neustria were to their Frankish heritage. Rather, historical actors respond to forces such as political relations at a local, dynastic or international level, economic advantage, religious ideology, and social processes that require belonging or greater prestige. In so doing, they may employ ethnic relations and boundaries, strengthening distinctions, creating hierarchies and disseminating their conceptions more widely. The meaning of viking or Scandinavian identity developed differently in England and Normandy because of the specifics of those local contexts, and the actions of their inhabitants, as they attempted to forge new societies from mixed populations.

---

[21] Wimmer, *Ethnic Boundary Making*, esp. pp. 4–5.

Appendix 1: The Date of Fulbert's *Vita Romani*

The date of composition of Fulbert's *Vita Romani* is important for the arguments contained in Chapter 3 of this book because of the particular narrative of viking invasion and domination that it contains – a narrative that is absent from all other texts related to the cult of Romanus. I believe that Fulbert wrote his text in the mid-tenth century, and therefore that this narrative represents an early vision of ethnic relations in Normandy, before a standard account had come to dominate: these arguments are rehearsed in Chapter 3. If I am wrong, and Fulbert wrote in the mid-eleventh century, then this would suggest that more varied narratives of the relations between vikings and local inhabitants continued to circulate long into the ducal period.

Fulbert's *Vita Romani* was largely unknown to modern scholarship until Felice Lifshitz completed her study of Romanus's dossier.[1] Although it now exists in only two manuscripts, the many other texts Lifshitz has surveyed which depend on it reveal a much wider medieval circulation. Lifshitz concluded that the *Vita Romani* was composed by a certain Fulbert in the mid-tenth century, probably in 943. If we accept this date, then the *Vita Romani* was one of the earliest literary products from Normandy and, alongside the *Planctus* of William Longsword, the earliest Norman text to refer to the viking period. Fulbert had previously been identified with either of two Fulberts who were active in Rouen in the mid-eleventh century.[2] More recently, several scholars have disputed Lifshitz's dating of Fulbert's *Vita*, and even returned to these identifications.[3] However, Lifshitz's argument is the only one to make sense of all the internal, contextual and manuscript evidence, a conclusion also reached recently by John Howe.[4]

Fulbert's *Vita Romani* is related to several other hagiographical texts. It is only through assessing the arguments for these connected texts' dates of composition that a conclusion regarding the date of the *Vita Romani* can be drawn. Here I lay out the crucial connections between Fulbert's *Vita Romani* and these texts, with a particular focus on issues of authorship.

---

[1] Lifshitz, 'Dossier of Romanus'.

[2] Maurists, *Histoire littéraire de France*, VIII (Paris, 1747), pp. 370–6.

[3] N. Gauthier, 'Quelques hypothèses sur la rédaction des vies des saints évêques de Normandie', *Memoriam Sanctorum Venerantes: Miscellanea in Onore di Monsignor Victor Saxer* (Vatican: Pontificio Istituto di Archeaologia Cristiana, 1992), pp. 449–68 (p. 454); Le Maho, 'La production éditoriale à Jumièges', pp. 31–2.

[4] Howe, 'Hagiography of Jumièges', pp. 105–7.

Gerard's letter and his *Vita Romani*

The first group of texts related to Fulbert's *Vita Romani* involves an alternative, shorter, version of the *Vita*, which exists in several copies.[5] This *Vita* is associated with a letter from Gerard, 'pater cenobitarum', addressed to Uuigo or Hugo, archbishop of Rouen.[6] In the letter, Gerard stated that he enclosed an abbreviated version of the Life of St Romanus which he procured for the archbishop. This original version, he says, was 'written in a historical style' ('hystorialiter est stilo depicta'), and he sent an 'abridgement, like it in style' ('hanc digestam stilo illius ad instar vobis transmitto'). Furthermore, he refers to a metrical *Vita Romani*, which may be the metrical version still in existence (BHL 7310).[7] Lifshitz and Jacques Le Maho agree that this letter is addressed to Archbishop Hugh (or, potentially, his predecessor Wito), and there is no eleventh-century bishop to whom it could be addressed. Lifshitz identified Gerard as the reformer Gerard of Brogne (fl. 919), who died in 959, thus overlapping with the episcopal reigns of Wito and Hugh.[8] Le Maho disagreed on the identification of Gerard, instead proposing Gerard, abbot of Saint-Crépin of Soissons around 960, but accepted the same dating of this version.[9] Gerard's text was, therefore, written in the mid-tenth century. However, Le Maho maintains that Fulbert's version was written around a century later.

Ultimately, the disagreement over the date of Fulbert's text comes down to its relationship with Gerard's version. Lifshitz sees Gerard's *Vita Romani* as an abbreviation of Fulbert's text, which must therefore have been written at some point prior to 959. On the other hand, Le Maho and Gauthier imply that Fulbert expanded Gerard's version in the eleventh century, and that the original *Vita Romani* is completely lost.

Lifshitz's identification of Fulbert's *Vita Romani* as the original is much more convincing. To her arguments, here I add some considerations of Fulbert's authorial style, based on the case of his other known text, the *Vita Secunda Aichardi*.

---

[5] Fulbert and Gerard's versions are both included under BHL 7313: see Lifshitz, 'Dossier of Romanus', p. 160.

[6] Lifshitz presents a transcription and translation of the letter in 'Dossier of Romanus', pp. 362–6.

[7] Lifshitz, 'Dossier of Romanus', pp. 46, 57–8 seems to identify BHL 7310 with Gerard's metrical *Vita*, but in *Pious Neustria*, p. 163, she asserts that the original metrical version is lost and that BHL 7310 is a later version produced at St-Ouen.

[8] Lifshitz, *Pious Neustria*, pp. 159–63.

[9] J. Le Maho, 'La Réécriture Hagiographique au Xe Siècle: Autour des *Libri Gerardi* de la Cathédrale de Rouen', in *La Place de la Normandie dans la Diffusion des Savoirs*, ed. J.-P. Hervieu, E. Poulle and P. Manneville (Rouen, 2006), pp. 23–55 (pp. 25–8).

Fulbert as author of the *Vita Secunda Aichardi*

It is clear that the same Fulbert also wrote the *Vita Secunda Aichardi* for the monks of Jumièges. In each case, the author identified himself as 'Fulbertus *peccator*' in the first line of the preface. Indeed, the prefaces are so similar as to leave us in no doubt that the author is the same person. They both contain numerous examples of similar phrasing, and describe Fulbert's reluctance to write the *vita* until convinced, in the case of the *Vita Secunda Aichardi* by a vision of an old man, and in the case of the *Vita Romani* by an unnamed

Fulbert's *Vita Romani*	*Vita Secunda Aichardi*
Dominis et con**fratribus suis** sancte Rothomagensis ecclesie matris filiis **Fulbertus peccator salutem.**	**Dominis suis**, Gimesiensis \Gemmeticensis/ coenobii scilicet **fratribus** sanctissimis, **Fulbertus peccator salutem.**
Quod a uobis fratres et domini mei **totiens rogatus**, historicam uitam beati patris nostri Romani ingenioli mei stilo illustrare quod inquam **totiens** rogatus, obstinantius huc usque recusaui, non simplex **causa** me dehortabatur, ex eo uidelicet quod nequaquam artis peritia suffultus, ad opus hoc me minus idoneum sentiebam, ideoque **tantam operis sarcinam** a peritissimis uiris pretermissam arripere metuebam, ne nobilis materia rustico stilo exarata uilesceret, si forte in manus peritorum incideret grammaticorum... ... **Non irrationabiliter** igitur, **ut putabam**, uiribus **onus** impar assumere detrectabam...	**Quod** in vita beati Aichadri manu[m] mittere **totiès à vobis iussus, totiès** distulisse accusor, si **causam** vobis libeat discutere, **non irrationabiliter, vt mihi videtur, tanti oneris sarcina[m]** subterfugisse reperiar.
Unde simulato **motu indignationis** paulo inestuans, "**Usquequo** te," **inquit**, "degener et ignaue mollis desidia, et dissolute mentis deicit hebitudo. **Usque** adeo intra antra silentii clausum seruas, quod multo melius ad publicum efferri profuisset?..."	Ille **motu indignantis**, me in hunc modum coërcuit: **Vsquequò, inquit,** serue piger, **vsquequò** ignauiter agis? **Vsquequò** inobediens eris?

friend.[10] The above table gives several incidences of verbal parallels in the two prefaces. As is apparent merely from these examples, Fulbert's *Vita Romani* preface mirrors that of the *Vita Secunda Aichardi* in content and structure, but is considerably more verbose and repetitive.

Similarities persist in the main hagiographical texts. Notably, Fulbert's treatment of demons in the main text of the *Vita Romani* is echoed in the *Vita Secunda Aichardi*, especially on one striking point of detail. Both works refer to the idea that demons convened a council, in which they would give account of their evil-doings and receive appropriate reward or punishment. The *Vita Romani* relates the following in its description of a ruined Roman amphitheatre outside the city:

> De quo loco aiebant sepe inmundorum spirituum murmur auditum, et quasi ad aggregatum concilium de longinquis terre partibus conuentum statutum, in quo rationem operum suorum pro se quisque reddere cogebatur, et pro magnitudine scelerum altius quisque honorabatur, pro inertia uero uerberibus afficiebatur.[11]

The *Vita Secunda Aichardi*, meanwhile, reports the following behaviour of a demon tormenting Aichard:

> Et eccè diabolus infrà tenebrosum cellæ angulum se continebat, nefandam cautionem in manibus tenens, et ut superat tonsa coma deorsùm influebat, ipse colligere et in numerum capillaturam omnem redigere videbatur; res tremenda et sollicitè pensanda!
> ... Ad hæc verba viri Dei impurus minister respondit: "Quod tu, velut rerum ignarus, requiris, si meum nescis esse officium, servorum Dei habitacula revisere, et offensas singulorum breviario meo annotare, et sic principi nostro referre, ne ad concilium ipsius revertentem vacuum me suppliciis durioribus jubeat excruciari...[12]

Although the precise account of what demons reported at such councils differs slightly, the same idea is represented in both texts. Moreover, the short passage about the demonic council appears only in Fulbert's versions of these *Vitae*, and not in Gerard's text or the *Vita Prima Aichardi*, so the conceit can clearly be recognized as Fulbert's own contribution.

From these verbal and substantive parallels, we are left in no doubt that the same Fulbert composed both the *Vita Romani* and the *Vita Secunda Aichardi*.

---

[10] While there is always the possibility that one text was a close copy or later forgery, nothing leads us to this conclusion. The preface to the *Vita Secunda Aichardi* is printed in L. Surius, *De Probatis Sanctorum Historiis*, 6 vols. (Cologne, 1570–75), V, 239–40; the *Vita* is in *Vie de Saint Achard*, in J. de Guyse, *Histoire de Hainaut...*, ed. le Marquis de Fortia, 16 vols. (Paris 1826–38), VIII, 40–139 (=BHL 182).

[11] Lifshitz, *Pious Neustria*, p. 248.

[12] *Vie de Saint Achard*, pp. 90–2.

Fulbert's *Vita Aichardi* as adaptation and *Vita Romani* as original composition

In writing the *Vita Secunda Aichardi*, Fulbert used an earlier hagiography as his source, the *Vita Prima Aichardi*.[13] His debt to the earlier text is clear, but Fulbert's approach was far more thorough than mere embellishment. Although he adhered to the original structure, Fulbert completely rewrote the *Vita Aichardi*. Let us consider the same passage, which relates Aichard's conversation with a demon who must report to the demonic council. While adhering closely to the events provided by the earlier *Vita*, Fulbert rephrased and extended his source material, leaving very little in the way of verbal parallels. Fulbert used nearly twice as many words as the original, considerably expanding the dialogue between Aichard and the demon – a hallmark of his approach throughout the text. Such a thorough process of editing corresponds to Fulbert's account of his own aims in his preface. Finding the *Vita Prima* unsatisfactory in style, Fulbert rejected the instruction to abridge it, and preferred instead to alter the entire work:

> Nam, vt vera fatear, vitæ ipsius textum, casu mihi repertum, aliquandò percurri, quem per loca sanè verborum inanibus flucturis, vt ità dicam, imprǫgnatum offendi.
>
> Quas si iuxta mandatum vestrum demere voluissem, & locum vacantem sine additamento dimisissem, dum interrupta verborum feries malè cohærentes efferret sententias, non castigatum, sed decurtatum potiùs, & totum inconueniens opus reliquissem...
>
> Ego igitur tam subtilis ingenij peritiam in me vigere non sentiens, decreui aut ex toto omittere, aut ex toto, si fas esset, innouare.[14]

Compare Fulbert's approach in rewriting the *Vita Aichardi* to the relationship between the two *Vitae Romani* in the table below.

This short passage typifies the relationship of the two versions: they are largely identical, except for coherent blocks of text which are present only in Fulbert's version. Compared to Gerard's text, many passages of Fulbert's version continue for longer and include more dialogue: perhaps the way they were written could be called 'hystorialiter', as Gerard described the original text in his letter. If a mid-eleventh-century Fulbert rewrote Gerard's version, then he simply added passages throughout, with little amendment or paraphrasing elsewhere: this approach would be considerably different to that he took when rewriting the *Vita Prima Aichardi*, in which he thoroughly revised each section, as well as expanding it. Indeed, such an

---

[13] *Vita Aichardi* (BHL 181), ed. J. Périer, *AASS*, Sept V (1755), pp. 85–100.
[14] Surius, *De Probatis Sanctorum Historiis*, V, 239.

Fulbert's *Vita Romani*	Gerard's *Vita Romani*
De quo loco aiebant sepe inmundorum spirituum murmur auditum, *et quasi ad aggregatum concilium de longinquis terre partibus conuentum statutum, in quo rationem operum suorum pro se quisque reddere cogebatur, et pro magnitudine scelerum altius quisque honorabatur, pro inertia uero uerberibus afficiebatur. Post fanum huiusmodi sub obscuro quodam loco spelunca horribilis erat, introrsum quidem spaciosa, sed angusta fauce inestimabilem profundi altitudinem celabat.* Sed neque uisu hominis aduerti poterat, quia hiatu ipso sulphureus uortex tetros uapores exalabat, et intolerabiles fetores, cum quibus flamme piceus horro erumpens, uicine urbis edificia seuo sepe uastabat incendio, multos uero fumifero necabat odore.	De quo loco aiebant sepe inmundorum spirituum murmur auditum. Sed neque uisu hominis aduerti poterat, quia hiatu ipso sulphureus uortex tetros uapores exalabat, et intolerabiles fetores, cum quibus flamme piceus horro erumpens, uicine urbis edificia seuo sepe uastabat incendio, multos uero fumifero necabat odore.

approach is precisely the kind of abridgement that Fulbert disapproved of in his preface to the *Vita Secunda Aichardi*. It seems more likely that it was Gerard who abridged the version written by a mid-tenth-century Fulbert, by cutting out sections of text that he deemed extraneous, but leaving the rest untouched – thus producing, as he stated in his letter, 'digestam stilo illius ad instar'.

Not only does this hypothesis fit with Gerard's explanation in his letter to Hugo, but also with Fulbert's stated aims in his own preface to the *Vita Romani*. Explaining that he was 'so many times asked, by you my brothers and lords, to illustrate the historical life of our blessed father Romanus in my feeble style', Romanus made no mention of a prior text.[15] Indeed, he implied that none existed, stating that the task of writing one had been 'overlooked' (*pretermissam*) and repeating that he was driven to write the *Vita* because, if he did not, then the deeds of Romanus would remain 'within the cloisters of silence'; the friend persuading him to write, he said, chastised him not to

---

[15] Lifshitz, *Pious Neustria*, p. 234: 'a uobis fratres et domini mei totiens rogatus, historicam uitam beati patris nostri Romani ingenioli mei stilo illustrare...' Lifshitz, 'Dossier of Romanus', p. 233.

'keep closed up within the caves of silence, that which would serve much more if proclaimed to the public'.[16] The intention, here, was not to improve the style of Romanus's *Vita*, but to record it for the public and for posterity for the first time.

This evidence reinforces Lifshitz's proposed dating for the composition of the *Vita Romani* and associated texts.[17] She believes the *Vita Prima Aichardi* and another text by the same author, the *Vita Hugonis*, to have been written by members of the Jumièges community in the second half of the ninth century.[18] Fulbert, she has argued, then wrote the *Vita Romani* (and presumably the *Vita Secunda Aichardi*) in the 940s, after William Longsword's restoration of the monastery of Jumièges. Fulbert, in this interpretation, wrote while the archbishop of Rouen was still abbot of St-Ouen, as was the case until the time of Archbishop Robert.[19] Fulbert depicted Romanus as inhabiting a monastery, surrounded by 'brothers', and so it is reasonable to assume that that was the situation with which he was familiar. Yet Lifshitz has described Fulbert as 'a thoroughly Romanized Frank', who may have come first to Jumièges with the monks of St-Cyprian of Poitiers installed there by William Longsword.[20] This would explain his interest in Aichard's life in Poitiers.

The evidence presented here militates against Le Maho's alternative model for the composition of these texts. Le Maho asserts that the two Jumièges *vitae* of Aichard and Hugh were written by a St-Cyprian monk after Jumièges's 942 restoration, probably the abbot Anno.[21] These, he has claimed, were some of the earliest products of a re-founded Jumièges scriptorium, alongside the *Planctus* for William Longsword. Given this date for the composition of the *Vita Prima Aichardi*, Le Maho reasoned that Fulbert must have been active

---

[16] Lifshitz, *Pious Neustria*, p. 235: 'intra claustra silentii'; '…intra antra silentii clausum seruas, quod multo melius ad publicum efferri…'. Lifshitz, 'Dossier of Romanus', p. 234.

[17] Lifshitz, 'Dossier of Romanus', pp. 3–10.

[18] J. Van der Straeten, 'La vie inédite de S. Hugues, évêque de Rouen', *Analecta Bollandiana* 87 (1969), 215–60 (pp. 232–60) (=BHL 4032a). Van der Straeten claims that they were written in exile: J. Van der Straeten, 'L'Auteur des Vies de S. Hugues et de S. Aycadre', *Analecta Bollandiana* 88 (1970), 63–73 (pp. 69–72); also Van der Straeten, 'Vie inédite de S. Hugues', p. 228. On the other hand, Howe argues that they must have been written before the community's departure: Howe, 'Hagiography of Jumièges', p. 101, but cf. pp. 124–5. Lifshitz, in a position which reflects her general argument for continuity, argues that there was a small community at Jumièges throughout the late ninth century: Lifshitz, *Pious Neustria*, pp. 125–9.

[19] Lifshitz, *Pious Neustria*, p. 188.

[20] Lifshitz, 'Dossier of Romanus', p. 94.

[21] J. Le Maho, 'Autour de la renaissance monastique du Xe siècle en Normandie: les Vies des saints Aycadre et Hugues de Jumièges', in *Livrets, collections et textes, études sur la tradition hagiographique latine*, ed. M. Heinzelmann (Stuttgart, 2006), pp. 285–322 (pp. 321–2); Le Maho, 'La production éditoriale'.

considerably later, especially given his scathing opinion of this first *Vita*. He claims that the Fulbert who was author of the *Vita Secunda Aichardi* and the *Vita Romani* was an archdeacon of Rouen cathedral who is attested in various documents of the time of Archbishop Maurillus (1055–67). Le Maho's argument rests on the Poitiers interest of the *Vita Prima Aichardi*, which he considers could only have been written by someone who knew the area well. However, it involves a revised dating of an important manuscript in which the earliest *Vitae* of Hugh and Aichard appear, Rouen BM MS 1377 (U 108), which is generally seen as late ninth century.[22] Gauthier has also asserted that the *Vita Romani* is more likely to be eleventh century, but neither of them has addressed some of Lifshitz's central arguments.[23]

To accept this model, we would have to believe that the author of the *Vita Prima Aichardi/Vita Hugonis* deliberately aimed to present the former text as written earlier than it was; and also that Fulbert, in direct contrast to his approach to the *Vita Aichardi*, denied the existence of a source-text, which in fact he used verbatim for the majority of his text – again, in a completely different style to his reworking of the *Vita Aichardi*. While it is undeniable that early medieval writers frequently borrowed without attribution and misrepresented their own roles in composition, it seems perverse to assume this degree of duplicity in so many of the relevant texts, when a simpler explanation that tallies with the authors' own statements is highly plausible. Therefore, Lifshitz's dating of Fulbert's *Vita Romani* to the 940s–950s should continue to be accepted.

---

[22] Howe, 'Hagiography of Jumièges', p. 60; Van der Straeten, 'L'Auteur des Vies', p. 73.

[23] Gauthier, 'Quelques hypothèses', p. 454; Le Maho, 'La production éditoriale', p. 24.

Appendix 2: The Dates of The Latin *Vita Prima Sancti Neoti* and The Old English Life of St Neot

In Chapter 4, I discuss two texts which relate the life and posthumous miracles of St Neot: the Latin *Vita Prima Sancti Neoti* and the Old English Life of St Neot.[1] Varied dates have been proposed for these texts' original composition. Research by Michael Lapidge on the Latin *Vita* and Malcolm Godden on the Old English Life proposed that they were written in the periods 975x1080 and 1004/1015x1030 respectively. Despite some challenges to their arguments having been raised, I believe that these dates should be upheld, and that the Latin life should be situated in the earlier part of the suggested period. In what follows, I lay out the historical evidence, internal and external, which supports a late tenth or early eleventh century composition for the two saint's lives; and then I consider the relationship between the two texts and a third, post-Norman Conquest version, the *Vita Secunda Sancti Neoti*. The relationship thus revealed between the two pre-Conquest Lives reinforces an early dating for both.

Historical evidence

Both hagiographies were long considered post-Conquest productions, until the reconsiderations by Lapidge and Godden.[2] The extant manuscripts date from the twelfth to fourteenth centuries,[3] but the evidence given by the texts themselves indicates earlier dates of composition.

The *Vita Prima Sancti Neoti* is difficult to date with precision, but it seems to have been composed in the late tenth or early eleventh century. It must have been written following the foundation of the priory at Eynesbury (modern St Neots) sometime after 975. Although Neot lived in Cornwall, the *Translatio* which follows the *Vita Neoti* (probably by the same author) tells of the translation of his relics to Huntingdonshire.[4] Bishop Æthelwold, the founder of the priory at Eynesbury, is given a role in Neot's life, however anachronistic this might be, again suggesting that the text was written at Eynesbury. Neot is said to rest at *Eanulfesbyrig* (Eynesbury/St Neots) in the second Resting

---

[1] VPSN; 'The Old English Life of Seinte Neote', ed. Warner; M. Richards, 'An Edition and Translation of the Old English Life of Seinte Neote' (unpublished doctoral dissertation, Wisconsin University, 1971).

[2] VPSN, pp. lxxv–cxxiv; Godden, 'The Old English Life of St Neot'.

[3] VPSN, pp. lxxviii–lxxxii, cxvi.

[4] VPSN, pp. cii, 134–42.

Places list, compiled in 1013 or slightly later.[5] This casts doubt on William of Malmesbury's suggestion that the relics were moved to Crowland during the years of viking turmoil in the early eleventh century.[6] Viking attacks later became a common reason to claim relics of rival houses, and all the evidence for the presence of Neot's relics at Crowland dates from the early twelfth century. Orderic Vitalis reported *c.* 1115 that the relics were moved to Crowland by Osketel, who witnessed charters in 1012 and 1022–23.[7] However, shortly after the monastery's re-foundation as a cell of Bec in 1080, Anselm had inspected the relics at Eynesbury and declared them complete.[8] It appears that, in the late eleventh and early twelfth centuries, there was some competition over the possession of Neot's relics.

The *Vita Prima* seems to have been produced before this rivalry began. Its style, which resembles the late Anglo-Saxon 'hermeneutic style' and includes lines of verse integrated into the narrative, places it decisively before the Conquest, as Lapidge has shown. Therefore it cannot have been written after the re-foundation of St Neots as a cell of Bec in 1080.[9] This is borne out by internal evidence, as there is no mention of Bec or Anselm's inspection of the relics, which surely would have been included had it been written out of competition with Crowland. We are left, then, with composition at St Neots, from 975 at the earliest, and the latest date being either the 1020s if we accept Orderic's evidence of translation to Crowland, or any time before the Conquest if Crowland's claim is considered to be a later development.

Previously, the Old English Life, which is in the form of a homily, was assigned to the twelfth century on grounds of language.[10] However, Godden has shown that later features in the English are merely a result of the date of copying, as is also the case in the other texts in the manuscript, which are mostly by Ælfric. Godden has demonstrated that, behind these later amendments, the expression and phrasing of the Life show such similarity with other Old English homilies that it must have been composed in the opening years of the eleventh century (after 1004, to allow influence from Wulfstan's writings, or after 1014 if we believe that the influence came from the *Sermo Lupi ad Anglos* specifically).[11] On the basis of the text's mention of Bishop Ælfheah, whom he identified as Ælfheah the Bald of Winchester (934–51),

---

[5] D. Rollason, 'Lists of Saints' Resting-Places in Anglo-Saxon England', *ASE* 7 (1978), 61–93 (p. 90).

[6] William of Malmesbury, *Gesta Pontificum Anglorum*, I, 486–7.

[7] VPSN, p. lxxxix; *The Ecclesiastical History of Orderic Vitalis*, ed. M. Chibnall, 6 vols. (Oxford, 1969–80), II, 342–3.

[8] VPSN, p. xc.

[9] VPSN, pp. xcvi–ci.

[10] VPSN, p. cxvi.

[11] Godden, 'Old English Life of St Neot', p. 209; *Sermo Lupi ad Anglos*, ed. D. Whitelock (Exeter, 1939; 3rd edn 1976), pp. 35–6.

Godden argued that the Life was written before around 1020, after which date
'St Ælfheah' would always refer rather to Ælfheah of Canterbury.[12]

Godden's conclusions have recently been disputed, in favour of twelfth-
century composition, by George Younge.[13] Younge's arguments relate
predominantly to the relevance of the text in mid-twelfth-century England.
But this relevance is not in dispute: the *c.* 1150 date of the manuscript which
contains the Old English Life is itself evidence for twelfth-century interest.
This does not exclude the possibility of earlier relevance and interest; the
comparison between Alfred and contemporary kings, for example, certainly
manifested itself around the year 1000. The Life may well, like other texts
in the same manuscript (Cotton Vespasian D. xiv), have been originally
composed at an earlier date.

The other key component of Younge's argument rests on the dependence
of the Old English Life on the Latin *Vita Prima*, which he states dates from *c.*
1050.[14] Yet this date is merely Lapidge's preferred option within his range of
975–1080 (based on the text's erroneous reference to Æthelwold, which he finds
unlikely at an earlier date),[15] and Godden has made compelling arguments for
a much earlier date of composition. Therefore, if we accept, with Lapidge and
Younge, that the Old English Life derived from the Latin *Vita Prima*, this does
not mean it necessarily dates from after 1050; indeed, following the discussion
above, it need only date from after 975. Godden's arguments, alongside the
likely early date of the Latin *Vita Prima*, remain convincing reasons to date the
Old English Life to the period 1004x1014 – 1020x1031.

Relationship between texts, including the *Vita Secunda Neoti*

Let us consider the relationship between the Old English Life and the Latin
Vita Prima in more detail. Neither is a straight translation of the other: the
Latin *Vita* is much longer and includes considerably more detail regarding
Neot's interactions with Alfred, while the Old English Life includes a miracle
performed by Neot in life that does not appear in the *Vita Prima*. Moreover,
there is a later Latin version of the *Vita*, composed after the Conquest, which
(following Godden and Lapidge) we may call the *Vita Secunda*.[16] Godden
has argued that the *Vita Secunda* shows similarities with the Old English

---

[12] Godden, 'Old English Life of St Neot', pp. 194–202, 206–7.
[13] G. Younge, '"Those were Good Days": Representations of the Anglo-Saxon Past in
the Old English Homily on Saint Neot', *The Review of English Studies* ns 63 (2012),
349–69.
[14] Younge, 'Those were Good Days', pp. 354, 358.
[15] VPSN, pp. xciv–xcvi.
[16] *De S. Neoto Confessore in Anglia*, ed. G. Culperus, *AASS*, July VII (1731), pp. 314–29
(BHL 6052; hereafter Vita II), ch. 1 opens with a reference to England, 'priusquam
debellata triumphali Nortmannorum subjugaretur ditioni'.

Life which the *Vita Prima* does not contain: the *Vita Secunda* includes miracle stories related to Neot's life in Cornwall which resemble passages of the Old English Life, and which have no parallel in the *Vita Prima*. Godden therefore suggested that all three texts were based on an earlier, now lost, *Vita Neoti*. This represents a return to an earlier view of the texts.[17] Lapidge, however, presented the *Vita Prima* as the first life, on which both the Old English Life and the *Vita Secunda* were based, and Younge has presented further evidence in support of this relationship.

In support of the latter view we may emphasize that the narrative of the *Vita Secunda* itself closely follows that of the *Vita Prima*, and there are numerous verbal parallels which seem to indicate that the *Vita Prima* was the source-text.[18] These verbal parallels even relate to the metrical sections of the *Vita Prima*, which suggests that the author of the *Vita Secunda* relied directly on this text, and not a common source as Godden proposed: it is unlikely that the author of the *Vita Prima* would have used the same phrasing as a prose source so often in composing verse. Moreover, the Old English Life also matches the structure of the *Vita Prima* at some points in the narrative – particularly the episodes involving King Alfred. It is the presence of additional material in the Old English Life and the *Vita Secunda* that poses the problem.[19]

Both the *Vita Secunda* and the Old English Life claimed that Neot's relics rested in Cornwall, and made no mention of the translation to Eynesbury. In fact, the *Vita Secunda* actually stated that Neot's miracles continued at that site up till the present day.[20] We may therefore conclude that this text was not written at Eynesbury or Crowland. Lapidge proposed a south-western origin, perhaps Glastonbury, given its prominence in the text.[21] The author may have denied that the relics were in eastern England, or been unaware of it: it is possible, perhaps, that he used a manuscript copy of the *Vita Prima* which lacked the *Translatio*. Similarly, Godden has suggested that the Old English Life was composed somewhere Neot's festival was celebrated in the West Country, such as Glastonbury, Exeter, Crediton or Sherborne.[22] The

---

[17] Richards, 'Medieval Hagiography of St Neot'.

[18] VPSN, p. cxiii. Younge, 'Those were Good Days', pp. 354–8, presents more evidence that the Old English homily and Vita II were independently based on the *Vita Prima*.

[19] Godden gives an additional argument, based on the *Vita Prima*'s use of the phrase 'uno integro lustro annisque duobus' for seven years; he argues that the Old English Life's 'seven times' could not have been derived from this phrase ('Old English Life of St Neot', pp. 203–4). However, this discrepancy could perhaps be explained by a correction or annotation in the manuscript used by the Old English hagiographer.

[20] Vita II, ch. 46.

[21] VPSN, pp. cxiv–cxv. Richards, 'Medieval Hagiography of Neot', p. 273, proposed Exeter.

[22] The Old English Life was written for delivery on Neot's feast day: it opens by referring to 'þyssen halgen, þe we todæig wurðigeð' (p. 129). Godden, 'Old English Life of St Neot', p. 211.

south-western origins of both the *Vita Secunda* and the Old English Life may suggest the reason why they include the miracle stories that the *Vita Prima* does not. It is likely that a collection of miracles performed by St Neot in Cornwall and at Glastonbury circulated independently in the south-west, either in written or oral form. The authors of the Old English Life and the *Vita Secunda* then separately incorporated some of these into the relevant sections of their narratives, which were otherwise derived from the *Vita Prima*. This explanation would account for the fact that their miracles in each of these texts are different, but are similar in theme and show Celtic influence.[23] Therefore, differences between the two early texts – the Old English Life of St Neot and the Latin *Vita Prima Sancti Neoti* – may be explained by their places of composition in the south-west and eastern England, respectively. Both were probably written in the years preceding around 1020, but the Latin text must have come first in order for it to be used by the Old English homilist.

[23] In fact, Godden, 'Old English Life of St Neot', p. 205 makes a similar suggestion, as does Younge, 'Those were Good Days', p. 358. Moreover, the author of the Old English Life refers to his sources as 'books' in the plural (p. 129).

Bibliography

Printed primary sources

Abbo of Fleury, *Life of St Edmund*, in *Three Lives of English Saints*, ed. M. Winterbottom (Toronto, 1972), pp. 65–87

Abbo of St-Germain, *Viking attacks on Paris: the Bella Parisiacae urbis of Abbo of Saint-Germain-des-Prés*, ed. and trans. N. Dass (Paris, 2007)

'*Acta Archiepiscoporum Rotomagensium*: Study and Edition', ed. R. Allen, *Tabularia 'Documents'* 9 (2009), 1–66

Adalbéron de Laon, *Poème au Roi Robert*, ed. C. Carozzi (Paris, 1979)

Ademar of Chabannes, *Chronicon*, ed. G. Waitz, *MGH, SS*, 4 (Hanover, 1891; repr. 1968), 106–48

Ælfric's Lives of Saints: being a set of sermons on saints' days formerly observed by the English church, ed. W. Skeat, 2 vols. (London, 1881–1900)

Alcuin of York, trans. S. Allott (York, 1974)

Alcuini sive Albini Epistolae, MGH, Epistolae, IV (Berlin, 1895), ed. E. Dümmler

Alfred the Great, ed. S. Keynes and M. Lapidge (London, 1983)

Anglo-Saxon Charters series (Oxford, 1973–)

The Anglo-Saxon Chronicle: A Collaborative Edition, ed. D. Dumville and S. Keynes (Cambridge, 1983–)

The Anglo-Saxon Chronicle: A Collaborative Edition, Volume 4. MS B, ed. S. Taylor (Cambridge, 1983)

The Anglo-Saxon Chronicle: A Collaborative Edition, Volume 17. The Annals of St Neots with Vita Prima Sancti Neoti, ed. D. Dumville and M. Lapidge (Cambridge, 1985)

The Anglo-Saxon Chronicles, trans. by Michael Swanton (London, 1996; rev. ed. 2000)

The Anglo-Saxon Missionaries in Germany…, trans. C. H. Talbot (London, 1954)

Les Annales de Saint Bertin, ed. F. Grat, J. Vielliard and S. Clémencet (Paris, 1964)

Anonymi Leidensis De Situ Orbis Libri Duo, ed. R. Quadri (Padua, 1974)

Asser's Life of King Alfred, ed. W. Stevenson (Oxford, 1904; repr. 1959)

Baedae Opera Historica, ed. J. E. King (London, 1930)

Beowulf: An Edition, ed. B. Mitchell and F. Robinson (Oxford, 1998)

The Book of Settlements: Landnámabók, trans. H. Pálsson and P. Edwards (Winnipeg, 1972)

Byrhtferth of Ramsey: the Lives of St Oswald and St Ecgwine, ed. M. Lapidge (Oxford, 2009)

Byrhtferth of Ramsey, *Vita Ecgwini*, in *Byrhtferth of Ramsey: the Lives of St Oswald and St Ecgwine*, ed. M. Lapidge (Oxford, 2009)

Byrhtferth of Ramsey, *Vita Oswaldi*, in *Byrhtferth of Ramsey: the Lives of St Oswald and St Ecgwine*, ed. M. Lapidge (Oxford, 2009)

Carmen de Exordio Gentis Francorum ed. E. Dümmler, *MGH*, Poetae Latini aevi Carolini, 2 (Berlin, 1884), pp. 141–5

Carmina in honorem Hludovici, ed. E. Dümmler, *MGH*, Poetae Latini aevi Carolini, 2 (Berlin, 1884), 5–79

Carolingian Civilization: A Reader, ed. P. Dutton (Peterborough, Ont., 1993)

Cartulaire de l'Abbaye de Redon en Bretagne, ed. A. de Courson (Paris, 1863)

Cartulaire de l'Abbaye de Saint-Père de Chartres, ed. B. Guérard, 2 vols. (Paris, 1840)

Cartularium Saxonicum, ed. W. de Gray Birch, 3 vols. (London, 1885–99)

The Cartulary of the Abbey of Mont-Saint-Michel, ed. K. Keats-Rohan (Donington, 2006)

Catalogi Regum Francorum Praetermissi, ed. B. Krusch, *MGH*, SS rer. Merov., 7 (Hanover, 1920), pp. 850–5

Charters of Burton Abbey, ed. P. Sawyer, Anglo-Saxon Charters 2 (Oxford, 1979)

Charters of Northern Houses, ed. D. Woodman, Anglo-Saxon Charters 16 (Oxford, 2012)

Charters of the New Minster, Winchester, Anglo-Saxon Charters 9, ed. S. Miller (Oxford, 2001)

Chartes de l'Abbaye de Jumièges (v.825 à 1204) conservées aux Archives de la Seine-Inférieure, ed. J. Vernier, 2 vols. (Rouen, 1916)

The Chronicle of Hugh Candidus, a Monk of Peterborough, ed. W. T. Mellows (London, 1949)

Chronicon Æthelweardi: The Chronicle of Æthelweard, ed. A. Campbell (London, 1962)

Constitutum Constantini, ed. H. Fuhrmann, *MGH*, Fontes iuris, 10 (Hanover, 1968), 69–74

Councils and Ecclesiastical Documents relating to Great Britain and Ireland, ed. A. W. Haddan and W. Stubbs, 3 vols. (Oxford, 1869–73)

De S. Neoto Confessore in Anglia (BHL 6052), ed. G. Culperus, *AASS*, July VII (1731), pp. 314–29

Die Briefe des heiligen Bonifatius und Lullus, ed. M. Tangl, *MGH*, Epp. sel., 1 (Berlin, 1916)

Die Gesetze der Angelsachsen, ed. F. Liebermann, 3 vols. (Halle, 1898–1916)

Dudo of Saint-Quentin, *De Moribus et Actis Primorum Normanniae Ducum: Auctore Dudone Sancti Quinini Decano*, ed. J. Lair (Caen, 1865)

Dudo of St Quentin, *History of the Normans*, trans. E. Christiansen (Woodbridge, 1998)

Bibliography

The Ecclesiastical History of Orderic Vitalis, ed. M. Chibnall, 6 vols. (Oxford, 1969–80)

The Electronic Sawyer: Online Catalogue of Anglo-Saxon Charters <http://www.esawyer.org.uk/> [accessed 19/05/2013]

English Historical Documents, I: c.500–1042, ed. D. Whitelock (London, 1955; 2nd edn 1979)

'Epistolae Ioannis Papae IX', in *Sacrosancta Concilia ad Regiam editionem exacta...*, ed. P. Labbé and G. Cossart, 16 vols. (Paris, 1671–72), IX, cols 483–94

Frechulfi Lexoviensis Episcopi Opera Omnia, ed. M. I. Allen, Corpus Christianorum Continuatio Mediaevalis CLXIX-CLXIXA, 2 vols. (Turnhout, 2002)

Geffrei Gaimar, *Estoire des Engleis*, ed. I. Short (Oxford, 2009)

Genealogiae Comitum Flandriae, ed. L. C. Bethmann, *MGH, SS*, 9 (Hanover, 1851), pp. 302–4

Genealogiae Karolum, ed. G. Waitz, *MGH, SS*, 13 (Hanover, 1881), pp. 245–6

The Gesta Guillelmi of William of Poitiers, ed. R. H. C. Davis and M. Chibnall (Oxford, 1998)

The Gesta Normannorum Ducum of William of Jumièges, Orderic Vitalis and Robert of Torigni, ed. E. van Houts, 2 vols. (Oxford, 1992)

Havelok, ed. G. V. Smithers (Oxford, 1987)

The Historia Brittonum: 3. The "Vatican" Recension, ed. D. Dumville (Cambridge, 1985)

Historia de Sancto Cuthberto, ed. T. Johnson South (Cambridge, 2002)

History and politics in late Carolingian and Ottonian Europe: the Chronicle of Regino of Prüm and Adalbert of Magdeburg, ed. S. Maclean (Manchester, 2009)

Inventio et Miracula Sancti Vulfranni, ed. J. Laporte, in *Mélanges. Documents publiés et annotés par Dom. J. Laporte et al.* 14th s. (Rouen, 1938), 1–87

Íslendingabok / Kristni Saga: The Book of the Icelanders / The Story of the Conversion, trans. S. Grønlie (London, 2006)

Íslendingabók, ed. J. Benediktsson, Íslenzk Fornrit 1, 2 vols. (Reykjavik, 1968)

Lamberti Ardensis historia comitum Ghisnensium, ed. J. Heller, *MGH, SS*, 24 (Hanover, 1879), pp. 566–8

Lambert of Ardres, *The History of the Counts of Guines and Lords of Ardres*, trans. L. Shopkow (Philadelphia, 2001)

Lamberti S. Audomari Canonici Liber Floridus, ed. A. Derolez (Ghent, 1968)

Landnámabók, ed. J. Benediktsson, Íslenzk Fornrit 1, 2 vols. (Reykjavik, 1968)

The Laws of the Earliest English Kings, trans. F. L. Attenborough (Cambridge, 1922)

The Laws of the Kings of England from Edmund to Henry I, trans. A. J. Robertson (Cambridge, 1925)

Liber Eliensis, ed. E. O. Blake (London, 1962)

Liber Historiae Francorum, ed. B. Krusch, *MGH, SS* rer. Merov., 2 (Hanover, 1888), 215–328

The Life of King Edward, ed. F. Barlow (Oxford, 1962; 2nd edn 1992)

The Life of St Anselm by Eadmer, ed. R. Southern (London, 1962)

Memorials of St Dunstan, ed. W. Stubbs (London, 1874)

Miracula Sancti Benedicti: Les Miracles de Saint Benoit, ed. E. de Certain (Paris, 1858)

'The Old English Life of Seinte Neote', in *Early English Homilies from the Twelfth Century MS Vesp.D.xiv*, ed. R. D. N. Warner, EETS os 152 (London, 1917 for 1915), 129–34

The Old English Orosius, ed. J. Bately, EETS, SS, 6 (London, 1980)

Óttarr svarti, *Knútsdrápa*, ed. M. Townend, in *Poetry from the Kings' Sagas 1: From Mythical Times to c.1035*, ed. D. Whaley, 2 vols. (Turnhout, 2012), II, 779

Pauli Warnefridi Liber de Episcopis Mettensibus, ed. G. Pertz, *MGH*, SS, 2 (Hanover, 1829), 260–68

The Planctus for William Longsword, ed. R. Helmerichs (1999–2002), <http://vlib.iue.it/carrie/documents/planctus/planctus/> [accessed 21/06/2013]

Poetry from the Kings' Sagas 1: From Mythical Times to c.1035, ed. D. Whaley, 2 vols. (Turnhout, 2012)

Poetry from the Kings' Sagas 2: From c.1035 to 1300, ed. K. E. Gade, 2 vols. (Turnhout, 2009)

Recueil des Actes de Louis IV, Roi de France (936–984), ed. P. Lauer (Paris, 1914)

Recueil des Actes des Ducs de Normandie (911–1066), ed. M. Fauroux, Mémoires de la Société des Antiquaires de Normandie, 36 (Caen, 1961)

Reginonis Abbatis Prumiensis Chronicon, ed. F. Kurze, *MGH*, SS rer. Germ. 50 (Hanover, 1890)

Regum Francorum Genealogiae, ed. G. Pertz, *MGH*, SS, 2 (Hanover, 1829), pp. 308–14

Richards, M., 'An Edition and Translation of the Old English Life of Seinte Neote' (unpublished doctoral dissertation, Wisconsin University, 1971)

Richer of St-Rémi, *Histories*, ed. J. Lake, 2 vols. (Cambridge, MA, 2011)

Rodulfi Glabri Historiarum libri quinque/ Rodulfus Glaber, The Five Books of the Histories, ed. J. France (Oxford, 1989)

Roger of Wendover, *Chronica sive Flores Historiarum*, ed. H. Coxe, 5 vols. (London, 1841–44)

Saxo Grammaticus, *Gesta Danorum: The History of the Danes*, ed. K. Friis-Jensen, trans. P. Fisher, 2 vols. (Oxford, 2015)

Sermo Lupi ad Anglos, ed. D. Whitelock (Exeter, 1939; 3rd edn 1976)

Sigvatr Þórðarson, *Knútsdrápa*, ed. M. Townend, in *Poetry from the Kings' Sagas 1: From Mythical Times to c.1035*, ed. D. Whaley, 2 vols. (Turnhout, 2012), II, 651–52

Sigvatr Þórðarson, *Vestrfararvísur*, ed. J. Jesch, in *Poetry from the Kings' Sagas 1: From Mythical Times to c.1035*, ed. D. Whaley, 2 vols. (Turnhout, 2012), II, 617

Snorri Sturluson, *Edda: Prologue and Gylfaginning*, ed. A. Faulkes (London, 2nd edn 2005)

Snorri Sturluson, *Heimskringla*, ed. B. Aðalbjarnarson, Íslenzk Fornrit 26–27, 2 vols. (Reykjavik, 1941)

Snorri Sturluson, *Heimskringla*, trans. A. Finlay and A. Faulkes (London, 2011)

Snorri Sturluson, *The Prose Edda*, trans. J. Byock (London, 2005)

Steinn Herdísarson, *Nizarvísur*, ed. K. E. Gade, in *Poetry from the Kings' Sagas 2: From c.1035 to 1300*, ed. K. E. Gade, 2 vols. (Turnhout, 2009), I, 363

Surius, L., *De Probatis Sanctorum Historiis*, 6 vols. (Cologne, 1570–75)

Symeonis monachi opera omnia, ed. T. Arnold, RS 75, 2 vols. (London, 1882–85)

Translatio Prima Sancti Audoeni (BHL 756), *AASS*, August IV (1752), pp. 820–2

Translatio Secunda Sancti Audoeni (BHL 757), *AASS*, August IV (1752), pp. 823–4

Translatio Severi, in *Texte français et latin des vies des Saints du diocèse de Coutances et Avranches avec des notions préliminaires et l'histoire des Reliques de chaque Saint*, ed. E.A. Pigeon, 2 vols. (Avranches, 1892–98), II, 56–77

Two Voyagers at the Court of King Alfred: The ventures of Ohthere and Wulfstan together with the Description of Northern Europe from the Old English Orosius, ed. N. Lund, trans. C. Fell (York, 1984)

Þjóðólfr Arnórsson, *Stanzas about Haraldr Sigurðarson's leiðangr*, ed. D. Whaley, in *Poetry from the Kings' Sagas 2: From c.1035 to 1300*, ed. K. E. Gade, 2 vols. (Turnhout, 2009), I, 154–7

Þórðr Kolbeinsson, *Eiríksdrápa*, ed. J. Carroll, in *Poetry from the Kings' Sagas 1: From Mythical Times to c.1035*, ed. D. Whaley, 2 vols. (Turnhout, 2012), I, 507

Une Translation de Reliques à Gand en 944: Le Sermo de Adventu Sanctorum Wandregisili, Ansberti et Vulframni in Blandinium, ed. N.-N. Huyghebaert (Brussels, 1978)

Van der Straeten, J., 'La vie inédite de S. Hugues, évêque de Rouen', *Analecta Bollandiana* 87 (1969), 215–60 (=BHL 4032a)

Vie de Saint Achard, in J. de Guyse, *Histoire de Hainaut...*, ed. le Marquis de Fortia, 16 vols. (Paris 1826–38), VIII, 40–139 (=BHL 182)

Vita Aichardi (BHL 181), ed. J. Périer, *AASS*, Sept V (1755), pp. 85–100

Vita Elphegi (BHL 2518–19), ed. D. van Papenbroeck, *AASS*, Apr. XIX (Antwerp, 1675), pp. 631–41

Vita Romani, in F. Lifshitz, *The Norman Conquest of Pious Neustria: Historiographic Discourse and Saintly Relics, 684–1090* (Toronto, 1995)

Warner of Rouen, *Moriuht: A Norman Latin Poem from the Early Eleventh Century*, ed. C. McDonough (Toronto, 1995)

William of Malmesbury, *Gesta Pontificum Anglorum*, ed. M. Winterbottom with R. M. Thomson, 2 vols. (Oxford, 2007)

William of Malmesbury, *Gesta Regum Anglorum*, ed. R. A. B. Mynors, R. M. Thomson and M. Winterbottom, 2 vols. (Oxford, 1998)

Wulfstan of Winchester, *The Life of St Æthelwold*, ed. M. Lapidge and M. Winterbottom (Oxford, 1991)

Secondary sources

Abrams, L., 'Diaspora and Identity in the Viking Age', *EME* 20 (2012), 17–38

Abrams, L., 'Early Normandy', *ANS* 35 (2013), 45–64

Abrams, L., 'Edward the Elder's Danelaw', in *Edward the Elder, 899–924*, ed. N. Higham and D. Hill (London, 2001), pp. 128–43

Abrams, L., 'England, Normandy and Scandinavia', in *A Companion to the Anglo-Norman World*, ed. C. Harper-Bill and E. van Houts (Woodbridge, 2003)

Abrams, L., 'Scandinavian Place-Names and Settlement-History: Flegg, Norfolk and East Anglia in the Viking Age', in *Vikings and Norse in the North Atlantic: Proceedings of the Fourteenth Viking Congress*, ed. A. Mortensen and S. Arge (Torshavn, 2005)

Abrams, L., 'The Anglo-Saxons and the Christianization of Scandinavia', *ASE* 24 (1995), 213–49

Aird, W. M., *St Cuthbert and the Normans: The Church of Durham, 1071–1153* (Woodbridge, 1998)

Albu, E., 'Dudo of Saint-Quentin: The Heroic Past Imagined', *HSJ* 6 (1994), 111–18

Albu, E., *The Normans in their Histories: Propaganda, Myth, and Subversion* (Woodbridge, 2001)

Amory, F., 'The Viking Hasting in Franco-Scandinavian Legend', in *Saints, Scholars and Heroes: Studies in Medieval Culture in Honour of Charles W. Jones*, ed. M. King and W. Stevens, 2 vols. (Collegeville, 1979), II, 265–86

Anlezark, D., 'Sceaf, Japheth and the Origins of the Anglo-Saxons', *ASE* 31 (2002), 13–46

Arnoux, M., 'Before the *Gesta Normannorum* and beyond Dudo: Some Evidence on Early Norman Historiography', *ANS* 22 (2000), 29–48

Arnoux, M., 'Les premières chroniques de Fécamp: de l'hagiographie à l'histoire', in *Les Saints dans la Normandie médiévale. Colloque de Cerisy-la-Salle (26–29 septembre 1996)*, ed. P. Bouet and F. Neveux (Caen, 2000), pp. 72–82

Ashley, S., 'The Lay Intellectual in Anglo-Saxon England: Ealdorman Æthelweard and the Politics of History', in *Lay Intellectuals in the Carolingian World*, ed. P. Wormald and J. L. Nelson (Cambridge, 2007), pp. 218–45

Bailey, R., *Viking Age Sculpture in Northern England* (London, 1980)

Bale, A., 'Introduction: St Edmund's Medieval Lives', in *St Edmund, King and Martyr: Changing Images of a Medieval Saint*, ed. A. Bale (York, 2009), pp. 1–25

Barker, E., 'The Anglo-Saxon Chronicle Used by Aethelweard', *Bulletin of the Institute of History Research* 40 (1967), 75–91

Barker, E., 'The Cottonian Fragments of Æthelweard's Chronicle', *Historical Research* 24 (1951), 46–62

Barrow, J., 'Chester's Earliest Regatta? Edgar's Dee-rowing Revisited', *EME* 10 (2001), 81–93

Barrow, J., 'Danish Ferocity and Abandoned Monasteries: The Twelfth-century View', in *The Long Twelfth-Century View of the Anglo-Saxon Past*, ed. M. Brett and D. A. Woodman (Aldershot, 2015), pp. 77–93

Barrow, J., 'Survival and Mutation: Ecclesiastical Institutions in the Danelaw in the Ninth and Tenth Centuries', in *Cultures in Contact: Scandinavian Settlement in England in the Ninth and Tenth Centuries*, ed. D. M. Hadley and J. E. Richards (Turnhout, 2000), pp. 155–76

Barth, F., 'Introduction', in *Ethnic Groups and Boundaries: The Social Organization of Culture Difference*, ed. F. Barth (London, 1969; reissued 1998), pp. 9–38

Bartlett, R., 'Medieval and Modern Concepts of Race and Ethnicity', *Journal of Medieval and Early Modern Studies* 31 (2001), 39–56

Bartlett, R., *The Making of Europe* (London, 1993)

Bartlett, R., *The Natural and the Supernatural in the Middle Ages* (Cambridge, 2008)

Bately, J., 'The Compilation of the Anglo-Saxon Chronicle Once More', *Leeds Studies in English* 16 (1985), 7–26

Bates, D., 'Britain and France in the Year 1000', *Franco-British Studies* 28 (1999), 5–22

Bates, D., *Normandy Before 1066* (London, 1982)

Bates, D., Review of Eleanor Searle, *Predatory Kinship, Speculum* 65 (1990), 1045–7

Bauduin, P., *La Première Normandie (Xe –XIe siècles): Sur les frontières de la Haute Normandie: Identité et construction d'une principauté* (Caen, 2004)

Bell, A., 'Gaimar's Early "Danish" Kings', *PMLA* 65 (1950), 601–40

Biddle, M., 'Excavations at Winchester, 1965', *Antiquaries Journal* 46 (1966), 308–32

Biddle, M., 'Narrative Frieze', in *The Golden Age of Anglo-Saxon Art, 966–1066*, ed. J. Backhouse, D. H. Turner and L. Webster (London, 1984), pp. 133–5

Bildhauer, B., 'Blood, Jews and Monsters in Medieval Culture', in *The Monstrous Middle Ages*, ed. B. Bildhauer and R. Mills (Toronto, 2003), pp. 75–83

Bisson, T., 'Nobility and Family in Medieval France: A Review Essay', *French Historical Studies* 16 (1990), 597–613

Blackburn, M., 'Expansion and Control: Aspects of Anglo-Scandinavian Minting South of the Humber', in *Vikings and the Danelaw: Papers from the Proceedings of the Thirteenth Viking Congress*, ed. J. Graham-Campbell and others (Oxford, 2001), pp. 125–42

Blair, J., 'A Handlist of Anglo-Saxon Saints', in *Local Saints and Local Churches in the Early Medieval West*, ed. A. Thacker and R. Sharpe (Oxford, 2002), pp. 495–565

Blair, J., 'The Chertsey Resting-Place List and the Enshrinement of Frithuwold', in *The Origins of Anglo-Saxon Kingdoms*, ed. S. Bassett (Leicester, 1989), pp. 231–6

Blair, J., *The Church in Anglo-Saxon Society* (Oxford, 2005)

Bloch, R. H., *Etymologies and Genealogies: A Literary Anthropology of the French Middle Ages* (Chicago, 1983)

Blunt, C., 'The St Edmund Memorial Coinage', *Proceedings of the Suffolk Institute of Archaeology* 31 (1969), 234–55

Blunt, C. E., Stewart, B. H. I. H., and Lyon, C. S. S., *Coinage in Tenth-Century England* (Oxford, 1989)

Bohannan, L., 'A Genealogical Charter', *African Journal of the International African Institute* 22 (1952), 301–15

Boje Mortensen, L., 'Stylistic Choice in a Reborn Genre: The National Histories of Widukind of Corvey and Dudo of St Quentin', in *Dudone di San Quintino*, ed. P. Gatti and A. Degl'Innocenti (Trento, 1995), pp. 77–102

Bouchard, C. B., *Those of My Blood: Constructing Noble Families in Medieval Francia* (Philadelphia, 2001)

Bouet, P., 'Dudo de Saint-Quentin et Fécamp', *Tabularia* 2 (2002), 57–70

Bouet, P., 'Les Translations de Reliques en Normandie (IXe–XIIe siècles), in *Les Saints dans la Normandie médiévale. Colloque de Cerisy-la-Salle (26–29 septembre 1996)*, ed. P. Bouet and F. Neveux (Caen, 2000) pp. 97–108

Bowden, G., Balaresque, P., King, T., and others, 'Excavating Past Population Structures by Surname-Based Sampling: The Genetic Legacy of the Vikings in Northwest England', *Molecular Biology and Evolution* 25.2 (2008), 301–9

Breese, L. W., 'The Persistence of Scandinavian Connections in Normandy in the Tenth and Early Eleventh Centuries', *Viator* 8 (1977), 47–61

Brown, P., *The Cult of Saints: Its Rise and Function in Latin Christianity* (Chicago, 1981)

Brown, R. A., *The Normans and the Norman Conquest* (Woodbridge, 1969; 2nd edn 1985)

Brubaker, R., *Ethnicity Without Groups* (Cambridge, MA, 2004)

Bruce, A. M., *Scyld and Scef: Expanding the Analogues* (London, 2002)

Burns, R., *Muslims, Christians and Jews in the Crusader Kingdom of Valencia: Societies in Symbiosis* (Cambridge, 1983)

Caerwyn Williams, J. E., *The Court Poet in Medieval Ireland*, Sir John Rhys Memorial Lecture 1971 (London, 1971)

Chaplais, P., 'The Anglo-Saxon Chancery: from the Diploma to the Writ', in *Prisca Munimenta. Studies in Archival and Administrative History Presented to Dr A. E. J. Hollaender*, ed. F. Ranger (London, 1973), pp. 43–62

Chaplais, P., 'The Origin and Authenticity of the Royal Anglo-Saxon

Diploma', in *Prisca Munimenta. Studies in Archival and Administrative History Presented to Dr A. E. J. Hollaender*, ed. F. Ranger (London, 1973), pp. 28–42

Chaplais, P., 'The Royal Anglo-Saxon "Chancery" of the Tenth Century Revisited', in *Studies in Medieval History Presented to R. H. C. Davis*, ed. H. Mayr-Harting and R. I. Moore (London, 1985), pp. 41–51

Chaplais, P., 'Who Introduced Charters into England? The Case for Augustine', in *Prisca Munimenta. Studies in Archival and Administrative History Presented to Dr A. E. J. Hollaender*, ed. F. Ranger (London, 1973), pp. 88–107

Chibnall, M., 'Charter and Chronicle: The Use of Archive Sources by Norman Historians', in *Church and Government in the Middle Ages: Essays Presented to C. R. Cheney on his 70th Birthday*, ed. C. N. L. Brooke and others (Cambridge, 1976), pp. 1–17

Chibnall, M., *The Normans* (Oxford, 2000)

Clark, C., 'The Narrative Mode of the Anglo-Saxon Chronicle before the Conquest', in *Words, Names and History: Selected Writings of Cecily Clark*, ed. P. Jackson (Woodbridge, 1995), pp. 3–19

Clayton, M., 'Ælfric and Æthelred', in *Essays on Anglo-Saxon and Related Themes in Memory of Lynne Grundy*, ed. J. Roberts and J. Nelson (London, 2000), pp. 65–88

Clemoes, P., 'The Chronology of Ælfric's Works', in *The Anglo-Saxons: Studies in Some Aspects of Their History and Culture, Presented to Bruce Dickins*, ed. P. Clemoes (London, 1960), pp. 212–47

Cohen, J. J., *Hybridity, Identity and Monstrosity in Medieval Britain: On Difficult Middles* (New York and Basingstoke, 2006)

Coon, L., *Sacred Fictions: Holy Women and Hagiography in Late Antiquity* (Philadelphia, 1997), pp. 1–25

Coumert, M., *Origines des Peuples: les récits du Haut Moyen Âge occidental (550–850)* (Paris, 2007)

Coupland, S., 'The Rod of God's Wrath or the People of God's Wrath?', *Journal of Ecclesiastical History* 42 (1991), 535–54

Cowen, A., 'Writing Fire and the Sword: The Perception and Representation of Violence in Viking Age England' (unpublished doctoral thesis, York University, 2004)

Crawford, B., 'The Vikings', in *From the Vikings to the Normans, 800–1100*, ed. W. Davies (Oxford, 2003), pp. 41–71

Crick, J., 'Edgar, Albion and Insular Dominion', in *Edgar, King of the English 959–975: New Interpretations*, ed. D. Scragg (Woodbridge, 2008), pp. 158–70

Cronan, D., '*Beowulf* and the Containment of Scyld in the West Saxon Royal Genealogy', in *The Dating of Beowulf: A Reassessment*, ed. L. Neidorf (Cambridge, 2014), pp. 112–37

Cross, K., '"And that will not be the end of the calamity": Why Emphasise Viking Disruption?', in *Stasis in the Medieval World*, ed. M. Bintley, M. Locker, V. Symons and M. Wellesley (London, 2016), pp. 155–78

Cross, K., 'Byrhtferth's *Historia regum* and the transformation of the Alfredian past', *HSJ* 27 (2015), 55–78

Crumplin, S., 'Rewriting History in the Cult of St Cuthbert from the Ninth to the Twelfth Centuries' (unpublished doctoral thesis, University of St Andrews, 2005)

Cubitt, C., 'Ælfric's Lay Patrons', in *A Companion to Ælfric*, ed. H. Magennis and M. Swan (Leiden, 2009), pp. 165–92

Cultures in Contact: Scandinavian Settlement in England in the Ninth and Tenth Centuries, ed. D. Hadley and J. Richards (Turnhout, 2000)

Curta, F., 'Linear Frontiers in the 9ᵗʰ Century: Bulgaria and Wessex', *Quaestiones Medii Aevi Novae* (2011), pp. 15–32

d'Avray, D., 'Method in the Study of Medieval Sermons', in *Modern Questions about Medieval Sermons*, ed. N. Bériou and D. d'Avray (Spoleto, 1994), pp. 3–29

d'Haenens, A., 'Les Invasions Normandes dans l'Empire Franc au IXe Siècle', in *I Normanni e loro espansione*, pp. 233–98

d'Haenens, A., *Les Invasions Normandes, Une Catastrophe?* (Paris, 1970)

The Dating of Beowulf, ed. C. Chase (Toronto, 1997)

Dass, N., 'Temporary Otherness and Homiletic History in the Late Carolingian Age: A Reading of the *Bella Parisiacae urbis* of Abbo of Saint-Germain-des-Prés', in *Difference and Identity in Francia and Medieval France*, ed. M. Cohen and J. Firnhaber-Baker (Farnham, 2010), pp. 99–113

Davis, C., 'An Ethnic Dating of *Beowulf*', *ASE* 35 (2006), 111–29

Davis, R. H. C., *The Normans and their Myth* (London, 1976), pp. 12–14

de Boüard, M., 'De la Neustrie Carolingienne à la Normandie féodale: Continuité ou discontinuité?', *Bulletin of the Institute of Historical Research* 28 (1955), 1–14

Documentary Culture and the Laity in the Early Middle Ages, ed. W. Brown, M. Costambeys, M. Innes and A. Kosto (Cambridge, 2013)

Dolley, M., 'An Introduction to the Coinage of Æthelraed II', in *Ethelred the Unready: Papers from the Millenary Conference*, ed. D. Hill (Oxford, 1978), pp. 115–33

Dolley, M., and Yvon, J., 'A Group of Tenth-Century Coins Found at Mont-Saint-Michel', *British Numismatic Journal* 40 (1971), 7–11

Dottelonde, P., 'Normandie: la chasse aux ancêtres vikings', *L'Histoire* 49 (1982), 99–102

Douglas, D., 'The First Ducal Charter for Fecamp', in *L'abbaye Benedictine de Fecamp* (Fécamp, 1959), pp. 45–56

Downham, C., '"Hiberno-Norwegians" and "Anglo-Danes": Anachronistic Ethnicities in Viking Age England', *Mediaeval Scandinavia* 19 (2009), 139–69

Downham, C., 'Viking Ethnicities: A Historiographic Overview', *History Compass* 10 (2012), 1–12

Downham, C., *Viking Kings of Britain and Ireland: the Dynasty of Ívarr to AD 1014* (Edinburgh, 2007)

Drögereit, R., 'Gab es eine angelsächsische Königskanzlei?' *Archiv für Urkundenforschung* 13 (1935), 335–436

Drögereit, R., 'Kaiseridee under Kaisertitel bei den Angelsachsen', *Zeitschrift der Savigny-Stiftung für Rechtsgeschichte, Germanistische Abteilung* 69 (1952), 24–73

Duby, G., 'Remarques sur la littérature généalogique en France aux XIe et XIIe siècles', in G. Duby, *Hommes et Structures de moyen âge* (Paris, 1973), pp. 287ff

Dudone di San Quintino, ed. P. Gatti and A. Degl'Innocenti (Trento, 1995)

Dumas, F., *Le Trésor de Fécamp et le Monnayage en Francie Occidentale Pendant le Seconde Moitié du Xe siècle* (Paris, 1971)

Dumville, D., 'The Anglian Collection of Royal Genealogies and Regnal Lists', *ASE* 5 (1976), 23–50

Dumville, D. N., *English Caroline Script and Monastic History: Studies in Benedictinism, A.D. 950–1030* (Woodbridge, 1993)

Dumville, D., 'Kingship, Genealogies and Regnal Lists', in *Early Medieval Kingship*, ed. P. Sawyer and I. Wood (Leeds, 1977), pp. 72–104

Dumville, D., 'The West Saxon Genealogical List: Manuscripts and Texts', *Anglia* 104 (1986), 1–32

Dunbabin, J., 'Discovering a Past for the French Aristocracy', in *The Perception of the Past in Twelfth-Century Europe*, ed. P. Magdalino (London, 1992), pp. 1–14

Dunbabin, J., *France in the Making, 843–1180* (Oxford, 2nd edn 2000)

Dutton, P., *The Politics of Dreaming in the Carolingian Empire* (Lincoln and London, 1994)

Eriksen, T. H., *Ethnicity and Nationalism* (London, 1993; 2nd edn 2002)

Ethnic Groups and Boundaries: The Social Organization of Culture Difference, ed. F. Barth (London, 1969)

Ethnicity, ed. J. Hutchinson and A. D. Smith (Oxford, 1996)

Faulkes, A., 'The Earliest Icelandic Genealogies and Regnal Lists', *Saga-Book* 29 (2005), 115–19

Fell, C., 'Edward King and Martyr and the Anglo-Saxon Hagiographic Tradition', in *Ethelred the Unready: Papers from the Millenary Conference*, ed. D. Hill (Oxford, 1978), pp. 1–13

Fellows-Jensen, G., 'Les noms de lieux d'origine scandinave et la colonisation viking en Normandie: Examen critique de la question', *Proxima Thulé* 1 (1994), 63–103

Fichtenau, H., *Arenga: Spätantike und Mittelalter im Spiegel von Urkundenformeln* (Graz-Cologne, 1957)

Foot, S., 'Reading Anglo-Saxon Charters: Memory, Record, or Story?', in *Narrative and History in the Early Medieval West*, ed. E. Tyler and R. Balzaretti (Turnhout, 2006), 39–65

Foot, S., Æthelstan: the First King of England (New Haven, 2011)

Foot, S., 'The Making of *Angelcynn*: English Identity before the Norman Conquest', *TRHS* 6th s. 6 (1996), 25–49

Foot, S., 'Remembering, Forgetting and Inventing: Attitudes to the Past in England at the End of the First Viking Age', *TRHS* 6th s. 9 (1999), 185–200

Frank, R., 'Germanic Legend in Old English Literature', in *The Cambridge Companion to Old English Literature*, ed. M. Godden and M. Lapidge (Cambridge, 1991; 2nd edn 2013), pp. 82–100

Frank, R., 'Skaldic Verse and the Date of Beowulf', in *The Dating of Beowulf*, ed. C. Chase (Toronto, 1997), pp. 123–39

Friese, E., 'Die "Genealogia Arnulfi comitis" des Priesters Witger', *Frühmittelalterliche Studien* 23 (1989), 203–43

Friis-Jensen, K., 'Dudo of St-Quentin and Saxo Grammaticus', in *Dudone di San Quintino*, ed. P. Gatti and A. Degl'Innocenti (Trento, 1995), pp. 11–28

Frontiers in Question: Eurasian Borderlands, 700–1700, ed. D. Power and N. Standen (Basingstoke, 1999)

Garipzanov, I. H., 'Introduction: History Writing and Christian Identity on a European Periphery', in *Historical Narratives and Christian Identity on a European Periphery: Early History Writing in Northern, East-Central and Eastern Europe (c. 1070–1200)*, ed. I. H. Garipzanov (Turnhout, 2011), pp. 1–11

Garipzanov, I., *The Symbolic Language of Authority in the Carolingian World (c.751–877)* (Leiden, 2008)

Garrison, M., 'Divine Election for Nations – a Difficult Rhetoric for Medieval Scholars?', in *The Making of Christian Myths in the Periphery of Latin Christendom (c.1000–1300)*, ed. L. Boje Mortensen (Copenhagen, 2006), pp. 275–314

Gatch, M. McC., 'The Achievement of Ælfric and his Colleagues in European Perspective', in *The Old English Homily and its Backgrounds*, ed. P. Szarmach and B. Huppé (Albany, 1978), pp. 43–63

Gauthier, N., 'Quelques hypothèses sur la rédaction des vies des saints évêques de Normandie', *Memoriam Sanctorum Venerantes: Miscellanea in Onore di Monsignor Victor Saxer* (Vatican, 1992), pp. 449–68

Geary, P., 'Ethnic Identity as a Situational Construct in the Early Middle Ages', *Mitteilungen der Anthropologischen Gesellschaft in Wien* 113 (1983), 15–26

Geary, P., *Furta Sacra: Thefts of Relics in the Central Middle Ages* (Princeton, 1978; rev. edn 1990)

Gelting, M., 'Predatory Kinship Revisited', *ANS* 15 (2003), 107–20

Genicot, L., *Les Actes Publics*, Typologie des Sources de Moyen Âge Occidental 3 (Turnhout, 1972)

Genicot, L., *Les Genealogies*, Typologie des Sources du Moyen Âge Occidental, 15 (Turnhout, 1975)

Genicot, L., 'Princes Territoriaux et Sang Carolingien: La Genealogia Comitum Buloniensium', in *idem, Études sur les Principautés Lotharingiennes* (Louvain, 1975), pp. 217–306

Gerberding, R., *The Rise of the Carolingians and the Liber Historiae Francorum* (Oxford, 1987)

Ghosh, S., 'The Barbarian Past in Early Medieval Historical Narrative' (unpublished doctoral thesis, University of Toronto, 2009)

Gillett, A., 'Ethnogenesis: A Contested Model of Early Medieval Europe', *History Compass* 4 (2006), 241–60

Ginzburg, C., 'Morelli, Freud and Sherlock Holmes: Clues and Scientific Method', *History Workshop* 9 (1980), 5–36

Gittos, H., 'The Audience for Old English Texts: Ælfric, Rhetoric, and "the edification of the simple"', *ASE* 43 (2014), 231–66

Glazer, N., and Moynihan, D., *Beyond the Melting-pot* (Cambridge, MA, 1963)

Glick, T., *Islamic and Christian Spain in the Early Middle Ages* (Boston, 2005)

Godden, M., 'Apocalypse and Invasion in Late Anglo-Saxon England', in *From Anglo-Saxon to Early Middle English: Studies Presented to E.G. Stanley*, ed. M. Godden, D. Gray and T. Hoad (Oxford, 1995), pp. 130–62

Godden, M., 'The Old English Life of St Neot and the Legends of King Alfred', *ASE* 39 (2010), 193–225

Goffart, W., *Barbarian Tides: The Migration Age and the Later Roman Empire* (Philadelphia, 2006)

Goffart, W., 'Does the Distant Past Impinge on the Invasion Age Germans?', in *On Barbarian Identity: Critical Approaches to Ethnicity in the Early Middle Ages*, ed. A. Gillett (Turnhout, 2002), pp. 21–37

Goffart, W., *The Narrators of Barbarian History (A.D. 550–800)* (Notre Dame, 2005)

Gransden, A., 'Abbo of Fleury's *Passio Sancti Eadmundi*', *Revue Benedictine* 105 (1995), 20–78

Gransden, A., *Historical Writing in England c. 550 to c. 1307* (London, 1974)

Gransden, A., 'The Legends and Traditions Concerning the Origins of the Abbey of Bury St Edmunds', *EHR* 100 (1985), 1–24

Gransden, A., 'Traditionalism and Continuity during the Last Century of Anglo-Saxon Monasticism', in A. Gransden, *Legends, Traditions and History in Medieval England* (London, 1992), pp. 31–79

Gretsch, M., *Ælfric and the Cult of the Saints in Late Anglo-Saxon England* (Cambridge, 2005)

Gretsch, M., 'Historiography and Literary Patronage in late Anglo-Saxon England: the Evidence of Æthelweard's *Chronicon*', *ASE* 41 (2012), 205–48

Grig, L., *Making Martyrs in Late Antiquity* (London, 2004)

Guillet, F., 'Le Nord Mythique de la Normandie: des Normands aux Vikings de la fin du XVIIIe siècle jusqu'à la Grande Guerre', *Revue de Nord* 360–1 (2005), 459–71

Guillot, O., 'La conversion des Normands peu après 911: Des reflets contemporains à l'historiographie ultérieure (Xe–XIe s.)', *Cahiers de Civilisation Médiévale* 24 (1981), 101–16, 181–219

Guyotjeannin, O., Pycke, J., and Tock, B.-M., *Diplomatique Médiévale* (Turnhout, 1993)

Hachmann, R., *Die Goten und Skandinavien* (Berlin, 1970), pp. 15–35

Hadley, D., '"Hamlet and the Princes of Denmark": Lordship in the Danelaw, c.860–954', in *Cultures in Contact: Scandinavian Settlement in England in the Ninth and Tenth Centuries*, ed. D. M. Hadley and J. D. Richards (Turnhout, 2000), pp. 107–32

Hadley, D., *The Northern Danelaw: Its Social Structure, c.800–1100* (London and New York, 2000)

Hadley, D., 'Viking and Native: Rethinking Identity in the Danelaw', *EME* 11 (2002), 45–70

Hadley, D., *The Vikings in England: Settlement, Society and Culture* (Manchester, 2006)

Hadley, D., and Richards, J., 'Introduction: Interdisciplinary Approaches to the Scandinavian Settlement', in *Cultures in Contact: Scandinavian Settlement in England in the Ninth and Tenth Centuries*, ed. D. Hadley and J. Richards (Turnhout, 2000), pp. 3–15

Hagger, M., *Norman Rule in Normandy, 911–1144* (Woodbridge, 2017)

Handelman, D., 'The Organization of Ethnicity', *Ethnic Groups* 1 (1977), 187–200

Harris, S., *Race and Ethnicity in Anglo-Saxon Literature* (New York, 2003)

Hart, C., 'Æthelwine (d. 992)', *Oxford Dictionary of National Biography*, Oxford, 2004; online edn, Oct 2005 [http://www.oxforddnb.com/view/article/8919, accessed 8 Sept 2016]

Hart, C., 'Athelstan "Half King" and his Family', in C. Hart, *The Danelaw* (London, 1992), pp. 569–604

Hart, C., *The Danelaw* (London, 1992)

Hart, C., 'Danelaw and Mercian Charters of the Mid Tenth Century', in C. Hart, *The Danelaw* (London, 1992), pp. 431–53

Hartmann, J., *The Göngu-Hrólfssaga: A Study in Old Norse Philology* (New York, 1912)

Heather, P., 'Disappearing and Reappearing Tribes', in *Strategies of Distinction: the Construction of Ethnic Communities, 300–800*, ed. W. Pohl and H. Reimitz (Leiden, 1998), pp. 95–111

Helmerichs, R., '*Princeps, Comes, Dux Normannorum*: Early Rollonid Designators and their Significance', *HSJ* 9 (2001), 57–77

Herrick, S. K., *Imagining the Sacred Past: Hagiography and Power in Early Normandy* (Cambridge, MA, 2007)

Herval, R., 'Un Moine de l'An Mille: Guillame de Volpiano, 1er abbe de Fecamp (962–1031)', in *L'abbaye Benedictine de Fecamp* (Fécamp, 1959), pp. 27–44

Hill, J., 'Ælfric: His Life and Works', in *A Companion to Ælfric*, ed. H. Magennis and M. Swan (Leiden, 2009), pp. 35–65

Hill, J., 'The Dissemination of Ælfric's *Lives of Saints*: A Preliminary Survey', in *Holy Men and Holy Women: Old English Prose Saints' Lives and Their Contexts*, ed. P. E. Szarmach (Albany, 1996), pp. 235–59

Hill, T. D., 'The Myth of the Ark-Born Son of Noe and the West-Saxon Royal Genealogical Tables', *Harvard Theological Review* 80 (1987), 379–83

Hirschman, E. C., and Panther-Yates, D., 'Peering Inward for Ethnic Identity: Consumer Interpretation of DNA Test Results', *Identity* 8 (2008), 47–66

Hofmann, P., 'Infernal Imagery in Anglo-Saxon Charters' (unpublished doctoral thesis, University of St Andrews, 2008)

Holman, K., 'Defining the Danelaw', in *Vikings and the Danelaw: Papers from the Proceedings of the Thirteenth Viking Congress*, ed. J. Graham-Campbell and others (Oxford, 2001), pp. 1–11

Howe, J., 'The Hagiography of Jumièges (Province of Haute-Normandie)', in *L'Hagiographie du Haut Moyen Âge en Gaule du Nord: Manuscrits, textes et centres de production*, ed. M. Heinzelmann (Stuttgart, 2001), pp. 91–125

Howe, N., 'An Angle on this Earth: Sense of Place in Anglo-Saxon England', *Bulletin of the John Rylands University Library of Manchester* 82 (2000), 3–27

Hudson, B., review of C. Downham, *Viking Kings of Britain and Ireland*, in *Speculum* 84 (2009), 703–05

Hudson, B., *Viking Pirates and Christian Princes: Dynasty, Religion, and Empire in the North Atlantic* (Oxford, 2005)

Huisman, G., 'Notes on the Manuscript Tradition of Dudo of St Quentin's Gesta Normannorum', *ANS* 6 (1983), 122–35

Innes, M., 'Danelaw Identities: Ethnicity, Regionalism and Political Allegiance', in *Cultures in Contact: Scandinavian Settlement in England in the Ninth and Tenth Centuries*, ed. D. Hadley and J. Richards (Turnhout, 2000), pp. 65–88

Innes, M., 'Teutons or Trojans? The Carolingians and the Germanic Past', in *The Uses of the Past in the Early Middle Ages*, ed. Y. Hen and M. Innes (Cambridge, 2000), pp. 227–49

Insley, C., 'Archives and Lay Documentary Practice in the Anglo-Saxon World', in *Documentary Culture and the Laity in the Early Middle Ages*, ed. W. Brown, M. Costambeys, M. Innes and A. Kosto (Cambridge, 2013), pp. 336–62

Insley, C., 'Charters and Episcopal Scriptoria in the Anglo-Saxon South-West', *EME* 7 (1998), 173–97

Insley, C., 'Charters, Ritual and Late Tenth-Century English Kingship', in *Gender and Historiography: Studies in the History of the Early Middle Ages in Honour of Pauline Stafford*, ed. J. Nelson and S. Reynolds with S. Johns (London, 2012), pp. 75–89

Insley, C., 'The Family of Wulfric Spott: an Anglo-Saxon Mercian Marcher Dynasty?', in *The English and Their Legacy, 900–1200: Essays in Honour of Ann Williams*, ed. D. Roffe (Woodbridge, 2012), pp. 115–28

Insley, C., 'Rhetoric and Ritual in Late Anglo-Saxon Charters', in *Medieval Legal Process: Physical, Spoken and Written Performance in the Middle Ages*, ed. M. Mostert and P. S. Barnwell (Turnhout, 2011), pp. 109–21

Insley, C., 'Where Did All The Charters Go? Anglo-Saxon Charters and the New Politics of the Eleventh Century', *ANS* 24 (2002), 109–27

Jesch, J., 'Skaldic Verse in Scandinavian England', in *Vikings and the Danelaw:*

Papers from the Proceedings of the Thirteenth Viking Congress, ed. J. Graham-Campbell and others (Oxford, 2001), pp. 313–25

Jezierski, W., 'Æthelweardus Redivivus', *EME* 13 (2005), 159–78

John, E., '"Orbis Britanniae" and the Anglo-Saxon Kings', in E. John, *'Orbis Britanniae' and Other Studies* (Leicester, 1966), pp. 1–63

Johnson, D., 'The Fall of Lucifer in "Genesis A" and Two Anglo-Latin Royal Charters', *The Journal of English and Germanic Philology* 97 (1998), 500–21

Johnson-South, T., 'The Norman Conquest of Durham', *Journal of the Charles Homer Haskins Society* 4 (1992), 85–95

Jordan, V., 'The Role of Kingship in Tenth-Century Normandy: Hagiography of Dudo of Saint Quentin', *HSJ* 3 (1991), 53–62

Kelly, S., 'Anglo-Saxon Lay Society and the Written Word', in *The Uses of Literacy in Early Medieval Europe*, ed. R. McKitterick (Cambridge, 1990), pp. 36–62

Kelly, S., *Charters of Abingdon Abbey*, Anglo-Saxon Charters 7–8, 2 vols. (Oxford, 2000–01)

Kershaw, J., 'Culture and Gender in the Danelaw: Scandinavian and Anglo-Scandinavian Brooches', *Viking and Medieval Scandinavia* 5 (2009), 295–325

Kershaw, J., *Viking Identities: Scandinavian Jewellery in England* (Oxford, 2013)

Kershaw, J., and E. C. Røyrvik, 'The "People of the British Isles" Project and Viking settlement in England', *Antiquity* 90 (2016), 1670–80

Kershaw, P., 'The Alfred-Guthrum Treaty: Scripting Accommodation and Interaction in Viking Age England', in *Cultures in Contact: Scandinavian Settlement in England in the Ninth and Tenth Centuries*, ed. D. Hadley and J. Richards (Turnhout, 2000), pp. 43–64

Keynes, S., *An Atlas of Attestations in Anglo-Saxon Charters, c.670–1066* (Cambridge, 2002)

Keynes, S., *The Diplomas of King Æthelred 'The Unready': A Study in Their Use as Historical Evidence* (Cambridge, 1980)

Keynes, S., 'King Æthelstan's Books', in *Learning and Literature in Anglo-Saxon England*, ed. M. Lapidge and H. Gneuss (Cambridge, 1985), pp. 143–201

Klapisch-Zuber, C., *L'Arbre des Familles* (Paris, 2003)

Klapisch-Zuber, C., *L'Ombre des Ancêtres: Essai sur l'imaginaire médiévale de la parenté* (Paris, 2000)

Kleinman, S., 'The Legend of Havelok the Dane and the Historiography of East Anglia', *Studies in Philology* 100 (2003), 245–77

Klepper, D. C., *The Insight of Unbelievers: Nicholas of Lyra and Christian Reading of Jewish Text in the Later Middle Ages* (Philadelphia, 2007)

Kopár, L., *Gods and Settlers: The Iconography of Norse Mythology in Anglo-Scandinavian Sculpture* (Turnhout, 2012)

Koziol, G., *The Politics of Memory and Identity in Carolingian Royal Diplomas: The West Frankish Kingdom (840–987)* (Turnhout, 2012)

La Fontaine, J., 'Descent in New Guinea: an Africanist View', in *The Character of Kinship*, ed. J. Goody (Cambridge, 1973), pp. 35–51

Lamb, S., 'Knowledge about the Scandinavian North in Ninth-Century England and Francia', *Quaestio Insularis* 8 (2007), 82–93

Lapidge, M., 'B and the Vita S. Dunstani', in *St Dunstan: his Life, Times and Cult*, ed. N. Ramsay, M. Sparks and T. Tatton-Brown (Woodbridge, 1992), pp. 247–59

Lapidge, M., 'The Hermeneutic Style in Tenth-Century Anglo-Latin Literature', *ASE* 4 (1975), 67–111

Lauer, P., 'Les Translations des Reliques de Saint Ouen et de Saint Leufroy du IXe au Xe siècle, et les deux abbayes de la Croix-Saint-Ouen', *Bulletin Philologique et Historique du Comité des Travaux Historiques et Scientifiques* (1921), pp. 119–36

Lavelle, R., *Aethelred II: King of the English 978–1016* (Stroud, 2002)

Lawson, M. K., *The Battle of Hastings 1066* (Stroud, 2002)

Le Maho, J., 'Après les Invasions Normandes', in *L'abbaye Saint-Ouen de Rouen, des origines à nos jours*, ed. J.-P. Chaline (Rouen, 2009), pp. 25–32

Le Maho, J., 'Autour de la renaissance monastique du Xe siècle en Normandie: les Vies des saints Aycadre et Hugues de Jumièges', in *Livrets, collections et textes, études sur la tradition hagiographique latine*, ed. M. Heinzelmann (Stuttgart, 2006), pp. 285–322

Le Maho, J., 'La production éditoriale à Jumièges vers le milieu du Xe siècle', *Tabularia 'Études'* 1 (2001), 11–32

Le Maho, J., 'La Réécriture Hagiographique au Xe Siècle: Autour des *Libri Gerardi* de la Cathédrale de Rouen', in *La Place de la Normandie dans la Diffusion des Savoirs*, ed. J.-P. Hervieu, E. Poulle and P. Manneville (Rouen, 2006), pp. 23–55

Le Maho, J., 'Les Normands de la Seine à la Fin du IXe Siècle', in *Les fondations scandinaves en Occident et les débuts du duché de Normandie: Colloque de Cerisy-la-Salle (25–29 septembre 2002)*, ed. P. Bauduin (Caen, 2005)

Le Maho, J., 'Les premières installations normandes dans la basse vallée de la Seine (fin du IXe siècle)', in *La progression des Vikings, des raids à la colonisation*, ed. A.-M. F. Héricher (Rouen, 2003), pp. 153–69

Legris, Canon, 'L'Exode des Corps Saints', *Revue Catholique de Normandie* 28 (1919), 125–36, 168–75, 209–21

Lévi-Strauss, C., *Totemism*, trans. R. Needham (London, 1964 [1962])

Lewis, A., *Royal Succession in Capetian France: Studies on Familial Order and the State* (Cambridge, MA, 1981)

Leyser, K., 'The Ottonians and Wessex', in K. Leyser, *Communications and Power in Medieval Europe: The Carolingian and Ottonian Centuries*, ed. T. Reuter (London and Rio Grande, 1994), pp. 73–104

Lifshitz, F., 'Beyond Positivism and Genre: "Hagiographical" Texts as Historical Narrative', *Viator* 25 (1994), 95–114

Lifshitz, F., 'The Dossier of Romanus of Rouen: the Political Uses of Hagiographical Texts' (unpublished doctoral thesis, Columbia University, 1988)

Lifshitz, F., 'Eight Men In: Rouennais Traditions of Archiepiscopal Sanctity', *HSJ* 2 (1990), 63–74

Lifshitz, F., 'The "Exodus of Holy Bodies" Reconsidered: The Translation of the Relics of St. Gildard of Rouen to Soissons', *Analecta Bollandiana* 110 (1992), 329–40

Lifshitz, F., 'The Migration of Neustrian Relics in the Viking Age: the Myth of Voluntary Exodus, the Reality of Coercion and Theft', *EME* 4 (1995), 175–92

Lifshitz, F., *The Norman Conquest of Pious Neustria: Historiographic Discourse and Saintly Relics, 684–1090* (Toronto, 1995)

Lifshitz, F., 'La Normandie carolingienne: essai sur la continuité, avec utilisation de sources négligées', *Annales de Normandie* 48 (1998), 505–24

Lifshitz, F., 'Translating "Feudal" Vocabulary: Dudo of Saint Quentin', *HSJ* 9 (2001), 39–56

Lifshitz, F., *Viking Normandy: Dudo of St Quentin's Gesta Normannorum* <http://www.the-orb.net/orb_done/dudo/dudintro.html> [accessed 10/02/2013]

Literacy in Traditional Societies, ed. J. Goody (Cambridge, 1968)

Lot, F., *Études critiques sur l'Abbaye de Saint-Wandrille* (Paris, 1913)

Loud, G. A., 'The *Gens Normannorum* – Myth or Reality?', *ANS* 4 (1982), 104–16

Loyn, H., 'The Imperial Style of the Tenth-Century Anglo-Saxon Kings', *History* 40 (1955), 111–15

Lund, N., 'King Edgar and the Danelaw', *Mediaeval Scandinavia* 9 (1976), 181–95

Maitland, F., *Domesday Book and Beyond: Three Essays in the Early History of England* (Cambridge, 1897; repr. 1987)

Malešević, S., *The Sociology of Ethnicity* (London, 2004)

Martínez Pizarro, J., 'Ethnic and National History ca. 500–1000', in *Historiography in the Middle Ages*, ed. D. M. Deliyannis (Leiden, 2003), pp. 43–87

Maurists, *Histoire littéraire de France*, VIII (Paris, 1747)

Mazet-Harhoff, L., 'The Incursion of the Vikings into the Natural and Cultural Landscape of Upper Normandy', in *Viking Trade and Settlement in Continental Western Europe*, ed. I. S. Klæsøe (Copenhagen, 2010), pp. 81–122

McKitterick, R., *History and Memory in the Carolingian World* (Cambridge, 2004)

McLeod, S., *The Beginning of Scandinavian Settlement in England: The Viking 'Great Army' and Early Settlers, c. 865–900* (Turnhout, 2014)

McNair, F., 'The Politics of Being Norman in the Reign of Richard the Fearless, Duke of Normandy (r. 942–996)', *EME* 23 (2015), 308–28

McTurk, R., *Studies in Ragnars Saga Loðbrókar and its major Scandinavian analogues* (Oxford, 1991)

Meaney, A., 'Æthelweard, Ælfric, the Norse Gods and Northumbria', *Journal of Religious History* 6 (1970), 105–32

Medieval Frontier Societies, ed. R. Bartlett and A. MacKay (Oxford, 1989)

Michelet, F. L., *Creation, Migration, and Conquest: Imaginary Geography and Sense of Space in Old English Literature* (Oxford, 2006)

Moesgaard, J. C., 'Saints, Dukes and Bishops: Coinage in Ducal Normandy, c. 930-c. 1150', in *Money and the Church in Medieval Europe, 1000–1200*, ed. G. E. M. Gasper and S. H. Gullbekk (Farnham, 2015), pp. 197–207

Molyneaux, G., 'The *Old English Bede*: English Ideology or Christian Instruction?', *EHR* 124 (2009), 1289–1323

Molyneaux, G., 'Why Were Some Tenth-Century English Kings Presented as Rulers of Britain?', *TRHS* 21 (2011), 59–91

Mostert, M., *The Political Theology of Abbo of Fleury* (Hilversum, 1987)

Murray, A. C., 'Beowulf, the Danish Invasions, and Royal Genealogy', in *The Dating of Beowulf*, ed. C. Chase (Toronto, 1981), pp. 101–11

Musset, L., 'Gouvernés et Gouvernants dans le Monde Scandinave et dans le Monde Normand', *Recueils de la Société Jean Bodin* 23 (1968), 439–68

Musset, L., 'L'Exode des Reliques du Diocèse de Sées au Temps des Invasions Normandes', *Société Historique et Archéologique de l'Orne*, 88 (1970), 3–22

Musset, L., 'Le satiriste Garnier de Rouen et son Milieu (Début du XIe siècle)', *Revue du Moyen Âge Latin* 10 (1954), 237–58

Musset, L., 'Les Domaines de l'Époque Franque et les Destinées du Régime Domanial du IXe au XIe Siècle', *BSAN* 49 (1946), 7–97

Musset, L., *Les invasions: le second assaut contre l'Europe chrétienne, VIIe–XIe siècles* (Paris, 1965; 2nd edn 1971)

Musset, L., 'Monachisme d'Époque Franque et Monachisme d'Époque Ducale en Normandie: Le Problème de la Continuité', in *Aspects du Monachisme en Normandie (IVe-XVIIIe siècles)*, ed. L. Musset (Paris, 1982), pp. 55–74

Musset, L., 'Pour l'étude comparative de deux fondations politiques des Vikings: le royaume d'York et le duché de Rouen', in L. Musset, *Nordica et Normannica: recueil d'études sur la Scandinavie ancienne et médiévale, les expéditions des Vikings et la fondation de la Normandie* (Paris, 1997), pp. 157–72

Musset, L., 'Un aspect de l'esprit medieval: la "cacogéographie" des Normands et de la Normandie', in L. Musset, *Nordica et Normannica: recueil d'études sur la Scandinavie ancienne et médiévale, les expéditions des Vikings et la fondation de la Normandie* (Paris, 1997), pp. 233–42 (first published in *Revue du Moyen Âge latin* II (1946), 129–38)

Nelson, J., 'England and the Continent in the Ninth Century: II, the Vikings and Others', *TRHS* 6th s., 13 (2003), 1–28

Nelson, J., 'Normandy's Early History since *Normandy Before 1066*', in *Normandy and Its Neighbours, 900–1250: Essays for David Bates*, ed. D. Crouch and K. Thompson (Turnhout, 2011), pp. 3–15

Nightingale, J., 'Oswald, Fleury and Continental Reform', in *St Oswald of Worcester: Life and Influence*, ed. N. Brooks and C. Cubitt (Leicester and London, 1996), pp. 23–45

Noble, T. X., *Charlemagne and Louis the Pious: Lives by Einhard, Notker, Ermoldus, Thegan, and the Astronomer* (University Park, 2009)

La Normandie vers l'an mil: études et documents, ed. F. de Beaurepaire and J.-P. Chaline (Rouen, 2000)

Oexle, O. G., 'Die Karolinger und die Stadt des heiligen Arnulf', *Frühmittelalterliche Studien* 1 (1967), 250–364

Parker, E. C., 'Anglo-Scandinavian Literature and the Post-Conquest Period' (unpublished D.Phil. thesis, University of Oxford, 2013)

Parker, E., '*Havelok* and the Danes in England: History, Legend, and Romance', *The Review of English Studies* n.s. 67 (2016), 428–47

Pinner, R., *The Cult of St Edmund in Medieval East Anglia* (Woodbridge, 2015)

Planavergne, D., 'Les Normands avant la Normandie: Les invasions scandinaves en Neustrie au IXe siècle dans l'hagiographie franque', in *Les fondations scandinaves en Occident et les débuts du duché de Normandie: Colloque de Cerisy-la-Salle (25–29 septembre 2002)*, ed. P. Bauduin (Caen, 2005), pp. 37–52

Pohl, B., *Dudo of St Quentin's* Historia Normannorum: *History, Tradition and Memory* (Woodbridge/York, 2015)

Pohl, B., 'Translatio imperii Constantini ad Normannos: Constantine the Great as a possible model for the depiction of Rollo in Dudo of St. Quentin's *Historia Normannorum*', *Millennium: Yearbook on the Culture and History of the First Millennium* 9 (2012), 297–339

Pohl, W., 'Telling the Difference: Signs of Ethnic Identity', in *Strategies of Distinction: the Construction of Ethnic Communities, 300–800*, ed. W. Pohl and H. Reimitz (Leiden, 1998), pp. 17–69

Pommeraye, J.-F., *Histoire de l'abbaye royale de St-Ouen de Rouen* (Rouen, 1662)

Potts, C., '*Atque unum ex diversis gentibus populum effecit*: Historical Tradition and the Norman Identity', *ANS* 17 (1995), 139–52

Potts, C., 'The Early Norman Charters: a New Perspective on an Old Debate', in *England in the Eleventh Century: Proceedings of the 1990 Harlaxton Symposium*, ed. C. Hicks (Stamford, 1992), 25–40

Potts, C., *Monastic Revival and Regional Identity in Early Normandy* (Woodbridge, 1997)

Potts, C., 'When the Saints Go Marching: Religious Connections and the Political Culture of Early Normandy', in *Anglo-Norman Political Culture and the 12th-Century Renaissance*, ed. C. W. Hollister (Woodbridge, 1997), pp. 17–31

Power, D., and Standen, N., 'Introduction', in *Frontiers in Question: Eurasian Borderlands, 700–1700*, ed. D. Power and N. Standen (Basingstoke, 1999), pp. 1–31

Prentout, H., *Essai sur les origines et la fondation du duché de Normandie* (Paris, 1911)

Prentout, H., Étude Critique sur Dudon de Saint-Quentin et son Histoire des Premiers Ducs Normands (Caen, 1916)

Property and Power in the Early Middle Ages, ed. W. Davies and P. Fouracre (Cambridge, 1995)

Quinn, J., 'From Orality to Literacy in Medieval Iceland', in *Old Icelandic Literature and Society*, ed. M. Clunies Ross (Cambridge, 2000), pp. 30–60

Rauer, C., 'The Sources of the *Old English Martyrology*', *ASE* 32 (2003), 89–109

Reimitz, H., 'Anleitung zur Interpretation: Schrift und Genealogie in der Karolingerzeit', in *Vom Nutzen des Schreibens: Soziales Gedächtnis, Herrschaft und Besitz*, ed. W. Pohl and P. Herold, Forschungen zur Geschichte des Mittelalters 5 (Vienna, 2002), pp. 167–81

Remensnyder, A., *Remembering Kings Past: Monastic Foundation Legends in Medieval Southern France* (Ithaca, 1995)

Reynolds, S., 'Medieval *Origines Gentium* and the Community of the Realm', *History* 68 (1983), 375–90

Reynolds, S., *Kingdoms and Communities in Western Europe, 900–1300* (Oxford, 1984)

Reynolds, S., 'What Do We Mean by "Anglo-Saxon" and "Anglo-Saxons"?', *Journal of British Studies* 24 (1985), 395–415 (repr. in S. Reynolds, *Ideas and Solidarities of the Medieval Laity* (Aldershot, 1995), no. III)

Richards, M., 'The Medieval Hagiography of St Neot', *Analecta Bollandiana* 99 (1981), 259–78

Ridyard, S., *The Royal Saints of Anglo-Saxon England* (Cambridge, 1988)

Roach, L., *Æthelred the Unready* (New Haven and London, 2016)

Roach, L., *Kingship and Consent in Anglo-Saxon England, 871–978: Assemblies and the State in the Early Middle Ages* (Cambridge, 2013)

Roesdahl, E., 'What May We Expect? On the Problem of Vikings and Archeology in Normandy', in *La progression des Vikings, des raids à la colonisation*, ed. A.-M. F. Héricher (Rouen, 2003), pp. 207–13

Rollason, D., 'The Cults of Murdered Royal Saints in Anglo-Saxon England', *ASE* 11 (1983), 1–22

Rollason, D., 'Lists of Saints' Resting-Places in Anglo-Saxon England', *ASE* 7 (1978), 61–93

Rollason, D., 'Relic-cults as an Instrument of Royal Policy c.900–c.1050', *ASE* 15 (1986), 91–103

Rollason, D., 'St Cuthbert and Wessex: The Evidence of Cambridge, Corpus Christi College Ms. 183', in *St Cuthbert, His Cult and His Community to AD 1200*, ed. G. Bonner, D. Rollason and C. Stancliffe (Woodbridge, 1989), pp. 413–24

Rollason, D., *Saints and Relics in Anglo-Saxon England* (1989)

Sawyer, P., *The Age of the Vikings* (London. 1962; 2nd edn 1971)

Sawyer, P., 'Scandinavians and the English in the Viking Age', H. M. Chadwick Memorial Lecture 5, 1994 (Cambridge, Department of ASNaC, 1995)

Schmid, K., 'Zur Problematik von Familie, Sippe und Geschlecht, Haus und Dynastie beim mittelalterlichen Adel. Vorfragen zum Thema: "Adel und Herrschaft im Mittelalter,"' *Zeitschrift für die Geschichte des Oberrheins* 105 (1957), 1–62

Searle, E., 'Fact and Pattern in Heroic History: Dudo of Saint-Quentin', *Viator* 15 (1984) 119–37

Searle, E., 'Frankish Rivalries and Norse Warriors', *ANS* 8 (1986), 198–213

Searle, E., *Predatory Kinship and the Creation of Norman Power, 840–1066* (Berkeley and Los Angeles, 1988)

Shopkow, L., 'The Carolingian World of Dudo of Saint-Quentin', *Journal of Medieval History* 15 (1989), 19–37

Shopkow, L., 'Dynastic History', in *Historiography in the Middle Ages*, ed. D. M. Deliyannis (Leiden, 2003), pp. 217–48

Shopkow, L., *History and Community: Norman Historical Writing in the Eleventh and Twelfth Centuries* (Washington, DC, 1997)

Sidebottom, P., 'Viking Age Stone Monuments and Social Identity in Derbyshire', in *Cultures in Contact: Scandinavian Settlement in England in the Ninth and Tenth Centuries*, ed. D. Hadley and J. Richards (Turnhout, 2000), pp. 213–35

Simpson, L., 'The King Alfred/St Cuthbert Episode in the *Historia de Sancto Cuthberto*: its significance for mid-tenth century English history', in *St Cuthbert, His Cult and His Community to AD 1200*, ed. G. Bonner, D. Rollason and C. Stancliffe (Woodbridge, 1989), pp. 397–411

Sisam, K., 'Anglo-Saxon Royal Genealogies', *PBA* 39 (1953), 287–348

Skinner, Q., *Visions of Politics I: Regarding Method* (Cambridge, 2002)

Smyth, A., *Scandinavian Kings in the British Isles 850–880* (Oxford, 1977)

Spiegel, G., 'The Cult of St Denis and Capetian Kingship', *Journal of Medieval History* 1 (1975), 43–69

Stafford, P., 'Political Ideas in Late Tenth-Century England: Charters as Evidence', in *Law, Laity and Solidarities: Essays in Honour of Susan Reynolds*, ed. P. Stafford, J. Nelson and J. Martindale (Manchester, 2001), pp. 68–82

Stafford, P., 'The Reign of Æthelred II, a Study in the Limitations on Royal Policy and Action', in *Ethelred the Unready: Papers from the Millenary Conference*, ed. D. Hill (Oxford, 1978), pp. 15–46

Stafford, P., *Unification and Conquest: A Political and Social History of England in the Tenth and Eleventh Centuries* (London, 1989)

Stenton, F., *Anglo-Saxon England* (Oxford, 1943, 1971; repr. 2001)

Stenton, F., *The Latin Charters of the Anglo-Saxon Period* (Oxford, 1955)

Stenton, F., 'The Scandinavian Colonies in England and Normandy', *TRHS* 4th s. 37 (1945), 1–12

Stewart, I., 'The St Martin Coins of Lincoln', *British Numismatic Journal* 36 (1967), 46–54

Stocker, D., 'Monuments and Merchants: Irregularities in the Distribution of Stone Sculpture in Lincolnshire and Yorkshire in the Tenth Century', in *Cultures in Contact: Scandinavian Settlement in England in the Ninth and Tenth Centuries*, ed. D. Hadley and J. Richards (Turnhout, 2000), pp. 180–212

Stodnick, J., '"Old Names of Kings or Shadows": Reading Documentary Lists', in *Conversion and Colonization in Anglo-Saxon England*, ed. C. E. Karkov and N. Howe (Tempe, 2006), pp. 109–31

Strategies of Distinction: the Construction of Ethnic Communities, 300–800, ed. W. Pohl and H. Reimitz (Leiden, 1998)

Tabuteau, E. Z., *Transfers of Property in Eleventh-Century Norman Law* (Chapel Hill and London, 1988)

Thacker, A., 'In Search of Saints: the English Church and the Cult of Roman Apostles and Martyrs in the Seventh and Eighth Centuries', in *Early Medieval Rome and the Christian West. Essays in Honour of Donald A. Bullough*, ed. J. Smith (Leiden, 2000), pp. 247–77

The Old English Homily and its Backgrounds, ed. P. Szarmach and B. Huppé (Albany, 1978)

Thomas, H., *The English and the Normans: Ethnic Hostility, Assimilation and Identity, 1066–c.1220* (Oxford, 2003)

Thompson, S., *Anglo-Saxon Royal Diplomas: A Palaeography* (Woodbridge, 2006)

Thornton, D., 'Orality, Literacy and Genealogy in Early Medieval Ireland and Wales', in *Literacy in Medieval Celtic Societies*, ed. H. Pryce (Cambridge, 1998), pp. 83–98

Townend, M., 'Contextualizing the "Knútsdrápur": Skaldic Praise-Poetry at the Court of Cnut', *ASE* 30 (2001), 145–79

Townend, M., *Language and History in Viking Age England: Linguistic Relations Between Speakers of Old Norse and Old English*, Studies in the Early Middle Ages 6 (Turnhout, 2002)

Townend, M., 'Whatever Happened to York Viking Poetry? Memory, Tradition and the Transmission of Skaldic Verse', *Saga-Book* 27 (2003), 48–90

Trafford, S., 'Ethnicity, Migration Theory and the Historiography of the Scandinavian Settlement in England', in *Cultures in Contact: Scandinavian Settlement in England in the Ninth and Tenth Centuries*, ed. D. Hadley and J. Richards (Turnhout, 2000), pp. 17–39

Treharne, E., 'Making Their Presence Felt: Readers of Ælfric, c. 1050–1350', in *A Companion to Ælfric*, ed. H. Magennis and M. Swan (Leiden, 2009), pp. 398–422

Trumbore-Jones, A., 'Pitying the Desolation of Such a Place: Rebuilding Religious Houses and Constructing Memory in Aquitaine in the Wake of the Viking Incursions', *Viator* 37 (2006), 85–102

Valtonen, I., *The North in the Old English Orosius: A Geographical Narrative in Context* (Helsinki, 2008)

Van der Straeten, J., 'L'Auteur des Vies de S. Hugues et de S. Aycadre', *Analecta Bollandiana* 88 (1970), 63–73

van Houts, E., 'Historiography and Hagiography at Saint-Wandrille: The *Inventio et Miracula Sancti Vulfranni*', *ANS* 12 (1990), 233–51

van Houts, E., 'Women and the Writing of History in the Early Middle Ages: the Case of Abbess Matilda of Essen and Aethelweard', *EME* 1 (1992), 53–68

Walker, I., *Harold: the Last Anglo-Saxon King* (Stroud, 1997)

Ward-Perkins, B., 'Why Did the Anglo-Saxons Not Become More British?', *EHR* 115 (2000), 513–33

Watson, C., 'Old English Hagiography: Recent and Future Research', *Literature Compass* 1 (2004) ME 100, 1–14

Webber, N., *The Evolution of Norman Identity, 911–1154* (Woodbridge, 2005)

Wenskus, R., *Stammesbildung und Verfassung. Das Werden der frühmittelalterlichen Gentes* (Cologne, 1961)

Werner, K., 'Quelques observations au sujet des débuts du "duché" de Normandie', in *Droit privé et institutions régionales: Études historiques offertes à Jean Yver* (Paris, 1976), pp. 691–709

Whatley, E. G., 'An Introduction to the Study of Old English Prose Hagiography: Sources and Resources', in *Holy Men and Holy Women: Old English Prose Saints' Lives and Their Contexts*, ed. P. Szarmach (Albany, 1996), pp. 3–32

Whitbread, L., 'Æthelweard and the Anglo-Saxon Chronicle', *EHR* 74 (1959), 577–89

Whitelock, D., 'The Dealings of the Kings of England with Northumbria in the Tenth and Eleventh Centuries', in *The Anglo-Saxons: Studies in Some Aspects of Their History and Culture, Presented to Bruce Dickins*, ed. P. Clemoes (London, 1960), pp. 70–88

Whitelock, D., 'Wulfstan and the So-called Laws of Edward and Guthrum', *EHR* 56 (1941), 1–21

Wickham, C., *Problems in Doing Comparative History* (Southampton, 2005)

Wickham, C., 'Property Ownership and Signorial Power in Twelfth-Century Tuscany', in *Property and Power in the Early Middle Ages*, ed. W. Davies and P. Fouracre (Cambridge, 1995), pp. 221–44

Wilcox, J., 'The Audience of Ælfric's *Lives of Saints* and the Face of Cotton Caligula A. XIV, fols. 93–130', in *Beatus Vir: Studies in Early English and Norse Manuscripts in Memory of Phillip Pulsiano*, ed. A. N. Doane and K. Wolf (Tempe, 2006), pp. 228–63

Williams, A., *Æthelred the Unready: the Ill-Counselled King* (London, 2003)

Wimmer, A., *Ethnic Boundary Making: Institutions, Power, Networks* (Oxford, 2013)

Winterbottom, M., 'The Style of Æthelweard', *Medium Ævum* 36 (1967), 109–18

Wolfram, H., *Intitulatio I: Lateinische Königs- und Fürstentitel bis zum Ende des 8. Jahrhunderts* (Vienna, 1967)

Wolfram, H., '*Origo et religio*. Ethnic Traditions and Literature in Early Medieval Texts', *EME* 3 (1994), 19–38

Wolfram, H., 'Political Theory and Narrative in Charters', *Viator* 26 (1995), 39–51

Wood, I., 'Beyond Satraps and Ostriches: Political and Social Structures of the Saxons in the Early Carolingian Period', in *The continental Saxons from the migration period to the tenth century: an ethnographic perspective*, ed. D. Green and F. Siegmund (Woodbridge, 2003), pp. 271–90

Wood, I., 'Defining the Franks: Frankish Origins in Early Medieval Historiography', in *Concepts of National Identity in the Middle Ages*, ed. S. Forde, L. Johnson and A. Murray (Leeds, 1995), pp. 47–57

Wood, I., 'Genealogy Defined by Women: the Case of the Pippinids', in *Gender in the Early Medieval World: East and West, 300–900*, ed. L. Brubaker and J. M. H. Smith (Cambridge, 2004), pp. 234–56

Wood, I., 'Missionaries and the Christian Frontier', in *The Transformation of Frontiers From Late Antiquity to the Carolingians*, ed. W. Pohl, I. Wood and H. Reimitz, The Transformation of the Roman World 10 (Leiden, 2001), pp. 209–18

Wormald, P., 'Æthelred the Lawmaker', in *Ethelred the Unready: Papers from the Millenary Conference*, ed. D. Hill (Oxford, 1978), pp. 47–80

Wormald, P., 'Æthelweard (*d.* 998?)', *Oxford Dictionary of National Biography* (Oxford: OUP, 2004) <http://www.oxforddnb.com/view/article/8918> [accessed 24 July 2013]

Wormald, P., '*Engla Lond*: The Making of an Allegiance', *Journal of Historical Sociology* 7 (1994), 1–24

Wormald, P., *The Making of English Law: King Alfred to the Twelfth Century. Volume I: Legislation and its Limits* (Oxford, 2001)

Wright, C., 'Old English Homilies and Latin Sources', in *The Old English Homily: Precedent, Practice, and Appropriation*, ed. A. Kleist (Turnhout, 2007), pp. 15–66

Yarrow, S., *Saints and Their Communities: Miracle Stories in Twelfth Century England* (Oxford, 2006)

Young, C., *Contemporary Ancestors: A Beginner's Anthropology for District Officers in Africa* (London, 1940)

Younge, G., '"Those were Good Days": Representations of the Anglo-Saxon Past in the Old English Homily on Saint Neot', *The Review of English Studies* ns 63 (2012), 349–69

Yver, J., 'Les Premières Institutions du duché de Normandie', in *I Normanni e loro espansione in Europa nell' alto medioevo* (Spoleto, 1969), pp. 299–366

Index